THE AGE OF ABUNDANCE

THE
AGE OF
ABUNDANCE

How Prosperity Transformed
America's Politics and Culture

— ◆ —

BRINK LINDSEY

Collins
An Imprint of HarperCollinsPublishers

HarperCollins books may be purchased for educational, business,
or sales promotional use. For information, please write:
Special Markets Department, HarperCollins Publishers,
10 East 53rd Street, New York, NY 10022.

FIRST EDITION

Designed by Joseph Rutt

Printed on acid-free paper

Library of Congress Cataloging-in-Publication Data
is available upon request.

ISBN: 978-0-06-0747664
ISBN-10: 0-06-0747668

07   08   09   10   11   /RRD   10   9   8   7   6   5   4   3   2   1

Contents

Introduction

———— •◆• ————

In the years after World War II, America crossed a great historical threshold. In all prior civilizations and social orders, the vast bulk of humanity had been preoccupied with responding to basic material needs. Postwar America, however, was different. An extensive and highly complex division of labor unleashed immense productive powers far beyond anything in prior human experience. As a result, the age-old bonds of scarcity were broken. Concern with physical survival and security was now banished to the periphery of social life.

To employ, with all due irony, the terminology of Karl Marx, America left behind the "realm of necessity" and entered the "realm of freedom."

Marx, of course, had imagined that this great transformation would be achieved under communism. But the dream of a centrally planned utopia turned out to be an unrealizable fantasy. Instead, the realm of freedom came as a new stage of capitalist development. And where America led, the rest of the world began to follow. The advanced societies of the English-speaking countries, western Europe, and Japan were closest behind. And in the recent decades of so-called globalization, many less-developed nations, including those of the former communist bloc, have entered or are fast approaching the golden circle of widespread prosperity. Yes, poverty is still a cruel scourge for billions of the world's inhabitants; in those less-fortunate regions of the globe, the path of capitalist development remains strewn with obstacles. Yet there are sound reasons to hope that the realm of freedom will continue to expand, and that one day in the not terribly distant future, the mass affluence that Americans have enjoyed for over a half century will extend around the world. As America's experience makes clear, such a state of affairs would by no means constitute a utopia. It would, however, represent an immense expansion in the range of life's possibilities and the scope of its promise.

This ongoing revolution cries out for greater attention and understanding. The liberation from material necessity marks a fundamental change in the human condition, one that leaves no aspect of social existence unaffected. As a result, many age-old verities no longer apply: truths and rules that arose and obtained during the 10 millennia when subsistence agriculture was the main business of mankind have been rendered obsolete. We are in uncharted territory. Consequently, we are in need of new maps.

In the six decades since the end of World War II, Americans have been busy exploring the new environs of mass affluence. Those decades have witnessed both exhilarating discoveries and tragic errors, as well as a great deal of blind groping and simple muddling through. There is much to be learned from a careful examination of this accumulated experience—not only about the altered nature and course of American life, but also about the broad direction in which the rest of the world is moving. This book represents an attempt to organize America's experience with mass affluence into some kind of coherent narrative, from which at least some hints for future mapmakers might be gleaned.

"Let me tell you about the very rich," wrote F. Scott Fitzgerald. "They are different from you and me."[1] Indeed they are. Born and raised in the bosom of material plenty, they face an environment far removed from that which confronts the common lot. Living in that rarefied environment, they become adapted to it. And as a result, their motivations, aspirations, morals, and worldviews diverge markedly from those of people who struggle every day in the shadows of deprivation.

While Fitzgerald was referring to the tiny Jazz Age upper crust, his words apply as well to postwar America's affluent society. Living amidst unprecedented material abundance, Americans in the age of abundance have been operating in an environment utterly different from that inhabited by the overwhelming majority of their fellow human beings, past and present. Specifically, the central and abiding imperative of human existence since the dawn of the species—securing the food, shelter, and clothing needed for survival—could now be taken for granted by all but a dwindling minority. As a result, Americans have become a different kind of people.

The story of postwar America is thus the story of adaptation to new social realities. Adaptation, in particular, to mass affluence. At the heart of this process was a change in the basic orientation of the dominant culture: from a culture of overcoming scarcity to one of expanding and enjoying abundance. From a more rigid and repressed social system focused on achieving prosperity to a looser and more expressive one focused on taking wider advantage of prosperity's possibilities. American capitalism is derided for its superficial banality, yet it has unleashed profound, convulsive social change. Condemned as mindless materialism, it has burst loose a flood tide of spiritual yearning. The civil rights movement and the sexual revolution, environmentalism and feminism, the fitness and health-care boom and the opening of the gay closet, the withering of censorship and the rise of a "creative class" of "knowledge workers"—all are the progeny of widespread prosperity.

Gifted contemporaries caught glimpses of these changes as they were unfolding. At the dawn of the postwar boom, David Riesman, in his 1950 classic *The Lonely Crowd*, revealed how economic development was promoting a shift in American social psychology: away from the absolutist "inner-directed" sensibility of the country's Protestant bourgeois tradition, and toward a more relativistic, "other-directed" outlook. Although Riesman was concerned that the new ethos tended toward conformism, he was alert to more liberating possibilities. "The more advanced the technology, on the whole, the more possible it is for a considerable number of human beings to imagine being somebody else," he wrote. "In the first place, the technology spurs the division of labor, which, in turn, creates the possibility for a greater variety of experience and of social character. In the second place, the improvement in technology permits sufficient leisure to contemplate change—a kind of capital reserve in men's self-adaptation to nature—not on the part of a ruling few but on the part of many."[2]

Later in the fifties, John Kenneth Galbraith famously proclaimed that mass prosperity was here to stay in *The Affluent Society*. And he saw correctly that the implications were momentous. "The discovery that production is no longer of such urgency . . . involves a major wrench in our attitudes," he wrote. "What was sound economic behavior before cannot be sound economic behavior now. What were the goals of individuals, organizations and, perhaps more especially, of government before may not be so now."[3] In particular, Galbraith grasped that a shift in priorities toward greater emphasis on personal fulfillment and quality of life was now in the works—even if, as an inveterate collectivist, he mistakenly believed that the new priorities were best pursued through the inexorable shrinkage of the competitive private sector.

By the 1970s, the tumult of cultural transformation was obvious to all. But it took the special insight of Tom Wolfe to trace this upheaval back to the same prosperity that earlier begat suburbia and tailfins. In the mid-seventies essay that dubbed the era the "me decade," Wolfe argued that the new temper of the times was inextricably connected "with this unprecedented post–World War II American luxury: the luxury enjoyed by so many millions of middling folk, of dwelling upon the self." "But once the dreary bastards started getting money in the 1940's," he explained, "they did an astonishing thing—they took the money and ran! They did something only aristocrats (and intellectuals and artists) were supposed to do—they discovered and started doting on *Me!* They've created the greatest age of individualism in American history!"[4]

No one has analyzed the process of cultural reorientation more exhaustively than University of Michigan political scientist Ronald Inglehart, who for decades has been using attitude surveys to track the progress of what he calls "postmodernization." And his research has examined cultural trends, not only in the United States, but in dozens of other countries as well. The best-documented aspect of postmodernization is a shift from "materialist" to "postmaterialist" values, in which the "emphasis on economic achievement as the top priority is now giving way to an increasing emphasis on the quality of life. In a major part of the world, the disciplined, self-denying, and achievement-oriented norms of industrial society are giving way to an increasingly broad latitude for individual choice of lifestyles and individual self-expression."[5]

According to Inglehart, the shift toward postmaterialist values is only one part of a broader process. Specifically, the heightened emphasis on subjective well-being as opposed to material security is highly correlated with a marked change in attitudes on a host of apparently unrelated issues, from adherence to traditional religion to trust in government to views on sex and sexual orientation. The central thrust of this "Postmodern shift" is a "broad de-emphasis on all forms of authority," whether political, economic, religious, or familial. Once the quest for personal fulfillment and self-realization becomes a dominant motivation, all cultural constraints that might pose obstacles to that quest come under sustained and furious assault.

Inglehart concurs in the judgment that mass affluence is behind the sweeping cultural changes of recent decades. "This shift in worldview and motivations," he explains, "springs from the fact that there is a fundamental difference between growing up with an awareness that survival is precarious, and growing up with the feeling that one's survival can be taken for granted." Once material accumulation is no longer a matter of life and death, its diminished urgency naturally allows other priorities to assert themselves. "This change of direction," Inglehart concludes, "reflects the principle of diminishing marginal utility." Meanwhile, material security reduces stress, and thus the appeal of inflexible moral norms. "Individuals under high stress have a need for rigid, predictable rules," Inglehart observes. "They need to be sure what is going to happen because they are in danger— their margin for error is slender and they need maximum predictability. Postmodernists embody the opposite outlook: raised under conditions of relative security, they can tolerate more ambiguity; they are less likely to need the security of absolute rigid rules that religious sanctions provide."[6]

The process of cultural adaptation has been anything but smooth. For his part, Inglehart notes that the "Postmodern shift" is frequently accompanied by an "authoritarian reflex." "Rapid change leads to severe insecurity, giving rise to a powerful need of predictability . . . ," he writes. "The reaction to change takes the form of a rejection of the new, and a compulsive insistence on the infallibility of old, familiar cultural patterns." Commenting on the growing prominence of religious fundamentalism in the United States and elsewhere, Inglehart argues that "it is precisely *because* traditional social and religious norms have been eroding rapidly in these societies during recent decades that people with traditional values (who are still numerous) have been galvanized into unusually active and disruptive forms of behavior, in order to defend their threatened values."[7]

The juxtaposition of a postmodern shift and an authoritarian reflex suggests a relationship of Newtonian simplicity: action and reaction, progress and backlash. Here in the United States at least, the reality has been rather more complicated. Here, mass affluence did trigger a mirror-image pair of cultural convulsions: on the countercultural left, a romantic rebellion against order and authority of every description; and on the traditionalist right, an evangelical revival of socially and theologically conservative Protestantism. Both arose around the same time, in the dizzying 1960s. Between them, these two movements have played decisive roles in shaping America's accommodation to mass affluence. But those roles cannot be fairly described as progressive and reactionary, or adaptive and obstructive. The countercultural left combined genuine liberation with dangerous antinomian excess, while the traditionalist right mixed knee-jerk reaction with wise conservation of vital cultural endowments.

The two movements thus offered conflicting half-truths. On the left were arrayed those elements of American society most open to the new possibilities of mass affluence and most eager to explore them—in other words, the people at the forefront of the push for civil rights, feminism, and environmentalism, as well as sex, drugs, and rock 'n' roll. At the same time, however, many on the left harbored a deep antagonism toward the institutions of capitalism and middle-class life that had created all those glittering new possibilities. On the right, meanwhile, were the stalwart defenders of capitalism and middle-class mores. But included in their number were the people most repelled by and hostile to the social and cultural ferment that capitalism and middle-class mores were producing. One side attacked capitalism while rejoicing in its fruits; the other side celebrated capitalism while denouncing its fruits as poisonous.

Between them, over the course of the sixties and seventies, the two movements wrecked the postwar liberal order that had presided over the coming of mass affluence and the resulting pacification of class conflict. And they wrecked the cultural unity sustained by a fuzzy, other-directed, "Judeo-Christian" version of American civil religion. Each movement struggled to claim the soul of American society and culture, but neither succeeded in forging a workable new consensus on its own terms.

America in the age of abundance has thus been roiled by ongoing and inconclusive ideological conflict. Though the country has made real and durable strides toward adapting to new social conditions, it has done so by lurching alternately leftward and rightward. And all the while, the emerging new modus vivendi has had to contend with scorn from both sides of the ideological divide. To the chagrin of those on the left, the embrace of more progressive values—in particular, greater equality for women and minorities—has been spoiled by the continued vitality of the competitive capitalist order and the ascendancy of conservatism in politics. And to the equivalent mortification of their counterparts on the right, the triumph of capitalism, and the resilience of core middle-class values regarding work and family and nation, have likewise been spoiled by the now-irreversible shift toward a more secular, hedonistic culture.

Consequently, American society's progress in adapting to mass affluence has come in defiance of prevailing ideological categories. Hence the nastiness of politics in recent years, a symptom of ideological stalemate. Contrary to the conventional wisdom, the raw and inflamed political divisions of the present day reflect not underlying social polarization, but instead the seething frustration of ideologues on both sides with the coalescing new cultural synthesis.

Since the hotly disputed presidential election of 2000, it has been fashionable to depict American society as divided into rival "red" (heartland, conservative) and "blue" (coastal, liberal) camps. "America is more bitterly divided than it has been for a generation," reported the *Economist* magazine in 2004. According to Matthew Dowd, a Bush campaign strategist, "You've got 80% or 90% of the country that look at each other like they are on separate planets." "The red states get redder, the blue states get bluer," fretted columnist E. J. Dionne, "and the political map of the United States takes on the coloration of the Civil War."[8] And humorist Dave Barry offered this priceless sketch of the opposing forces: on the red side, "ignorant racist fascist knuckle-dragging NASCAR-obsessed cousin-marrying roadkill-eating tobacco-juice-dribbling gun-fondling religious fanatic rednecks"; and on the blue side, "godless unpatriotic pierced-nose Volvo-driving France-loving left-wing communist latte-sucking tofu-chomping holistic-wacko neurotic vegan weenie perverts."[9]

Without a doubt, political loyalists are in a nasty mood. "I hate President George W. Bush . . . ," wrote Jonathan Chait a few years back in the normally sedate *The New Republic.* "I hate the way he walks—shoulders flexed, elbows splayed out from his sides like a teenage boy feigning machismo. I hate the way he talks—blustery self-assurance masked by a pseudo-populist twang. I even hate the things that everybody seems to like about him."[10] Voices on the right have been every bit as shrill. Consider, by way of illustration, this sampling of recent book titles by prominent conservative provocateurs: Ann Coulter's *Treason: Liberal Treachery from the Cold War to the War on Terrorism;* Sean Hannity's *Deliver Us from Evil: Defeating Terrorism, Despotism, and Liberalism;* Hugh Hewitt's *If It's Not Close, They Can't Cheat: Crushing the Democrats in Every Election and Why Your Life Depends on It;* and Michael Savage's *Liberalism Is a Mental Disorder.* In this season of distemper, a Gresham's law of rhetoric is replacing polemics with witch-hunting paranoia.

It is also true that ordinary Americans' political loyalties have grown polarized over the past several years. A high point was reached in early 2005, when 94 percent of Republicans, but only 18 percent of Democrats, expressed approval of the job President Bush was doing.[11] Partisan chauvinism more generally has been on the rise, albeit fairly modestly. For example, the National Election Survey asks Republicans and Democrats to rate the two parties on a 0 to 100 scale. For Republicans, the average difference between the two ratings rose from 23 points in 1998 to 32 points in 2004; for Democrats, the average difference inched up from 33 to 35 points over the same period.[12]

Nevertheless, it does not follow that American society is cloven into two cohesive and hostile subnations. Cultural diversity, cultural conflict—to be sure, both are abundant in contemporary America. But for all the country's jostling, bumptious plenitude of worldviews and ways of life, a viable center manages to hold. While opinions and habits of the heart are scattered over a wide space, the distribution follows a classic bell curve pattern: the hump in the middle dominates the tails of left and right. Among others, sociologist Alan Wolfe and political scientist Morris Fiorina have documented in careful detail the prevailing ideological centrism.[13]

Most Americans, it turns out, stand on a common ground whose coloration is not recognizably red or blue. On the one hand, they embrace the traditional, Middle American values of patriotism, law and order, the work ethic, and commitment to family life. At the same time, however, they hold attitudes on race and sex that are dramatically more liberal than those that held sway a generation or two ago. Likewise, they are deeply skeptical of authority, and are so strongly committed to open-mindedness and tolerance as to be almost absolutist in their relativism. Such an amalgamation of views is flatly inconsistent with current definitions of ideological purity. Despite all the talk of raging "culture wars," most Americans are nonbelligerents.

In his delightful *Bobos in Paradise*, David Brooks described the contemporary American mainstream as a novel confluence of the bourgeois and the bohemian, once widely divergent and mutually antagonistic ways of life. "I found that if you investigated people's attitudes towards sex, morality, leisure time, and work, it was getting harder and harder to separate the antiestablishment renegade from the pro-establishment company man," Brooks wrote. "Most people, at least among the college-educated set, seemed to have rebel attitudes and social-climbing attitudes all scrambled together. Defying expectations and maybe logic, people seemed to have combined the countercultural sixties and the achieving eighties into one social ethos."[14] With his light-hearted foray into what he called "comic sociology," Brooks identified a profoundly significant development. Today's culturally dominant "bobo" worldview represents a synthesis of the two great ideological responses to mass affluence: the bohemian rebellion against convention and authority on the one hand, and the unapologetic defense of the old Protestant bourgeois virtues on the other.

But if this analysis is correct—if a new kind of cultural unity now defines the American mainstream—why has political debate grown so fractious and surly? The answer is that politics has become a lagging indicator of social change. The culture-war contretemps that have injected such acrimony into political life reflect the fact that ideological partisans of the countercultural left and religious right now constitute major, if not dominant, factions within the country's two great political parties. Winning political representation, however, has proved a hollow triumph, as neither movement has achieved its ultimate goal: to remake American society in its own image. The measure of their mutual failure can be seen in the hostility directed from both ends of the political spectrum toward contemporary America. To the true believers of the ideological left, America is disfigured by endemic racism, sexism, and materialism; to their counterparts on the right, the country has been corrupted by godlessness and rampant immorality.

There are many causes that contribute to the caustic tone of today's politics—the greater ideological consistency of the two parties (i.e., the comparative rarity now of conservative Democrats and liberal Republicans), the close partisan balance, the fact that superheated rhetoric attracts the money and media attention that feed modern political causes and campaigns. In addition to these other factors, however, surely this cause is fundamental: from their widely divergent positions, the ideologues of left and right share a dyspeptic frustration with the prevailing culture—and with the fact that most people are much less frustrated than they are!

The curdled politics of recent years thus represent a kind of triumph. The American cultural mainstream has succeeded at containing within tolerable bounds the ideological dissatisfactions of both the countercultural left and religious right. The ideologues are articulate and well organized, but they remain minority factions. Having gained tantalizing access to the levers of political power, these noisy dissenters have discovered that they lack the mass to budge those levers very far. And so they rail against each other, when their true complaint is with the recalcitrant center that defies them both.

A kind of triumph, perhaps, but hardly complete or satisfying. A new cultural synthesis has been forged, but this post-scarcity version of *e pluribus unum* remains unrepresented in the political forum. Indeed, it remains unacknowledged and anonymous in the current political vocabulary. Today's American mainstream could perhaps most naturally be described as liberal, in the broader sense of the great liberal tradition of individualism and moral egalitarianism that this country has embodied throughout its existence. Alternatively, it could also with justice be called conservative, if the object of conservation is understood to be that same liberal tradition. But the ideologies that pass for liberalism and conservatism today are far too weighted down with illiberal elements—on the left, hostility to commerce; on the right, narrow-minded populism—for either to lay rightful claim to what has become the new American center. Under present circumstances, it probably makes most sense to refer to that center as libertarian, given that the new cultural synthesis is committed to wide scope for both economic and cultural competition.

For the time being, however, the center remains ideologically up for grabs. Or to change the metaphor, the new world we have been creating does not yet appear on the political map. And that is a real problem. America has much work to do if it is to make the most of the opportunities of mass affluence, but the task would be considerably more manageable if we had a better idea of where we are and how we got here. It is my hope that this book will prove of some value in describing the journey thus far through this unmarked terrain.

AFTER WRITING THIS book, I owe much to many. First of all, I am grateful to Ed Crane, president of the Cato Institute, for believing in this book and allowing me to devote much of my time over the past several years to researching and writing it. I

also want to express my deepest thanks to my agent, Rafe Saga-
lyn, and my editor at HarperCollins, Marion Maneker, for helping me to turn what started as an inchoate grab bag of ideas
into, for better or worse, this final product. David Boaz, Will
Wilkinson, Dan Griswold, Brian Doherty, and Reihan Salam
read preliminary drafts and offered challenging and helpful
comments. They deserve credit for improving the book and receive full absolution for all errors and flaws that remain. Matt
Klokel, Tanja Stumberger, and Tom Blemaster provided valuable
research assistance.

Most of the sources I used while researching and writing are
acknowledged in the notes and bibliography, but two exceptions
deserve mention here. First, I have generally omitted citations to
often ephemeral Web sites. However, this book in its present
form would not have been possible without access to the incredibly rich array of primary and secondary sources available on
the Internet. Second, to avoid tedious repetitiveness, I generally
did not cite information obtained or derived from the Bureau of
the Census's invaluable *Statistical Abstract of the United States*
and *Historical Statistics of the United States,* which are also available online. For anyone interested in American social history,
they are indispensable reference tools.

My wife, Debbie, deserves special commendation for enduring another long stint of book widowhood. Let me also mention
Matthew, Michael, and Jack, my three sons. They are my pride
and joy in the present, and my great hope for the future. Finally,
in writing a book about an era largely coincident with my own
lifetime, I have had frequent occasion to reflect on my own personal past. So let me close with love for my parents, Bill and
Linda Lindsey, two of the millions of intrepid adventurers in
postwar America's realm of freedom. For my place and bearings
in this strange and wondrous world, I thank them.

ONE

The Realm of Freedom

On July 24, 1959, in the depths of the Cold War, Vice President Richard Nixon and Soviet premier Nikita Khrushchev stood face-to-face, close enough to smell each other's breath. Dozens of journalists and dignitaries crowded around them in increasingly nervous silence as the two argued heatedly. Khrushchev, the bald, brash son of Ukrainian peasants, raised his booming voice and waved his stubby hands in the air. Nixon, nearly a head taller, hovered over him, struggling to maintain his composure but then jabbing a finger into his adversary's chest. Precipitating this superpower showdown was a disagreement over . . . washing machines.

Nixon was in Moscow for the opening of the U.S. National Exhibition, a bit of Cold War cultural exchange cum oneupmanship that followed on the heels of an earlier Soviet exhibition in New York. He and Khrushchev were now in the fair's star attraction: a six-room, fully furnished ranch house, bisected by a central viewing hallway that allowed visitors to gawk at American middle-class living standards. The Soviet press referred to the house dismissively as the "Taj Mahal," contending that it was no more representative of how ordinary Americans lived than the Taj Mahal was of home life in India. Actually, it was priced at

$14,000, or $100 a month with a 30-year mortgage—as Nixon put it, well within the reach of a typical steelworker.

Pausing before the model kitchen, packed with all the latest domestic gadgetry, Khrushchev blustered, "You Americans think that the Russian people will be astonished to see these things. The fact is that all our new houses have this kind of equipment." He then proceeded to complain about the wastefulness of American capitalism—in particular, how foolish it was to make so many different models of washing machines when one would do. Nixon countered, "We have many different manufacturers and many different kinds of washing machines so that the housewives have a choice." From there he expanded to broader themes: "Isn't it better to be talking about the relative merits of our washing machines than the relative strength of our rockets? Isn't this the kind of competition you want?"

Whereupon Khrushchev erupted, "Yes, this is the kind of competition we want. But your generals say they are so powerful they can destroy us. We can also show you something so that you will know the Russian spirit." Nixon took the threat in stride. "We are both strong not only from the standpoint of weapons but from the standpoint of will and spirit," he shot back. "Neither should use that strength to put the other in a position where he in effect has an ultimatum."[1]

What came to be known as the "kitchen debate" was a moment of almost surreal Cold War drama. Had it been written as a piece of fiction, the scene could be criticized justly for the belabored obviousness of its symbolism. Here the great historic confrontation between capitalism and communism presented itself in distilled miniature—as a duel of wits between two of the era's leading political figures. Just as the Cold War combined ideological conflict with great power rivalry, so this odd, unscripted exchange fused both elements, as the disputants jumped from household appliances to nuclear doom without so much as a good throat clearing. Topping it all off, the spontaneous staging of the encounter in a transplanted American kitchen foreshadowed the Cold War's eventual outcome: communism's collapse in the face of capitalism's manifest superiority in delivering the goods. In capitalism, it turned out, lay the fulfillment of communism's soaring prophecies of mass affluence.

Richard Nixon made precisely this point during his formal remarks later that day at the official opening of the exhibition. He noted with pride that the 44 million American families at that time owned 56 million cars, 50 million television sets, and 143 million radios, and that 31 million of them owned their own homes. "What these statistics demonstrate," Nixon proclaimed, "is this: that the United States, the world's largest capitalist country, has from the standpoint of distribution of wealth come closest to the ideal of prosperity for all in a classless society."[2] However casual his commitment to honesty over the course of his career, on that particular occasion Richard Nixon spoke the truth.

A century earlier, Karl Marx had peered into the womb of history and spied, gestating there, a radical transformation of the human condition. The traditional "idiocy of rural life," the newfangled misery of urban workers, would be swept away. The normal lot of ordinary people throughout history—to stand at the precipice of starvation—would be exchanged for a share in general abundance. In the new dispensation, the advanced development of productive forces would allow humanity's physical needs to be met with only modest effort. Consequently, the "realm of necessity" would yield to the "realm of freedom."

In that brave new realm, according to Marx, "begins that development of human energy which is an end in itself."[3] A forbidding bit of Teutonic abstraction: what exactly could it mean? Marx was notoriously cryptic about his vision of utopia, but through the darkened glass of his dialectics we glimpse a future in which ordinary people, at long last, could lift their sights from the grim exigencies of survival. Freed from the old yoke of scarcity, they could concentrate instead on the limitless possibilities for personal growth and fulfillment.

It was Marx's genius to see this coming transformation at a time when the main currents of economic thought led toward altogether drearier forecasts. Thomas Malthus, of course, made his name by arguing—with ample justification in the historical record—that any increase in wages for the poor would be dissipated by a swelling birth rate. Meanwhile, David Ricardo, second only to Adam Smith in the pantheon of classical economists, posited an "iron law of wages" that mandated bare subsistence as the equilibrium toward which labor markets tended. With prophetic insight, Marx grasped that the progress of industrialization would render such fatalism obsolete. On the other hand, it was the world's tragic misfortune that Marx's vision of widespread abundance was married to a profoundly misconceived rejection of competitive markets. According to Marx, the total centralization of economic decision making, in which markets and even money have been abolished and all production is "consciously regulated . . . in accordance with a settled plan," was the only path by which the realm of freedom could be reached.

History had other ideas. In a colossal irony, Marx's miracle did come to pass, but only by the grace of everything he hated. That day of the kitchen debate, "Tricky Dick" Nixon hammered the irony home. The realm of freedom had emerged, not in the bleak, dead end of communist tyranny, but in the capitalist United States.

America in the years after World War II was the scene of a great revolution in human affairs: the advent of mass affluence. With its vast natural wealth and beckoning, unsettled spaces beyond the frontier, America had always been known as a land of plenty. But here was something entirely new: comforts, conveniences, and opportunities previously only dreamed of, or at best the preserve of a tiny few, were now made available to the broad mainstream of a sprawling, populous nation. Having surmounted the stern challenges of depression and global war, American capitalism now burst forth with heightened productive forces that opened a "new frontier," an unexplored realm of dizzying choices and proliferating possibilities. In other words, the realm of freedom.

It is no exaggeration to say that in postwar America, the terms of human existence were being rewritten. The fulfillment of basic material needs, once the central and abiding challenge of life, was now assured for most of the population and moreover was increasingly taken for granted. Nothing of the kind had ever occurred before, though soon other countries would follow America's lead. It was all but inevitable, then, that a change of such fundamental importance would trigger a host of profound consequences. In particular, cultural norms and political ideologies would have to adapt to the new and unprecedented social realities. The age of abundance was therefore destined to be an age of improvisation, confusion, conflict, and high adventure.

In that respect, at least, there was continuity. The curtain was raised on the drama of mass affluence just as it fell on another wild and contentious episode: that of the transition from poverty to plenty. The transition saw the development in America of a social order dedicated with unsurpassed intensity of focus to the task of overcoming material scarcity; what followed was the development of a new, quite different social order dedicated to making the most of abundance. To make sense of the latter period, which brings us to the present day, it is necessary first to get some handle on the former.

D REAMS OF MATERIAL abundance did not begin with Marx. For millennia they consoled—and tormented—mankind with imagined glimpses of life freed from want. "And the LORD God planted a garden in Eden, in the east; and there he put the man whom he had formed. Out of the ground the LORD God made to grow every tree that is pleasant to the sight and good for food. . . ." Here at the fabled dawn of time, toil and deprivation were as yet unknown. They came soon enough, of course, inflicted as divine punishment for sinful disobedience: "By the sweat of your face you shall eat bread until you return to the ground. . . ."[4] The Fall of Man was a descent into the realm of necessity.

As the Hebrews pined for lost Eden, the ancient Greeks looked back wistfully at a long-gone golden age. "[A]nd they lived like gods, with carefree heart, remote from toil and misery . . . ," wrote Hesiod in *Works and Days*. "All good things were theirs, and the grain-giving soil bore its fruits of its own accord in unstinted plenty, while they at their leisure harvested their fields in contentment amid abundance."[5]

Popular throughout medieval Europe were tales of Cockaigne, a mythical land of comical excess and ease. "This is the land of the Holy Ghost; / Those who sleep longest earn the most," relates a Dutch rhyme from the fifteenth century. "No work is done the whole day long, / By anyone old, young, weak, or strong."[6] Pieter Brueghel the Elder's *The Land of Cockaigne* (1567) depicts the scene in typical fashion. In the center of the painting, three men—peasant, soldier, and merchant—are lolling about on the ground in gorged and stuporous repose. A legged egg and a half-eaten pig run by, both stuck with knives for the convenience of whoever eventually consumes them. A goose lies down on a platter, offering itself to be eaten. A nearby house is roofed with cakes, and in the distance a visitor is just entering the kingdom, having tunneled his way through the encircling mountains of pudding.

Recalling these old legends is a useful prod to the historical imagination. There is no making sense of the world we now inhabit until we confront the yawning chasm that separates our age from the vast bulk of human experience. The mundane, everyday, taken-for-granted circumstances of life in contemporary America's affluent society are, from the perspective of the other side of the chasm, the stuff of flightiest fantasy. We live on the far side of a great fault line, in what prior ages would have considered a dreamscape of miraculous extravagance.

Consider the most basic indicator of human welfare: life expectancy. A baby born in the Roman Empire during the reign of Augustus could look forward to an average life span of around 25 years; a baby born in medieval Europe could expect no better. As to living standards more generally, world output per head was essentially unchanged from the birth of Jesus to 1500 or so, hovering dismally at a few hundred U.S. dollars per year. Economic growth did occur, of course, but at a glacial pace relative to modern times—and, in good Malthusian fashion, it manifested itself through rising numbers rather than improvements in average welfare. Total world output expanded between two- and three-fold from AD 1 to 1500, while the global population climbed in corresponding fashion from roughly 200 million to 500 million.[7] All the works and glories that we call civilization fed off this aggregate growth, as a tiny landowning elite siphoned off perhaps a third of total production to fund, in addition to its own personal consumption, arts and letters and monuments for posterity. Those magnificent achievements, however, were but a flickering beacon in the general gloom—a shadowland of toil and suffering occupied by the masses of illiterate, unchronicled humanity.

It is entirely understandable that medieval Europeans would fantasize about a make-believe land of gluttony and sloth. Their own lives, after all, afforded precious few occasions for indulging in either vice. While actual death from starvation was relatively uncommon, food shortages were a normal part of life—especially during the spring and summer months, as stocks from the previous year's harvest began to dwindle. Lenten fasting was more than pious asceticism; it was frequently a practical necessity. And even if quantities were serviceable, quality rarely was. Regular meat eating grew increasingly common in Europe after 1300, but beforehand most people subsisted on grain and little else. The prayer for one's daily bread was meant literally.

The discovery of America gave new life to the age-old dreams of plenty—and those dreams have had a special resonance here ever since. "[I]t is a veritable Cockaigne!" Columbus wrote to the king during his third voyage to the New World.[8] Enthralled by similar fantasies, Orellana voyaged down the Amazon in search of El Dorado, while Ponce de León scoured Florida for a Fountain of Youth. Captain Arthur Barlowe, coleader of an expedition sent by Walter Raleigh, proclaimed that the natives of the Carolina coast "lived after the manner of the golden age."[9]

While America's natural bounty may have dazzled newcomers

from Europe, what passed for plenty was bleak indeed by present-day standards. Prior to the Industrial Revolution, American abundance consisted merely of a sufficiency of the most rudimentary necessities. A typical farmhouse in early nineteenth-century America was a cold and dark affair. A single fire commonly provided the only heat in the house and was also used for cooking; one or two candlesticks offered the only additional light at night. Beds were strewn around the house, even in the kitchen; many still slept on scratchy, irritating mattresses of straw tick. Carpets were rare, and the kitchen floor might be covered with sand. The battle against household dirt was hardly waged; mass-produced brooms were still a novelty. Other than one or two framed mirrors, the walls were bare. Around the home, according to an English visitor in 1818, "was a sort of out-of-door slovenliness. . . . You see bits of wood, timber, boards, chips, lying about, here and there, and pigs tramping about in a sort of confusion." [10]

Such homes at least provided basic shelter from the elements, but there was no refuge from illness and death.[11] One out of six or seven white babies did not live to see his first birthday, and few people made it past their mid-60s. In between, the hazards of disease were a constant menace. Diphtheria, whooping cough, and scarlet fever robbed many a family of young children, as did measles, mumps, and chicken pox and the secondary infections that came in their wake. Typhoid fever, bacterial dysentery, and pneumonia claimed victims of all ages.

Malaria and tuberculosis were endemic. Malaria, or "the ague," afflicted victims throughout the South with violent, shaking paroxysms. "To have the ague is in some places so common," concluded an account from the 1830s, "that the patient can hardly claim the privilege of sickness."[12] Tuberculosis, meanwhile, ravaged the Mid-Atlantic and northern states. "Consumption" probably claimed the distinction of being antebellum America's single biggest killer.

Most terrifying of all were the occasional epidemics that devastated whole communities. Yellow fever usually struck seaports, sometimes with savage results; a particularly awful outbreak in Philadelphia in 1793 killed one-tenth of the city's inhabitants. In 1832, cholera took advantage of the country's improving transportation networks to kill thousands nationwide. Some 2,500 people died in New York City alone in the space of two months.

Adding to the harshness of preindustrial life, physical violence and cruelty were ubiquitous. Dog and cock fights, bull- and bear-baiting were popular amusements, as was no-holds-barred fighting, in which gouging out the eye of one's opponent was a well-established strategem. Stocks and whipping posts stood as regular fixtures in New England town squares, and the punishments meted out there were supplemented by branding and the removal or cropping of ears. Public executions commonly drew large and boisterous crowds, peppered with young boys held aloft by their fathers to give them a better view. Back at home and in the schoolhouse, whippings and beatings and ear boxings were liberally administered to misbehaving children. All of this brutality was fueled by widespread drunkenness: consumption of pure, 200-proof alcohol by Americans over 14 years old averaged seven gallons a year during the early nineteenth century—twice the current level. In the 1820s, an estimated half of adult men were drinking at least six shots of liquor daily.[13]

Circumstances were far grimmer for the millions of Americans who lived as slaves. One-room, dirt-floored family huts were the rule, without windows or candles or much in the way of furniture. One out of three African American children died as infants; little better than half survived to adulthood. Those who cheated death and endured privation still had to contend with the whip, and worse, inflicted at the whim of their overseers and masters. And compounding all the material afflictions was the profound spiritual degradation that was slavery's cruelest curse. "The slave is a human being, divested of all rights—" wrote Frederick Douglass, "reduced to the level of a brute—a mere 'chattel' in the eye of the law—placed beyond the circle of human brotherhood—cut off from his kind—his name, which the 'recording angel' may have enrolled in heaven, among the blest, is impiously inserted in a *master's ledger,* with horses, sheep, and swine."[14]

B Y T H E C L O S E of the nineteenth century, America was in the throes of an economic revolution.[15] The country's population bulged to 76 million in 1900, more than triple what it had been a half century before. New immigrants were pouring in by the hundreds of thousands every year. Meanwhile, energy consumption quadrupled over the same period to nearly 10 quadrillion Btu annually. With their numbers and powers thus multiplied, Americans began concentrating in cities. The country contained only 10 cities with populations above 50,000 in 1850; by 1900, the total had soared to 78. The pell-mell rush to urbanization was propelled by the launching of great new industrial enterprises. Manufacturing output increased over sixfold between 1860 and 1900, and the number of production workers more than tripled from 1.3 million to 4.5 million during the same period. Americans linked their burgeoning cities to each other and to their rural hinterlands through sprawling networks of transport and communication. Over a quarter-million miles of railroad track cobwebbed the country as the twentieth century dawned, while Western Union handled more than 60 million messages a year. In all these ways—through greater numbers, denser concentration, boosted energies, mechanized muscle, and expanding interconnections—Americans ignited an efflorescence of brainpower. The number of patents issued annually for new inventions first exceeded 1,000 in 1854; in 1900 nearly 40,000 new patents were awarded. The upshot of this revolution was a fantastic increase in the country's capacity to generate wealth. Gross domestic product per capita quadrupled over the course of the nineteenth century.

The vast riches that had been created were on ostentatious display in the aristocratic luxury enjoyed by the new industrial and financial magnates and their families. For all the stately splendor of Fifth Avenue and the posh pomp of Newport, nothing surpassed George Vanderbilt's Biltmore for over-the-top, Gilded Age excess. The youngest grandson of the famous Commodore located his Xanadu on a 125,000-acre estate in the Blue Ridge Mountains near Asheville, North Carolina. The home, modeled after sixteenth-century French châteaux, took six years to construct and was formally opened on Christmas Eve 1895. Surrounded by 250 acres of landscaped gardens designed by Frederick Law Olmsted, the house covered 175,000 square feet—250 rooms in all. The library boasted 23,000 volumes; a household staff of 40 to 50 servants, along with George's voracious reading habit, kept them from gathering dust.

The indulgence in Old World opulence was new for America, but new for mankind—and thus immeasurably more significant—was the proliferation of mass-produced comforts and conveniences for the nation's large and growing middle classes. Let there be light: that primeval desire was now fulfilled as never before. Coal and kerosene oil burned 15 times brighter than candles; gas lighting, four times brighter than kerosene. On September 4, 1882, the first commercial power station began supplying electric light and power in a square-mile area around Pearl Street in lower Manhattan, thus inaugurating the era of around-the-clock, artificial daylight.

Store-bought clothing made a rapid transition from novelty to norm. In 1880, less than half of men's clothing was purchased off the rack; by 1900, the figure had shot up to 90 percent. Before the mid-nineteenth century, the only factory-made shoes were "straights" that were the same for left and right foot alike. The move to making "crooked shoes," combined with new mass-production techniques, brought comfortable, inexpensive footwear first to the working classes and then up the socioeconomic scale.

Mechanized food processing made cornucopias of affordable products available for purchase. U.S. production of wheat flour rose from 40 million barrels in 1860 to 106 million in 1900, while refined-sugar production increased from 790 million pounds to

4.9 billion over the same period. A little over a million cases of canned corn were produced in 1880; by 1900, the figure had jumped to 6.5 million. American tobacco companies produced 16 million cigarettes in 1870; thirty years later, annual production had skyrocketed to 3.9 billion.

A profusion of new goods for the home—drapes and curtains, wallpaper, carpets, rugs, clocks, furniture, dinnerware—issued forth from America's teeming factories. "We have pickle and olive forks, strawberry and ice cream forks, oyster and fish forks," observed Emily Fogg Mead, sociologist and mother of Margaret, in 1901; "we have also berry spoons, sugar spoons, soup spoons, salt spoons, mustard spoons in ever-increasing variety"—although perhaps her table was unusually well appointed.[16] Indoor plumbing, with running water and flush toilets, was becoming commonplace in nicer homes by the end of the nineteenth century. Eastman Kodak's Brownie camera hit the market in 1900; sold for $1, using film at 15 cents a roll, it brought photography to the general public. Home libraries swelled as new book titles published (including new editions) tripled from 2,076 to 6,356 between 1880 and 1900. Over the same period, the total circulation of daily newspapers climbed from 3.6 million to 15.1 million. Between 1890 and 1904, the number of pianos sold jumped from 32,000 to 374,000.

Conveying all the bounty of mass production to eager buyers were new, fast-flowing channels of mass distribution. Springing up in cities across America, like so many Cockaignes in miniature, were the dream palaces known as department stores. In New York, R. H. Macy & Company began in 1858 as a small dry-goods outlet; by 1877, it was occupying space in 11 adjacent buildings, and in 1902, it moved uptown to its present-day location at the corner of Broadway and 34th Street. In Philadelphia, John Wanamaker commenced construction of his Grand Depot store in 1876 on the site of an abandoned rail station—but only after first sanctifying the grounds by hosting a major revival that featured famed evangelist Dwight Moody. Marshall Field's in Chicago, Filene's in Boston, Meier & Frank in Portland, Hudson's in Detroit, Burdine's in Miami—all had their beginnings in the waning decades of the nineteenth century. Thanks to recent advances in glassmaking, the new department stores were able to entice customers with large, street-level window displays. The writer Edna Ferber, in high puritanical dudgeon, denounced a Chicago store window that caught her eye as "a breeder of anarchism, a destroyer of contentment, a second feast of Tantalus."[17]

One didn't need to live in a big city to be tantalized. Another retailing innovation, the mail-order catalog, brought the new consumerism's urbanities to small-town and rural America. The pioneers of selling without salesmen were based, logically enough, in Chicago, the nerve center of the nation's rail networks. Aaron Montgomery Ward went into business in 1872 with a single-page price sheet and order form; by 1884, the company's catalog ran 240 pages and offered almost 10,000 items. Richard Warren Sears and Alvah Curtis Roebuck started out in the watch business, selling discounted merchandise through railroad station agents, who, being bonded, made ideal middlemen. By 1893, Sears, Roebuck and Company had moved into general merchandise; within a dozen years, the circulation of the company's bulging catalog topped 2 million. The "nation's wish book" quickly became a beloved American icon: the promise of plenty for the land of plenty.

That promise, however, extended only so far. The new industrial economy produced great wealth—but, alas, not enough. Outside the golden circle of machine-made prosperity, millions of Americans endured lives of wretched hardship and squalor; many more struggled uncertainly on the edges of the abyss. It is not simply that the conditions they faced were appalling by the standards of today—though, of course, they were. Worse, the overall character of American life now suffered in comparison to its past. The frontier had closed, and with it the old opportunities for sturdy self-sufficiency that free land and open spaces once afforded. In the past, diligence and hard work had sufficed to guarantee (for white Americans, at least) some decent share of America's natural plenty. Now, a large and impoverished working class labored with little realistic chance of escape from want's iron grip.

Jacob Riis escaped, but he did not forget. Through his books and photographs, he afflicted the comfortable with haunting portraits of urban misery. The third of 14 children from a small town in Denmark, Riis arrived in New York in 1870 at the age of 22. For the next three years, he sought without success to gain solid footing in his adopted country. He built shacks for Pennsylvania ironworkers, worked as a brickmaker in New Jersey, assisted a country doctor, ran muskrat traps in upstate New York, worked in the lumberyards of Buffalo, sold furniture and flatirons, and, in one desperate interlude, was reduced to begging scraps from Delmonico's restaurant in New York City. Eventually, he found steady work as a police reporter for the *New York Tribune*, and thus began his career of chronicling *les misérables* of the Lower East Side.

In his 1890 classic, *How the Other Half Lives*, Riis bore witness to the huddled crush of suffering in New York's tenements. Some three-quarters of New York's 1.6 million inhabitants lived in these dismal structures—four- to six-story buildings laid out to squeeze several families onto each floor, with most of the rooms windowless and thus dark and unventilated. In the 10th, 11th, and 13th Wards downtown, 180,000 people were crammed 430 to the acre, almost quadruple the density for Manhattan as a whole. Riis told the story of one 7th Ward family of "honest, hard-working Germans, scrupulously neat, but poor." The family had nine members: husband, wife, six children, and a grandmother. "All nine lived in two rooms, one about ten feet square that served as parlor, bedroom, and eating room, the other, a small half room made into a kitchen."[18] The monthly rent for these quarters consumed more than a week's wages for the father. Riis arrived on the scene after the mother had killed herself by leaping from the window.

In an age that idealized feminine frailty, some 150,000 women and girls in the city earned their own living—many as seamstresses in the tenement sweatshops, where the workday stretched as long as 16 hours during peak seasons. Sixty cents a day was a typical wage, disposed of as follows in one representative case: "Pays $1.50 for her room; for breakfast she has a cup of coffee; lunch she cannot afford. One meal a day is her allowance."[19] Approximately 100,000 children lived on the streets, surviving by selling newspapers, blacking boots, begging, and stealing. "In warm weather a truck in the street, a convenient outhouse, or a dugout in a hay barge make good bunks," Riis reported. "Two were found making their nest once in the end of a big iron pipe up by the Harlem Bridge, and an old boiler at the East River served as an elegant flat for another couple. . . ."[20]

Alcohol provided a temporary refuge for many—and, of course, a means to deeper ruin. Riis counted 4,065 saloons below 14th Street, as compared to 111 Protestant places of worship. The final refuge awaited all, of course, but many were forced to enter as pathetically as they had lived: roughly 10 percent of all burials in New York City during 1889 took place in potter's fields.

The slums of New York were especially foul and degraded, but working-class life was strapped and harsh everywhere. Annual earnings for most workers of this era, even assuming they had steady jobs throughout the year, did not quite suffice to maintain their families at a minimal level of subsistence. Accordingly, working-class households had to rely on their children for one-fourth to one-third of total family income. Renting out a room to boarders was another common expedient for making ends meet. Even with these supplements, over 90 percent of family spending went to food, clothing, and shelter.[21] Clearly, there was little margin for error here: any period of prolonged unemployment, due to lack of work or sickness or injury, could be ruinous. In particular, unskilled workers with children too young to work lived on a knife's edge.

Work's meager recompense was matched by its brutal physical toll. Ten hours a day, six days a week were the norm for factory jobs at the end of the nineteenth century, and longer hours were by no means unheard of. Extremes of hot and cold, debilitating heavy lifting, and poisonous coal or cotton dust were among the afflictions visited routinely on America's workers. Also, ever-present danger: the annual body count for workplace deaths and injuries was around a million. In 1890, one railroad worker out of 306 was killed; one out of 30 was injured. "It is a reproach to our civilization," said President Benjamin Harrison of railway carnage, "that any class of American workmen should in the pursuit of a necessary and useful vocation be subjected to a peril of life and limb as great as that of a soldier in time of war." [22] The cruelties of the workplace were all the worse for the widespread presence of children. Some 1.75 million children between the ages of 10 and 15 were earning a living in 1900, or a little shy of one-fifth of all children that age. About one-quarter of workers in southern cotton mills were children, half under the age of 12.

Thomas Hobbes wrote famously that life in the state of nature was solitary, poor, nasty, brutish, and short. For ordinary Americans at the dawn of the twentieth century, the only noticeable improvement over that primordial state of affairs was that misery had found company. All the dazzling riches heaped up by industrial production had thus far failed to provide a significantly better quality of life for the mass of Americans. Consider, in this regard, the most basic, physiological measures of living standards: life expectancy and height (a proxy for nutrition). From 1800 to 1900, life expectancy for males registered almost no gain, inching upward from 45.5 years to 46.3. Over the same period, the average height of a native-born, white American adult male actually fell by an inch or so.[23] Stunted growth was only one obvious sign of generally poor health: in World War I, roughly one-third of the men who volunteered to fight were turned away because of chronic medical problems.[24]

And, as usually was the case, things went hardest for those not of white Protestant stock. Life expectancy for whites (male and female) in 1900 stood at 47.6 years; for nonwhites, 33.0. That same year, 40 percent of African Americans found themselves in the bottom tenth of the income distribution, as did 36 percent of Italian-born Americans and 43 percent of those born in Russia.[25] As of 1910, only 17 percent of native-born whites slept three or more to a room; for African Americans, the figure was 34 percent; for Jews, 43 percent; for the Italian-born, 44 percent; for the Romanian-born, 81 percent.[26]

A MERICA IN 1900 was writhing and shuddering to break the bonds of necessity. A diligent, determined, and sometimes ruthless vanguard had already managed to slip free, and many others were aspiring and struggling to follow their lead. But this partial and outward-rippling liberation still depended on the toil and sweat and broken bodies of laboring, suffering multitudes, for whom the dreams of factory-produced affluence were as unattainable as the kingdom of Cockaigne. Thus the simultaneously inspiring and degrading spectacle of the Gilded Age: a nation of brilliant light and dispiriting shadow, soaring highs and abysmal lows, haves and have-nots. And thus, likewise, the deep confusion of the era, as many of the brightest minds of the age mistook the engine of eventual mass deliverance—the competitive market system—for the chief bulwark of domination and oppression.

By the middle of the twentieth century, a new era in human history had begun. In the Cape Cods and ranch houses of the new suburban sprawl, in the office buildings filled with white-collar knowledge workers, on the highways and airwaves that wove a sprawling continent into a unified consuming culture, humanity's relationship with nature was being redefined and the old rules of social interdependence rewritten. A chain reaction of mutually reinforcing scientific and technological progress was making possible a life of material abundance to be shared, not just by a privileged elite, but by the vast bulk of the American populace. The realm of freedom had arrived.

In the new dispensation, Americans benefited from breathtaking gains in longevity and physiological well-being. Thanks to breakthroughs in public health and medical science, average life expectancy stood at 68.2 years in 1950—21 years longer than at the turn of the century. The improvement was especially dramatic for nonwhites: their life expectancy at birth was now 89 percent of whites', up from 70 percent a half century earlier. The most invidious of all inequalities was thus ebbing. From 1900 to 1950, one deadly disease after another was brought to heel: the annual number of deaths caused by tuberculosis plummeted from 194.4 per 100,000 people to 22.5; the death rate for typhoid dropped from 31.3 per 100,000 to 0.1; for scarlet fever, from 9.6 to 0.2; for diphtheria, from 40.3 to 0.3; for whooping cough, from 12.2 to 0.7; for measles, from 13.3 to 0.3. The overall death rate from all causes was cut nearly in half from 17.2 per 1,000 people at the turn of the century to 9.6 five decades later. All of these blessings were reflected in a happy inversion of spending patterns: in 1900, Americans collectively spent nearly twice as much on funerals as on medicine; 50 years later, the ratio was reversed.[27] Meanwhile, Americans were living healthier as well as longer lives, as average height increased nearly three inches between 1900 and 1950.[28]

The workplace was no longer the punishing meat grinder of old. With a standard 40-hour workweek and paid holidays and vacations, Americans averaged 1,903 hours on the job in 1950—or 36.6 hours per week. Child labor was quickly becoming a painful memory, as the average age for starting work now stood at 17.6 years, up from 13.0 years in 1870.[29] Workplace hazards had abated considerably. In manufacturing industries, the average number of disabling injuries per million man-hours was cut in half—from 24.2 to 12.1—between 1926 and 1955. The improvements in safety were even more dramatic for railroad workers, as the injury rate fell from 23.9 to 7.2 over the same period. Mining remained relatively dangerous, but the injury rate in 1955 (38.3 per million man-hours) was half of what it had been a mere quarter century earlier.

Public utilities and domestic appliances had rescued home life from much of its age-old drudgery. Only 24 percent of homes had running water in 1890; by 1950, the figure was 83 percent. No longer was it necessary to lug some 9,000 gallons of water into the house every year. Central heating by oil and gas (and later electricity) had become the norm: by 1960, only 5 percent of U.S. homes were heated by wood, only 12 percent by coal. Gone was the need to cut and carry 20 tons of wood every year for fireplaces and stoves, or haul 7.5 tons of coal to the stove and then spend hundreds of hours cleaning the dust off floors, furniture, and drapes. Electric lighting illuminated 94 percent of homes in 1950, up from 3 percent five decades earlier. By 1960, nine out of 10 U.S. households had mechanical refrigerators, and 73 percent owned washing machines. Those appliances had not been available to anyone, rich or poor, a half century earlier.[30]

Other new appliances came into the home—and changed everything. In 1920, Westinghouse Electric Company hit upon a novel idea for selling the radios it was producing: it would offer scheduled programming to supplement the normal one-to-one communications of ham operators. Westinghouse vice president Harry Davis teamed up with company engineer and local ham operator Dr. Frank Conrad to build a 100-watt transmitter at one of the Westinghouse plants in East Pittsburgh. On the evening of November 2, 1920, station KDKA made the first commercial radio broadcast, covering the presidential election that day and allowing listeners to learn that Warren G. Harding had defeated James M. Cox before their neighbors read about it in the newspapers the next morning. Within four years, 600 commercial stations dotted the country; by 1930, 46 percent of American homes contained a radio, and a decade later penetration had climbed to 81 percent.

Philo T. Farnsworth was a Mormon farm boy whose family had recently moved from Utah to Rigby, Idaho. In 1922, at the age of 15, the young prodigy sketched out for his high school science teacher an idea he had been working on for the past year: electronic television, in which an "image dissector" vacuum tube would beam electrons one line at a time toward a fluorescent screen. Five years later, on September 7, 1927, in a San Francisco lab, Farnsworth demonstrated that his idea worked by transmitting an image of a single straight line. The subsequent development of commercial television was slowed by World War II, but then "the tube" quickly exploded onto the scene. When the *I Love Lucy* episode "Lucy Goes to the Hospital" aired on January 19, 1953, 44 million Americans tuned in to watch the birth of Little Ricky. By 1960, television was a fixture in 87 percent of American homes.

TV and radio were just part of the profusion of novelties designed to fill Americans' expanding leisure time. In 1900, fewer than 2 percent of Americans took vacations, Christmas and Independence Day were the only two widely observed holidays, and the church and the saloon provided just about all the recreation that most people knew. By midcentury, things were radically different. In 1950, national parks, monuments, and historical areas received more than 30 million visits; attendance at horse races topped 29 million; over 17 million people went to major-league baseball games; nearly 18 million people held hunting or fishing licenses; more than 320,000 different teams competed in men's bowling leagues; and weekly attendance at movie theaters averaged 60 million.

Whether at work or play, Americans were on the move. In their pathbreaking study of "Middletown" (Muncie, Indiana) during the 1920s, Robert and Helen Lynd encountered one local resident who dismissed their meticulous fact-gathering as so much overkill. "Why on earth do you need to study what's changing this country?" he asked. "I can tell you what's happening in just four letters: A-U-T-O!"[31] The automobile was just becoming a mass consumer product at that time, and its use continued to boom as the century progressed. The number of vehicles on the road climbed from 23 million in 1930 to 62 million in 1960. Meanwhile, air travel received a huge boost on July 15, 1954, with the initial prototype flight of the Boeing 707, the nation's first commercial jetliner. Air traffic volume more than tripled during the 1950s, reaching 34 billion passenger miles in 1960.

As Americans extended themselves through space, they began to stretch intellectually as well. In 1890, the ratio of new high school graduates to 17-year-olds came to only 3.5 percent; by 1950, it had climbed to 57.4 percent. In the old days, school attendance had been a catch-as-catch-can affair, as the average student enrolled in elementary or secondary school attended only 86 days of class. In 1950, average school attendance had nearly doubled to 158 days. That same year, 2.3 million people were enrolled in colleges or other postsecondary institutions— 14.2 percent of 18- to 24-year-olds, as compared to 1.8 percent back in 1890. By the end of the fifties, America had more college students than farmers.

By the middle years of the twentieth century, America was the scene of a million raging mutinies against the material limitations of the past. Together, they added up to nothing less than the conquest of scarcity. Economists will wince at this formulation, since in the manner in which they use the word, scarcity remains as endemic in the affluent society as it was in any lean and hungry yesteryear. As long as there are trade-offs, as long as a little more of this requires a little less of that, there is scarcity in the economists' definition. Scarcity, in that sense, is an ineradicable feature of the human condition.

From a sociological perspective, however, the conquest of scarcity was real—and an historical achievement of the first order. For all the preceding millennia, physical survival stood front and center as *the* overriding problem that most people had to confront, day in and day out, for all of their lives. Paul's injunction that "if any would not work, neither should he eat" required no civil authority for its enforcement. Even in the rude natural plenty of agrarian America, most people stood face-to-face with nature, wresting their sustenance from it or, should they fail to do so, suffering directly at its hands.

In this state of affairs, choices were relegated to the margins of life. What to do, how to contribute to the great social enterprise, where to live, whom to associate with, how to spend one's resources—these were questions that, for most people, required little thought, since the options were few and the relative desirability of this or that alternative was usually obvious. As John Kenneth Galbraith observed in his 1958 book, *The Affluent Society:* "Few people at the beginning of the nineteenth century needed an adman to tell them what they wanted."[32] As with consumption decisions, so with most of the rest: limited choices, and little vexation in picking among them.

The reign of scarcity was thus one in which most people interacted directly with nature and biological imperatives were the dominant concerns of life. By contrast, in the new world of abundance, most Americans were insulated from nature by an enormous edifice of human-created technologies and institutions. And within that edifice, choices among the bewildering products of the human imagination became the dominant concerns of life—and certainties about how to select among them grew ever wispier.

With such thoughts in mind, the felicity of Marx's prophetic phrasing begins to become apparent. The old world of scarcity was a realm dominated by necessity: nature and its stern dictates set the basic terms of human existence. The new abundance, meanwhile, opened up a mad proliferation of choices—and what, in the end, is freedom but the ability to choose?

THE PRECEDING PAGES offer a brief sketch of America's rapid rise to mass affluence: from the meager, preindustrial circumstances of the early nineteenth century to the throes of industrialization at the outset of the twentieth, and on to the conquest of scarcity a mere half century later. But what propelled this dizzying ascent? What elements within American society combined to power such an astonishing transformation?

In Marx's dialectical vision, the bourgeoisie held the key that would unlock the riddle of history. This revolutionary class was the catalyst for the great revolution to come. Its unswerving dedication to profit and accumulation, and its relentless assault on all obstacles that stood in its way, would summon and ignite the energies needed to escape necessity's gravitational pull. The familiar and rousing words of *The Communist Manifesto* are worth repeating here. "The bourgeoisie, during its rule of scarce one hundred years, has created more massive and more colossal productive forces than have all preceding generations together," wrote Marx and Engels. "Subjection of Nature's forces to man, machinery, application of chemistry to industry and agriculture, steam-navigation, railways, electric telegraphs, clearing of whole continents for cultivation, canalisation of rivers, whole populations conjured out of the ground—what earlier century had even a presentiment that such productive forces slumbered in the lap of social labour?"[33]

But the bourgeois epoch, for all its immense creativity, was only a transitional phase. According to Marx, the internal contradictions at the heart of bourgeois rule would eventually overwhelm its accomplishments, and so its distinctive brand of revolutionary, exploitative dynamism would pass from history's stage. The bourgeoisie would lead humanity to the promised land, but it was not destined to reign there.

When we look back at how mass affluence in America was actually achieved, we can see that much of the Marxian narrative still rings true. Only up to a point, of course: Marx was profoundly, irredeemably wrong about what would follow the bourgeois capitalism of his day. However, since his errors are now so obvious, we are at last in a position to give proper due to those things Marx managed to get right. It is too much to say, as Hazlitt did of Burke, that "in arriving at one error he discovered a hundred truths"; but it is a fair judgment to say that if Marx was able to lead a whole century disastrously astray, it was only because he saw so much farther than most.

First and foremost, the mass affluence that Marx foretold did indeed come to pass. Further, as he predicted, the bourgeoisie of his day did play the critical role in the drama. In particular, it was the American contingent of that class who led the world in building the economic institutions of mass production and mass distribution—institutions whose ongoing development would eventually secure the conquest of scarcity. The American business class was able to lead the revolutionary charge precisely because it, to a greater extent than its counterparts anywhere else, succeeded in weaving that ever-more-intricate web of commercial relationships that Marx (following Carlyle) called the "cash nexus." As Marx argued, this revolutionary vanguard presented two faces. On the one hand, it was "constantly revolutionising the instruments of production, and thereby the relations of production, and with them the whole relations of society"; at the same time, it was not above engaging in "naked, shameless, direct, brutal exploitation."[34] Moreover, the American bourgeois ascendancy was beset by profound, internal contradictions—if not those Marx imagined. In the end, those contradictions brought America's bourgeois era to a close. By the time the realm of freedom dawned in the middle of the twentieth century, new classes, with dramatically different values, stood poised to assume leadership at the forefront of American society.

The Americans who led the way to the mass-production economy, and thus to the mass affluence it ultimately created, did so by virtue of a notable and paradoxical achievement: they united the worship of God and Mammon into a single, world-transforming faith. Known commonly as the Protestant work ethic, that faith forged its adherents into a cohesive, crusading force of calculating daredevils, straightlaced hustlers, and priggish, wild-eyed dreamers. Under the circumstances, they were precisely what was needed to rescue mankind from poverty.

"There is, probably, no people on earth with whom business constitutes pleasure, and industry amusement, in an equal degree with the inhabitants of the United States," wrote Francis Grund, a Bohemian-born immigrant to Boston, in 1837. "Business is the very soul of an American: he pursues it, not as a means of procuring for himself and his family the necessary comforts of life, but as the fountain of all human felicity."[35] Tocqueville, who was visiting America at around the same time, concurred: "I know no other country where love of money has such a grip on men's hearts."[36]

America's buzzing, ceaseless money fever went far beyond simple avarice. Here was a full-blown ethos, and one that imposed severe intellectual and moral demands on its devotees. Its intellectual component was a commitment to precise and rigorous calculation—of the flows of profit and loss, and the stocks of accumulating wealth. The moral component was a steely self-discipline whose hallmark was deferred gratification: business before pleasure, hard work and accomplishment before rest, attention to reputation and social standing before the impulses of the moment, frugality and saving before expenditure. "He that kills a breeding sow, destroys all her offspring to the thousandth generation," wrote Benjamin Franklin, the great archetype and popularizer of American bourgeois virtue. "He that murders a crown, destroys all that it might have produced, even scores of pounds."[37] This was the attitude that Max Weber called the "spirit of capitalism," or "the *duty* of the individual to work toward the increase of his wealth, which is assumed to be an end to itself."[38]

By the time that Grund and Tocqueville were making their observations, the American commercial ethos was soaring to new heights—uplifted and invigorated by a major religious revival. Religious enthusiasm in America was as old as the landing at Plymouth, but by the early days of the new republic its future seemed uncertain. Enlightenment rationalism had gained significant ground among the educated elite, as evidenced by the large number of deists among the Founding Fathers. The burgeoning frontier West, meanwhile, was raw and wild and largely unchurched. Writing in 1822, Thomas Jefferson stated confidently, "I trust that there is not a young man now living in the United States who will not die an Unitarian."[39]

Events already under way as Jefferson wrote would put the lie to his prediction. During the early decades of the nineteenth century, a surge of evangelical fervor that came to be known as the Second Great Awakening swept over the young nation. In New England, Nathaniel Taylor and Lyman Beecher (Harriet's father) spearheaded the development of "New School" Presbyterian theology. Charles Grandison Finney honed soul winning into a science with his massive revival campaigns in New York and the Midwest; Finney's ministries were credited with achieving hundreds of thousands of conversions. Camp meetings in the South and the Appalachians sparked explosive growth of the Baptist and Methodist denominations. Between 1780 and 1820, Americans built 10,000 new churches; over the next four decades, they added 40,000 more.[40]

The revitalized American Protestantism that emerged from the Second Great Awakening broke decisively with the Calvinist past. Specifically, it rejected Calvinism's central dogma of predestination and asserted the individual's free moral agency. "Let a man look into his own breast," declared Nathaniel Taylor, "and he cannot but perceive inward freedom—*inward freedom*—for if freedom be not in the *mind* it is nowhere."[41] In its more optimistic strains, the new American religion went beyond mere free will to claim the possibility of human perfectibility. Spiritual rebirth in Christ, Charles Finney argued, marked "a change from selfishness to benevolence, from having a supreme regard to one's own interest to an absorbing and controlling choice of the happiness and glory of God's Kingdom."[42] Consequently, the spread of salvation could turn America into an earthly paradise—and prepare the way for Christ's return. "If the church will do all her duty," Finney proclaimed in 1835, "the millennium may come in this country in three years."[43]

The effect of the Protestant revival was to democratize Ben Franklin's bourgeois ethos by casting it as Christian virtue—and raising its promised rewards beyond mere material success to the achievement of God's kingdom on earth. Under the sway of the new religiosity, American manners underwent a stunning transformation. A highly organized—and insufferably scolding—temperance movement brought about a revolution in drinking habits: average alcohol consumption for Americans over 14 dropped from seven gallons in 1830 to less than two gallons 15 years later.[44] Gambling, horse racing, bear-baiting, and cockfighting all experienced corresponding declines. Flogging and mutilation gave way to imprisonment in new state penitentiaries; Connecticut's last public whipping occurred in 1828. Sexuality succumbed to the new self-restraint. In New England towns, one bride in three was pregnant in the late eighteenth century; by 1840, the ratio had been cut to one in five or six.[45] Yankee ministers John Todd and Sylvester Graham (best known today for his crackers) led a crusade against the "filthy vice" of male masturbation—to what end, though, remains unclear, since reliable statistics on the campaign's effectiveness are unfortunately unavailable.[46]

The energy once dissipated in the old, wild pleasures was now channeled into godlier and more profitable pursuits. "In 1800, good men slumbered over the desecration of the Sabbath," wrote Emerson Davis in 1851. "They have since awoke."[47] School attendance surged along with churchgoing: the percentage of New York's under-20 population enrolled in school shot from around 40 percent at the turn of the century to 70 percent in the 1830s.[48] Meanwhile, the general shift from impulse to duty fed a controlled frenzy of expansive commercialism. "Work is here the Patron Saint," John Greenleaf Whittier concluded in a description of Lowell, Massachusetts. "Here is no place for that respectable class of citizens called gentlemen, and their much vilified brethren, familiarly known as loafers." Imbued with what Whittier called "the gospel according to Poor Richard's Almanac," Americans in every section of the country pooled their efforts to construct a great commercial empire.[49] New England textile mills and armament factories pioneered the techniques of mass production; roads and canals and railways lured the farmers of the sprawling interior out of subsistence and into the cash nexus; King Cotton made the South an exporting power. The Holy Spirit and the spirit of capitalism advanced in lockstep.

In the new Protestant consensus, America's unique and divinely blest mission became an article of faith. No one confessed the faith with greater gusto than John O'Sullivan, the Jacksonian editorialist who contributed "manifest destiny" to our lexicon. "Christianity and democracy are one," he declared in 1839. "What, indeed, is democracy but Christianity in its earthly aspect, Christianity made effective among the political relations of men." America, in the romantic nationalism of the time, was nothing less than the agent of Providence. "Yes, we are the nation of progress, of individual freedom, of universal enfranchisement," O'Sullivan wrote later that year. "All this will be our future history, to establish on earth the moral dignity and salvation of man—the immutable truth and beneficence of God."[50]

From a contemporary perspective, it is easy to see the massive hypocrisies on which such smugness should have choked. In a country supposedly brimming with Christian benevolence, little attention was paid to the moral dignity of the country's indigenous tribespeople as they were driven off their lands and herded west of the Mississippi. The land of individual freedom made sweeping exceptions for women, who could neither vote nor, once married, own land nor enter into legally binding agreements. Other exceptions applied to Catholics and Mormons, who faced persecution and recurrent mob violence. And, of course, the gravest assaults on both liberty and Christian charity were reserved for the millions of African Americans forced to live and work as human chattel.

Notwithstanding its tragic blind spots, and to a considerable degree because of them, the American civil religion of bourgeois Protestantism proved a near-ideal vehicle for launching the great drive toward mass affluence. The escape from necessity's clutches required the summoning and expenditure of enormous human energies that previously had "slumbered in the lap of social labour"—energies needed to press forward, relentlessly, with the transformation of both the natural and social environments. The necessary powers had been gathering for centuries in the restless, searching dynamism of modernizing Europe—in scientific investigation and technological innovation, exploration and colonization, commercial adventure and economic development, nationalism and political power sharing, speculative inquiry and cultural expression. In America, in the middle of the nineteenth century, bourgeois Protestantism focused these energies on moneymaking, supercharged them with millennial religious zeal, and made them the birthright of a large and fast-growing populace. The result was escape velocity.

The support provided by Protestant pieties to entrepreneurial activity is by now familiar ground. As Weber and countless successors have noted, the equation of business success and Christian virtue lent great encouragement to the development of the profit-seeking faculty. Furthermore, the dour abstemiousness of the bourgeois ethos was highly functional in an age still characterized by grinding scarcity. The stern mandates of thrift and ceaseless industry, as with the suspicion of all forms of sensual pleasure, may have been irrational from the standpoint of personal happiness; they were, however, ideally suited to the needs of group advancement. Any income spent frivolously was income unavailable for investment; any time spent frivolously was time invested unprofitably. Such grim single-mindedness harnessed the power of compound interest to accelerate exponentially the amassing of capital—and with that, the productivity of enterprise; and with that, the overall standard of living. The "worldly asceticism" of the bourgeoisie thus hastened the coming of mass hedonism.

Reaching the realm of freedom required innumerable contributions of individual talent and hard work—contributions that the Protestant work ethic steeled Americans to make. But individual effort, however inspired or dedicated, was not enough. Also required were organization and cooperation on a scale and level of complexity beyond anything in prior human experience. The conquest of scarcity depended on radical alteration, not only of humanity's relationship with nature, but also social relationships as well. Here again, America's civil religion helped the country to rise to the occasion.

Industrialization was as much an organizational as a technological revolution, and at the center of the action was the development of the large-scale business enterprise. Prior to 1850, it didn't really exist. Nicholas Biddle ran the Second Bank of the United States during the 1820s and 1830s with only two assistants.[51] Around the same time, John Jacob Astor, the richest man in America, employed just a handful of clerks to manage his American Fur Company.[52] A century later, everything had changed. "What we look for in analyzing American society today is therefore the institution which sets the standard for the way of life and the mode of living of our citizens; which leads, molds, and directs; which determines our perspective on our own society; around which crystallize our social problems and to which we look for their solution," wrote Peter Drucker in his seminal 1946 book, *Concept of the Corporation.* "And this, in our society today, is the large corporation."[53] The numbers supported Drucker: by 1947, the 200 largest industrial corporations accounted for 30 percent of total U.S. value added in manufacturing and 47.2 percent of corporate manufacturing assets.[54]

The modern, multiunit business corporation was only the most visible product of industrialization's great organizing drive. The standardization of time zones, weights and measures, railroad track gauges, and commodity grades; the professionalization of law, medicine, architecture, engineering, accounting, and teaching; the establishment of research universities; the emergence of labor unions and trade associations; the development of insurance, credit reporting, and tradable securities markets— all these and other innovations, along with the mass migration to the cities, helped to create the new social landscape in which Big Business held sway.

That dramatically altered social landscape—urbanized, organized, rationalized, bureaucratized—was the seedbed of mass abundance. In it, people were able to trust each other even in the absence of personal knowledge or family or communal ties. Perfect strangers, often scattered across miles and years, were willing to stake their money, their economic futures, and even their lives on the assumption that unknown others were doing their part. And thus were made possible the large-scale, long-term investments that generate the wealth of the affluent society.

If the organizational revolution raised dramatically the level of trust in the economic sphere, it also presupposed a basic capacity for trust already present in the broader culture. The very idea of collaborating with others across blood or geographical lines requires a leap of the moral imagination that has been exceptional in human history. Most people in most times and places have lived in the narrow ambit of tightly restricted moral horizons: the circle of empathy and trust within which the force of reciprocal obligations was felt did not extend much beyond family or tribe. Dealings with those outside the circle were seen as a zero-sum affair. Outsiders were to be feared and appeased if powerful, despised and exploited if weak.

The expansion of commerce and the rise of national consciousness in Europe had been gradually widening moral horizons for centuries. Americans, though, developed a capacity for trust—and therefore collaboration—beyond anything ever before achieved. "Americans of all ages, all stations of life, and all types of disposition are forever forming associations," wrote Alexis de Tocqueville. "There are not only commercial and industrial associations in which all take part, but others of a thousand different types—religious, moral, serious, futile, very generous and very limited, immensely large and very minute."[55] Fired by religious certitude, and buzzing with commercial zeal and a sense of national mission, Americans (or the white Protestant majority, at any rate) embraced a democratized moral community that extended across a continent.

At the time Tocqueville was writing, the American flair for organizing was still mainly confined to the local or regional level. Until the later decades of the nineteenth century, the country remained, in historian Robert Wiebe's words, "a society of island communities"—a nation of largely autonomous small towns.[56] At the same time, deep-seated sectional differences sliced up the country like so many fault lines. Over time, though, the resistance of traditional localism could not compete with the driving, expansive dynamism of the bourgeois Protestant consensus. Once the greatest challenge to that consensus—the southern slave economy—was destroyed in the fire and slaughter of the Civil War, the way was clear for a hurtling juggernaut of economic development and social change.

The starchy bourgeois obsession with "respectability"—which today looks so frightfully fusty and dull—was a vital aid in greasing the juggernaut's wheels. The remaking of the social landscape shifted the locus of personal loyalties from inherited bonds with kin and community to chosen, affiliational ties based on occupation and shared values. The punctilious probity of bourgeois morality eased that transition by allowing people to signal to each other their unswerving commitment to upright dealings in all phases of life—and thus their trustworthiness. "The most trifling actions that affect a man's credit are to be regarded," advised Benjamin Franklin. "The sound of your hammer at five in the morning or nine at night heard by a creditor makes him easy six months longer, but if he sees you at a billiard-table or hears your voice at a tavern, when you should be at work, he sends for his money the next day." As the "gospel according to Poor Richard's Almanac" became the national creed, reputation for clean living substituted for personal knowledge, blood, and locality as the primary basis of trust.

The intertwined growth of faith and credit was showcased in the careers of brothers Arthur and Lewis Tappan. Born in Northampton, Massachusetts, during the 1780s and raised, in a fitting coincidence, in Jonathan Edwards's old house, they moved to New York during the 1820s and entered the silk-importing business. Striking it rich, the Tappans became generous benefactors of the Second Great Awakening. They donated the stately Manhattan headquarters of the American Tract Society, which distributed over 30 million pieces of Christian literature between 1825 and 1835; they converted a sleazy New York theater into a church and installed evangelist Charles Finney as pastor; they later helped to establish Oberlin College, where Finney was to serve as president. In addition to their strictly Christian charities, Arthur and Lewis served as leaders of the abolitionist cause, founding the American Anti-Slavery Society and financing the Underground Railroad.

After their silk business went bust in the Panic of 1837, the brothers Tappan hit upon a way to combine their twin passions of caring for souls and making money. In the 1840s they formed the nation's first commercial credit-rating service, the Mercantile Agency, that still exists today as Dun & Bradstreet. The agency's credit reporters acted as capitalism's moral guardians, ensuring that resources flowed to people of "character" and away from those with "intemperate habits." Comments in credit reports like "leads a sporting life," "got mixed up with a bad woman," or "likes to drink too much" could send lenders running; on the other hand, "industrious young men, formerly clerks" and others like the gentleman who "has been pretty wild but has recently married and will probably be more steady now" could expect to profit from the agency's seal of approval.[57] Thus were God and Mammon reconciled: virtue and vice went straight to the bottom line.

T H E   R I S E   T O mass affluence was anything but a smooth and pleasant journey. The way forward led through brutal hardships and roiling antagonisms, at the root of which lay the transitional nature, now clear in retrospect, of the early industrial economy. Here was great new wealth, but not nearly enough. Although immense productive forces had been unleashed, they remained insufficient at this early stage to secure general abundance. As a necessary result, the new social order was a steep and tottering hierarchy in which the few prospered on the backs of a suffering multitude. That harsh reality could be ameliorated around the edges, but at its core the problem was intractable—there simply wasn't enough to go around.

As long as scarcity reigned, there was no escape from the cruel dilemma of lifeboat ethics. The lucky few who had found safety could fight off those struggling to climb aboard, or else they could allow the craft to be capsized and all to be lost. Few were willing to face this abysmal choice squarely, so comforting delusions were seized upon instead. Defenders of the bourgeoisie's fortunate position claimed that it reflected either God's will or the laws of nature. On the other side, supporters of the working class's claims contended that the persistence of mass poverty amidst all the new wealth was due to deep-seated flaws in the competitive market system—due, in other words, to the very system that was the only hope for alleviating poverty in the long run.

In addition to the fundamental conflict between the haves and have-nots, the messy, disruptive dynamism of the mass-production economy opened up nasty divisions within the upper and middle classes. Small business versus big, country versus city, old money versus new, intelligentsia versus commercialism—here again, market competition and the consumer society it was creating were at the center of raging controversy. Amidst rife confusion about how the new economic order really worked, a host of social reforms—ranging from salutary to crackpot— were advanced and resisted in pell-mell fashion. All too often, babies were tossed while bathwater was retained.

All of these stresses and strains exposed the contradictions at the heart of the bourgeois Protestant consensus. That consensus had formed in an agrarian America of small towns and free land on the frontier; it formed before waves of immigration brought Catholics and Jews in large numbers; it formed before Darwin and the sophisticated, new "higher criticism" of biblical scholarship shook the old, unquestioning faith in the literal truth of Holy Writ. In an urbanizing, industrializing America—with its complex webs of highly organized interdependence, its Babel of diverse faiths and cultures, and its stark and invidious contrasts between rich and poor—the old-time civil religion grew increasingly embattled. The great appeal of the old creed, and the source of its energizing power, had been its democratic universality: the gospel according to *Poor Richard's Almanac* promised eternal salvation and worldly success to all comers. By the last decades of the nineteenth century, however, the pretense of universality was coming unglued—and with it the ascendancy of the old consensus.

It had, of course, been a pretense from the beginning. Exploitation of the weak and powerless was not new to the industrial era. The expropriation of the aboriginial population and the enslavement of Africans were far darker crimes than any committed against the working class. The laborers who left the countryside and the peasants who crossed the Atlantic streamed into America's factories, as grim as they were, because they offered a better life than what had been left behind. The bargains they struck with their employers were hard ones, but there was a fundamental and qualitative difference between "wage slavery" and the real thing.

Hard bargains are generally unstable, however, and they certainly were in this case. With their backs against the wall of destitution, workers fought however they could to wring some mitigation from their employers. They demanded higher pay, shorter working hours, better working conditions, greater autonomy on the job, compensation for injuries, the right to organize into unions—anything to inch forward and create a little breathing space.

Acting on their own, workers staged countless private rebellions. Often, they just didn't show up. "Our mill operatives are much like other people, and take their frequent holidays for pleasure and visiting," complained a textile maker in 1878. "Blue Mondays" were commonplace in the coalfields; during World War I, absenteeism rates of 10 percent or more were typical for many industries. Quitting was another option. According to the U.S. Bureau of Labor Statistics, the "normal" turnover rate in American factories was 115 percent during 1913–1914; in other words, manufacturers had to replace their entire workforce in less than a year. Prior to the announcement of the $5 day, Ford Motor Company was plagued with a chaotic turnover rate of 370 percent.[58]

Acting together, workers sought strength in solidarity. A welter of trade unions formed to augment the bargaining power of those with specific skills. Often, though, these narrow craft-based associations worked at cross-purposes: what was good for the Brotherhood of Locomotive Engineers might not be good for the Brotherhood of Locomotive Firemen, or the conductors'

or brakemen's organizations, either. To overcome such problems, some labor organizers sought to unite skilled and unskilled
workers on an industry-wide basis. The Knights of Labor, under
the leadership of Terence Powderly, were the most successful effort along those lines during the nineteenth century; at their
high-water mark in 1886, the Knights boasted over 700,000
members. In the early twentieth century, the radical Industrial
Workers of the World, or "Wobblies," combined revolutionary
rhetoric with efforts to organize unskilled workers in the mining, lumber, and textile industries. Whatever their size, scope, or
ideology, labor unions employed a standard arsenal of pressure
tactics, including slowdowns, boycotts, strikes, and even sabotage.

In addition to flexing their economic muscle, workers sought
to advance their interests through the political process. In 1847,
New Hampshire became the first state to pass maximum hours
legislation, declaring 10 hours to be the legal workday; the next
year, Pennsylvania followed suit and also outlawed factory work
for children under 12 years old. Similar laws would be passed
repeatedly at the state level, though their mandates were typically honored in the breach. More successful was the later wave
of workmen's compensation laws, initiated by Wisconsin in
1911, which instituted regular benefits for workers and their de-
pendents in the event of job-related injury, illness, or death.
Labor also won important victories on restricting immigration
and its downward pressure on wages: first, in the nineteenth
century, with bans on Chinese immigration and importing workers under contract; finally, in the 1920s, with strict, across-the-
board limits that brought to a close the era of mass migration to
America.

Employers, for their part, fought at every turn to break the
resistance of their unruly workers. They enforced workplace discipline with harsh fines—a half day's pay for being late or talking
on the job. They rejected calls for shorter workdays as morally
suspect. "It is not the hours per day that a person *works* that
breaks him down," commented one Massachusetts manufac-

turer, "but the hours spent in dissipation." [59] Demands for higher pay met with equal disdain. "Everyone but an idiot knows that the lower classes must be kept poor or they will never be industrious"—that brutal assessment by the English writer Arthur Young in 1771 was still a widely shared view more than a century later. If workers are paid too much, wrote Frederick Winslow Taylor, the father of "scientific management," to Upton Sinclair, they "work irregularly and tend to become more or less shiftless, extravagant and dissipated. Our experiments showed . . . that for their own best interest it does not do for most men to get rich too fast." [60] Reassured by this highly convenient view of their workers' interests, employers fended off unions with "yellow dog" contracts and blacklists; they broke strikes with replacement workers and enforcers from Pinkerton's. When their own considerable resources proved insufficient, they fortified their cause with the armed might of the state, obtaining injunctions and the assistance of militias and federal troops to quell labor unrest.

Confrontations between capital and labor were frequently bloody. In the Pennsylvania coalfields, the murder of dozens of mine officials during the 1860s and 1870s led to the dubious conviction and execution of 20 alleged members of the "Molly Maguires." The Great Railroad Strike of 1877 quickly erupted into a nationwide spasm of violence, with riots in Baltimore, Chicago, Kansas City, Pittsburgh, St. Louis, and San Francisco. The strike sputtered after a few weeks, but by then over a hundred people had been killed and some $10 million in property destroyed. On May 3, 1884, labor trouble at the McCormick Harvester Works on the outskirts of Chicago sparked a confrontation between locked-out workmen and strikebreakers; four men were killed in the riot. The next evening, some 3,000 people turned out for a protest meeting in Haymarket Square; a bomb exploded, police opened fire, and another 10 people were killed. On July 5, 1892, 300 armed Pinkertons were shipped by barge up the Monongahela River to guard the Homestead steel mills during a lockout. Steelworkers were waiting for them at the mills when they arrived, and the resulting clash left a dozen dead on each side. In June 1894, a strike of the Pullman Palace Car Company escalated dramatically when railroad workers staged a sympathetic boycott, paralyzing rail traffic around the country. By the time the strike was put down in August, some 34 people had been killed, most in confrontations with state and federal troops in Chicago. On June 6, 1904, a bombing by members of the Western Federation of Miners killed 13 strikebreakers in Cripple Creek, Colorado; a retaliatory attack on the union hall by the local employers' association killed a half-dozen men. Ten years later, Colorado mine workers were once again on strike, and 74 people died before it was over. The darkest day was April 20, 1914, when National Guard troops attacked and burned an encampment of workers in what became known as the Ludlow massacre; among the victims were 11 children and two women.

The recurrent outbreaks of class warfare—only the most notorious melees have been mentioned here—reflected the grim, zero-sum logic of the lifeboat. American entrepreneurial culture was committed with religious certitude to a social project of profit, accumulation, reinvestment, and growth. Immersed in that culture, employers had no interest in diverting potential profits toward the marginal amelioration of their workers' lot. They paid as little as they could get away with, and that was very little indeed. On Sundays, they might have proclaimed the brotherhood of man; but for the rest of the week, it was the brotherhood of the bourgeoisie that counted.

Facing the disconnect between their Christian creed and their capitalist practice, with no foreknowledge of the general affluence to come, was psychologically unbearable for the bourgeois ruling classes. They soothed their consciences with faith that their exalted station was in accordance with divine providence— or, the next best thing, the laws of nature. "[N]o man in this land suffers from poverty unless it be more than his fault—unless it be his *sin*," declared the famous minister Henry Ward Beecher (son of Lyman, brother of Harriet). "It is said that a dollar a day is not enough for a wife and five or six children," Beecher commented during the 1877 railroad strike. "No, not if the man smokes or drinks beer. . . . But is not a dollar a day enough to buy bread with? Water costs nothing; and a man who cannot live on bread is not fit to live."[61] The great revivalist Dwight Moody sang from the same hymnal. "It is a wonderful fact," he claimed, "that men and women saved by the blood of Jesus rarely remain the subjects of charity, but rise at once to comfort and respectability."[62]

The proclamations of Christian moralists were seconded by social scientists, who secularized the traditional Protestant work ethic by dressing it up in Darwinian garb. "They do not perceive that here 'the strong' and 'the weak' are terms which admit of no definition unless they are made equivalent to the industrious and the idle, the frugal and the extravagant," wrote William Graham Sumner, Yale sociologist and leading light of the American "social Darwinist" school, in response to claims that capitalist competition was hard on the weak. "They do not perceive, furthermore, that if we do not like the survival of the fittest, we have only one possible alternative, and that is the survival of the unfittest. The former is the law of civilization; the latter is the law of anti-civilization." From this perspective, any departure from the strictures of laissez-faire was condemned as quixotic defiance of natural law. Competition in the race for survival, wrote Sumner, "can no more be done away with than gravitation."[63]

Such rationalizations provided comfort to the comfortable, but they could not hold up under sustained intellectual scrutiny. The gathering intensity of such scrutiny was another emerging contradiction of the bourgeois order. Just as that order gave rise to an external threat in the form of a large, impoverished working class, so it created an internal threat—a growing intelligentsia of scholars and writers, and their audience of educated professionals, who were *in* the bourgeois world but not *of* it. This "adversary culture" enjoyed the perquisites of middle- or upper-class affluence, but was increasingly disaffected from the values and priorities of the old Protestant consensus.

The main currents of thought in the late nineteenth and early twentieth centuries were moving swiftly away from the complacency and fatalism of the bourgeois establishment. Leading theologians, confronting Darwin and German higher criticism, gave up the old dogmatic insistence on biblical inerrancy and sought to reorient an overhauled, liberal Protestantism in the direction of social activism. "The gospel has been very imperfectly heard by anyone to whom it has brought no other tidings than that of personal salvation," wrote Washington Gladden, a prominent adherent of the new "social gospel." "For in truth the individual is saved only when he is put into right relations to the community in which he lives, and the establishment of these right relations among men is the very work that Christ came to do."[64] Meanwhile, a new breed of social scientists scoffed at the notion that existing social institutions reflected in their every detail the immutable workings of natural law and thus were beyond improvement. "It is only through the artificial control of natural phenomena that science is made to minister to human needs," argued Lester Ward, a vociferous critic of the laissez-faire school; "and if social laws are really analogous to physical laws, there is no reason why social science may not receive practical applications such as have been given to physical science."[65]

Adherents of the new thinking rejected utterly the equation of wealth and personal merit. "[T]he money-strong represent, in some sense, the survival of the fittest—not necessarily the best . . . ," wrote the sociologist Charles Cooley. "They are not necessarily the ablest in other regards, since only certain kinds of ability count in making money; other kinds, and those often the highest, such as devotion to intellectual or moral ideals, being even a hindrance."[66] By the same token, poverty was not necessarily evidence of moral unfitness. "[T]he only consolation, the only hope," Lester Ward contended, "lies in the truth . . . that as far as the native capacity, the potential quality, the 'promise and potency,' of a higher life are concerned, those swarming, spawning millions, the bottom layer of society . . . are by nature the peers of the boasted 'aristocracy of brains' that now dominates society."[67]

In its criticism of bourgeois Protestant dogmas, the new thinking was devastatingly on target. Though it was certainly possible to improve one's station in American society, the fact is that most of the bourgeoisie were born into it, and thus their primary moral claim to the fruits and opportunities of relative affluence lay in their skill at choosing parents. And for many at the bottom, unflagging diligence and backbreaking toil were repaid with only the barest sustenance; absence of education and connections, and the vagaries of boom-and-bust cycles, could overwhelm even the most heroic of individual efforts.

Furthermore, the idea that the existing political and legal system represented some kind of sacrosanct, natural order was self-serving fantasy. The newborn industrial economy was the product of a long and tortuous process of historical development—and, thank heavens, was the final word in nothing. Moreover, despite all their fulminations about the inviolability of private property, America's business classes were happy to play fast and loose with property rights when it suited them. Land grants for railroads and protective tariffs for manufacturers were only the most obvious instances of picking pockets to fatten profits. More fundamentally, new common-law doctrines on nuisance, negligence, foreseeable damages, and negotiable instruments ushered in sweeping redefinitions of property rights—all to make way for industrial expansion.[68]

Yet, in advancing their own positive agenda, the social gospelers and pragmatic reformers fell into deeper delusions than those that afflicted the defenders of laissez-faire. They could not accept the brutal fact that there wasn't enough wealth to go around; they could not credit their stodgy, philistine, bourgeois nemeses with discovering the path to eventual deliverance. Instead, they fooled themselves into thinking that the poverty and misery that they saw all around them were caused by the competitive market system—and, in particular, by the large business enterprises that now played a leading role within that system. They despised business rivalry. "Competition, which is the instinct of selfishness, is another word for dissipation of energy,

while combination is the secret of efficient production," wrote
Edward Bellamy, whose utopian socialist novel, *Looking Backward*, was the best-selling American book of the late nineteenth
century.[69] They despised the profit motive. According to Thorstein Veblen, perhaps the most brilliant and most influential of
the new school of economists, the dominance of "pecuniary interests" was responsible for "chronic derangement, duplication,
and misdirected growth."[70] They believed, fantastically, that
public spiritedness could substitute for the prospect of gain as
the primary motivation in economic life. And they believed, even
more fantastically, that the centralization of economic decision
making in the hands of a dramatically expanded government
would accomplish that change in motivation.

And so overlaying the bitter class struggle was a howling ideological confusion within the socioeconomic elite. On one side
stood defenders of capital who believed that the status quo in all
its particulars was divinely ordained. On the other stood defenders of labor who, seduced by crackpot utopian schemes, sought
to junk the current system altogether. In the middle, difference
splitters and opportunists tacked this way and that. Truth and
error were distributed haphazardly among the contending factions. The defenders of laissez-faire, for their part, were correct
that competition was essential for economic progress. The locus
of competition, however, was not overall moral merit or quality
of bloodlines, as the social Darwinists presumed; rather, it was
ideas about what consumers want and how best to deliver it to
them—ideas whose originators and implementers could be
scoundrels as well as saints. The champions of the working class
were right that the poor could be lifted up, but their hostility to
profit-seeking enterprise was misplaced and their faith in government's beneficence grossly and naïvely overblown. Big Business and its supporters understood the creative power of
large-scale production, but scanted the critical importance of
business rivalry; the trustbusters presented the mirror image.

Such was the muddle of American political economy during
the messy transition to mass affluence. The system endured its

gravest crisis during the economic catastrophe of the 1930s, but in the end the competitive market order survived intact—modernized with innovations in corporate governance and regulatory oversight, stabilized with social policies to mitigate poverty and economic dislocation, and deranged with heavy doses of collectivist mismanagement. By surviving, the market order was ultimately able to amass sufficient resources to extend prosperity to all but the margins of American society—and thus to buy, for a brief time at least, social and ideological peace.

In the years after World War II, America reached the realm of freedom. The project of growth and accumulation launched a century earlier by a spiritually energized Protestant bourgeoisie had succeeded—in material terms, at least—beyond its instigators' wildest expectations. But America gained the world only to transform its own soul. The economic revolution triggered a revolution in values—one in which the old bourgeois Protestant consensus would be turned on its head.

Climbing Maslow's Pyramid

———•◆•———

"It is quite true that man lives by bread alone—when there is no bread," observed Abraham Maslow in his pathbreaking 1943 article, "A Theory of Human Motivation." "But what happens to man's desires when there *is* plenty of bread and when his belly is chronically filled?"[1]

Writing during the depths of World War II, Maslow had put his finger on what would be the fundamental issue in postwar American life. There was plenty of bread in the affluent society—so now what? What new challenges would emerge, and what new motivations would rise to the fore, now that the age-old struggle against scarcity had been won?

Abraham Maslow was born in New York City in 1908, the son of Russian Jewish immigrants and the oldest of seven children.[2] Young Abraham grew up in modest, lower-middle-class comfort—and withering emotional barrenness. His father, Samuel, ran a barrel-repair business in Manhattan and spent little time at home, absorbed in his work and steering clear of his shrewish wife. Rose, Abraham's mother, was nothing short of a horror. Intensely miserly despite the fact that her husband earned a decent living, she kept a lock on the refrigerator to prevent her children from snacking. Her penny-pinching, furthermore, was embellished by a vicious cruel streak. Once, as a young child, Abraham came upon two stray kittens and decided to take them home. When Rose discovered the kittens in the basement, drinking milk from her dishes, she killed them right in front of her little boy, bashing their skulls against the basement wall. Maslow thus discovered early in life that bread alone was not enough: economic security was no consolation for a love-starved boy.

Like so many other bright young New Yorkers of his day, Abraham took advantage of that broad avenue of upward mobility, City College. He tried other, conventional routes of further ascent—law school and medical school—but was unable to stick with either. Intellectual passions won out over economic ambitions, and he ended up earning a PhD in psychology from the University of Wisconsin. Entering the job market in the middle of the Great Depression meant that finding a position would be difficult, and the reflexive anti-Semitism that then prevailed in academia made matters still worse (several advisers urged him to change his first name to something more . . . acceptable). Overcoming all obstacles, Maslow was eventually able to land a job at unprestigious Brooklyn College. He later moved to the newly formed Brandeis University, established as a refuge for Jewish scholars and students.

Maslow's early research focused on animal behavior—specifically, how different basic drives interact and influence each other's expression. In one experiment, he showed that monkeys would continue to eat treats like chocolate or peanuts well after they were full from consuming their regular diet. Even animals, he concluded, were motivated by drives other than simple, physiological survival. For his doctoral dissertation, Maslow conducted an extensive study of sexual and dominance behavior among monkeys. Through observation of zoo animals as well as controlled experiments, he determined that a monkey's relative power status in its social group has a powerful influence on its sexual behavior—a ho-hum commonplace today, but at the time an important discovery.

Maslow soon moved away from animal research and began exploring the broader implications of drive interaction for human psychology. The result was his famous theory of the hierarchy of needs, first outlined in "A Theory of Human Motivation." What happens when there is plenty of bread? *"At once other (and higher) needs emerge* and these, rather than physiological hungers, dominate the organism. And when these in turn are satisfied, again new (and still higher) needs emerge, and so on."[3]

Maslow's hierarchy is conventionally depicted as a pyramid. At the base are physiological needs, followed by the need for safety and security. When those elementary drives are unsatisfied, they move urgently to the center of attention. When gratified, they are usually taken for granted. Moving up the pyramid, people focus on love and belonging needs as well as the desire for self-respect and social status. At the summit, according to Maslow, is the drive to achieve self-actualization. "Even if all these [other] needs are satisfied, we may still often (if not always) expect that a new discontent and restlessness will soon develop, unless the individual is doing what he is fitted for," he wrote. "A musician must make music, an artist must paint, a poet must write, if he is to be ultimately at peace with himself."[4]

Maslow was attempting to explain individual psychology, not social development, but his insights went to the very heart of the great changes in American life unleashed by widespread prosperity. Freed from physical want and material insecurity, Americans in their millions began climbing Maslow's pyramid. They threw over the traditional Protestant ethos of self-denial and hurled themselves instead into an utterly unprecedented mass pursuit of personal fulfillment, reinventing and reinvigorating the perennial quests for belonging and status along the way. The realm of freedom, once imagined as a tranquil, happily-ever-after utopia, turned out to be a free-for-all of feverish and unquenchable desire.

As secure access to the fruits of mass production permeated the expanding middle classes and then spread out into the rest of society, the American character began to change. The alteration was gradual, but over the course of decades the cumulative effect was fundamental. By the 1950s, when the postwar boom ushered in the age of abundance, America's dominant culture was far, far removed from the preindustrial Protestant consensus of a century before. The transition to mass affluence had entailed a transition to a new ethos.

The substance of the change was this: from a scarcity-based mentality of self-restraint to an abundance-based mentality of self-expression. The aversion to material luxury was the first thing to go, as Americans reveled in wave after wave of new, factory-made comforts and conveniences. Across classes and religions and ethnic backgrounds, "enough" proved an ever-receding horizon, and the common commitment to chase that horizon became the glue that held an increasingly pluralistic society together. With the general triumph of consumerism came a host of related changes, as the liberation of desire spilled over into one area of life after another. Sexuality grew less inhibited, while physical fitness and mental health became the objects of increasingly fervent attention. Meanwhile, the continuing expansion and growing complexity of the division of labor, impelled forward by the consumerist consensus, worked to undermine traditional resistance to the new mass hedonism. More and more women were lured out of the home and into the workforce; rising educational levels bred deepening skepticism about received dogmas of any kind.

Social conservatives today frequently look back on the 1950s as a halcyon period of stability and innocence. Lift away the nostalgic fog, though, and a very different picture emerges. Beneath the gray flannel moderation and genial civility of the Eisenhower years was a social order in the throes of cultural commotion. It is no accident that the modern conservative movement was born during the fifties: the founding fathers of the contemporary right understood clearly that the old, absolutist, bourgeois ethos was collapsing around them. And they were as powerless to stop it as they were to imagine what would come next.

T HE ASCENT OF Maslow's pyramid had its beginnings back in the Gilded Age, when stern Protestant morality first started to crumble under the weight of machine-made bounty. Among the nation's industrial elite, a new conception of economic life began to emerge. The old suspicion of luxury and sensual pleasure relaxed and gave way; the ascetic restraints of thrift and deferred gratification loosened and unwound. In the traditional bourgeois ethic, work was its own reward and wealth served only as a sign of virtue and a security buffer against scarcity. Now, affluence became a playground chase for self-assertion and personal fulfillment.

Thorstein Veblen skewered the new lifestyle in his *The Theory of the Leisure Class*. Veblen understood that "[i]ndustrial efficiency is presently carried to such a pitch as to afford something appreciably more than a bare livelihood to those engaged in the industrial process." Under those novel conditions, motivations were changing. "[S]o far as regards those members and classes of the community who are chiefly concerned in the accumulation of wealth," he wrote, "the incentive of subsistence or of physical comfort never plays a considerable part."

No longer pressed by physical needs, the upper reaches of the bourgeoisie now constituted a new kind of aristocracy, or "leisure class," in which "pecuniary emulation" and "conspicuous consumption" replaced the old struggle for military glory. Within this class, "[i]t becomes indispensable to accumulate, to acquire property, in order to retain one's good name." Such a competition, Veblen understood, could go on indefinitely: "But as fast as a person makes new acquisitions, and becomes accustomed to the resulting new standard of wealth, the new standard forthwith ceases to afford appreciably greater satisfaction than the earlier standard did." And as the business elite chased the will-o'-the-wisp, the middle and lower classes began to follow in their train. In the burgeoning pecuniary culture, the leaders of the race sought "popular esteem," while those trailing the pack longed merely for the "complacency which we call self-respect."[5]

Veblen despised this commercialized status seeking, but his

contemporary Simon Patten took an altogether sunnier view. Largely forgotten now but a prominent economist in his day, Patten enthusiastically embraced the historic shift from an economy of "deficit" and "pain" to one of "surplus" and "pleasure." Industrialization, he saw presciently, was ushering in a new era of abundance—a "new basis of civilization," as he titled his most widely read work. Over the long run, he believed, economic advance would lead to cultural and spiritual uplift, as satiation with creature comforts and baser amusements would prompt the cultivation of higher aspirations and more refined tastes. Patten therefore rejected as outmoded the old "ideal of restraint, denial, and negation." "We encourage self-denial when we should encourage self-expression," he wrote. "We try to suppress vices when we should release virtues." According to Patten, "The new morality does not consist in saving, but in expanding consumption. . . . We lack . . . courage to live joyous lives, not remorse, sacrifice, and renunciation."[6]

It is an interesting question whether Veblen or Patten left the bigger mark. Veblen's name has survived, his famous turns of phrase remain in general currency, and his books are still in print. Patten, on the other hand, has faded into obscurity. Yet his legacy lives on in an institution he did much to build: the Wharton School of the University of Pennsylvania, the nation's first business school. Every newly minted MBA bears Patten's stamp, as do all the anonymous contributions of business-school graduates to the triumph of the money culture that Veblen so reviled.

Whatever his hand in the matter, it is inarguable that events broke Patten's way. The progress of industrialization exposed a fundamental conflict between the two great expressions of the bourgeois Protestant ethos: the highly organized yet raucously competitive commercial order on the one hand, and the religiously inspired repression of individual desire on the other. Technological breakthroughs were opening up exhilarating vistas of comfort, convenience, and luxury—and immense profits and power for those who charged ahead and seized command of the new terrain. But wasn't it sinful to indulge in worldly pleasures—and, worse, to traffic in corruption? Caught between the contradictory demands of God and Mammon, America's business vanguard finessed the dilemma by reinterpreting the divine will.

The evolving message of Henry Ward Beecher reflected the general drift of thought. In his widely read *Seven Lectures to Young Men* of 1844, Beecher reiterated the traditional view that idle hands are the devil's workshop. "The indolent mind," he warned, "is not empty, but full of vermin."[7] A few decades later, he was taking a decidedly softer line. Religion, he stated approvingly, was "getting rid of the old ascetic side" and becoming "more joyful, more loving, more genial, humane and sympathetic."[8] As it happened, Beecher may have gone too far in shedding his own ascetic side. In 1874, he was accused of committing adultery with Elizabeth Tilton, the wife of a friend and a member of his church. Although a civil jury failed to reach a verdict and the church later cleared him, the scandal dogged Beecher for the rest of his life.

When it came to making Christianity safe for consumerism, no one could match the exuberant efforts of Bruce Barton. The son of a Congregational minister, Barton shot to the top of the best-seller lists in 1925 with his *The Man Nobody Knows,* a reinterpretation of Jesus's life as "the story of the founder of modern business." Barton rejected the "sissified" image of Jesus as a "weakling" and a "kill-joy"; on the contrary, the Lamb of God was a he-man and raconteur who "spread health wherever he went" and offered "a happier, more satisfying way of living." Above all, Jesus was a superb executive who "picked up twelve men from the bottom ranks of business and forged them into an organization that conquered the world." His parable of the good Samaritan was "the most powerful advertisement of all time." "He would be a national advertiser today, I am sure, as he was the great advertiser of his own day."[9] On that subject, Barton spoke with considerable authority, since, in addition to his accomplishments as author and armchair theologian, he was a founder of Batten, Barton, Durstine & Osborn (BBDO)—the advertising giant that created Betty Crocker and gave us the jingles "Mmm mmm good," "Ring around the collar," and "Have it your way."

Thus was the Protestant work ethic reimagined. "It speaks to us only of ourselves, our pleasures, our life," wrote the merchant Herbert Duce in 1912. "It does not say, 'Pray, obey, sacrifice thyself, respect the King, fear thy master.' It whispers, 'Amuse thyself, take care of yourself.' "[10] No longer dammed by puritanical restraint, the newly permissive commercial culture began to spread, overflowing its source in the sophisticated elite and rippling throughout the larger ranks of society. In small towns and the urban working class, Americans dropped old habits and loyalties to heed the seductive whisper.

Commerce began to colonize ground formerly occupied by religion. Strict observance of the Sabbath buckled under pressure from a host of new temptations: baseball, golf at the country club, nickelodeons and motion pictures, amusement parks, and taking the car out for a Sunday drive. "Sunday is becoming more a day of recreation than of rest every week," harrumphed a Muncie, Indiana, newspaper in 1890.[11] Two years earlier, representatives of six major Protestant denominations gathered in Washington, D.C., and founded the American Sabbath Union, later renamed the Lord's Day Alliance, in an effort to agitate for a federal Sunday rest law. That initiative came to nought, and by the 1920s state Sabbath laws in the industrial North were being scrapped or becoming dead letters. Meanwhile, Christmas underwent a similar transition from holy day to holiday. By 1891, F. W. Woolworth was sending out the word to his store managers, "This is our harvest time. Make it pay."[12] No retailer did more to create the new, commercialized holiday tradition than R. H. Macy & Company. In 1874, Macy's prepared its first Christmas-themed window displays; exactly 50 years later, it inaugurated the annual Macy's Thanksgiving Day Parade to kick off the Christmas shopping season. By 1926, 5,000 children a day were filing through the store's Christmas grotto. Thus did the miracle in Bethlehem make way for the miracle on 34th Street.

Unbuttoned consumerism impinged on family life as well. Canning, baking, and sewing in the home went into decline; new appliances offered deliverance from the unremitting drudgery of housework. Parental authority weakened as children spent more time at school—and under the influence of a mesmerizing popular culture. Perfume, cosmetics, and form-fitting new fashions stoked the fires of youthful prurience, and the darkened privacy of automobiles and movie theaters lent opportunity to motive. A high school boy in "Middletown" proclaimed confidently, "The most important contribution of our generation is the one-piece bathing suit for women."[13]

The transformation of the family from a unit of production to one of consumption had enormous consequences. "[S]ince the head of the family is no longer in control of the economic process through which the family gets its living," wrote retailing pioneer Edward Filene with warm approval, "he must be relieved of many ancient responsibilities and therefore many of his prerogatives."[14] The toppling of the old paterfamilias could be seen in the ongoing elimination of legal disabilities for women, culminating in 1920 with the extension of suffrage under the 19th Amendment. With increasing female independence came a loosening of the marital bond: between 1870 and the 1920s, the divorce rate climbed over 30 percent per decade.[15]

Consumerism's relentless assault on traditional verities advanced apace with economic development. Industry waxed and cities bulged, while agriculture, that great bastion of social conservatism, retreated inexorably to the margins of national life. Between 1900 and 1950, farming's contribution to gross domestic product shrank from 23 to 7 percent, while Americans living in rural areas declined from 60 percent of the population to 36 percent. Those economic and demographic shifts progressively sapped cultural resistance to the getting-and-spending ethos. Uprooted from its native farm soil, the agrarian sensibility—with its instinctive belief in thrift and self-sufficiency, and its patient acceptance of the slow-paced rhythms of nature—could not long survive. "[T]he culture of the soil is the best and most sensitive of vocations," declared the Twelve Southerners in their 1930 manifesto, *I'll Take My Stand*.[16] Notwithstanding their passion and eloquence, only a dwindling few stood with them.

As the new commercial spirit took hold in the old-stock American heartland, so, too, did it gradually co-opt the urban, immigrant-dominated working classes. Abandoning the conventional wisdom that the great unwashed could be kept in line only through poverty and iron discipline, business leaders began to look at their workers in a new and considerably more favorable light. Instead of seeing revolutionary masses, or threats to Yankee culture, they saw potential customers. And they saw that the phenomenal increases in productivity made possible by technological advance would come to little if increases in demand failed to follow suit. An article in *Printer's Ink*, the trade journal for the advertising industry, expressed the view that had become conventional business wisdom by the 1920s: "[M]odern machinery . . . made it not only possible but imperative that the masses should live lives of comfort and leisure; that the future of business lay in its ability to *manufacture customers* as well as products."[17] Cultural resistance to granting workers higher pay and shorter hours gave way to the recognition, in the words of Edward Filene, that "mass production can produce consumers by creating buying power."[18]

As living standards steadily rose, and enticing and affordable mass-market products continued to proliferate, American workers gradually surrendered the dream of toppling the bourgeoisie—and concentrated instead on joining it. Terence Powderly, head of the Knights of Labor, had sought nothing less than to "to forever banish that curse of modern civilization—wage slavery."[19] In Powderly's vision, worker-owned cooperatives would eventually replace the capitalist wage system. Such utopian naïveté soon faded, however, as the sputtering cooperative movement failed to establish a serious alternative to the modern business corporation. What carried the day instead was the "pure and simple unionism" of Samuel Gompers and his American Federation of Labor. "We are operating under the wage system," Gompers said in 1899. "As to what system will ever come to take its place I am not prepared to say. . . . I know that we are living under the wage system, and so long as that lasts it is our purpose to secure a continually larger share for labor."[20]

Over the half century that followed Gompers's pragmatic statement, many within the labor movement—especially in the new Congress of Industrial Organizations—continued to push for some fundamental alteration of the employment relationship in the direction of worker control over production. In the end, however, Gompers's more modest ambitions defined the limits of the movement's success. By the end of World War II, union representation and collective bargaining had become the rule in American industry, as some three-quarters of the blue-collar workforce was unionized. Excluded from the scope of collective bargaining, however, was anything that fell within the "managerial prerogative," including production schedules, pricing, investment, and technological change.

The terms of the uneasy peace were set by the 1950 "Treaty of Detroit" between Walter Reuther's United Automobile Workers and Charles Wilson's General Motors. GM offered a five-year contract with cost of living adjustments and real wage increases to reflect productivity gains, and Reuther—whose socialist ideals had led him to spend two years in the Soviet Union during the 1930s—accepted. "GM may have paid a billion for peace. It got a bargain," wrote Daniel Bell, Reuther's former colleague in the Socialist Party, in *Fortune*. "It is the first major union contract that explicitly accepts objective economic facts—cost of living and productivity—as determining wages, thus throwing overboard all theories of wages as determined by political power and of profits as 'surplus value.'"[21] The class struggle had made its accomodation with consumerism, surrendering control over production in exchange for gains in consumption.

The attenuation of class conflict was greatly aided by a sustained boom in office work. In the middle and upper echelons,

a fast-growing corps of managers and professionals supervised and directed the complex activities of business enterprises,
large and small alike, and maintained the intricate interconnections among them. At the bottom, armies of clerical
and administrative workers collected and recorded the torrents
of information upon which managerial and professional coordination depended. In 1900, white-collar workers constituted
only 18 percent of the labor force, compared to 36 percent for
blue-collar workers. By 1950, the white-collar share had jumped
to 37 percent, just below the 41 percent share for blue-
collar workers. The emergence of a large bloc of office workers
blurred the old distinctions between capital and labor, and hos-
tilities dissipated in the less-polarized environment. Working-
class radicalism had fed off of the physical pain and danger that
were suffered routinely in the factory. Desk jobs, however menial or tedious, did not inspire the same sense of oppression.

The triumph of the new, consumerist work ethic spelled the
abandonment of what had been a central goal of the labor movement since its inception: shorter working hours. From petition
drives for a 10-hour workday in the 1840s, to agitation for an
eight-hour day during the 1880s, to the campaign for a five-day
workweek in the 1920s, reducing the time consumed in toil had
always stood at or near the top of workers' aspirations. Radical
champions of labor believed that the trend toward shorter hours
still had far to go. According to Bill Haywood of the Industrial
Workers of the World, "Everybody now realizes that it is ridiculous for sane people to work all day and every day. 'The less work
the better,' is the motto which the workers must set themselves."[22] In the shining socialist future that Haywood anticipated, working four months a year would suffice to produce all
the abundance anybody would desire.

The last hurrah for shorter hours occurred during the Great
Depression, when various "share-the-work" schemes were proposed in response to massive joblessness. The AFL drafted a bill
that would mandate a 30-hour week; Hugo Black introduced it

and the Senate passed it in April 1933. Franklin Roosevelt, newly inaugurated, flirted with supporting the measure but ultimately decided against it. The path to recovery, he concluded, lay in restarting the engines of production and employment, not reallocating a shrunken and static lump of labor. The National Industrial Recovery Act that preempted the 30-hour legislation made some noises about promoting shorter hours, but when the Supreme Court struck down the NIRA in 1935, even that half-hearted effort was halted. With the Fair Labor Standards Act of 1938, the 40-hour workweek (and time and a half for overtime) settled in as a stable American institution, never to be seriously challenged again.

Instead of restricting and reducing work, the labor movement and its political supporters in the Democratic Party switched directions and favored more. Full employment became the rallying cry; unemployment and underemployment alike were problems to be solved. In the new Keynesian economic vision, the solution was to be found in expansionary policies that stimulated aggregate demand—in other words, consumption. "Consumption," declared Alvin Hansen, one of the first Keynesians of prominence among American economists, "is the frontier of the future."[23] Hansen was a principal author of the Employment Act of 1946, which committed the federal government to maintaining "the propensity to consume" at a fever pitch with appropriately accommodating fiscal policies.

With that landmark piece of legislation, the consumerist work ethic was officially enshrined as political and economic orthodoxy. What had begun as a cultural innovation within the bourgeoisie was now the common faith of business and working classes alike. A century earlier, the Second Great Awakening had forged a broad social consensus on the basis of the Protestant work ethic, thereby creating the cultural momentum that launched the eventual escape from scarcity. Over the course of the harrowing transition, the combination of industrialization, urbanization, and mass immigration provoked bitter and sometimes violent conflicts over a growing but still insufficient pie.

Now, as America entered the era of mass affluence, the old rifts mended and a new social consensus prevailed.

In postwar America, cultural unity rested once again on the work ethic. This time, however, the impassioned pursuit of profit and accumulation had broken free from puritanical repression of desire. As a result, the whole thrust and focus of economic life changed. In the nineteenth century, on the farm and in the factory, most Americans worked for basic physical sustenance. Now they worked for comforts, conveniences, amusements, status, and fulfillment—in other words, for personal pleasure and self-realization. It had sometimes been imagined that with the conquest of scarcity, the economic "problem" would be "solved." Instead, the problem was simply reinvented. Economic relations and considerations remained the glue that held society together, but now they embraced an entirely new set of concerns. In the realm of freedom, Americans used capitalism as the main engine for climbing Maslow's pyramid.

"WE ARE NOW confronted with the problem of permitting the average American to feel moral even when he is flirting, even when he is spending, even when he is not saving, even when he is taking two vacations a year and buying a second or third car," intoned Ernest Dichter, a motivational researcher and business adviser.[24] The problem was quickly remedied. As the postwar boom gathered momentum and dispersed its heaping largesse, what remained of the old cultural inhibitions on getting and spending sloughed off and fell away.

The main features of modern consumerism had been in place by the 1920s, but at that time the new ethos was not yet triumphant. Beneath the glitz and flash of the Jazz Age, roughly 40 percent of all nonfarm families were still submerged in poverty; over 40 percent of the nation's population still lived in rural areas. Thus, despite the rise in stock prices and flappers' hemlines, economic and social conditions in much of the country offered little encouragement to free-spending hedonism. Then, during the trials of the 1930s and 1940s, the harsh privations of the Great Depression were succeeded by wartime shortages and rationing. Under those strapped circumstances, the scarcity mentality staged a general comeback, and scrimping and saving and reusing and doing without were once again the order of the day.

But not for long. Impelled by pent-up demand after a decade and a half of hardship, the ebullience of the peacetime economy soon put parsimony to rout. "[T]hrift is becoming a little un-American," declared William Whyte in his celebrated 1956 work, *The Organization Man.*[25] Seconding that sentiment was *Bride's* magazine, which instructed prospective newlyweds that when you purchase "the dozens of things you never bought or even thought of before . . . you are helping to build greater security for the industries of this country. . . . [W]hat you buy and how you buy it is very vital in your new life—and to our whole American way of life."[26] Historian David Potter, in his insightful 1954 account, *People of Plenty,* noted the revolution in attitudes. How is the well-adjusted individual supposed to act "once abundance is secured"? "In his personal economy," Potter wrote, "society expects him to consume his quota of goods—of automobiles, of whiskey, of television sets—by maintaining a certain standard of living, and it regards him as a 'good guy' for absorbing his share, while it snickers at the prudent, self-denying, abstemious thrift that an earlier generation would have respected."[27] In line with revised expectations, by 1957, two-thirds of American households were in debt of some kind, and half of them were paying off installment purchases.[28]

The consumer society reveled in materialism—to the point that things took on a life of their own. They served not merely as utilitarian objects, but as symbols and signifiers of identity and status. Catering to consumers' runaway imaginations—their desire for things to mean more than simple functionality—were two great industries unknown in the preindustrial age of scarcity: entertainment and advertising. One aimed to amuse, the other to persuade; together, they embellished materialism with fantasy and romance. Max Weber had depicted capitalism as a dull and dreary affair, an "iron cage" in a rationalized, bureaucratized, "disenchanted" world. Hollywood and Madison Avenue retorted with commercialized reenchantment—shallow and banal, perhaps, but not without its charms.

Is it going too far to call such slight stuff a kind of secular religion? If it is, what are we to make of screen "idols," sports "legends," action "heroes," sex "goddesses," and other assorted deities in the pantheon of celebrity? And what are Tony the Tiger, the Marlboro Man, and Allstate's "good hands"—all, by the way, created by the Leo Burnett agency during the 1950s—but advertising "icons"? This thin and whimsical idolatry enlivened the culture of consumption by creating mythologized objects of desire. Celebrities and the make-believe worlds they inhabited offered visions of the good life in all its hedonistic splendor; branding and packaging conjured up more make-believe worlds in which inanimate things acquired personalities.

These flights of fancy lent color and verve to the central cult of the affluent society: the worship of the American Dream. The expression was coined in 1931 by the historian James Truslow Adams, who described it as "that dream of a land in which life should be better and richer and fuller for every man, with opportunity for each according to his ability or achievement. . . . It is not a dream of motor cars and high wages merely, but a dream of social order in which each man and each woman shall be able to attain to the fullest stature of which they are innately capable. . . ."[29] At the heart of the American Dream was the notion that material and spiritual betterment are somehow intertwined—that dedication to improving one's condition is the basis for a good and decent and meaningful life. The Burnett agency's logo—a hand reaching for the stars—captured the idea well enough. "When you reach for the stars," Leo Burnett explained, "you may not quite get one, but you won't end up with a handful of mud either." In the American Dream, hustling and high-flown aspiration were often one and inseparable.

The entertainment and advertising industries dated back to the early decades of industrialization, but the advent of television fused the two into a cultural force of titanic power. Adoption of the new technology proceeded at breakneck speed after the return to peacetime production. In 1947, there were only 44,000 television sets in the country; by 1953, half of all American families owned one. In 1954, Swanson introduced the "TV dinner" and sold more than 10 million of them during the first year of nationwide distribution—a clear indication that what started as an appliance quickly had become something like a member of the family. Radio, too, had combined entertainment and advertising and transmitted the mixture directly into the intimacy of the home, but television added the hypnotic lure of the broadcast image. The result was a "selling machine in every living room," according to an early NBC instructional film for advertisers.[30] For every audience, its appointed time slot: children received the morning, housewives the daytime, teenagers the afternoon, adults the evening, and families Sunday night. Advertisers targeted accordingly, and viewers were enthusiastic victims of the saturation bombing; commercial jingles were nearly as popular as the programming.

Unraveling restraints on desire gave freer rein to Cupid as well as mere cupidity. On January 3, 1948, the medical publisher W. B. Saunders released an 804-page tome entitled *Sexual Behavior in the Human Male*. The study's author was Alfred C. Kinsey, a zoology professor at Indiana University who was previously best known for writing *Edible Wild Plants of Eastern North America* and assembling a superb collection of gall wasps. With its dry recitation of statistics on extramarital sex, masturbation, and homosexuality, the Kinsey report blew the lid off the prevailing code of sexual silence. The book reached its sixth printing within 10 days, and sales eventually topped a quarter-million copies. Five years later, Kinsey released the companion volume, *Sexual Behavior in the Human Female*, to a similarly thunderous reception. Moralists were outraged by the lack of public outrage. Henry Pitney Van Dusen, head of the Union Theological Seminary, bemoaned the two reports' revelation of "a prevailing deg-radation in American morality approximating the worst decadence of the Roman Empire."[31]

Just as the second Kinsey report was climbing the best-seller lists, another midwesterner was launching his contribution to decline and fall. In December 1953, Chicagoan Hugh Hefner published the debut issue of *Playboy* magazine, featuring the classic centerfold of Marilyn Monroe sprawled on red velvet. Hefner's genius was to transform the skin magazine from cheap and squalid into something upscale and sophisticated. "We like our apartment," Hefner wrote in that initial issue. "We enjoy mixing up cocktails and an hors d'oeuvre or two, putting a little mood music on the phonograph, and inviting in a female acquain-tance for a quiet discussion on Picasso, Nietzsche, jazz, sex."[32] Within three years, the magazine's circulation stood at 600,000.

As the decade wore on, the demand for titillation proved inex-haustible. In 1956, a young housewife and mother named Grace Metalious exposed the seamier side of small-town America with her salacious blockbuster, *Peyton Place*. Alcoholism, infidelity, promiscuity, and contempt for organized religion show up in the book's first five pages; illegitimacy, abortion, and incest make their appearances in due course. Dog-eared copies were soon lurking under beds all across the country, and by 1958 *Peyton Place* passed *Gone with the Wind* as the nation's all-time best-selling novel. "I didn't find out about masturbation until I was eighteen," recalled rock star Grace Slick, who would later carry cultural provocation to new heights. "I was lying down on the bed, reading a book called *Peyton Place*, and it was a horny book. . . . For the next two weeks I went bananas with it."[33] Meanwhile, the 1956 release of Brigitte Bardot's *And God Cre-ated Woman* helped to establish a mass market for the bikini, the daring swimwear created in 1946 by French engineer Louis Reard and named for the nuclear tests that year in the South Pa-cific. In 1960, Brian Hyland's infectious "Itsy Bitsy Teenie Weenie Yellow Polka Dot Bikini" hit number one on the pop charts and pushed sales even higher.

Relaxed repression of carnal appetites went hand in hand with greater attention to physical health and emotional well-being. Sponsored by a Bay Area yogurt maker, Jack LaLanne's exercise program first hit the local San Francisco airwaves in 1951. Two years later, the bodybuilder and fitness guru took his television show into national distribution, and housewives across the country began doing "trimnastics" along with the jumpsuited LaLanne. Children, too, were being put through their paces. The March 1956 issue of *American* magazine featured an article entitled "Are We Becoming a Nation of Weaklings?" by Jack Kelly (Grace's father). "American youngsters today are weaker and flabbier than those in many other countries, and they are growing softer every year," Kelly warned. "Their physical fitness or lack of it constitutes one of our gravest problems." Responding to such concerns, President Eisenhower established the President's Council on Youth Fitness (later renamed the President's Council on Physical Fitness) in July 1956 to promote better physical education and sports programs in the nation's schools.

Americans were striving to tone up their minds as well, as the dramatic increase in schooling produced a vibrant and growing demand for intellectual stimulation. In 1948, Columbia Records unveiled the $33\frac{1}{3}$ rpm long-playing record, an innovation that helped bring recorded classical music to a mass audience. Meanwhile, Pocket Books created a new market for "quality" paperbacks, offering literature and serious nonfiction in a format formerly reserved for lurid pulp. The number of local art museums soared from 600 in 1930 to 2,500 three decades later; symphony orchestras doubled during the 1950s.[34] Reproductions of art masterpieces adorned many a suburban living room, while bookshelves proudly displayed a set of Harvard Classics and Will and Ariel Durant's *The Story of Civilization*. It was the age of middlebrow, and snobs turned up their noses while millions expanded their horizons.

A newfound concern for mental health grabbed the country's attention. "The more conservative psychoanalysts maintain as a rule of thumb that about a third of all adults are neurotic," reported Ernest Havemann in a five-part *Life* magazine series on psychology that ran during January and February of 1957.[35] Not to worry, though: the problems of the American psyche were now the focus of unprecedented scientific and medical attention. "The capital of psychoanalysis used to be Freud's native Vienna," reported Havemann. "But now the United States has more psychologists and psychiatrists, engaged in more types of inquiry and activity, than all the rest of the world put together."[36] In a March 1955 article entitled "Pills for the Mind," *Time* magazine declared, "The treatment of mental illness is in the throes of a revolution. For the first time in history, pills and injections . . . are enabling some psychiatrists to . . . nip in the bud some burgeoning outbreaks of emotional illness . . . [and] treat many current cases far more effectively. . . ."[37] Just a month later, Wallace Laboratories obtained FDA approval for a new antianxiety medication called meprobamate, which it marketed under the trade name Miltown. The drug became an instant sensation, as television star Milton Berle began calling himself "Miltown" and parties featuring the "dehydrated martini" started popping up in suburbia. By 1956, one American in 20 was taking Miltown or some other tranquilizer at least once a month.

Popularizers followed in the specialists' wake. "If the syndicate figures are to be believed," wrote Havemann in *Life*, "a column called 'Child Behavior' has a circulation of 9.5 million; 'The Worry Clinic,' 19 million; 'Mirror of Your Mind,' 20 million."[38] In 1952, the minister Norman Vincent Peale fused feel-good Protestantism with pop psychology lingo to produce the self-help classic, *The Power of Positive Thinking*. "Ten times each day practice the following affirmation, repeating it out loud if possible," advised Peale. " 'I can do all things through Christ which strengtheneth me' (Philippians 4:13). Repeat those words NOW. That magic statement is the most powerful antidote on earth to inferiority thoughts."[39]

The psychology boom and the broader "triumph of the therapeutic"[40] had made it possible, among other things, for a young intellectual like Abraham Maslow to build a career on the scientific study of emotional health. In 1920, the American Psychological Association could claim only 400 members; by the 1950s, APA membership had climbed to 16,000. Within the swelling ranks of practitioners was room for those, like Maslow, who pushed beyond the prevailing concern with treating dysfunction and promoting "adjustment" and tackled instead the more ambitious challenges of attaining fulfillment and self-actualization. And within the larger populace that hungered for psychological guidance was a ready following for such trailblazers. The very fact of Maslow's career thus supplied evidence for the fundamental veracity of his famous thesis. Freed from physical want and insecurity, Americans had begun taking the pursuit of happiness *seriously*.

THE FIRST GENERATION to experience mass affluence feared it was too good to last. Americans entered the realm of freedom with fresh memories of hard times—and a gnawing dread of hard times' return. The young adults of the fifties had come of age amidst the misery and menace of depression and war; now they faced the devastating prospect of nuclear conflict with the Soviets. The good life they were just beginning to enjoy was thus shadowed by anxiety, and those shadows did much to shape Americans' conception of the happiness they were now so intently pursuing.

"I've been through one war. Maybe another one's coming," explained Tom Rath, the title character in *The Man in the Gray Flannel Suit*. "If one is, I want to look back and figure I spent the time between wars with my family, the way it should have been spent."[41] Millions of the fifties generation agreed with him. After the waste and destruction of the thirties and forties, they longed for simple, humble pleasures—peace and quiet and relief from the trials and tensions of life. They had had their share of extremes: the turbulent politics and class conflicts of the Depression years; the totalitarian ideologies that had plunged the world into chaos and threatened to do so again; the searing intensity of combat. Enough of all that, they declared, and sought fulfillment in the stability of home and family.

In the years after World War II, the pursuit of happiness—the quest for the American Dream—launched a mass migration to suburbia. During the 1940s and 1950s, nearly 40 million Americans lit out for the "crabgrass frontier."[42] The construction of single-family homes exploded, from 114,000 in 1944 to 937,000 in 1946 to 1,692,000 in 1950. In 1946, Levitt & Sons—run by Bill Levitt along with his brother Alfred and their father, Abraham—began buying up 4,000 acres of potato farms in Hempstead, Long Island, for a massive housing development. Originally called Island Trees, what was soon redubbed Levittown boasted more than 17,000 homes and 75,000 residents when construction was completed in 1951. By July 1948, at the peak of the building frenzy, 36 new homes were completed every day. Each of the identical Cape Cod houses, priced uniformly at $7,990, featured two bedrooms, a 12-by-16-foot living room, a kitchen, and a bath. Also included in the purchase price were a built-in refrigerator, a stove, a Bendix washer, a fireplace, and an eight-inch Admiral television set.[43]

Scorned as soulless hives of conformism by the *bien-pensant* set, the suburbs meant freedom for the millions who moved there: freedom from the aggravation and intrusiveness of urban congestion, freedom to work in the city without living there, freedom to move around, freedom to raise children in wholesome surroundings, freedom to own your own home, freedom to tend your own garden, freedom to make new friendships and build new communities. Among the original Levittowners was one Wilbur Schaetzl, a veteran who had been living with his wife and another family member in a one-room apartment. "That was so awful I'd rather not talk about it," he recalled. "Getting into this house was like being emancipated."[44]

More than a place to live, the suburbs offered a new way to live. Residents embraced the novelty of this strange synthesis of rural and urban; they were creating a new lifestyle and they took to the challenge with a sense of adventure. In Park Forest, a planned community outside Chicago, sharing of books, silverware, and children's toys was commonplace. "We laughed at first at how the Marxist society had finally arrived," observed one resident, "but I think the real analogy is to the pioneers."[45] The seemingly mundane tasks of making and maintaining a home were anything but in those early days of affluence. "We have a new house and we want to keep it up nice; this is not work but enjoyment," said a working-class man who had left the city for the third Levittown, this one in New Jersey. "I've never been more content. . . . Working in the yard is like fishing, so relaxing. I have more pep here than in Philadelphia."[46] As one alumnus of Park Forest reminisced, "It all got pretty hectic at times, but one thing's sure—we were *living*."[47]

Part of suburbia's novelty lay in how it united people across regional, class, ethnic, and religious lines. Blasted by critics for their white-bread homogeneity, suburbs took the myth of the American melting pot and made it a living social reality. Sociologist Herbert Gans lived in the New Jersey Levittown as a participant-observer from 1958 to 1960, during the community's first two years. Here were his neighbors: "Two were Anglo-Saxon Protestant couples from small towns, the breadwinners employed as engineers; one an agnostic and a golf buff, the other a skeptical Methodist who wanted to be a teacher. Across the backyard lived a Baptist white collar worker from Philadelphia and his Polish-American wife, who had brought her foreign-born mother with her to Levittown; and an Italian-American tractor operator (whose ambition was to own a junkyard) and his upwardly mobile wife, who restricted their social life to a brother down the street and a host of relatives who came regularly every Sunday in a fleet of Cadillacs. One of my next-door neighbors was a religious fundamentalist couple from the Deep South whose life revolved around the church; another was an equally religious Catholic blue collar worker and his wife, he originally a Viennese Jew, she a rural Protestant, who were politically liberal and as skeptical about middle class ways as any intellectual.

Across the street, there was another Polish-American couple, highly mobile and conflicted over their obligations to the extended family; another engineer; and a retired Army officer."[48]

The demographic shift to suburbia was accompanied by the demographic bulge of the baby boom. Birthrates had been falling steadily since the establishment of the republic, due to a combination of social changes and declining infant mortality, but the downward trend steepened markedly in the years after World War I. In 1916, the birthrate for women between the ages of 15 and 44 stood at 123 per 1,000 women; 20 years later, in the bleak depths of the Great Depression, it had fallen all the way to 76 per 1,000. In 1947, the birthrate shot up to 113 per 1,000 as the war's end allowed pent-up demand of a particular sort to be satisfied at last. Instead of settling back down, however, fertility held steady and then proceeded to rise even higher. In 1957, the birthrate once again reached 123 per 1,000 women. In that year, the peak of the baby boom, 4.3 million Americans were born—a figure never equaled before or since.[49]

The surging birthrate reflected a broader social turn toward family-centered life. People began marrying younger. In 1930, the median age when wedding bells first chimed stood at 24.3 years for men and 21.5 for women; by 1956, it had fallen to 22.5 and 20.1, respectively. Meanwhile, marriages split up less frequently. Divorce rates surged with the stresses and separations caused by World War II, peaking in 1946 at 17.9 per 1,000 married women. By 1958, the divorce rate had sunk to 8.9 per 1,000. *McCall's* magazine proclaimed it the era of family "togetherness." "For the first time in our history the majority of men and women own their own homes and millions of these people gain their deepest satisfaction from making them their very own," the magazine observed in a May 1954 editorial. "But the most impressive and the most heartening feature of this change is that men, women and children are achieving it *together*. They are creating this new and warmer way of life not as women *alone* or men *alone*, isolated from one another, but as a *family* sharing a common experience."

The new culture of affluent domesticity was affirmed and promoted by the great new cultural medium of television. Technological progress and economic growth had fostered an enthusiastic commitment to home and family, and television—a technological marvel, a growth industry, a home appliance, and a focus of family life—combined all of those momentous social developments in one magical, flickering box. How could it help but celebrate the values that had brought it into being and provided its raison d'être? Suburban family life was relentlessly idealized in that new dramatic form, the sitcom. Antiseptic yet nonetheless compelling shows like *Ozzie and Harriet, Leave It to Beaver, The Donna Reed Show,* and *Father Knows Best* offered suburban pioneers reassurance that the nuclear family could thrive without the nurture of hometown roots and extended kinship ties, that the stresses of Dad's rat race could be shucked off with a pipe and slippers, and that the submersion of Mom's identity in the concerns of husband and children was the sure foundation of durable happiness.

Meanwhile, shows like *Texaco Star Theater, The Colgate Comedy Hour,* and *Goodyear Television Playhouse* trumpeted with their very names the paternity of prosperity: corporate enterprise. Consider, in particular, *General Electric Theater,* one of the more successful and long-running efforts in this genre. Developed by Bruce Barton's ad agency, BBDO, and airing on Sunday nights from 1953 to 1962, the show featured drama, comedy, adventure, fantasy, and music in an anthology format. Tying it all together was the genial host, whose introductions, segues, and closing comments were peppered with GE huckstering and paeans to progress. "In the meantime, remember," he instructed viewers during the November 4, 1956, telecast, "from electricity comes progress; progress in our daily living; progress in our daily work; progress in the defense of our nation." During the closing segment of the February 10, 1957, episode, he stood with his wife in the kitchen of a "Total Electric" home. "When you live better electrically," he observed, "you lead a richer, fuller, more satisfying life. And it's something all of us in this modern age can have." And so it went, endless variations on the theme encapsulated in GE's motto: "Progress is our most important product." The show's host, of course, was the actor Ronald Reagan, who in his subsequent career would continue to preach the interdependence of economic dynamism and family values.

The American embrace of that interdependence was consecrated by a flurry of religious expression. As affluence spread, so did church membership. Between 1926 and 1950, formal affiliation with religious bodies increased at better than twice the rate of population growth. As of 1950, over 85 million Americans, or some 57 percent of the citizenry, claimed membership in a church or synagogue; by 1958, the figure had leapt to nearly 110 million, or 63 percent. Sunday school enrollment grew faster than church membership, with over 41 million enrolled as of 1958. According to a Gallup poll published in January 1956, roughly half of adult Americans attended church during the average week—up from just over a third in a similar survey conducted in 1940. The building of suburbia entailed a boom in church construction, as the value of new religious structures soared from $76 million in 1946 to $409 million in 1950 to $868 million in 1957.[50]

Protestantism remained the dominant creed, claiming the allegiance of roughly 70 percent of Americans in the early 1950s. But at least in its main currents, it bore little resemblance to the old-time religion of the Second Great Awakening. Less judgmental than therapeutic, less concerned with self-restraint than with peace of mind, the leading Protestant denominations aimed at providing comfort, not making demands. The triumph of science and technology had made belief in the literal truth of the Bible impossible for many; the assimilation of large minorities of Catholics and Jews had deprived Protestantism of its former status as *the* American religion; and of course, the alluring possibilities of affluence had rendered the old repressive morality unbearably confining. And so the once-fiery faith settled down into something more sophisticated and tolerant—and prone to fuzzy-minded complacency. The Methodist minister Roy Eckardt, writing in 1954, criticized what he called the "cult of the Man Upstairs": "God is a friendly neighbor who dwells in the apartment just above. Call on him anytime, especially if you are feeling a little blue. He does not get upset over your little faults. He understands. . . ."[51]

Meanwhile, the major non-Protestant confessions had been substantially assimilated and Americanized. Roman Catholics, who made up some 20 percent of the population, came to square their faith in a Universal Church with their adopted country's irrepressible religious pluralism. Likewise, they learned to reconcile their submission to Rome with the American tradition of church-state separation. The British writer (and Catholic convert) Evelyn Waugh, on a visit to this country, noted the distinctive attitudes of American Catholics. In Chicago, he went to see the Italian film *Paisan,* which he had previously seen in London. In the movie, three American chaplains—the proverbial minister, priest, and rabbi—visit a small, remote community of Franciscans. When the friars learn that two of their guests are not Catholic, they begin a fast for the pair's conversion. "In London," Waugh related, "the audience was mainly non-Catholic, but its sympathy was plainly with the friars. In Chicago, the audience was composed mainly of Italian speakers, presumably Catholics of a sort, and to them the friars seemed purely comic."[52]

American Jews, for their part, adapted their religious services to conform with Protestant norms, complete with sermons, choirs, organs, singing by the congregation, and responsive readings. Their synagogues, likewise, developed a Protestant-style institutional structure that included youth groups, Sunday schools, dinners, brunches, and discussion groups. And Hanukkah was elevated from obscurity into a full-scale Christmas counterpart.[53]

In what Will Herberg called the "triple melting pot," Protestantism, Catholicism, and Judaism now assumed a new identity as the three branches of a common American religion. This ecumenical synthesis amounted to a kind of faith in faith—a belief in the power of religion divorced from any specific religious content. "Our government makes no sense," President Eisenhower remarked famously, "unless it is founded in a deeply felt religious faith—and I don't care what it is."[54] In a similar vein, the minister Daniel Poling noted in a 1954 issue of *Parade* magazine that in his youth "I formed a habit that I have never broken. I began saying in the morning two words, 'I believe.' Those two words with nothing added . . . give me a running start for my day, and for every day."[55] Amidst the tensions of the vague and menacing Cold War, Americans rallied to their generic religiosity as the antidote to godless communism. "One nation under God" went the revised words of the Pledge of Allegiance, amended in 1954. Here was faith stripped of all dogma—all, that is, save unshakeable commitment to the American Dream.

FIFTIES AMERICA HAS received unsparing criticism—from contemporaries and ever since—for its shallowness, complacency, and conformism. And, indeed, those shortcomings, and many others besides, were much in evidence at the time. Yet despite all its flaws, American society at midcentury represented an astonishing historical achievement. Most obviously, its technological virtuosity surpassed anything in human experience. The harnessing of natural processes to human ends had been carried to a degree that in the relatively recent past would have been indistinguishable from magic or even divinity. The result was the richest, most productive, and most powerful civilization in history—and the first society in history in which the vast bulk of the populace was spared the ravages of poverty and disease, and afforded the opportunities of material abundance.

At the same time, and relatedly, the American social order was more complex than anything that had come before. Its highly elaborate and intricately organized division of labor provided the matrix for achieving an imperfect but still workable integration of widely varying religions, regions, ethnicities, classes, cultures, and worldviews. The complexity of American society was, of course, the key to its technological triumphs. Only by pushing the division of labor relentlessly forward was it possible to achieve the level of specialization needed to produce all the marvels of the age. And only through a series of fortuitous and inspired cultural and political improvisations was it possible to maintain and advance this finely grained division of labor in spite of all the internal differences and conflicts of interest it encompassed and produced.

Leading the way were the country's large and growing middle classes. Though their roots traced back to the old Protestant bourgeoisie, they had now evolved into something the old guard of the Second Great Awakening would have found unrecognizable. What remained intact was the capacity for trusting and working with people outside one's intimate circle of family and friends—in other words, for forming and maintaining relationships on the basis of shared, abstract values and purposes. But the values and purposes that were shared had changed dramatically. The Protestant bourgeoisie had founded its economic dynamism on a common adherence to a particular and rigid set of religious beliefs and moral strictures. That old-time religion, with its galvanizing sense of absolute certainty and unabashed bigotry against other races and faiths, could not maintain its hold on the nation's socioeconomic elite. What emerged in its place was a creed that was both more amorphous and more inclusive.

In his landmark 1950 study, *The Lonely Crowd,* David Riesman identified the change in values as a shift from an "inner-directed" to an "other-directed" ethos. In the former, individuals live according to a specific and inflexible code absorbed during childhood; in the latter, they change their mores with the times, taking their cues from contemporaries known to them either personally or through the mass media. According to Riesman, the rise of the other-directed ethos was a product of growing affluence. "Increasingly," he wrote, *"other people* are the problem, not the material environment."[56] As a result, the pugnacity and intolerance of the old Protestant bourgeoisie had become outdated and dysfunctional. In the kinder, gentler world of the office place and suburban block party, a more genial, tolerant, relativistic frame of mind was needed. "The other-directed person must be able to receive signals from far and near; the sources are many, the changes rapid. What can be internalized, then, is not a code of behavior but the elaborate equipment needed to attend to such messages and occasionally to participate in their circulation."[57] In Riesman's evocative metaphor, the inner-directed character acts as a kind of gyroscope, while the other-directed mind-set operates as a radar.

As Riesman observed so acutely, the new middle classes were struggling to find their bearings in a world where the old certainties were rapidly crumbling away. As early as 1914, a survey of leading American scientists found that nearly 70 percent of them disbelieved or doubted the existence of God; a repeat of the survey 20 years later found only 15 percent who were willing to profess belief in the Almighty.[58] The impiety of the scientific community was like a rock dropped in a pond; ripples of doubt propagated throughout all the better informed segments of society. Faith of some kind or other persisted for the overwhelming majority, but the dominant middle-class Protestantism now smacked more of whistling past the graveyard than anything vital or energizing.

The continued commitment to the work ethic was also tinged with doubts. With the ebbing of religious zeal, worldly success no longer signaled proof of divine favor. And with the ebbing of scarcity, the once-obvious prudence of hard work and incessant accumulation was no longer unquestionable. Middle-class Americans sensed, if only dimly, that they were now in the realm of freedom—that continued participation in the extended division of labor was a choice, not a necessity. Though it was easy enough to suspend disbelief and get caught up in the shared fantasies of the consumer society, Americans were occasionally able to step back—whether in moments of anxious desperation or philosophical reflection—and see through the charade. However much they often seemed otherwise, climbing the company ladder and winning the rat race and keeping up with the Joneses were not matters of life and death. They were elaborate games, freely chosen—which meant that other choices were possible.

Even a character as self-satisfied as Sinclair Lewis's Babbitt could not escape the occasional longing for escape from the artifice of modern living. In his sleep, he sought out the elusive fairy child, "a dream more romantic than scarlet pagodas by a silver sea." "He slipped away, ran down the paths of a midnight garden, and at the gate the fairy child was waiting."[59] A generation later, the man in the gray flannel suit found not frustration, but solace, in recognizing the arbitrariness that lurks within every choice. "It really doesn't matter. . . . Here goes nothing. . . . It will be interesting to see what happens" had been Tom Rath's whispered mantra on every parachute jump during the war. Back home, he found himself repeating the old incantation after accepting a new, high-paying, high-pressure job. If he could treat the stark horror of kill-or-be-killed as a game, he could do the same with the penny-ante stresses of peacetime.

Despite their doubts, the new middle classes soldiered on. Often, it is true, they simply evaded their uncertainty with the frantic diversions of hustle and bustle, the pap of positive thinking, and the sweet and easy sedative of popular entertainment. But it is entirely too harsh a judgment to condemn the new middle-class culture as nothing but self-delusion and "false consciousness." The Americans of the fifties generation had known poverty and war, and they were sure that peace and prosperity were better. The returning veterans had known the pain of separation from loved ones, and they were sure that family life, whatever its shortcomings and compromises, was better. The Levittowners had known the lack of privacy and inconvenience of cramped apartment living, and they were sure that suburbia was better. The millions who left farms and small towns had known the crushing boredom that haunts rural life, and they were sure that the buzz and excitement of consumerism was better.

Precisely because their vision of the good life was blurred by a doubting relativism, the new middle classes were able to amass and exercise social powers their inner-directed predecessors never dreamed of. Liberating their knack for organizing from the petty specifics of sect or surname, they were free to build large national organizations and new suburban communities that knitted together regions and religions and ethnic groups. It is easy to poke fun at the glad-handing and groupthink of the "organization man," or the near-obssessive preoccupation with fitting in and getting along that dogged the denizens of suburbia. But the middle classes of the early postwar years were learning to make their way in an "outside world" that now included people with widely different backgrounds, experiences, and values. The situation was hardly conducive to an ethos of sharp elbows and bristling self-assertion. What is remarkable, in retrospect, is not that those early efforts at living with pluralism were awkward and sometimes insipid; what is remarkable is how well they succeeded.

The commitment to building a pluralistic, middle-class society was evident in one of the era's defining acts of legislation: the Servicemen's Readjustment Act of 1944, otherwise known as the GI Bill of Rights. What the mass draft and shared experiences of combat had done to promote social solidarity during the war, the GI Bill carried forward into peacetime. By the time the original program ended in 1956, over 2 million veterans had received a college education using GI Bill benefits, and another 5 million had obtained education or training of other kinds.

Meanwhile, the nation's elites were embracing pluralism as well. In a remarkable bow to principle over privilege, the quasi-hereditary East Coast WASP establishment quietly made arrangements for its own liquidation—or, at least, its dilution into a new and altogether different upper stratum. In 1952, two-thirds of applicants to Harvard got in; the acceptance rate rose to nearly 90 percent when the applicant's father was an alumnus. The mean SAT verbal score of the incoming freshman class was 583—respectable, but hardly stellar. By 1960, the situation was dramatically different. The acceptance rate had dropped to less than one out of three, and the average SAT verbal score now stood at 678. The share of incoming freshmen from New England was down by a third, and there were more graduates of public schools than private schools.[60] "The figures report the greatest change in Harvard admissions, and thus in the Harvard student body, in a short time—two college generations—in our recorded history," concluded Dean of Admissions Wilbur J. Bender.[61] At Harvard and other top schools, the old-boy network was being dismantled in favor of a more diversified, and more talented, meritocracy.

Americans at midcentury liked to think of themselves as members of a uniformly middle-class society. "The rich man smokes the same sort of cigarettes as the poor man, shaves with the same sort of razor, uses the same sort of telephone, vacuum cleaner, radio and TV set," boasted a 1947 article in *Harper's*. "Our houses are all on one level, like our class structure," *House Beautiful* observed in 1953.[62] The success of the labor movement "has made the worker to an amazing degree a middle-class member of a middle-class society," according to *Fortune* in 1951.[63]

Despite having made real strides, the country was far less socially and economically integrated than people liked to think. In particular, the large urban working classes remained outside the golden circle of middle-class trust. In purely material terms, of course, conditions had improved dramatically. But culturally, the working classes still lacked the ability to work effectively with strangers in furtherance of common abstract loyalties. In return for material benefits, they had accepted the consumer society and middle-class leadership of it. But within that consensus, the working classes pursued their own distinct version of the American Dream—one in which loyalties extended not much beyond those acquired through birth, childhood, and marriage. In working-class culture, personal identity was inseparable from the peer group into which one was born and married into; there was little development of values or interests independently of this group, and thus little pursuit of such values or interests with like-minded outsiders. The world outside the peer group was inevitably hostile territory. As sociologist Herbert Gans observed in his study of the working-class Italian "urban villagers" of Boston's old West End, "the West Ender always expects to be exploited in his contact with the outside world, and is ready to exploit it in return."[64]

Working-class life thus unfolded within relatively narrow horizons. Blue-collar workers had little notion of a lifelong career with advancement and personal development along the way. Work was simply a means to a paycheck; a clean job without heavy lifting, a decent and fair-minded boss, and coworkers who were good company defined the outer limits of realistic expectations. With this kind of static future in store for their charges, schools were content to offer not much more than rote learning and rigid discipline. Parents, likewise, made little effort to train their children to thrive in an outside world that they themselves found alien. So long as kids stayed out of trouble, they were left to the devices of their siblings, cousins, and neighborhood pals. The public sphere, as well, was lacking in higher aspirations. Politics in working-class areas had little to do with ideology or other such rarefied abstractions. Rather, the great urban political machines ran off patronage and exchanges of favors—and heavy doses of graft. The working classes, in sum, lived on the cultural periphery of American life—deriving real advantages from hiring out their labor, but cut off from full participation in all the challenges and opportunities of middle-class society.

Though differently positioned to take advantage of mass affluence, the middle and working classes both actively supported the choice to push ahead with the division of labor—to maintain the mobilization of social energies and build the modern mass-consumption economy. Other groups, however, stood outside that choice. Some were excluded, denied by legal and cultural barriers the chance to pursue their own versions of the American Dream. Other groups dissented from the choice, either because they preferred what had been left behind or because they imagined paths not taken. These alienated outsiders lurked in the shadows of the affluent American consensus; in time, they would challenge that consensus and shatter it. Perhaps the gravest threat to the postwar social order, however, lay not on the margins of American life, but in its very bosom. It lay in the quiet night of suburbia, slumbering in the children's bedrooms.

THREE

Howl

———— •◆• ————

"In the West, among the intellectuals, the old passions are spent."[1] So declared Daniel Bell in *The End of Ideology,* and he wrote from personal experience. Bell had grown up poor in New York City; his father died when he was a baby, and his mother worked in a garment factory. As a kid, he would steal potatoes from the vegetable markets on the West Side, or scavenge bruised tomatoes that had been discarded, and eat them with his gang of buddies around street fires made from broken boxes.

The bookish young Daniel burned with the hope that the world might someday be different—and the belief that radical political change would be necessary to achieve that end. In 1932, at age 13, he joined the Young People's Socialist League, the youth organization of Norman Thomas's Socialist Party. He pored over the sociology books at the New York Public Library's Ottendorfer branch, and attended a reading group on Marx at the Rand School of Social Science. And he pondered how best to take his radicalism to the next level: should he follow his friends who had joined the Young Communist League, or his other friends who had signed up with the Trotskyists?

He decided to do neither. Instead, Daniel read Alexander Berkman's memoirs of the Kronstadt rebellion—and that, for him, put an end to flirtations with communism of any stripe. The tale is a useful reminder of the hysterical temper of those times. Only in the red thirties was it possible for someone like Berkman—best known for shooting and stabbing Henry Clay Frick after the Homestead riots—to end up exerting a moderating influence on anybody. However odd the teacher, the lesson stuck. Although Bell would remain a self-described socialist for his entire career, he had acquired a lifetime immunity to ideological enthusiasm.[2]

Writing at the end of the fifties, Daniel Bell found that the country as a whole now shared his disillusionment. Having spent the decade as labor editor at *Fortune,* Bell had chronicled the endgame of the great class conflicts that had roiled the transition from scarcity to affluence (it was Bell who dubbed the 1950 deal between the UAW and GM the "treaty of Detroit"). With the working classes successfully joined in pursuit of the American Dream, the old fighting faiths of the left had lost their primary constituency. "The irony, further, for those who seek 'causes' is that the workers, whose grievances were once the driving energy for social change, are more satisfied with the society than the intellectuals," Bell wrote. "The workers have not achieved utopia, but their expectations were less than those of the intellectuals, and the gains correspondingly larger."[3] Looking ahead, Bell foresaw a politics of prosaic problem solving—mature, responsible, and dull. The raptures and horrors of the old apocalyptic visions were over and done with.

While Daniel Bell saw exhaustion on the left, Lionel Trilling peered in the other direction and found only grumbling incoherence. "In the United States at this time liberalism is not only the dominant but even the sole intellectual tradition," he wrote in a famous passage from *The Liberal Imagination.* "For it is the plain fact that nowadays there are no conservative or reactionary ideas in circulation." Conservative impulses existed, he conceded, but they expressed themselves "only in action or in irritable mental gestures which seek to resemble ideas."[4]

Trilling, a founding member of "the Family" of New York intellectuals that Bell later joined, was one of America's foremost literary critics at a time when that profession wielded formidable cultural influence. The first Jew granted tenure in Columbia's illustrious English department, Trilling had dabbled in radical politics in the thirties, but his innate caution and sense of nuance made him ill-suited to the enterprise. Allying himself with the postwar political consensus, and the social consensus on which it was based, he assumed the role of liberalism's sympathetic critic.

In that capacity, Trilling regarded the absence of a conservative intellectual opposition with worry rather than gloating. "[L]iberalism is concerned with the emotions above all else, as proof of which the word happiness stands at the very center of its thought," he noted, "but in its effort to establish the emotions, or certain among them, in some kind of freedom, liberalism somehow tends to deny them in their full possibility." In other words, the American Dream, while decent and humane, lacked sufficient ambition; it had pulled up short, content to wade in the shallows of self-realization. To avoid becoming "stale, habitual, and inert," liberalism needed to confront and plumb the dark and unruly depths of the human psyche, remaining ever alert to the fact that "the world is a complex and unexpected and terrible place which is not always to be understood by the mind as we use it in our everyday tasks."[5] Which is to say, it needed confrontation with the conservative temperament, a turn of mind acutely alive to the tragic dimensions of human life. In the absence of a living opposition, Trilling proposed more active engagement with the troubled, troubling meditations of modern literature.

Decades before Francis Fukuyama, Bell and Trilling had succumbed to the mirage of endism. What they mistook for liberalism's final, if problematic, triumph was in fact only the ticking calm before the bomb blast. While they rehashed the last war, the consensus that seemed so unshakeable was about to be convulsed from both left and right. The wild-eyed certainties of radical ideology would once again tempt a generation, and the daily headlines would proclaim with depressing regularity that the world is indeed complex and unexpected and terrible.

The triumph over scarcity had made possible the pacification of class conflict and the emergence of a new and broader cultural synthesis. Working classes and business classes, immigrant groups and old-stock WASPs, had found in capitalism's mounting plenty the materials for fashioning a durable peace. It was a great accomplishment, no doubt—especially since America had been spared the totalitarian nightmares that arose out of the class conflicts of Europe. But other, unresolved social conflicts remained, and consequently the reigning cultural synthesis was both incomplete and unstable.

Now, rather than serving as a balm, affluence acted as instigator and rabble-rouser. The ethos of self-realization, unleashed by prosperity and empowered by the technologies and trust networks of the mass-consumption economy, would follow its own ineluctable logic—and the prudence and self-restraint born of the Depression and war years would soon be swept away. Now that the mass pursuit of happiness had begun in earnest, Americans grew increasingly restive in the face of any obstacle or constraint, no matter how deeply rooted or time-honored. In the logic of affluence, once physical necessity receded, the confinements of *conventional* necessity—the dictates of custom and established authority—began to crack and crumble.

Under the placid surface of Eisenhower-era America, insurgencies of discontent gathered strength and stoked their smoldering grievances. African Americans, still cruelly excluded from the nation's widening ethnic pluralism, began to conclude that their long-delayed emancipation could wait no longer. However terrible the price, it had to be paid *now*. Housewives unreconciled to suburban purdah struggled with where to put the blame for their maladjustment—on themselves, or on a sexual division of labor that declared broad realms of endeavor to be "man's world" and off-limits. Conservative devotees of old-style bourgeois mores, disoriented in a world that had passed them by, railed against cultural corruption and the decadence of the liberal establishment. Bohemians and radicals, disaffected by a world whose priorities they thought absurdly misguided, groped in search of alternatives to consumerism. And the middle-class young, the largest generation in American history and the first in all of history born into broad-based prosperity, mixed adolescent rebellion with the larger cultural assault on authority of any kind. Brimming with that combustible concoction, they danced to rock 'n' roll and waited for a spark.

"No . . . something has changed," Lena Younger replied, turning toward her son Walter Lee. "You something new, boy. In my time we was worried about not being lynched and getting to the North if we could and how to stay alive and still have a pinch of dignity too . . . Now here come you and Beneatha—talking 'bout things we ain't never even thought about hardly, me and your daddy. You ain't satisfied or proud of nothing we done."[6]

Electrifying Broadway when it opened in the spring of 1959, Lorraine Hansberry's *A Raisin in the Sun* told the story of a struggling African American family in postwar Chicago. Living together in a cramped and run-down apartment were Lena, or Mama, the widowed matriarch; her two children, Walter Lee and Beneatha; and Walter's wife and son. Mama's husband, a manual laborer all his life, had recently died, and a life insurance check for $10,000 simultaneously offered hope for a better life and threatened to tear the family apart.

Walter and Beneatha exemplified the rising expectations and seething frustrations of African Americans in the fifties. Beneatha, a college student with dreams of becoming a doctor, moved restlessly from one fleeting enthusiasm to the next. "What is it you want to express?" Mama asked, taking her to task for indulging in guitar lessons. "Me!" she shouted back. Channeling Abraham Maslow, Beneatha's African boyfriend nicknamed her Alaiyo, or "One for Whom Bread—Food—Is Not Enough." Walter, meanwhile, was stuck in a dead-end job as a chauffeur while his wife and mother had to work as domestic servants to make ends meet.

"Sometimes it's like I can see the future stretched out in front of me—just plain as day...," he complained to his mother. "Just waiting for me—a big, looming blank space—full of *nothing*. Just waiting for *me*. But it don't have to be."[7] Feverishly, desperately, he longed to own his own business and hit it big.

The escalation from Mama's humble aspirations to her children's straining impatience was sweeping through black America in the years after World War II. In the face of degrading and entrenched oppression, capitalism's advance toward mass affluence was propelling African Americans to challenge their oppressors and assert themselves. In the ensuing confrontation, the quest for self-realization would raise itself to physical and spiritual heroism—and plunge into heartbreaking self-destructiveness.

Blacks had been released from slavery after the Civil War, but they had not won their freedom. The Reconstruction years saw concerted efforts to secure political equality for African Americans, but with the reversion to southern home rule conditions swiftly deteriorated. Beginning in the 1890s, one member of the old Confederacy after another moved to codify white supremacy as the law of the land. First came disenfranchisement of blacks (as well as many poor whites) through literacy tests, property qualifications, poll taxes, and all-white primaries. In Louisiana, for example, the number of registered black voters fell from 130,334 in 1896 to 1,342 eight years later.[8] Next came a baroque profusion of segregation laws and practices. The public schools had generally remained segregated even during Reconstruction, but now Jim Crow laws extended apartheid to trains, waiting rooms in train stations, streetcars, buses, restaurants, lunch counters, pool halls, theaters, public parks, circuses, textile factories, toilets in places of employment, hospitals, mental institutions, prisons, and graveyards. Miscegenation, or interracial sex and marriage, was outlawed, notwithstanding which white men could rape black women more or less with impunity. Florida and North Carolina even required that the school textbooks used by white children be kept separate from those used by black children; Atlanta courts used special Bibles for swearing in black witnesses.

Official Jim Crow buttressed a broader social consensus among whites that African Americans were inferior and were to be treated as such. Restrictive covenants maintained residential segregation. Blacks were called by their first names, like children, and could not enter a white person's home by the front door. Any signs of "uppitiness," especially by black men toward white women, were deemed intolerable. Extralegal enforcement of that intolerance was swift and brutal: between 1890 and 1920, some 2,500 African Americans were lynched.

Groaning under the weight of such mistreatment, African Americans endured severe material deprivation. The overwhelming prevalence of black poverty was starkly visible in the mortality statistics: in 1900, the average life expectancy of a black newborn was only 33 years, nearly a third below that of the average white baby. Perhaps the greatest injury inflicted by Jim Crow, however, was spiritual deprivation. Members of a despised and subjugated race, African Americans faced overwhelming psychological pressure to accept as valid the racism of the white majority—to be ashamed of their own identities. In *The Souls of Black Folk,* W. E. B. DuBois gave the name of "double-consciousness" to this affliction—"this sense of always looking at one's self through the eyes of others, of measuring one's soul by the tape of a world that looks on in amused contempt and pity." [9] Could there be a graver disability in a society increasingly oriented toward self-realization?

Yet if America's ongoing economic transformation made blacks' condition even more difficult to bear, it also rendered the structures of oppression less stable. As the twentieth century dawned, nearly 90 percent of African Americans still lived in the South, and almost 80 percent of the black population was located in rural areas. Economic development, however, would lead blacks out of the countryside and into the cities—in particular, the cities of the industrial North. Northern factories had shunned black workers in the past, but labor shortages created by America's entry into World War I prompted a change of heart. Faced suddenly with the opportunity to multiply their incomes manyfold, approximately half a million African Americans ventured to the North during the war years. The imposition of tight immigration restrictions during the twenties ensured that demand for cheap black labor would continue.

If capitalism first pulled blacks out of the South with the lure of factory jobs, it later pushed them out with technological change. On October 2, 1944, at the Hopson Plantation in Clarksdale, Mississippi, International Harvester field-tested the first mechanical cotton picker suitable for factory production. The public demonstration was a rousing success: each of the eight Harvester machines tested that day picked as much cotton as 50 people could have done, at a cost per bale less than one-seventh that of using manual labor.[10] Within a few years, the mechanical cotton picker was sweeping the South, the sharecropping system that had prevailed since the Civil War was starting to disintegrate, and African Americans were being thrown off the land. Between 1940 and 1970, 5 million African Americans left the South—more than the total number of Italians or Irish or Jews or Poles who came to this country during the heyday of immigration.

Conditions in the North were hardly idyllic for blacks. Discrimination was rampant and sometimes violent. In the race riots that erupted in over 20 cities during the "Red Summer" of 1919, the worst violence occurred in Chicago. After five days of bloodshed, 38 people were dead, 500 were injured, and 1,000 African Americans were left homeless. Nevertheless, by comparison with what they had left behind, blacks found the growing ghettoes of the North abuzz with opportunity, excitement, temptation—and freedom. Robert Abbott, publisher of the *Chicago Defender* and an indefatigable champion of the black migration, referred to the move north as the "flight out of Egypt" and Chicago as the "promised land." According to Abbott, blacks in northern cities "could get the wrinkle out of their bellies and live like men."[11] Black-owned businesses flourished, from small shops to sizeable corporations like Chicago's Supreme Liberty Life Insurance, which by the 1950s boasted 36 offices in 28 cities, 600 employees, and $18 million in assets.[12] And Harlem and "Bronzeville" on the south side of Chicago became the capitals of a burgeoning new African American culture. The rising black spirit expressed itself in a thriving literary scene and, of course, the breathtaking new musical forms of jazz and the blues.

The black exodus began to reshape American politics. Northern blacks could vote, and in the 1930s they abandoned their historical allegiance to the Republican Party and threw their support overwhelmingly behind FDR. In so doing, they drove a wedge between the oddest bedfellows of the Democratic Party's New Deal coalition: northern liberals, who increasingly supported civil rights for blacks, and segregationist southern whites. Although FDR did almost nothing to challenge segregation, perceptive southerners could see that the new alliance between African Americans and Democrats meant trouble for Jim Crow. "To any discerning person, it is perfectly obvious that the so-called Democratic party at the North is now the negro party, advocating actual social equality for the races," Senator Carter Glass of Virginia complained bitterly in 1937; "but most of our Southern leaders seem to disregard this socialistic threat to the South in their eagerness to retain Mr. Roosevelt in power."[13]

Harry Truman would confirm such fears with bolder moves in favor of black rights—most notably, his 1948 executive orders desegregating the armed forces and prohibiting discrimination in federal employment. Meanwhile, the federal courts, increasingly liberal after two decades of appointments by Roosevelt and Truman, turned away from the old separate-but-equal doctrine. In the 1944 case of *Smith v. Allright,* the Supreme Court held the white primary to be unconstitutional; two years later, in *Morgan v. Virginia,* it ruled against segregation in interstate travel; in 1948, it struck down restrictive covenants in *Shelley v. Kraemer.* And on May 17, 1954, the Supreme Court issued its unanimous ruling in *Brown v. Board of Education.*

By the end of the fifties, when *A Raisin in the Sun* debuted on

Broadway, African Americans had benefited from decades of real and steady progress. Average life expectancy nearly doubled, increasing by 30 years during the first six decades of the twentieth century. The literacy rate rose from 55 percent to just under 90 percent. By 1960, 40 percent of blacks breathed the relatively free air of the North and the West; with increasing economic opportunity, the black poverty rate plunged to 40 percent, down from 75 percent just two decades before.[14] Black musicians and athletes had become leading figures in American popular culture.

And yet . . . Notwithstanding all these gains, Jim Crow still reigned in the South. Few southern blacks could vote, the vast bulk of segregation policies remained unchallenged, and federal court rulings in favor of civil rights went largely unenforced by local authorities. Precisely because progress had been made, the continuation of this state of affairs became unbearable. Because pride in real accomplishments made bowing and scraping even more humiliating, because service in the war meant that full-fledged citizenship had been earned in blood, because partial victories over oppression stoked hunger for more, African Americans reached the boiling point. In a country in which classless equality was now the national mantra, and the pursuit of personal fulfillment had become the new civil religion, the persistent torment of double consciousness now demanded immediate redress. Soothing counsels of patience by sympathetic but ineffectual white liberals would no longer suffice. And so, eschewing the proper channels of litigation and legislation, African Americans began to act directly. Rather than petitioning white authorities for action, they would act on their own to claim their freedom—and dare their oppressors to stop them if they could.

As the sun came up on Monday, December 5, 1955, the city buses of Montgomery, Alabama, rolled through their appointed rounds. The morning routine, however, was anything but: on that day, and for many days thereafter, the buses were largely empty. Late afternoon on the previous Thursday, a 42-year-old seamstress named Rosa Parks had been arrested for refusing to surrender her bus seat to make room for white passengers. The next day, about 50 black community leaders met in the basement of the Dexter Avenue Baptist Church and agreed to call for a one-day bus boycott to protest Parks's arrest. On Monday afternoon, after the protest's success had exceeded all expectations, leaders met again, agreed to continue the boycott until various demands were met, and formed the Montgomery Improvement Association to coordinate the effort. Elected as president of the MIA was Dexter Baptist's young minister, the 26-year-old Martin Luther King Jr. Addressing a crowd of thousands that night, King proclaimed, "The only weapon we have in our hands this evening is the weapon of protest." [15]

The 40,000 African Americans of Montgomery would wield that weapon for a total of 382 days. Not until December 21, 1956, did the boycott finally end—and it ended only because, the day before, U.S. marshals had served notice on city officials to desegregate the city's bus lines by order of the U.S. Supreme Court. Over the course of that year and change, participants in the boycott endured hardship and harassment as they figured out how to get to and from work, and attend to all life's pressing chores, without their usual mode of transportation. Initial reliance on black taxicabs was thwarted when the police commissioner announced he would arrest any driver who charged less than the minimum 45-cent fare. Some 150 car owners then volunteered their cars to serve in a massive car pool; each car was used to supply over a hundred rides a day. Many, meanwhile, simply walked wherever they had to go. One elderly woman, Mother Pollard, was urged by friends to go ahead and take the bus in light of her frail health. "My feets is tired," she replied, "but my soul is rested." [16]

The defenders of segregation fought ferociously to disrupt this unprecedented challenge. Car-pool drivers were hounded by the police with tickets for trivial and bogus infractions (King himself was arrested for driving 30 miles per hour in a 25 miles per hour zone); 89 indictments for violations of an obscure antiboycott law were handed down (in the end, King was the only one tried and convicted); the homes of King and other leaders were bombed. On the day that the Supreme Court ruled Alabama's bus segregation laws unconstitutional, a state court judge granted an injunction against the car pool as an unlicensed municipal transportation system. It took five weeks for the Supreme Court's official order to reach Montgomery, during which time the boycotters continued their resistance on foot.

In April 1956, Martin Luther King collaborated with Bayard Rustin to write a preliminary assessment and defense of the boycott then in progress. "Gradually the Negro masses in the South began to re-evaluate themselves—a process that was to change the nature of the Negro community and doom the social patterns of the South," King wrote. "We discovered that we had never really smothered our self-respect and that we could not be at one with ourselves without asserting it. From this point on, the South's terrible peace was rapidly undermined by the Negro's new and courageous thinking and his ever-increasing readiness to organize and to act."[17]

The Montgomery bus boycott was the opening drama in the coming mass movement for black civil rights. As King's words reveal, that social revolution had its origins in a psychic revolution. The external triumph over Jim Crow was preceded by the internal triumph over the old self-loathing of double consciousness. Excluded from full participation in the nationwide quest for self-realization, African Americans made their own quest out of battling the exclusion. And it was especially fitting that in this cause born of economic progress, the first great victory relied on an exercise of consumer power.

" WORK THAT ENTICES women out of their homes and provides them with prestige only at the price of feminine relinquishment, involves a response to masculine strivings," warned sociologist Ferdinand Lundberg and psychoanalyst Marynia Farnham in their 1947 best seller, *Modern Woman: The Lost Sex*. "The more importance outside work assumes, the more are the masculine components of the woman's nature enhanced and encouraged. In her home and in her relationship to her children, it is imperative that these strivings be at a minimum and that her femininity be available both for her own satisfaction and for the satisfaction of her children and husband."[18]

"Women have many careers but only one vocation—motherhood," Agnes Meyer chimed in with similar views in the August 1950 issue of the *Atlantic*. "Women must boldly announce that no job is more exacting, more necessary, or more rewarding than that of housewife and mother," she proclaimed, and then lambasted those "mothers who neglect their children because they find some trivial job more interesting."[19]

Popular women's magazines of the era—*Ladies' Home Journal, McCall's, Good Housekeeping, Woman's Home Companion*—echoed and reinforced such thinking. Typical headlines included "Femininity Begins at Home," "It's a Man's World Maybe," "Have Babies While You're Young," "How to Snare a Male," "Should I Stop Work When We Marry?" "Are You Training Your Daughter to Be a Wife?" "Careers at Home," "Do Women Have to Talk So Much?" "Really a Man's World, Politics," "Don't Be Afraid to Marry Young," "Cooking to Me Is Poetry," and "The Business of Running a Home."[20]

In the years after World War II, the claim that a woman's place is in the home was reasserted with a vehemence that smacked of desperation. Since the outset of industrialization, capitalism's advance toward mass affluence had been challenging that claim with ever-increasing vigor. Economic opportunities outside the home multiplied just as economic obligations inside the home dwindled; pull and push factors thus combined to undermine the sexual division of labor. In the posttraumatic aftermath of depression and war, however, events took an odd turn. The longing for the simple pleasures of hearth and home gave renewed plausibility to the notion that women's pursuit of happiness need not extend beyond the front yard. This revival of what Betty Friedan later called the "feminine mystique" would be short-lived, though. After all, when cultural norms and social realities veer off in opposite directions, the results are seldom stable.

Capitalism's restless development had long been working to redefine the terms of family life. Before making fundamental changes in the nature of women's work, however, it would first transform the nature of work for men. In traditional agrarian society, the family had been the primary unit of economic production. Indeed, the word economy comes from the Greek *oikonomia*, which means "household management." Each household, each family, was a largely self-sufficient enterprise. But with the emergence of the industrial economy, home production began to give way to the marketplace and its far-flung division of labor. Men left home to work in factories, shops, and offices, and surrendered their roles as directors of the family enterprise.

Industrialization's early advances thus gave rise to the new duality of work and home—the "man's world" of the exchange economy and the feminine sphere of domesticity. The home came to be seen as an oasis of emotional intimacy, a refuge from the competitive rigors of the outside world. It was the woman's job to maintain that refuge: to keep a clean, orderly, and elegant home, raise the children and oversee their education, and offer love and understanding to the harried family breadwinner.

That neat and tidy bifurcation fell under assault from the moment it emerged, for it assumed a sexual division of labor that capitalism's progress was rendering ever more artificial. In the early industrial era, the home was outside the cash nexus, but it remained a place of work—exhausting, never-ending drudgery, to be more specific. Over time, however, many of the tasks that constituted traditional women's work would be outsourced to the marketplace. The growing ranks of the affluent employed small armies of domestic servants to do the cooking, cleaning, and laundry; later, household appliances made the mechanical equivalents of such servants available to the masses. Textile factories ended home spinning, the garment industry displaced home sewing, and the introduction of mass-production techniques to food processing transformed home baking and canning into hobbies.

Over the first half of the twentieth century, the time required for traditional housework dwindled markedly. As a result, increasing numbers of women took advantage of the opening to pursue paid work in the marketplace. They had to contend, of course, with unabashed discrimination; reigning cultural attitudes flatly denied that women and men should share an equal footing in the job market. It was widely assumed, for instance, that women should not receive the same pay as a man who held the same job, since, after all, the man was supporting a family and women were only supplementing family incomes. Likewise, wide swaths of the job market were considered exclusively male domains; most women, consequently, had to settle for "pink-collar" jobs as schoolteachers, nurses, secretaries, clerks, or shop assistants.

Nevertheless, despite all obstacles, female participation in the labor force climbed inexorably. Between 1890 and 1940, the proportion of women in the job market rose from 18.9 percent to 25.8 percent; for married women, the participation rate more than tripled from 4.6 percent to 15.6 percent. The greater independence that came from a paycheck of one's own lent further momentum to the ongoing campaign for women's rights. Already, the breakdown of preindustrial patriarchy had triggered the abolition of the most egregious legal disabilities. The common-law doctrine of coverture—which disallowed married women from owning property, signing contracts, or being a party to a lawsuit—had been gradually modified, limited, and finally abolished over the course of the nineteenth century. Two decades into the new century, formal legal equality between the sexes made its greatest single advance when voting rights for women were finally achieved.

Notwithstanding such developments, the division of the world into separate male and female preserves remained deeply engrained in the American mind. Indeed, women's special role in their designated sphere became increasingly idealized and romanticized. The family, for millennia the basic unit of economic production, had now assumed a new identity as the primary locus of consumption. Unsurprisingly, then, the consumerist ethos of self-realization and personal fulfillment made home life central to its concerns and aspirations. Men were now expected to seek emotional rewards from participating actively in the family, but for women the expectations soared much higher. Being a wife and mother—managing the family's consumption, attending to the emotional needs of Dad and the kids, and generally choreographing and producing the suburban idyll of harmonious togetherness—came to be regarded as the highest and best outlet for female self-expression. If the nineteenth-century housewife was expected to do her duty, her twentieth-century counterpart was expected to do her duty and *love* it.

Such expectations, however, were increasingly at odds with underlying social realities. As America entered the 1950s, the necessity for women to stay at home had all but succumbed to affluence and technology. Yes, it was still very much possible to make a full-time job out of being a wife and mother: creativity in the kitchen, artistry in home decoration, hands-on involvement in children's upbringing and education, and active participation in social and community activities could easily consume all the hours in the day. The point, however, was that spending one's time in such pursuits had clearly become a choice—in a way that boiling water for laundry, hauling wood for the stove, and scrubbing filthy floors had not been. The choice to engage in homemaking now had to contend with a proliferating array of rival choices supplied by the job market.

The acute labor shortages that arose during World War II prompted a dramatic spike in female employment. Between 1940 and 1944, the number of women in the workforce jumped from 14.2 million to 19.4 million. After the war, however, Rosie the Riveter lost her job to returning servicemen, and over 2.5 million women dropped out of the labor market by 1946. The retreat, however, was only temporary. In 1953, the number of women in the workforce exceeded the 1944 peak. Notwithstanding the strong cultural pressures to stick to the kitchen and nursery, participation in the job market by married women with minor children rose from 28.3 percent to 39.0 percent over the course of the 1950s.

The majority of women, however, went with the cultural flow of the postwar years: embracing the renewed emphasis on home life, marrying younger, having more babies, staying with their husbands through thick and thin. And millions found real and lasting happiness by doing so. Others, however, paid a heavy price for choosing to live out the 1950s sitcom ideal. Far from achieving self-realization in their domestic roles, they came to believe that their confinement to those roles condemned them to lives that were empty and trivial. Feeling frustrated and trapped, they pined for greener grass on the other side of the picket fence.

As the fifties wore on, those subterranean discontents slowly seeped up to the surface. In December 1956, *Life* magazine featured an article entitled "Changing Roles in Modern Marriage." In it, the author identified (with condemnation rather than sympathy) a phenomenon referred to as the "suburban syndrome," in which "the wife, having worked before marriage or at least having been educated and socially conditioned toward the idea that work (preferably some kind of intellectual work in an office, among men) carries prestige" falls prey to depression on account of being "just a housewife."[21] That same year, *McCall's* ran a story called "The Mother Who Ran Away" and received an avalanche of supportive letters. "It was our moment of truth," an editor at the magazine later recalled. "We suddenly realized that all those women at home with their three and a half children were miserably unhappy."[22] By 1962, a Gallup poll revealed that only 10 percent of mothers hoped that their daughters would follow the choices they had made in life.[23]

In 1957, a suburban housewife and mother of three was looking forward to the 15th reunion of her class at Smith College. A freelance writer, she sold *McCall's* on the idea of an article, tentatively entitled "The Togetherness Woman," that would be based on a survey of her classmates. With the help of two friends, she prepared a detailed questionnaire that included, in addition to the typical fare, such deeper questions as "What difficulties have you found in working out your role as a woman?" "What are the chief satisfactions and frustrations of your life today?" "How do you feel about getting older?" "How have you changed inside?" "What do you wish you had done differently?" The 200 responses she received revealed a panoply of "suburban syndrome" symptoms. In particular, 80 percent expressed regret that they had not put their education to better use in professional work.[24]

McCall's, which had expected a celebratory piece on how education enriched women's lives, rejected the altogether different article that was actually submitted. *Ladies' Home Journal* agreed to publish it, but then rewrote the piece so thoroughly as to make it say the opposite of what the author intended. Finally, the freelancer tried *Redbook,* but the editor who read it was incredulous. Writing the author's agent, the editor fumed, "But she must be going off her rocker. Only the most neurotic housewife will identify with this."[25]

Stymied by the string of disappointments and rejections, Betty Friedan decided to give up on women's magazines and write a book instead. Six years later, *The Feminine Mystique* was published and a new feminist movement was born. Significantly, the book included an extensive discussion of the theories of Abraham Maslow, and Friedan made her case in explicitly Maslovian terms. "Despite the glorification of 'Occupation: housewife,' " she wrote, "if that occupation does not demand, or permit, realization of woman's full abilities, it cannot provide adequate self-esteem, much less pave the way to a higher level of self-realization."[26]

IN THE MIDDLE of the twentieth century, American capitalism was just emerging from decades of class conflict and ideological struggle. Radical alternatives to capitalism had ultimately failed to carry the day, and thus the basic system of market competition and corporate enterprise survived intact. Nevertheless, far-reaching changes in the interaction between political and economic life had occurred. Some of those changes constituted genuine improvements over the old Gilded Age order. In particular, social safety nets now offered some relief for the poor and jobless, and new regulatory structures provided better protection against disease, physical injury, and fraud. Less dramatic, though perhaps more consequential, were the large investments in public health and education that boosted life expectancies and substantially upgraded the nation's human capital.

All too often, however, what passed for reform was in fact an unmitigated botch. At the root of the problem was the failure to appreciate the continuing, vital role of competition in the new industrial economy. "So long as related industrial units are under different business managements," opined Thorstein Veblen, "they are, by the nature of the case, at cross-purposes."[27] Such thinking was widely shared among the Progressives and New Dealers whom Veblen inspired and influenced. Yet it was by no means confined to the leftward end of the political spectrum, as support for the centralization of economic decision making was also quite popular in Big Business circles. "I do not believe that competition is any longer the life of trade," concluded J. P. Morgan's chief lieutenant, George Perkins. "I have long believed that cooperation through large industrial units properly supervised and regulated by the Federal Government, is the only method of eliminating the abuses from which labor has suffered under the competitive method."[28] Henry Harriman, president of the U.S. Chamber of Commerce at the outset of the New Deal, observed along similar lines that "the laissez-faire economy which worked admirably in earlier and simpler industrial life must be replaced by a philosophy of planned national economy."[29]

What was the reason for this widespread enthusiasm for technocratic control? The answer lies in the perils of extrapolation. With the coming of the Machine Age, the immense productivity of large-scale business enterprise gave rise to a plausible but utterly wrongheaded notion about how the new industrial economy should be organized. Charles Proteus Steinmetz, the four-foot-tall engineering genius who pioneered the development of alternating current while at General Electric—and who, as a committed socialist, proudly displayed an autographed portrait of Lenin on his laboratory wall—expressed that notion in typical fashion. "All that is necessary," Steinmetz wrote in *America and the New Epoch*, "is to extend methods of economic efficiency from the individual industrial corporation to the national organism as a whole."[30]

Here was the essence of the collectivist delusion: if bureaucratic organization and rationalized, top-down control had achieved such wonders on the factory floor, just imagine what they could accomplish when applied to all of society! The idea's appeal transcended class and ideology. Sympathizers with the struggling working classes could not bear to face the truth that the country was still too technologically backward to alleviate mass poverty, so they convinced themselves that substitution of public administration for profit seeking was a magic cure-all. Meanwhile, the new tycoons and their functionaries, armed with the mighty hammer of corporate organization, imagined that all the world was a nail. The two sides differed merely as to how far centralization should be carried: the antibusiness left rested their hopes on the state, while Big Business argued that its cartels and trade associations should be vested with planning authority.

By the end of World War II, the American economy had amassed sufficient productive power to fund the purchase of industrial peace. Ideological passions cooled, and calls for radical reorganziation of production faded. But considerable damage had already been done. Over the course of the Progressive and New Deal bouts of reform, competitive vigor in broad areas of the economy was seriously compromised by restrictionist policies. Price controls or limits on new competitors, or both, extended to aviation, trucking, railroads, oil and gas, banking, stockbroking, broadcasting, and telephone service. Agriculture was enmeshed in a tangle of price supports and production controls. Manufacturers were stuck with labor policies that bloated payrolls and reduced flexibility on the shop floor. Fair-trade laws inhibited retail discounting. Selective antitrust enforcement targeted aggressive companies while leaving sleepy, stagnant oligopolies undisturbed. And in complete indifference to the effect on work incentives and new business creation, federal income tax rates topped out at 90 percent.

During the 1950s, the damage was well concealed. With the continued diffusion of mass-production techniques and modern forms of business organization, the United States now enjoyed living standards without historical precedent. Meanwhile, the country's lead over the rest of the world, which would have been considerable in any case, was compounded by the devastation inflicted elsewhere by World War II. Technological break-throughs accelerated by the war—in aerospace, electronics, nuclear energy, and plastics—were opening up exhilarating new possibilities for economic advance. The return of macroeconomic stability, the decline of radical politics, and the dissipation of labor tensions all served to bolster animal spirits and extend investors' time horizons. And pent-up demand after the privations of the thirties and forties set the stage for a mass-consumption binge.

Under such circumstances, complacency was irresistible. "Now we have as much government activity as is necessary, but not enough to stifle the normal motivations of private enterprise," boasted Eisenhower adviser Arthur Larson. "And we have a higher degree of government concern for the needs of people than ever before in our history, while at the same time pursuing a policy of maximum restoration of responsibility to individuals and private groups."[31] In other words, we like Ike and all's right with the world. With no appetite for a renewal of ideological conflict, Americans embraced the tepid pleasures of the mixed economy's happy medium.

Self-satisfaction was especially smug in the corridors of corporate power. "The best of all monopoly profits is a quiet life," the economist John Hicks once observed. In fifties America, with competitive pressures conveniently subdued, William Whyte's "organization men" reaped those profits with three-martini bonhomie. Progress was on autopilot, they believed, and the only real challenge was to keep the whole machine humming along smoothly with artful salesmanship and human relations. "From company to company, trainees express the same impatience," Whyte wrote. "All the great ideas, they explain, have already been discovered and not only in physics and chemistry but in practical fields like engineering. The basic creative work is done, so the man you need—for every kind of job—is a practical, team-player fellow who will do a good shirtsleeves job." [32]

The quiet life would not last. Beyond the confines of the New Deal consensus, beneath the notice of gray-flannel groupthink, forces of economic dynamism were pushing and straining for release. Just as the progress of capitalist development was undermining the repressive structures of Jim Crow and the feminine mystique, so was it launching an assault on the soft, safe collectivism of the postwar mixed economy. The demolition of the Big Business/Big Labor/Big Government edifice would not occur until the 1970s, but some of the fuses were lit right under Ike's nose.

One flame ignited in September 1957, when Robert Noyce, Gordon Moore, and six other colleagues bolted from their brilliant but erratic boss, William Shockley, to form Fairchild Semiconductor. The year before, Shockley, the Nobel Prize–winning developer of the transistor, had founded Shockley Semiconductor in Mountain View, California, where he had moved to be near his elderly mother in Palo Alto. Shockley assembled a team of topflight young engineers, but his imperious, paranoid manner soon proved too much for some of them. In one notorious incident, when his secretary cut her finger on a broken thumbtack, Shockley decided that the accident had actually been part of a plot to attack him, and he ordered employees to take lie detector tests to clear themselves. Fed up, the group that Shockley bitterly dubbed the "traitorous eight" set out on their own—and made history.

Fairchild, more than any other company, was responsible for creating what became known as Silicon Valley. First and foremost, it constructed the basic building block of the microelectronics revolution when, in the spring of 1959, Robert Noyce developed the first silicon integrated circuit. Fairchild also pioneered the valley's distinctive corporate culture. In reaction against Shockley's tyrannical manner, the eight founders decided to do without titles, dress codes, and assigned parking spaces; they even did without separate offices, preferring instead to work together in an open room. Each of the eight founders had an equal equity stake in the venture, and as Fairchild grew it made liberal use of stock options to attract talented technologists and managers. And over the years to come, Fairchild spin-offs—known as the "Fairchildren"—would spring up all over the valley. The most important of those offspring was born in 1968 when Noyce, Moore, and a young engineer named Andy Grove left Fairchild to start a new company called Intel.

Another fuse was lit on July 15, 1959, when the United Steelworkers of America launched a nationwide strike. Steel strikes were nothing new: since the USWA's creation in 1942, walkouts had occurred in 1946, 1949, 1952, 1955, and 1956. In what became a regular pattern, management would eventually agree to fat wage increases well in excess of those in other industries. Steel producers then levied hefty price hikes to cover the added costs—and with no effective foreign competition in a war-ravaged world, they got away with it. Between 1947 and 1957, steel prices actually increased 25 to 50 percent faster than unit labor costs. Management was unabashed about taking its share of the loot. In the 1958 *Business Week* listing of top-paid executives, Bethlehem Steel claimed six positions in the top 10. One Bethlehem alumnus recalled, "Bethlehem at that time had the reputation that its hallways were lined with gold, and when you became employed there they gave you a pick to mine [it]."[33]

By 1959, with the three-year union contract set to expire, Big Steel decided it was time to take a firmer line. A recession the year before had put a dent in profits, and in response industry leaders were rediscovering the virtues of cost control—in the mills, at least, if not in the executive suites. Their main target was Clause 2B from the 1956 agreement, which provided that "established labor practices"—that is, the number of people as-

signed to do a particular job—could not be changed without ne-
gotiations. The clause was enforced with absurd punctiliousness.
In a fit of exasperation, a Bethlehem engineer once tore away
the newspaper of an office worker who spent hours every day
working on the crossword puzzle instead of answering the
phone. The engineer was informed that doing the crossword
puzzle constituted an established practice and was dressed down
for taking the worker's personal property.

The union refused to budge. Why should workers tighten their
belts while the bosses gorged? The strike dragged on for 116
days, the longest in the industry's history, ending only because of
a Taft-Hartley injunction issued by the Supreme Court. During
the ensuing cooling-off period, management crumbled, agreeing
to a big increase in both wages and fringe benefits and dropping
its demands to scuttle Clause 2B. The wage-price spiral would
continue unabated—for the time being.

But the 1959 strike opened the door for gate-crashers who
would ultimately spoil the party. Increasingly desperate as the
production shutdown continued into the fall, steel buyers began
turning to European and Japanese suppliers. Imports, which
had amounted to only 2 million tons the year before, jumped to
5 million tons. And they never returned to prestrike levels. "The
big customers came back," one plant manager related, "but we
began to lose the by-products—nails, field fence and barbed
wire. It was a nickel-and-dime impact at first but it started to affect the cost structure because we were now selling a smaller
piece of the product."[34] Within a decade of the strike, foreign
steel shipments exceeded 15 million tons a year.

The New Deal regulatory state attempted to tame capitalism
by subduing the bumptious, unruly forces of competition. Economic life was to become more stable, more *manageable*. And so
technocratic managerialism settled in to the predictable rou-
tines of administering the status quo—and, over time, much of
American industry grew bloated and stagnant. In the seventies
and eighties, the combination of globalization and high technology upended that status quo with ferocious blasts of unexpected

change and unaccustomed competition. Blindsided by the challenge, the once vibrant industrial heartland was reduced to the reeling, clattering Rust Belt.

Even when the New Deal system was still functioning smoothly, the country's economic center of gravity began to shift. At the time America entered the realm of freedom, vast stretches of the continental nation remained underdeveloped. The Southeast was a rural backwater, its latent energies sapped by the exploitation of blacks and white addiction to exploited black labor. The West was largely empty, with an economy based primarily on the extraction of natural resources. Yet as competitive vigor waned in the Northeast and the Midwest, and opportunities began to narrow, new chances beckoned in what would become known as the Sunbelt—the burgeoning heartland of the postwar boom.

Florida, Texas, Arizona, and California were the pacesetters. Between 1940 and 1960, the combined population of the four states doubled from 15.7 million to 31.6 million. Over half of that bulge was due to migration: in just two decades, more than eight million people moved to those states from elsewhere in the country. Throughout the region, cities and their surrounding suburbs mushroomed. As of 1940, only two cities of the South and the West—Los Angeles and New Orleans—ranked in the nation's top 20. Two decades later, seven cities—Los Angeles, Houston, Dallas, New Orleans, San Antonio, San Diego, and Seattle—made the list.

The rise of the Sunbelt had many causes. For one thing, expansive and free-spending government played an important role. Major new dams, power plants, and irrigation projects provided necessary infrastructure; the proliferation of military bases, shipyards, and defense contracts during World War II and then the Cold War pumped billions of federal dollars into previously sleepy communities. Technological change was another major factor. In particular, the continued mechanization of southern agriculture finally spelled the end of the plantation's socially retrograde dominance. As a result, the countryside emptied and cities swelled: in the states of the old Confederacy, people living in urban areas rose from 35 percent of the population in 1940 to 58 percent in 1960. Meanwhile, the pell-mell pursuit of happiness unleashed by mass affluence led inevitably toward sunnier climates. Tourists flocked to warm-weather resorts, while retirees sought out golden sunshine for their golden years. The Sunbelt's growth was also greatly aided by the spread of air-conditioning, which allowed pleasant winters to be followed by bearable summers.[35]

The region's rapid ascent was also propelled by the paradoxical advantages of backwardness. Because economic takeoff in the South and the West occurred later than in the Northeast and the Midwest, it took place at a more advanced stage of overall capitalist development. As a result, economic growth did not exact the brutal human toll that it did in the Gilded Age, nor did it provoke the same anguished backlash. The factory work that came to the Sunbelt was incomparably safer, cleaner, and better paying than that which confronted the struggling immigrant masses at the turn of the century. Meanwhile, most of the rollicking expansion in employment came in the form of white-collar office jobs.

The Sunbelt was therefore able to boom untroubled by the class conflict and political turmoil that afflicted the old industrial heartland. Pro-business boosterism was the dominant creed, and without the presence of an impoverished, urbanized working class, no countervailing adversarial movement of any consequence emerged. In particular, labor unions made little headway. From 1946 to 1953, the CIO's "Operation Dixie" strove to organize the South, but the effort ended in dismal failure. "Right-to-work" laws, which undercut organized labor's power by prohibiting compulsory union membership, became the norm throughout the Sunbelt.

Just as the South avoided the economic and political trauma of early industrialization, it also missed out on the associated cultural transformation. The great wave of Gilded Age immigration all but bypassed Dixie: as of 1910, at the height of that wave, the South accounted for a mere 5.5 percent of the nation's foreign-born population. And while the industrial heartland's leading universities were located in big cities or had strong urban connections, Dixie's centers of learning were nestled in remote hamlets like Oxford, Mississippi, and Chapel Hill, North Carolina. Accordingly, southern intellectual life maintained a romantic, literary sensibility and avoided engagement with the grubby materialism of scientific and technological advance. Poor, rural, far removed from the cultural ferment of the nation's new ethnic pluralism, indifferent or hostile to the intellectual ferment at the frontiers of human knowledge, the South began its postwar growth spurt as a land that time forgot.

The West also served as a refuge for old-style values—at the same time that it was incubating radical breaks with tradition. The lack of settled social structures in the West made the region open to extreme movements in either direction. Yet despite the emergence of immensely influential enclaves of cultural radicalism, most especially in California's Bay Area, on the whole the traditionalist impulse predominated. As migrants from the South and the small towns of the Northeast and the Midwest headed westward, they brought their conservative values with them and transplanted them in new soil. Indeed, Southern California was nicknamed the "seacoast of Iowa" because of the preponderance of Farm Belt expatriates. "Here the alien patrimony is not European, but American," wrote Cary McWilliams in *Southern California Country*. "The nostalgia is for an America that no longer exists, for an America that former Kansans, Missourians and Iowans literally gaze back upon." [36]

New conditions and old traditions proved a good match, as individualism and self-reliance were well suited to the emptiness and rootlessness of the West. Likewise, enthusiastic religiosity beckoned to settlers groping for a sense of community. Southern California in particular was fertile ground for evangelical fervor. Between 1910 and 1915, Los Angeles oil millionaires Lyman and Milton Stewart bankrolled the publication of a 12-volume series of pamphlets called *The Fundamentals*. With three million copies printed and distributed, the old literalist faith acquired a new name: fundamentalism. Also in Los Angeles, the Azusa Street revival of 1906—led by William Seymour, the son of former slaves, in a ramshackle abandoned warehouse that had recently served as a livery stable—launched the modern Pentecostal movement.

Consequently, the Sunbelt's rise forged a curious but powerful alliance between economic dynamism and cultural conservatism. The marriage was decidedly incongruous. Scientific rationality, upon which capitalism's advance ultimately depended, had no place for belief in biblical inerrancy, while the therapeutic hedonism that capitalism's advance had unleashed did not sit well with pleasure-denying abstemiousness. Yet the cunning of history often makes sport of earnest philosophical distinctions, and here was a case in point. Also, to be fair, the union was no more theoretically incoherent than the industrial heartland's combination of cultural liberalism and economic collectivism.

Hitched to capitalism's immense motive power, the old Protestant bourgeois ethos began to stage a major comeback. Dethroned during the coming of mass affluence, the old-time religion had stayed alive in small towns and the nation's vast underdeveloped periphery. Now, as the Sunbelt started to boom, the keepers of the flame found their voice again. This time, however, it was not the voice of America's established, educated elite. This time, it was the cry of insurgency. Stripped of their social and cultural leadership, exiled from the centers of power, the devotees of old-fashioned bourgeois virtues denounced the apostasy and decadence into which the country had sunk. And they tossed and turned with dreams of winning their country back.

In the right-wing insurgency that took shape during the 1950s, culturally dispossessed Protestants made common cause with conservative Catholics to form a larger traditionalist camp organized around a trio of interrelated discontents. Hostile to the increasing permissiveness of the affluent society, unreconciled to the New Deal's domestic political settlement, and impatient with the indecisiveness of Cold War containment, the insurgents fused their specific grievances into an overarching charge that the country was in moral decline—and consequently in mortal peril. And they focused their blame for the nation's dire predicament on the political and cultural elites who, in their view, had abandoned the true faith and now worshipped at the altars of secularism, relativism, collectivism, internationalism, and appeasement.

During the fifties, fear of communist infiltration and takeover lent an apocalyptic intensity to the gathering conservative backlash. That fear certainly had a basis in fact, as documents recovered from Soviet archives now confirm the considerable extent to which American communists were involved in espionage on Moscow's behalf. But with the advent of the Cold War, communism's American presence went into wholesale retreat. Membership in the CPUSA plunged from around 60,000 in 1948 to 25,000 in 1953 and then to 10,000 by 1957. Meanwhile, communist-controlled unions accounted for around 20 percent of U.S. union membership in 1944, but only about 5 percent by 1952.

Yet even as the actual threat diminished, well-founded concerns spilled over into paranoia. Anxiety about conflict with the Soviets merged with misgivings about political and cultural developments at home. In the resulting synthesis, the rise of Big Government and the loosening of moral restraints came to be seen as evidence of foreign-backed subversion. "Something utterly new has taken root in America during the past generation, a communist mentality representing a systematic, purposive, and conscious attempt to destroy Western civilization . . . ," wrote J. Edgar Hoover in *Masters of Deceit*. "Communist thought control . . . has spread the infection, in varying degrees, to most phases of American life."[37]

This brand of hysterical anticommunism proved a handy cudgel for striking back against the nation's liberal elites. "Tailgunner Joe" McCarthy, a working-class Irish Catholic from small-town Wisconsin, built up a nationwide following by embellishing his red-baiting burlesque with healthy doses of antiestablishment resentment. "The reason why we find ourselves in a position of impotency . . . is the traitorous actions of those who have been treated so well by this nation," McCarthy thundered. "It is not the less fortunate or members of minority groups who have been selling this nation out but rather those who have had all the benefits the wealthiest nation on earth has had to offer—the finest homes, the finest college educations, and the finest jobs in the government that we can give."[38] Conservative elite bashing reached its crackpot apotheosis in the person of Robert Welch, the retired Massachusetts candy maker who founded the John Birch Society in 1958. According to Welch, Ike himself was a "conscious, dedicated agent of the Communist Conspiracy," as were John Foster Dulles and Allen Dulles (Eisenhower's secretary of state and CIA director, respectively) and Chief Justice Earl Warren.

All the strange convergences of the postwar right-wing insurgency could be found in the story of the Californian entrepreneur and political activist Walter Knott. His grandfather had moved the family to Southern California by covered wagon some 20 years before Walter's birth in 1889. Knott grew up in Pomona, married his high school sweetheart, Cordelia, and began farming in Orange County's Buena Park in 1920. In the early 1930s, he succeeded in cultivating a new berry invented by Rudolph Boysen, then the Anaheim parks superintendent. Knott named the new fruit—a cross among the blackberry, the red raspberry, and the loganberry—a "boysenberry," and began selling the berries and preserves made by Cordelia at his roadside stand. Struggling to keep afloat during the Great Depression, Cordelia started offering fried-chicken dinners as well. They were an immediate hit, and Knott quickly expanded his restaurant operations. By 1940, as many as 4,000 chicken dinners were being served on a Sunday evening.

To entertain the long lines of waiting diners, Knott opened what is regarded as the nation's first theme park—a re-created western ghost town that preceded its neighbor and imitator, Disneyland, by more than a decade. The first attraction was the Gold Trails Hotel, moved from its original location in Prescott, Arizona, and reassembled on the Knotts' property. Soon to follow were a little red schoolhouse from Kansas, a blacksmith's shop, a gristmill, and Boot Hill graveyard (featuring one "spooky" grave from which a heartbeatlike thumping emanated). The whole complex received the name Knott's Berry Farm in 1947 and continued to add new attractions, including a narrow-gauge rail line, a wagon camp, a saloon (offering sasparilla and, inevitably, boysenberry punch), an electronic shooting gallery, the Bird Cage Theatre, and even a panning-for-gold area. The park also boasted two houses of worship: the Little Adobe Chapel by the Lake (complete with a glowing painting of the Transfiguration that was revealed to visitors by automatically opening doors) and the Church of Reflections, which actually held Sunday services.

Knott's Berry Farm was a shrine to old-fashioned values: homey hospitality, the pioneer spirit of the Old West, and religious faith. At the same time, it was the epitome of go-go consumerism, catering to the affluent society's voracious appetite for new products and new diversions. Having made his fortune in a classic Sunbelt mix of entrepreneurial innovation and cultural conservatism, it was entirely fitting that Walter Knott would then spend a good chunk of his fortune on promoting that same mix in the political realm. He founded the California Free Enterprise Association, which then was housed in a two-story "Freedom Center" erected across the highway from the Berry Farm. In 1961, Knott served as honorary chairman for the five-day Orange County School of Anti-Communism that ended with a rally for 7,000 young people at Anaheim's La Palma Park stadium. A couple of years later, Knott was one of the Goldwater campaign's major backers, and it was at his insistence that on October 27, 1964, the campaign aired a speech entitled "A Time for Choosing" on national television. The speech was delivered by a former actor turned GE spokesman named Ronald Reagan, who was transformed overnight into a national political figure.

"TRUST YOURSELF. YOU know more than you think you do."[39] In those opening lines of *Baby and Child Care*, Dr. Benjamin Spock set the tone for his whole book—and for the generation raised on it. The year was 1946, the dawn of the baby boom, and for the millions of young couples who were settling down and starting families, Dr. Spock's gentle, tolerant common sense provided exactly the kind of guidance they longed to hear. Seldom in the history of publishing has a book so perfectly matched its moment, and the results of that match were impressive: in its first quarter century in print, *Baby and Child Care* sold well over 20 million copies.

Benjamin Spock was born in 1903 in New Haven, Connecticut, the oldest of six children in a well-to-do family. As a Yale undergraduate, he focused more on rowing than studying; though his grades were indifferent, he ended up winning a gold medal at the 1924 Olympics in Paris. After that triumph, he started medical school at Yale, but later transferred to Columbia, from which he graduated first in his class in 1929. Appropriately for an icon of the therapeutic age, Spock did his residency in psychiatry and psychoanalysis. He then opened a private pediatric office in New York, making him the first practicing physician in his field with psychiatric training. In 1943, he agreed with Pocket Books, the upstart publisher of quality paperbacks, to author a child-care manual that would sell for just 25 cents. Spock spent the next three years, including two on active duty in the Navy, dictating the book off the top of his head to his wife, Jane. The end result, which Spock hoped would sell 10,000 copies, quickly became an American institution.

In striking contrast with the prevailing medical style, Spock dispensed with the conceit that scientific expertise could pronounce the one best way to take care of babies and raise children. Instead, he urged parents to loosen up and do what came naturally. "It may surprise you to hear," Spock wrote, "that the more people have studied different methods of bringing up children the more they have come to the conclusion that what good mothers and fathers instinctively feel like doing for their babies is usually best after all."[40]

In Dr. Spock's comforting view, the same healthy instincts that whispered in parents' ears would also serve to guide children in their development. Children learned to behave and assume increasing responsibilities, not in response to external restraints and discipline, but by tapping into their own innate, natural goodness. "I disagree with the grim or irritable parent who seriously believes that punishment is a good regular method of controlling a child," Spock maintained.[41]

"What makes a child learn table manners?" the good doctor asked. "Not scolding—that would take a hundred years—but the fact that he wants to handle a fork and knife the way he sees others doing it. . . . What makes him considerate and polite with his parents? Not the fear that they will punish him if he's rude, but the loving and respecting feeling he has for them. What keeps him from lying and stealing? Not the fear of the consequences. . . . The thing that keeps us all from doing 'bad' things to each other is the feelings we have of liking people and wanting them to like us. In other words, if a child is handled in a friendly way, he wants to do the right thing, the grown-up thing, most of the time."[42]

In ways he never could have imagined, Benjamin Spock's sunny confidence in his millions of young charges was going to be put to the test. The baby-boom generation—the Dr. Spock generation—would grow up with external restraints of all kinds reduced to unprecedented laxity. Born into mass affluence, the middle-class children of the postwar years were spared the cruel restraints of disease and ignorance and poverty; they were excused from physical toil, whether on the farm or in the factory; and, in accordance with doctor's orders, they were largely exempted from the corporal discipline and stern moralism that previously had defined good parenting. The restrictive bonds of economic necessity had been blasted away; those of conventional necessity were fraying badly.

The fraying accelerated with the development during the fifties of a distinctive new youth market. Rallying to the banner of "nothing's too good for our kids," the immense productive forces of consumer capitalism began to redirect their energies toward serving the desires of the purest and most uninhibited of consumers. A landmark in the process occurred on December 15,

1954, when ABC's new television series *Disneyland* aired "Davy Crockett: Indian Fighter," the first of a three-part series on the life of the famous frontiersman. By February 23, 1955, when the final episode closed with Davey's swinging his rifle "Old Betsy" at the Alamo's last stand, a national craze was in full frenzy. Coonskin caps became de rigueur; at the height of the fad, some 5,000 a day were being sold. In addition, buckskins, chaps, rifles, powder horns, and lunch boxes flew off assembly lines and into suburbia, and Bill Hayes's "The Ballad of Davy Crockett" became a huge hit. All told, sales of Crockett-related merchandise reached $100 million. In the age of abundance, kids' wishes were the world's commands.

The booming youth market did not rely only on indulgent parents. In addition, young people were becoming big spenders on their own behalf. By 1956, America's 13 million teenagers boasted a combined income of $7 billion—a 26 percent jump over three years before. The average teenager's income of $10.55 a week now matched the disposable income of the typical American *family* in the early 1940s.[43] Young people quickly became the darlings of advertisers, not just because they had money to burn, but because their loyalties were up for grabs. "The people who want things the most and have the best prospects to get them are the young," the advertising expert James Twitchell observed. "They are also the ones who have not decided which brands of objects they wish to consume."[44] The potential rewards of appealing to teenagers were therefore huge, since their spending decisions could determine consumption patterns for a lifetime. As a result, advertisers began to chase the young—and the advertising-supported mass media followed right behind.

The emerging youth culture drew from the confluence of psychological and social developments. In the years after puberty, the urgings of the body are at their most insistent, while the internalization of society's norms remains a work in progress. It is during this time of life, therefore, that the counsel of passion seems wisest and that of authority and tradition most suspect.

Impetuosity has always been the coin of youth—winsome boldness on the one side, foolhardy rashness on the other.

The natural hot-bloodedness of the young was brought to a
boil by the peculiar circumstances of American adolescence. Indeed, the whole concept of adolescence was an American invention. As the industrializing country began to spread the blessings
of affluence, entry into the workaday world was postponed in
favor of more extensive education, and, consequently, the transition from childhood to adulthood became so protracted that it
acquired its own name and separate identity. Specifically, it was
in 1904 that American psychologist G. Stanley Hall brought the
term "adolescence" into general usage with his two-volume work
on the subject. By the 1950s, the vast majority of American kids
were spending their teenage years in high school, and a rapidly
growing fraction opted to continue their educations in college
and beyond. Accordingly, the awkward interval between childhood dependency and adult responsibility—and between biological and social maturity—dragged on ever longer.

Caught in this extended no-man's-land, brimming with energy
yet prevented from taking full part in the larger society around
them, America's young could not help but be restless. In the full
flush of postpubescent vigor, the teenagers of the fifties longed to
start living the new ethos of self-expression and personal fulfillment they had absorbed since birth. Instead, they found themselves warehoused in high schools, cut off from the "real world"
around them. Not allowed to start careers, not allowed to start
families, they stewed in pent-up desire and free-floating frustration. Thus emerged that now-familiar feature of the affluent society: teen angst.

For the first generation born into the realm of freedom, the affliction struck with particular severity. The baby boomers were
separated from their parents by what would come to be known
as the "generation gap"—in other words, the great historical divide between scarcity and abundance. Conflict between parents
and children has been the stuff of drama since the days of Oedi-
pus, but here was something extraordinary. The parents of the

baby boomers grew up amidst unusual hardships and immersed in traditional values—whether those of the Protestant bourgeoisie or the old-country ways of working-class immigrant groups. Their children, by contrast, were the original natives of a whole new world. Small wonder, then, that the perennial self-pitying complaint that "nobody understands me" found such resonance amongst postwar adolescents. Or that those adolescents would come to feel that their parents' values were hopelessly out-of-date.

The central and abiding theme of the new youth culture was, consequently, rebellion. Hand-wringing about "juvenile delinquency" became a national pastime—not because of any discernible uptick in criminal activity by minors, but because of a more general, and entirely well-founded, concern that kids were not reliably assimilating their parents' values and priorities. Hollywood quickly cashed in, sensing that whatever worried Mom and Dad was sure to thrill their children. In 1953's *The Wild One*, Marlin Brando sounded all the basic notes as Johnny, the brooding leader of a gang of motorcycle toughs. "What are you rebellin' against, Johnny?" a girl asks as he rolled into town. "Whaddya got?" was the immortal reply. If truth be told, the film has not held up particularly well over the decades. The hokey rear-screen projections during the bike-riding scenes, the now-archaic hipster lingo, and the fact that none of the young thugs ever has a speck of dirt on him—all combine to make the movie seem sweetly, comically innocent rather than menacing or disturbing. Nevertheless, at the time it sufficed to set the proper mood.

A better offering in the same genre was made two years later with James Dean's *Rebel without a Cause*. By the time the movie premiered on October 26, 1955, the young star was already dead, having crashed his silver Porsche Spyder into an oncoming car just the month before. The tragedy instantly transformed Dean into a cult figure and ensured that the second of his three film performances would forever define his character, Jim Stark, as an icon of misunderstood youth. With belabored symbolism, a planetarium—a man-made cosmos—provided the setting or backdrop for much of the movie's action. In a relatively early scene, at a school field trip to the planetarium, kids wisecracked under the artificial stars. As Jim, the new kid in school, struggled to fit in with the cool crowd, the lecturer intoned off screen: "Through the infinite reaches of space, the problems of Man seem trivial and naïve indeed. And Man, existing alone, seems to be an episode of little consequence."

Rebel without a Cause, in its heavy-handed way, proclaimed the full depths of juvenile discontent. In technological society's triumph of artifice over nature, how do we know what is genuine and authentic? In a world stripped of all its old certainties, how do we find the truth? In the realm of freedom, how shall we act when all is permitted? Those same existential doubts vexed adults as well: Tom Rath, the man in the gray flannel suit, and Jim Stark were peering into the same void. Yet grown-ups were shielded from the full force of such anxieties by the demands—or distractions?—of adult responsibility. Adolescents, by contrast, had nowhere to hide.

The culture of rebellion expressed itself in a rising, corrosive tide of cynicism and ridicule. Being hip, being cool, meant seeing through all the pretensions, hypocrisies, and corrupt compromises of the grown-up world. In J. D. Salinger's *The Catcher in the Rye*, published in 1951, Holden Caulfield led the way with his aversion to all things "phony"—including his headmaster ("a phony slob"), his former school ("I was surrounded by phonies"), movies ("If there's one thing I hate, it's the movies"), the word "grand" ("I could puke every time I hear it"), and the Christmas pageant at Radio City Music Hall ("old Jesus probably would've puked if He could see it").[45] A year later, William Gaines of EC Comics debuted a new comic book called *Tales Calculated to Drive You Mad: Humor in a Jugular Vein*. In 1955, the comic book became *Mad* magazine, and soon jug-eared, vacant-stared, gap-toothed Alfred E. Neuman became the grinning face of goofball, teenage-boy nihilism.

Meanwhile, a rising generation of comedians, collectively

dubbed the "sick comics," was scoring big with younger audiences. Abandoning the comfortable ruts of double entendres,
ethnic stereotyping, and mother-in-law jokes, they chose to explore the fresher, rawer material of observation, introspec-
tion, social satire, and political commentary. In so doing, Tom
Lehrer, Mort Sahl, Mike Nichols and Elaine May, Shelley Ber-
man, and, of course, Lenny Bruce used humor's immense subversive power to reshape cultural sensibilities. What is genuine
in a world of artifice? The disillusioned and irreverent sought
the answer through a process of elimination. "My humor is
mostly one of indictment," Bruce once said. "I'm a surgeon with
a scalpel for false values." Cut away all the puffery and decep-
tion and cant, and whatever is left must be authentic. (It should
be noted in passing how strikingly unfunny Lenny Bruce is to a
contemporary ear. The intelligence and wit are evident, but
whatever context made him *funny*—and the laughter on the old
recordings sounds genuine—has now been lost, apparently irre-
trievably.)

The youth culture of rebellion expressed itself as well in a dramatic turn toward romanticism—a celebration of the wild, the
primitive, the spontaneous. A celebration, in other words, of the
instinctual realm in which Benjamin Spock invested so much
hope. Here was a complementary approach to the search for authenticity: rather than looking outward at existing social institutions and tearing them down, turn inward instead. Shuck off the
carapace of technology and bureaucracy, and reassert the primacy of the primal.

Thus arose rock 'n' roll, the music of libidinal release. It got its
name in 1951, courtesy of Cleveland disk jockey Alan Freed. A
local record store owner named Lee Mintz had told Freed about
an interesting new development: white kids were starting to
spend some of their growing discretionary income on black
rhythm-and-blues music, often called "race music" or "sepia
music." Sensing an opportunity, Freed abandoned his classical-
music format and, calling himself "Moondog," began playing
R & B instead. Wanting to give the music a name that avoided

racial connotations, he started calling it rock and roll—which, amusingly and fittingly, was actually black slang for sex.

What Freed named, Elvis Presley transformed. When the young Memphis truck driver walked into Sam Phillips's Sun Records studio in August 1953, the secretary asked him, "What kind of singer are you?" "I sing all kinds," he replied nervously. "Who do you sound like?" she pressed further. To which Elvis responded, "I don't sound like nobody." Which, in the event, turned out to be exactly the point. Somehow, this slight, shy figure—who looked like a street tough with his pomaded hair and black clothes, but whose demeanor was sweetly humble and unfailingly polite—channeled through his voice the previously separate streams of R & B, gospel, and country music. On July 5, 1954, Elvis cut his first record with Phillips, a cover of Arthur Crudup's "That's All Right (Mama)." A couple days later, the record aired on the local *Red, Hot and Blue* radio show, and the switchboard lit up so fast that the disk jockey whisked Elvis into the station that night for a live interview. By September 9, 1956, when he made his first appearance on *The Ed Sullivan Show*, Elvis was a national sensation. And American mores would be forever changed.

How big was Elvis? "Before Elvis, there was nothing," John Lennon once said. And according to Leonard Bernstein, "Elvis Presley is the greatest cultural force in the twentieth century. He introduced the beat to everything and he changed everything—music, language, clothes." Hyperbole, perhaps, but not too far off the mark. The music that he pioneered and popularized possessed an intense power unlike anything that had come before, a power rooted in the ability to awaken and give expression to the instinctual urgings of the body. Rock and roll, indeed: the insistent, throbbing bass beat made feet move almost against their will and radiated a palpable sexual energy. And Elvis himself—with his good looks and sly charm, and, of course, his gyrating hips—was a dynamo of sexual charisma. But there was more to his immense appeal than simple prurience. Elvis was, in short, a natural. Everything about him—his country-boy simplicity, the stripped-down rawness of his sound, and the screaming, swooning pandemonium that surrounded him—proclaimed the rude vitality of the primitive. He was Rousseau's noble savage, updated with a swivel and a sneer.

While Elvis was upending the musical world, the Beats were experimenting with new literary forms. In the process, they created a whole rebel subculture. "I saw the best minds of my generation destroyed by madness, starving hysterical naked, / dragging themselves through the negro streets looking for an angry fix, / angelheaded hipsters burning for the ancient heavenly connection to the starry dynamo in the machinery of night, / who poverty and tatters and hollow-eyed and high sat up smoking in the supernatural darkness of cold-water flats floating across the tops of cities contemplating jazz." It was October 7, 1955, and Allen Ginsberg was giving his first public reading of "Howl" at the Six Gallery, a small San Francisco art gallery that once was an auto-repair shop. Starting quietly at first, he soon let the mood of the crowd and the wine in his veins take over, swaying back and forth and intoning in a singsong. Jack Kerouac was in the audience, slugging California Burgundy from a gallon jug and yelling "Go!" at the end of long lines. The rest of the crowd joined in, shouting encouragement with the cadence of the poem. By the time Ginsberg finished, tears were streaming down his face.

Ginsberg's "Howl" was one of protest—the howl of a wounded romantic sensibility that recoiled from American corporate consumerism in unabashed horror. Together, Ginsberg and Kerouac would become the leading voices of a radical cultural alternative, one that rejected things for experience, analysis for insight, and the past and future for the now. Integrating style with substance, they found inspiration in music—not rock 'n' roll, but the free-flowing improvisations of bebop jazz. Kerouac referred to his stream-of-consciousness avalanches of words as "spontaneous prose"; Ginsberg, who followed in Kerouac's footsteps, spoke of "composing on the tongue." The idea was to capture on the page the raw power of the spontaneous, bypassing to the maximum extent possible the overcautious censorship of the conscious mind. Drugs, especially marijuana and Benzedrine, proved useful in attaining the appropriate, trancelike state. Pioneering the new method, Kerouac pounded out what would become *On the Road* in April 1951, typing the whole manuscript on a single 120-foot scroll during a three-week frenzy sustained by coffee and speed.

The Beats sought to write as they lived, free and loose and in the moment. They then used their underground, bohemian existence as the raw material for their art. Such was their notion of authenticity and integrity: lives as works of art and art that was true to life, all in a seamless whole. Showing them the way was another Rousseauian natural man, Neal Cassady, who acted as both lifestyle mentor and artistic muse for his friends Kerouac and Ginsberg.

Neal Cassady had grown up in Denver's skid row, raised by an alcoholic father. From his chaotic upbringing, which included stints in reform schools and juvenile prisons, he emerged with a street hustler's charm and a manic energy that propelled him into incessant, restless motion. Blessed as well with natural athleticism—it was said he could throw a football 70 yards and run a hundred yards in under 10 seconds—Cassady possessed an immense animal magnetism that made him almost irresistibly attractive to men and women alike (although he preferred heterosexual relationships, he was happy to sleep with men from time to time). On top of everything else, he was a gifted car thief: by the time he moved to New York in 1946 at the age of 20, he had stolen some 500. "And his 'criminality' was not something that sulked and sneered," Kerouac wrote of him in *On the Road;* "it was a wild yea-saying overburst of American joy; it was Western, the west wind, an ode from the Plains, something new, long prophesied, long a-coming (he only stole cars for joy rides)." [46]

Cassady came to New York to visit a friend who had enrolled at Columbia. Once in town, he soon met Ginsberg, who was also a Columbia student, and Ginsberg's friend Kerouac (Kerouac was himself a Columbia dropout who had come to the school on a football scholarship but broken his leg during his first season). To the two aspiring young writers, Cassady seemed larger than life. He and Kerouac became close friends, and their cross-country adventures together in the late forties would later be immortalized in *On the Road*. What is more, Kerouac's distinctive "spontaneous prose" style was borrowed from the torrential word flow of Cassady's letters. Ginsberg actually fell in love with Cassady, who obliged him with a brief affair—a tribute to which appears in "Howl" ("who went out whoring in Colorado in myriad stolen night-cars, N.C., secret hero of these poems").

Out of the Beats' romantic resolve to live on the edge—and their ability to share with the world what they found there—arose a vibrant bohemian scene filled with admirers and imitators. Young hipsters and sophisticates who wore black, smoked dope, listened to jazz, and sprinkled their coffee-house conversations with references to Sartre and Camus, they became known as the "beatniks," thanks to Herb Caen's lampooning characterization not long after Sputnik took to the skies.

Norman Mailer, on the other hand, took approving note of the new avant garde. In a remarkable 1957 essay entitled "The White Negro," he began with a grim nod to "the psychic havoc of the concentration camps and the atom bomb," and then proceeded to an obligatory denunciation of fifties conformity. "It is on this bleak scene," he reported, "that a phenomenon has appeared: the American existentialist—the hipster." According to Mailer, the "life-giving answer" supplied by this new breed was "to divorce oneself from society, to exist without roots, to set out on that uncharted journey into the rebellious imperatives of the self."

In typical romantic fashion, Mailer idealized the backward and underdeveloped as spiritually exalted. In particular, African Americans, because they were poor and uneducated, were to be envied for their freedom from stifling, middle-class repression. "Knowing in the cells of his existence that life was war, nothing but war," Mailer wrote, "the Negro (all exceptions admitted) could rarely afford the sophisticated inhibitions of civilization, and so he kept for his survival the art of the primitive, he lived in the enormous present, he subsisted for his Saturday night kicks, relinquishing the pleasures of the mind for the more obligatory pleasures of the body." (When, in a similar vein, Kerouac wrote in *On the Road* of "wishing I were a Negro, feeling that the best the white world has offered was not enough ecstasy for me, not enough life, joy, kicks, darkness, music, not enough life," James Baldwin replied contemptuously that "I would hate to be in Kerouac's shoes if he should ever be mad enough to read this aloud from the stage of Harlem's Apollo Theater.") "The hipster," Mailer claimed, "had absorbed the existential synapses of the Negro, and for practical purposes could be considered a white Negro."

Warming to his runaway antinomianism, Mailer pushed beyond the primitive to embrace anything marginal and outré— even crime and madness. The vitality of the Beat scene, he wrote, arose from "the decision . . . to encourage the psychopath in oneself." Transgression of any kind, however brutal and sordid, had some redeeming quality. "It can of course be suggested that it takes little courage for two strong eighteen-year old hoodlums, let us say, to beat in the brains of a candy-store keeper . . . ," Mailer mused in an infamous passage. "Still, courage of a sort is necessary, for one murders not only a weak fifty-year old man but an institution as well, one violates private property, one enters into a new relation with the police and introduces a dangerous element into one's life."

In the end, Mailer's indiscriminate hostility to conventional limits of any kind—the very hostility that drove the whole youth culture of rebellion—hung on the same faith that sustained gentle, commonsensical Dr. Spock: that human beings are naturally good, and that therefore the instinctual and the virtuous are ultimately reconciled. "[T]he nihilism of Hip," Mailer argued, "proposes as its final tendency that every social restraint and category be removed, and the affirmation implicit in the proposal is that man would then prove to be more creative than murderous and so would not destroy himself."[47]

From philosophy's lofty perches, Herbert Marcuse was proclaiming the same reconciliation. In his highly influential synthesis of Freud and Marx, *Eros and Civilization*, Marcuse sought to challenge the Freudian proposition that "[f]ree gratification of man's instinctual needs is incompatible with civilized society."[48] According to Freud, civilization rests on the conquest of the id by the ego and superego—the subjugation of the "pleasure principle" to the "reality principle." But, Marcuse noted, the reign of repression has been based on economic necessity. "Scarcity," he wrote, "teaches men that they cannot freely gratify their instinctual impulses, that they cannot live under the pleasure principle."[49] It therefore followed, Marcuse argued, that the elimination of scarcity made possible the overthrow of repression.

Consequently, the moment of liberation was at hand. The reconciliation between pleasure and reality principles could be found at the two poles of history: "one would be located at the primitive beginnings of history, the other at its most mature stage." There was thus a deep symmetry between "matriarchal phases of ancient society" and the "rational organization of fully developed industrial society after the conquest of scarcity." Echoing Marx, Marcuse predicted that "[u]nder the 'ideal' conditions of mature industrial civilization, alienation would be completed by general automation of labor, reduction of labor time to a minimum, and exchangeability of functions." As a result, "the quantum of instinctual energy still to be diverted into necessary labor . . . would be so small that a large area of repressive constraints and modifications, no longer sustained by external forces, would collapse."[50] Capitalism's elaborate, soul-deadening disciplines could then be left behind, and civilization would advance into enlightened neoprimitivism. In Marcuse's conception, the realm of freedom was to be a playground of uninhibited instinct.

Eros and Civilization was published in 1955, shortly after Herbert Marcuse began teaching at Brandeis University. Born 56 years earlier to wealthy Jewish parents in Berlin, he fled the Nazis in 1933, escaping first to Switzerland before moving to the

United States and becoming an American citizen in 1940. At Brandeis, he became friends with Abraham Maslow, and the two lunched frequently together on campus. Maslow, for his part, did not share Marcuse's radical antipathy to American consumer capitalism. But his emphasis on self-realization—and, in particular, his belief that the instinctual impulses that lead people up the hierarchy of needs are fundamentally healthy—made him, along with Marcuse, a hero of the gathering romantic rebellion.

While studying at Brandeis during the fifties, one young psychology major fell deeply under the influence of both Marcuse and Maslow. "Most of all, I loved Professor Abe Maslow," he wrote later. "I took every class he gave and spent long evenings with him and his family." His exposure to Marcuse, however, led him to see Maslow's message as incomplete. "Maslow, a true pioneer, was far from a social radical . . . ," he observed. "Still I've found everything Maslow wrote applicable to modern revolutionary struggle in America, especially when corrected by Marcuse's class analysis." After college, Abbie Hoffman would apply his own personal touch to the lessons of his two mentors, but he never forgot his intellectual debt. "It doesn't take a great deal of insight," acknowledged the clown prince of the student revolt, "to see the entire sixties (myself included) as the synthesis of these two teachers."[51]

Signs and Wonders

———•◆•———

O n April 5, 1967, in a converted firehouse at 1757 Waller
Street, representatives of the *San Francisco Oracle*, the Diggers, the Family Dog, the Straight Theater, and other assorted
members of the Haight-Ashbury hippie scene held a press conference to announce the formation of the Council for a Summer
of Love. Anticipating a huge influx of pilgrims from all over the
country once schools let out, the council sought to mobilize the
community in preparation for the coming onslaught.

The event scored friendly press notices for its organizers. The
next day's *San Francisco Chronicle* described them as "a group of
the good hippies," defined as the ones who "wear quaint and en-
chanting costumes, hold peaceful rock 'n' roll concerts, and draw
pretty pictures (legally) on the sidewalk, their eyes aglow all the
time with the poetry of love." Singled out for especially favorable attention was "a winsome young thing in tights and a skirt
clear up to h-e-r-e" who was passing out coffee and pastries.[1]

By the time the storied Summer of Love arrived, the hippie
phenomenon had been incubating in the Bay Area for several
years. The Beat presence had been strong there from the days of
Allen Ginsberg's reading at the Six Gallery. And since October 1,
1964, when Jack Weinberg was arrested in Sproul Plaza on tres-

passing charges—he was soliciting contributions for the Congress of Racial Equality without permission—student unrest had been roiling the Berkeley campus. Romantic rebelliousness was in the air, but now it took a new twist, following the mental corkscrew turns triggered by a few hundred micrograms of LSD.

Ken Kesey was introduced to the drug in 1960, serving as a guinea pig for hire at a Veterans Administration hospital in Menlo Park. "When we first took those drugs in the hospital," he recalled, "it was like the books God keeps. You had heard about the Bible and the Akashic records, but suddenly you had a glimpse of them." He ended up getting a job at the hospital as a psychiatric aide, working the midnight-to-eight shift while high on mescaline or LSD. An aspiring writer, he decided to set his first novel in a mental ward—and to tell a story that would diagnose what he had come to see as a sickness in the American soul. "It was something to do with the American dream," he said. "How the American Dream gave us our daily energy and yet the dream was perverted and not allowed to develop fully."[2] The result was *One Flew Over the Cuckoo's Nest*, published in 1962 to both popular and critical acclaim.

A couple of years later, in June 1964, Kesey and an entourage of fellow seekers known as the Merry Pranksters set out on a cross-country trip in a 1939 International Harvester bus. The bus, swathed in a lurid rainbow of Day-Glo paint, was named "Furthur," and at the wheel was none other than Neal Cassady, on the road once again. In a summer of nonstop, drug-induced mayhem, all captured on endless hours of film, the Pranksters managed to catch a spark of something new—an exuberant, anarchic madness capable of transforming a whole culture. Once they returned home, they set about fanning that spark into a conflagration. Most famously, they held a series of "acid tests," crazed happenings fueled by LSD-spiked Kool-Aid and featuring bizarre spectacles of multimedia sensory overload. The house band for the acid tests was a rock group, formerly called the Warlocks, that had just changed its name to the Grateful Dead.

In April 1966, Jerry Garcia and the rest of the band moved into a communal home at 710 Ashbury Street, in the middle of the Haight-Ashbury district. Filled with elegantly ramshackle Victorians offering dirt-cheap rents, "the Haight" attracted students from nearby San Francisco State and a youthful, bohemian crowd. Rejecting the dour black of their Beat forerunners, Haight residents—variously referred to as "heads," "freaks," and "hippies"—preferred the Edwardian and Old West getups they scrounged from local thrift shops, and later the sunburst shades of riotous, Prankster-inspired Day-Glo. Guys' hair grew longer and longer; girls' skirts, shorter and shorter. Pot was ubiquitous in the Haight and, thanks to the Grateful Dead's patron and sound engineer, LSD was catching up fast. Augustus Owsley Stanley III, known simply as Owsley, was an Air Force radar technician turned illegal drug chemist extraordinaire. After getting turned on at the Muir Beach Acid Test, Owsley ditched his old methedrine lab and set about making the most powerful, and cheapest, LSD on the planet. Blue Cheer, White Lightning, Orange Sunshine, and, of course, Purple Haze—these Owsley products made San Francisco the world headquarters of psychedelia.

The Bay Area cultural revolution was a largely underground affair until January 14, 1967, when "A Gathering of the Tribes for a Human Be-In" grabbed national attention. The event was conceived as a show of unity between hippies and Berkeley radicals: "a union of love and activism previously separated by categorical dogma and label mongering," according to the official statement of purpose.[3] Just a few weeks earlier, a glimpse of that union had been seen on the Berkeley campus. At an antiwar mass meeting, a sing-along of "Solidarity Forever" faltered as too few knew the words, whereupon someone broke in with "Yellow Submarine" and the whole room joined in. The next day, a leaflet decorated with a little submarine appeared around the school. "Last night we celebrated the growing fusion of head, heart and hands; of hippies and activists . . . ," the broadside read. "And so we made a resolution which broke into song. . . ."[4]

Held on a brilliant blue-sky Saturday at the Polo Field in Golden Gate Park, the Be-In was kicked off by Allen Ginsberg and fellow Beat poet Gary Snyder. They led the early arrivals in a Hindu rite of *pradakshina*, walking clockwise around the field and chanting blessings. As 20,000 people gradually filled the park, the Diggers—a radical community-action group—distributed Owsley-donated turkey sandwiches and White Lightning acid. All the big San Francisco bands played—the Dead, Jefferson Airplane, Quicksilver Messenger Service, and Janis Joplin's Big Brother and the Holding Company—while the Hells Angels guarded the PA system's generator. Yippie leader Jerry Rubin gave a speech, and Timothy Leary and Richard Alpert, the two Harvard psychology professors who had been kicked off the faculty for their drug experiments, were both there. Leary eventually made his way to the microphone and tried out his new mantra, "Turn on, tune in, drop out." And in the middle of all the pandemonium, Shunryu Suzuki-roshi of the San Francisco Zen Center sat meditating on the stage. "The Be-In was like witnessing the prophecy of *Howl* being fulfilled," Allen Ginsberg gushed.

Because of all the media interest it generated, the Be-In served as a kind of coming-out party for the "Love Generation" (the term was coined, humorously enough, by San Francisco police chief Thomas Cahill). The organizers of the Summer of Love were reacting to the Be-In's fallout, and in the process they transformed the publicity boomlet into a full-fledged sensation. In May, Scott McKenzie's "San Francisco" ("If you're going to San Francisco / Be sure to wear some flowers in your hair") was released to cash in on the craze, eventually hitting number four on the charts. By the end of the summer, some 50,000 to 75,000 kids had responded to the call and made the trek. In the process, the Haight's anarchic innocence was destroyed, as the district was overrun by gawking tourists, crass opportunists, and criminal predators. Its special magic never really returned; instead, it dispersed throughout the country and a thousand sparks began to blaze.

Three days before the Summer of Love press conference, 1,500 miles away in Tulsa, Oklahoma, another, very different countercultural movement was holding a coming-out party of its own. On April 2, 1967, a crowd of about 18,000 people—far in excess of the 4,000 anticipated—gathered for the formal dedication ceremonies at Oral Roberts University. Oklahoma's governor, a U.S. senator, two members of Congress, and Tulsa's mayor were on hand for the festivities. And delivering the dedication address, "Why I Believe in Christian Education," was Billy Graham himself, the dean of American evangelists.

The audacious idea of founding a university had come to Oral Roberts just seven years earlier, during a June 1960 visit to Richmond, Virginia. In the middle of dinner with a young Pat Robertson, Roberts began scribbling on a napkin—not his own words, he believed, but words straight from God. "Raise up your students to hear My voice, to go where My light is dim," his inner voice instructed, "Where My voice is small and My healing power is not known. To go even to the uttermost bounds of the earth. Their work will exceed yours and in this I am well pleased."[5]

Hearing the voice of God had marked other key turning points in Oral Roberts's remarkable life. At age 17, young Oral, the son of a Pentecostal Holiness preacher, was fighting for his life. Diagnosed with tuberculosis, the six-foot-tall youth had wasted away to 120 pounds and been bedridden for nearly five months. One evening in late July 1935, his family dressed him, piled him into a borrowed Model T, and carried him to nearby Ada, Oklahoma, to appear before a traveling faith healer. Propped up in the back seat, the desperate young man suddenly found himself in the divine presence. "Son, I am going to heal you," Oral heard, "and you are going to take My healing power to your generation."[6] That night in the tent revival, as the evangelist George Moncey stood before him and commanded the disease to leave his body, Oral experienced a blinding flash and an electric sensation—and then felt his lungs open up and the ability to breathe deeply return. He knew he would recover, and that God had performed a miracle.

In 1947, Roberts—now a minister with his own little Pente-costal Holiness church in Enid, Oklahoma—found himself once again in crisis. This time, his torment was spiritual, not physi-cal. Believing he was destined for great things, he felt frustrated and trapped as a dirt-poor, small-town preacher with a pleasant but complacent congregation. One harried morning as he was hurrying to catch the bus, he realized he had not done his cus-tomary morning Bible reading. Picking up his copy of the Good Book and flipping it open to a random page, his eyes fell on III John 1:2: "I wish above all things that thou mayest prosper and be in health, even as thy soul prospereth." Roberts had read the New Testament countless times before, but that verse had never made an impression on him. Now it did, and it changed in an instant his whole understanding of God. God is good, Roberts now saw as he had never seen before: God wants us to be healthy, God wants us to succeed, God wants us to be rich! Not long af-terward, Oral Roberts once again heard God speak to him, com-manding him to follow Jesus' example and "bring healing to the people as he did."[7]

Roberts went on to achieve great success as a revivalist and faith healer—which is to say, he became a central figure in a marginal movement. As a Pentecostal, Roberts stood well off the mainline of respectable Protestantism. With their wild, exuber-ant worship that included speaking in tongues, "Holy Rollers" recruited their ranks from people on the wrong side of the tracks—the poor, the uneducated, the beaten, the desperate. By becoming a faith healer, Roberts ventured even farther beyond the pale—into the circus-sideshow realm of con artists, wild-eyed true believers, and combinations of the two. Yet all the same, he developed a massive following, drawn to his message of exuberant optimism. Roberts, unlike the typical revivalist, left the fire and brimstone alone. Instead, "Expect a miracle!" and "Something good is going to happen to you!" became his inces-santly repeated catchphrases.

Oral Roberts' ministry soon transcended Pentecostalism's lowly origins. Not content with success as a traveling tent preacher, he built a far-flung empire of evangelical outreach, complete with television and radio programs, magazines, newspaper columns, and even comic books. And now, as he was being sworn in as president of the university he built from scratch, Oral Roberts knew that he had brought his upstart faith into the American mainstream. Government officials were present to pay their respects to him, as were officials from 120 of the nation's colleges and universities. And best of all, Billy Graham was there to give his blessing. From the days of his first, breakthrough "crusade" in Los Angeles back in 1949, Graham had been instrumental in reviving the fortunes of theologically conservative Protestantism. Now, in this highly public way, Graham was lending some of his own lofty public standing to the Pentecostal enterprise.

The events in San Francisco and Tulsa that spring of 1967 revealed an America in the throes of cultural and spiritual upheaval. The postwar liberal consensus had shattered, and vying to take its place were two great, opposing movements—two sides of an enormous false dichotomy. Both were animated by gigantic outbursts of spiritual energy, comparable in intensity and influence to Great Awakenings past. On the one hand, the counterculture; on the other, the evangelical revival—those two eruptions of millenarian enthusiasm would inspire the left-right division that persists to this day.

Alas, that division pitted one set of half-truths against another. On the left gathered those who were most alive to the new possibilities created by mass affluence but who, at the same time, were hostile to the social institutions responsible for creating those possibilities. On the right, meanwhile, rallied those who staunchly supported the institutions that created prosperity but who shrank from the social dynamism they were unleashing. One side denounced capitalism but gobbled up its fruits; the other cursed the fruits while defending the system that bore them. Both causes were quixotic, and consequently neither was able to realize its ambitions. Out of their messy and confused dialectic, however, the logic of abundance would eventually fashion, if not a reworked consensus, then at least a new modus vivendi.

AS ALLEN GINSBERG noted at the San Francisco Be-In, the counterculture of the sixties had its roots in the fifties—specifically, in Beat bohemianism and the larger youth culture of adolescent rebellion. The Beats, though, never would have imagined that they were the vanguard of a mass movement. Theirs was the dissent of resignation and withdrawal; passively accepting their own marginality, they proudly considered themselves loners and misfits. "In the wildest hipster, making a mystique of bop, drugs, and the night life, there is no desire to shatter the 'square' society in which he lives, only to elude it," wrote the Beat author John Clellon Holmes. "To get on a soapbox or write a manifesto would seem to him absurd."[8]

What, then, begat the transformation from apolitical fringe to passionately engaged mass movement? First and foremost, a mass movement requires mass—in this case, a critical mass of critically minded young people. The sixties supplied that prerequisite, of course, as baby boomers began to come of age. Between 1960 and 1970, the number of Americans between the ages of 18 and 24 jumped from 16.2 million to 24.4 million. Meanwhile, as capitalism's ongoing development rendered economic life ever more technologically and organizationally complex, the demand for highly educated managers and professionals continued to grow. Consequently, among the swelling ranks of college-age young people, the portion who actually attended college ballooned from 22.3 percent to 35.2 percent over the course of the decade.

With their wider exposure to history, literature, philosophy, and science, recipients of higher education were more likely to see beyond the confines of their upbringing—to question the assumptions and values they were raised to accept, to appreciate the virtues of other cultures, to seek out the new and exotic for their own sake. By triumphing over scarcity, capitalism had launched the large-scale pursuit of self-realization. Now, by demanding that more and more people be trained to think for themselves, capitalism ensured that the pursuit would lead in new and unconventional directions—and that any obstacles on those uncharted paths would face clever and resourceful adversaries. In the culture as in the marketplace, the "creative destruction" of competitive commerce bred subversives to challenge the established order.

So the tinder was there. But what sparks would set it ablaze? In particular, what caused so many young people to seek such radical departures from the status quo? In retrospect, it is clear that the Eisenhower years were anything but uneventful: mass-produced plenty was fostering wholesale changes in American values and institutions. Yet even so, the process was constrained by a prevailing sense that limits should be nudged rather than pushed too hard. Gradualism was the watchword; patience, the counsel to the hotheaded few; sunny, sensible meliorism, the expectation for the future.

Within a few short years, the national mood had changed completely. No limits seemed to hold anymore; no line was uncrossable. Reason had surrendered the field to revelation and revolution. And the primary catalysts for the change were an odd couple, indeed. Both the civil rights struggle, on the one hand, and the psychedelic drug scene, on the other, inducted their participants into the realms of what can fairly be called religious experience; both acted on the minds of the young to dramatically alter the sense of what seemed possible. Social realities previously seen to be imperturbably rock solid now appeared fluid and malleable. A single bold stroke could change the world.

By the middle of the twentieth century, belief in racial equality was more or less de rigueur for liberals in good standing. Yet, notwithstanding liberalism's towering intellectual and political dominance, progress toward full civil rights for blacks remained exasperatingly modest. Despite their frustration, most liberals saw no alternative but to put their trust in steady gains over time. In his hallmark 1944 study of the racial problem, *An American Dilemma*, Swedish economist Gunnar Myrdal documented the glaring conflict between the "American creed" of equality for all and the actual practice of institutionalized racism. In the face of all the depressing detail he accumulated, Myrdal remained resolutely optimistic. The conflict, he was sure, would eventually be resolved in favor of the American creed. Education and gentle persuasion, according to Myrdal, would awaken white consciences in the end. "[A] great majority of white people in America would be prepared to give the Negro a substantially better deal if they knew the facts . . . ," Myrdal asserted confidently. "I have become convinced also that a majority even of Southerners would be prepared for much more justice to the Negro if they were really brought to know the situation."[9]

History did not follow Myrdal's script. Patient advocacy by white liberals was not what gave the cause of civil rights its irresistible energy and momentum. Instead, what made the movement move was the decision by African Americans, beginning with the Montgomery bus boycott, to push past liberal nostrums and take matters into their own hands. Moral suasion was not enough; confrontation and coercion, nonviolent but deliberately provocative, were needed to force the issue. In the words of Robert Moses, the heroic leader of voter registration efforts in Mississippi, "no privileged group in history has ever given up anything without some kind of blood sacrifice."[10] And to steel themselves to offer that sacrifice—to muster the courage to, as the saying went, "put your body on the line"—African Americans called on sources of strength more profound than social-science empiricism.

They called on religious conviction or its functional equivalent—not mere rational assent, but "the evidence of things not seen." Black churches were therefore indispensable to the movement's success, not just because they provided organization and fostered solidarity, but because the simple, powerful faith they propounded gave ordinary people the heart to do extraordinary things. Meanwhile, even those who lacked the consolation of literalist faith still found something, some lifeline beyond reason for hope to cling to.

Martin Luther King was a theological liberal, but in the awful stress of the Montgomery boycott he experienced a psychic crisis that he interpreted as divine intervention. Awakened one night by a telephone death threat, he sat forlornly at his kitchen table, shaken and overwhelmed, and began to confess his doubts aloud. "I am at the end of my powers," he said. "I have nothing left. I've come to the point where I can't face it alone." Whereupon an "inner voice" began to give him "quiet assurance" that he should do what he thought was right. "Almost at once my fears began to go," King recalled. "My uncertainty disappeared. I was ready to face anything."[11] Others, like Bob Moses, turned to existentialism, with its stark recognition that we are forced to create our own meaning through ultimately arbitrary choice, and found there the basis for putting commitment to the cause above all other considerations. Whatever the specifics of cosmology, and regardless of whether the supernatural was invoked at all, the prophetic imperative was the same: to set onself apart from the compromises and corruptions of everyday life and defy with all one's might the authority of unrighteousness.[12]

That defiance was sublime in its absolute audacity. On February 1, 1960, four black students from North Carolina Agricultural and Technical College, dressed in jackets and ties, walked into a Woolworth's in Greensboro and sat down at the whites-only lunch counter. Within two months, similar "sit-ins" had occurred in 54 cities in nine states.[13] Along with the subsequent "freedom rides" and voter registration efforts, these protests did not settle for merely denouncing the evil of segregation, nor did they credit the authority of their oppressors by targeting them with violence. Instead, protesters took the truly radical step of acting as if segregation did not exist—ordering lunch, getting on the bus, signing up to vote as if Jim Crow were already gone.

With a movement grounded in such extreme commitment, religiosity was always in the air. Marches, stately and solemn, were redolent of religious ritual; beatings, jailings, water-cannon dousings, tear gassings, and killings sanctified the movement by providing it with martyrs. John Lewis, a leader of the Student Nonviolent Coordinating Committee known for his almost boundless courage, looked back at the early sit-ins as "like a holy crusade"; the eve of his first freedom ride was "like the Last Supper, all thirteen of us that went on the Ride." [14] Of Martin Luther King's exalted stature among blacks, Lewis observed that King "lifted them so high they just can't help but think he is a Messiah. They can't help it, no matter how smart they are." [15] Meanwhile, among the backwoods poor of Mississippi, Bob Moses became known as "Moses of the Bible." Eventually, the modest activist changed his name to Robert Parris to avoid the comparison.

For America's liberal-minded young, the prophetic grandeur of the civil rights movement was electrifying. Many joined the movement; many more were inspired to take up other causes and make their own stands. "[W]ithout the civil rights movement, the beat and Old Left and bohemian enclaves would not have opened into a revived politics," concluded Todd Gitlin, a leader of Students for a Democratic Society, the premier organization of the student New Left. "Youth culture might have remained just that—the traditional subculture of the young, a rite of passage on the route to normal adulthood—had it not been for the revolt of black youth, disrupting the American celebration in ways no one had imagined possible." [16] The actor Peter Coyote, who when still known as Peter Cohon was prominent in the Haight as one of the Diggers, agreed. "By and large, white people felt completely trumped by black people at the time, who went out and set this incredibly courageous moral example by putting their lives on the line," he recalled. "And I think that those of us who were not actively involved with freedom marches in the South were pressed to come up with an identity and self-image of equal integrity. . . ." [17]

At the same time the civil rights movement was firing young minds with the possibilities of prophetic dissent, the emerging drug scene was blowing those minds with visions of mystical experience. Marijuana, which grew in popularity with the spread of the bohemian subculture during the fifties, served as the chemical gateway. Heightening sensory pleasures and lubricating free-associative thinking, "tea," as it was then called, fit perfectly with the Beat cult of intense experience. Allen Ginsberg's first time getting high culminated, in typical enough fashion, with an intensified appreciation of food's simple pleasures—in his case, a hot fudge sundae at a Broadway ice cream parlor. "It all just seemed so perfectly joyful and gay," he recalled, "and what came upon me at that moment in time was . . . the only way to describe it was that it was all like one great shattering moment of synchronicity!" [18] Ever the romantic, the young poet got a case of the munchies and thought himself beatified.

Pot offered an alternative form of intoxication for the emerging alternative culture. Under its influence, consciousness seemed not merely altered, but expanded; aggression melted away, and shared wonder and laughter took its place. "A whole philosophy was evolving out of marijuana," the writer Ishmael Reed observed. "There was a connection—political, cultural, and otherwise—with the feeling that people were becoming less uptight and that marijuana could bring more peace, could somehow relax what was essentially a violent and racist culture. . . . At the time, all the problems of the world were attributed to whiskey drinkers. The political and cultural leadership of the United States drank alcohol; the establishment culture, whose drug of choice had always been alcohol, was evil; the emerging hip culture thought that love and liberation were embodied in marijuana." [19]

Psychedelic drugs—peyote, mescaline, psilocybin, LSD—took consciousness expansion to an entirely new level. The phantasmagoric hallucinations induced by those substances frequently led people into the realm of something like religious experience. Certainly that was the case in the famed Good Friday experiment, conducted on April 20, 1962, at Marsh Chapel on the Boston University campus. Organized by Walter Pahnke, a Harvard graduate student in theology who was working under the supervision of Timothy Leary and Richard Alpert, the experiment sought to test whether drugs could produce mystical insights of lasting value under the proper "set and setting." The subjects were 20 divinity students who gathered in the chapel's basement while Good Friday services proceeded overhead. Ten received placebos while 10 ingested psilocybin; the event was staged as a double-blind study, but it was soon crashingly obvious who had taken what. Half sat dutifully and listened to the piped-in services; the other half were lying around, moaning, striking crucifixion poses while staring at the altar, and playing random chords on the organ. Nine of the psilocybin 10 reported mystical experiences; questioned again six months later, half of them claimed continuing spiritual benefits, including greater empathy and a renewed sense of wonder. Deus ex machina, indeed.

If psychedelics promised a new religion, Timothy Leary and Richard Alpert were its leading prophets. Together, the two psychology professors directed the remarkable Harvard Psilocybin Project, which ran from 1960 until Leary and Alpert were both dismissed by the university in 1963. From the moment of their own first personal experiences with the drugs, both became convinced that psychedelics were powerful agents of personal and social transformation.

"Cultural stability is maintained by keeping the members of any cultural group from seeing that the roles, rules, goals, rituals, language and values are game structures. . . ," Leary asserted during a 1961 address to the International Congress of Applied Psychology entitled "How to Change Behavior." "The nationality game. It is treason not to play. The racial game. The religious game. And that most tragic and treacherous game of all, the game of individuality. The ego game. The Timothy Leary game. Ridiculous how we confuse this game, overplay it." According to Leary, psychedelics allowed people to see the games they play for what they really are, and thereby gave them the insight to stop playing bad, self-defeating games and start playing better ones. "The most efficient way to cut through the game structure of Western life is the use of drugs. Drug-induced satori. In three hours, under the right circumstances, the cortex can be cleared."[20]

Cut loose from academia, Alpert and Leary gave up the scholar game and took up the guru game instead. The energies that took them to the top of their field they now turned to their new International Foundation for Internal Freedom. Located on an idyllic 2,500-acre estate in Millbrook, New York, the IFIF was dedicated to the proposition that FDR's four freedoms should be supplemented with a fifth: the freedom to expand your consciousness. "Our precise surgical target," Leary stated, "was the Judeo-Christian power monolith, which had imposed a guilty, inhibited, grim, anti-body, antilife repression on Western civilization."[21] With that religious revolution in mind, the two did more than anybody to draw the connection between drug-induced "turning on" and mystical religious traditions, especially those of the East. The Tibetan Book of the Dead was an early enthusiasm: the pair's 1964 book, *The Psychedelic Experience*, coauthored with former Harvard colleague Ralph Metzner, was a "trip" manual based on that ancient Buddhist text. Alpert, for his part, eventually converted to Hinduism and changed his name to Baba Ram Dass. In his New Age classic *Be Here Now*, he described how drugs had launched him on the path to spiritual awakening.

Both the civil rights movement and the drug culture were outgrowths of the logic of mass affluence. In a society devoted to self-expression and personal fulfillment, African Americans found their second-class status intolerable and latched onto resistance as their own path to self-realization. And their efforts to topple Jim Crow succeeded in large part because one product of technological abundance—television—carried their struggle into America's living rooms and rallied critical elements of the majority population to their cause. Meanwhile, the newly unrestrained pursuit of happiness led ineluctably to the pursuit of broadened experience—including the experience of altered states of consciousness. LSD may have been invented in a Sandoz lab in the 1940s, but marijuana, peyote, and magic mushrooms had been around a long, long time. What made them suddenly popular, what made increasing numbers of young people eager to try them and receptive to their pleasures, was the basic cultural shift wrought by the triumph over scarcity.

But these two outgrowths now spiraled back and raised the logic of mass affluence to a new level of intensity. Both acted as solvents that cut through the felt necessity of the status quo. The struggle for civil rights showed that rapid, dramatic social progress was possible, that deeply entrenched evil could be uprooted. It showed, in other words, that social reality was more fluid than imagined and that committed collective action could change the world for the good. Likewise, pot and psychedelics revealed to their users wildly different visions of reality from the "straight" one everybody took for granted. If our most basic categories of experience could be called into question, so could everything else.

Stripping away the prevailing social reality's illusion of inevitability created a state of mind that was especially susceptible to transports of religious-style fervor. Both the civil rights movement with its prophetic stance, and the drug culture with its promise of mystic satori, probed deeply into psychic realms beyond reason. Guided into those transcendent realms, many young and impressionable minds were set aflame with visions of radical change. From that psychic agitation, one assault after another on conventional wisdom and authority gained momentum. Antiwar protesters, feminists, student rebels, environmentalists, and gays all took their turns marching to the solemn strains of "We Shall Overcome"; all portrayed themselves as inheritors of the legacy of Montgomery and Birmingham and Selma. And in the dizzying multiplicity of rallies and demonstrations, was not the perfume of pot smoke nearly always in the air?

UNDER THE INFLUENCE of the new, radicalized sensibility, partisans of social change soon whipped themselves into a millenarian frenzy. "I think the cultural disjuncture that generational dissent is opening out between itself and the technocracy is . . . as great in its implications (though obviously not as yet in historical import) as the cleavage that once ran between Greco-Roman rationality and Christian mystery," proclaimed Theodore Roszak in his 1969 work, *The Making of a Counter Culture*.[22] Talk of revolution was incessant; agendas grew ever more grandiose. And a bit of astrological hokum—that the earth was entering the enlightened and harmonious Age of Aquarius—was appropriated by the popular culture as a tagline for the era. A New Age was dawning, and utopia was just around the corner.

What emerged was a revived and reimagined mass movement of the radical left. Though rooted in the past, it was entirely newfangled, with new passions and new priorities. It was, in a word, a post-scarcity left.

Herbert Marcuse's philosophical speculations in the fifties anticipated the events of the decade that followed. Inspired by the civil rights struggle and egged on by the drug culture, various proponents of social change came to see themselves as united in a larger, common cause. That cause, they believed, was nothing less than utopia—the utopia made possible by modern technology. Using Marcuse's terminology, the goal was the end of all "surplus repression" and free rein for the "pleasure principle." In other words, "Question authority" and "Do your own thing."

The radicals of the sixties believed that they were redeeming the miscarried promise of the ill-starred socialist dream. The old left, like its Aquarian successor, arose out of a profound yearning for community—for a social order in which all are united by bonds of mutual respect and affection. Edward Bellamy, America's most successful popularizer of socialist ideas, wrote in 1888 of a utopia in which "[t]here was no more either arrogance or servility in the relations of human beings to one another. For the first time since the Creation every man stood up straight before God."[23] Three-quarters of a century later, the Port Huron Statement of the Students for a Democratic Society launched the student New Left by echoing similar sentiments. "Human relationships should involve fraternity and honesty," the 1962 document stated. "Human interdependence is contemporary fact; human brotherhood must be willed, however, as a condition of future survival and as the most appropriate form of social relations."[24]

The socialist movement had imagined that the full blessings of fraternity could be secured through a fundamental reorganization of economic life. The capitalist system of incessant competition and unequal rewards had to be uprooted; in its place, a system of common provision would be established in which all worked together for mutual support. By the alchemy of socialism, what had been base would now be ennobled, as public service rather than private gain became the motivation for participating in the great social enterprise. Selfishness would wither away in the absence of capitalism's useless conflict, and brotherly love could at long last reign supreme.

Or so went the fantasy. Reality, of course, was an altogether different story. In those countries where something like full-fledged socialism was attempted in earnest, the result was monstrous tyranny rather than the peaceable kingdom. Meanwhile, the great, tangible promise made by socialism to the working classes—the elimination of mass poverty—was ultimately fulfilled by capitalism. Yes, capitalism had been substantially altered by the influence of social democracy, though to a lesser extent in the United States than in other industrialized countries. That influence, however, was of little comfort to those whose sympathies ran to the far left. The welfare and regulatory state, after all, preserved and even bolstered the underlying competitive, commercial order. And its cold, distant bureaucracies were a poor simulacrum of living, breathing fraternity.

Thus a new left for new circumstances. The same old yearning for community remained, as did the antipathy to capitalism's impersonal forces and instrumental, mercenary relationships. Gone, however, was the old focus on expanding material production. Capitalism was no longer charged with immiserating the workers; instead, it was blamed for quite the opposite. Possessions, not confessions, were the new opiate of the masses.

And gone as well was the socialist conceit that alienation could be cured simply by transferring ownership of the means of production. No technical fix, however grand the scale, could possibly suffice. "If the melancholy history of revolution over the past half-century teaches us anything," Theodore Roszak argued, "it is the futility of a politics which concentrates itself single-mindedly on the overthrowing of governments, or ruling classes, or economic systems. This brand of politics finishes with merely redesigning the turrets and towers of the technocratic citadel. It is the foundations of the edifice that must be sought."[25]

What was needed instead was the kind of revolution envisioned by Marcuse: the overthrow not merely of capitalist hierarchy, but of *all* hierarchy. To be accomplished, in Roszak's evocative coinage, by "the making of a counter culture." Capitalism still had to go, of course, but that was just for starters. "The revolution that ushers us into a post-scarcity society must be a complete revolution or it will be no revolution at all . . . ," argued anarchist Murray Bookchin in a 1969 essay entitled "Toward a Post-Scarcity Society." "[I]f we do not decentralize our cities into ecologically balanced communities, if we do not produce for human needs instead of profit, if we do not restore the balance of nature and find our place in it, if we do not replace hierarchy, the patriarchal family and the state by genuine, open, human relations, social life itself will be annihilated."[26] Talk about raising the stakes!

Here was a utopian vision for the discontents of an affluent society. And it appealed to a very different constituency than that which had rallied to the socialist banner. "Then it was the horny-handed virtues of the beer hall and the trade union that had to serve as the medium of radical thought," Theodore Roszak observed. "Now it is the youthful exuberance of the rock club, the love-in, the teach-in."[27] Of course, only a small fraction of America's young was consumed with revolutionary passion. According to a Harris poll, the percentage of students calling themselves "radical or far Left" peaked in the spring of 1970 (i.e., at the time of the U.S. invasion of Cambodia) at 11 percent.[28] But radiating out from that hard core were millions who to some degree or another shared the Aquarian sensibility: opposing the war and the corrupt "system" that waged it, and reveling in the Dionysian pleasures of sex, drugs, and rock 'n' roll.

The countercultural rebellion of the sixties was nothing if not audacious. Never before in American history had any mass movement dissented so profoundly from the country's reigning values and institutions; never before had any movement pushed for such a dramatic widening of the country's cultural horizons. It was only natural, then, that the new, rebellious sensibility would show similar audacity in its reformulation of sacred symbols, myths, and rituals. The spirit of dissent prompted a radical break from America's Christian traditions; the spirit of openness, an insatiable hunger for new sources of inspiration.

Buddhism, Hinduism, the *I Ching*, yoga, *tai chi*, tarot cards, witchcraft, shamanism, astrology, alternative medicine—exotica of every kind was stirred into the bubbling stew of sixties syncretism. Also added to the mix was the humanistic, "third-wave" psychology pioneered by Carl Rogers, Frederick Perls, and, of course, Abraham Maslow. The resulting mélange of East and West, of ancient superstition and cutting-edge science, was obviously a breathtaking departure from the insipid, play-it-safe religiosity that dominated American life the decade before. Less obvious, but no less real, were the deep and important continuities between the two.

In several critical respects, the cult of Aquarius served to extend and radicalize innovations that had led to fifties-style "faith in faith." By the fifties, mainstream American religion had largely dispensed with dogmatic theological certainty. Protestant fundamentalism, or the belief in biblical inerrancy, had been rooted out of most mainline demoninations. Doctrinal nitpicking between denominations and naked bigotry against Catholics and Jews were fading fast, replaced by the bland and congenial "I don't care what it is" religiosity so memorably celebrated by Ike. The broad-mindedness of the "triple melting pot" offered spiritual accommodation to the country's ethnic pluralism, and America's traditionally Protestant identity gave way to the inclusive abstraction of the "Judeo-Christian heritage."

The spiritual seekers of the sixties picked up the trend toward ecumenism and pushed it as far as they could go. In need of a sacred vocabulary that expressed their radical discontent with the status quo, they struck out beyond the confines of Western monotheism and groped their way toward a kind of globalized eclecticism. Such fearless openness to the Other made their new sensibility a powerful liberating force. The relativism of the fifties-style "other-directed" mentality, while a significant advance over the old "inner-directed" absolutism, was still constrained by a "go along to get along," "don't make waves" passivity. Aversion to conflict bred deference to long-standing conventions. By contrast, the new, globalized relativism burned with critical passion. From that passion came the spiritual resources to challenge and upend basic, core taboos on race relations, sex roles, and sexual identity.

The push beyond native religious traditions also lent new intensity and exuberance to the pursuit of self-realization. In particular, the baby boomers' conception of what constitutes self-realization differed markedly from that of their parents. For the generation that grew up during the Great Depression and World War II, achieving and enjoying material security had seemed adventure enough. Getting a college education, building suburbia, detonating the baby boom, pursuing careers in the burgeoning white-collar economy—all of these were novel and fresh; all represented invigorating challenges and opportunities for personal growth.

The baby boomers, however, couldn't help but take postwar prosperity for granted. After all, they had never known anything else. Consequently, the prospect of simply following in their parents' footsteps struck many of them as a dispiriting dead end. A good, steady job wasn't enough; the work itself had to be interesting and personally meaningful. Getting married and having the requisite two-point-something kids weren't enough; romantic attachment should be a union of soul mates, and sex was too magical to confine to marriage. A nice house with two cars in the garage wasn't enough; quality of experiences, not quantity of possessions, was the benchmark for a life fully lived.

The new spirituality went hand in hand with the change in attitudes about personal fulfillment. The heavy emphasis on mysticism, with its quest for purity of experience and contempt for material values, naturally appealed to the restive adolescents of suburbia. Of course, the Aquarian enthusiasts for Eastern religions conveniently ignored the fact that for millennia those religions had served as props for steeply hierarchical, deeply traditional social orders. Ransacking ancient faiths for useful jargon and imagery, they remade mysticism in their own image— as carte blanche for getting high, getting laid, and getting out of the materialistic rat race. Alan Watts, the great popularizer of Buddhism who himself was derided by purists as the "Norman Vincent Peale of Zen," found fault with the "beat Zen" of Kerouac and Ginsberg that "confuses 'anything goes' at the existential level with 'anything goes' at the artistic and social levels."[29] He was writing in 1958, and the cow was already well out of the barn.

Abraham Maslow's psychology of "self-actualization" and "peak experiences" was also remodeled to suit countercultural tastes. In his analysis of self-actualizing individuals, Maslow had focused on fairly conventional liberal role models: Thomas Jefferson, Albert Einstein, Eleanor Roosevelt. Successors, however, would show considerably more daring. In a wonderful synchronicity of the type so beloved in the sixties, Maslow actually passed the torch in person. While on vacation during the summer of 1962, he and his wife, Bertha, were driving down the scenic Highway 1 along California's Pacific coastline. Looking for a spot to spend the night, they found a little lodge near Carmel. The Asian attendant at the front desk was indifferent, even brusque, until he saw the signature on the register. Looking up wide-eyed and excited, he asked, "Maslow? *The* Abraham Maslow?" Whereupon he began bowing and exclaiming, "Maslow! Maslow! Maslow!"[30] The little lodge, it so happened, was Big Sur Hot Springs, soon to be renamed the Esalen Insti-tute—ground zero of the nascent "human potential" movement.

During its heyday in the sixties, Esalen was the straw that stirred the Aquarian drink. A who's who of cutting-edge thinkers passed through and conducted seminars: Maslow, Norman Brown, Alan Watts, Timothy Leary, Richard Alpert, Carlos Cas-taneda, Gregory Bateson, Joseph Campbell, Ashley Montagu, Arnold Toynbee, Paul Tillich, Linus Pauling, S. I. Hayakawa, and Buckminster Fuller, among many others. Fritz Perls and Will Schutz were therapists in residence, conducting gestalt and en-counter group sessions; Ida Rolf offered her eponymous mas-sage therapy; Gia-Fu Feng, the front desk attendant when the Maslows walked in unexpectedly, ran the mineral spring baths and conducted tai chi exercises. The spectacular natural set-ting—and the casual nudity, sex, and drug use at the baths—completed the scene.

Intellect, emotions, and senses all received their due at Esalen, and the unifying theme was personal growth through height-ened experience. "Know thyself" was the *summum bonum*; everything else was a ball and chain. Distilling Esalen's ethos of hot-tub spirituality was Fritz Perls' "Gestalt Prayer," made fa-mous for a time as the inscription of a popular wall poster: "I do my thing, and you do your thing. / I am not in this world to live up to your expectations / And you are not in this world to live up to mine. / You are you and I am I, / And if by chance we find each other, it's beautiful. / If not, it can't be helped." [31]

How could such extreme, atomistic individualism coexist with—indeed, feed off of—an equally fervent commitment to community? The answer to the puzzle lay in the Aquarian world-view's naïve romanticism. Heirs to Rousseau, the radicals of the sixties believed that human virtue is natural, spontaneous, in-stinctual—and that all vice and evil are products of repressive civilization. If that were true, then social harmony and the total liberation of individual desire must go together—they simply must! "The new wrinkle," Todd Gitlin commented in retrospect, "was to assert that the very act of engorging the self, unplugging from all the sacrificial social networks, would transform society. An audacious notion, that id could be made to do the work of superego!"[32]

For a flashback to that fantasy at its over-the-top, self-parodying wackiest, consider the beatific vision that concludes Jerry Rubin's Yippie manifesto *Do It!* "At community meetings all over the land, Bob Dylan will replace the National Anthem," Rubin hyperventilated. "There will be no more jails, courts or police. The White House will become a crash pad for anybody without a place to stay in Washington. The world will become one big commune with free food and housing, everything shared. All watches and clocks will be destroyed. Barbers will go to rehabilitation camps where they will grow their hair long. There will be no such crime as 'stealing' because everything will be free. The Pentagon will be replaced by an LSD experimental farm. There will be no more schools or churches because the entire world will become one church and school. People will farm in the morning, make music in the afternoon, and fuck wherever and whenever they want to."[33]

Such swaggering anarchism was no doubt exhilarating. It was also delusional folly of the first order. Regardless of what its votaries believed, Aquarius could not be consummated by a return to the state of nature. On the contrary, the very possibility of countercultural ferment was created and maintained in relentless, unbending defiance of nature. The quest for wider horizons and the fulfillment of higher needs, so exuberantly pursued during the sixties, had occurred only as a result of mass affluence. And mass affluence, in turn, was achieved and sustained only by virtue of a vast mobilization of social energies through an immensely complex and intricate division of labor. In short, there could be no counterculture without capitalism. And capitalism requires discipline and deferred gratification; it requires bureaucracy and hierarchy; it requires abstract loyalties and impersonal authority; it requires the stress of competition.

The partisans of the reimagined left recognized, correctly, that the coming of widespread abundance marked a watershed in human history. And they grasped that in the new conditions, wider horizons for human existence were now possible—and that hoary constraints of law and custom were needlessly inhibiting the promise of the age. Such important truths, however, were stretched and distorted by runaway romanticism. In the overheated moment, perceptive and intelligent people convinced themselves that all the conflicts and contradictions of life could be eliminated, all the agonizing trade-offs transcended, and that intoxicating moments of ecstatic rapture could somehow fill up all the moments of everyday reality.

The Aquarian radicals of the sixties thus pushed simultaneously in opposite directions. Propelling forward, they pressed into the unprecedented and unknown, exploring realms of experience shunned by knee-jerk convention and neglected by shallow, dogmatic scientism, and expanding sympathies and fellow feeling beyond the confining boundaries of blood, nation, class, and creed. Tugging backward at the same time, they shrank from the empowering discipline and rigor of modern life, pretending that the post-scarcity environment they took for granted was possible without large-scale organization and specialization, confusing deviance and dysfunction with dissent, and wallowing in the lazy pseudo-profundities of unreason.

THE ROMANTIC EXCESSES of the Aquarian left ensured that its impact on American society would be baleful as well as beneficent. Those excesses likewise guaranteed that the counterculture's influence, for good and ill, would be contested more successfully than otherwise might have been the case. With its misguided hostility to the capitalist system that brought it into being, the counterculture created an opening for hostile worldviews that allied themselves with capitalism's titanic power. In an astonishing reversal of fortune, conservative Protestantism took advantage of the opportunity and reclaimed a place on society's center stage. Counterculture thus begat counterrevolution; antinomianism created the opening for dogma to reassert itself.

The evangelical revival made for the unlikeliest of comeback stories. In the middle years of the nineteenth century, the bourgeois Protestant worldview had enjoyed unquestioned cultural primacy and matchless self-confidence. America was God's country, and the millennium—no metaphor, mind you, but the real deal—was edging closer every day. The ensuing decades, however, hammered America's old-time religion with setback after setback: Darwin and German higher criticism shook belief in biblical inerrancy; mass immigration filled the country with rival faiths; urbanization bred cesspools of sin and temptation. Under assault, conservative Protestants grew increasingly defensive and pessimistic.

Specifically, many of them fell under the sway of a theological innovation known as "dispensational premillennialism." Developed by the British evangelist John Nelson Darby during the 1820s, dispensationalism gained American adherents through the Niagara Bible Conferences of the 1880s and 1890s and the proselytizing of men like Dwight Moody and C. I. Scofield. Dispensationalists claimed that Christ's return would occur not after the establishment of his kingdom on earth (as postmillennialists believed), but beforehand. First would come "the Rapture," as Christ appeared in the skies and all believers then alive were suddenly transported by him to heaven. Next would follow a seven-year period of tribulation, climaxing with the Battle of Armageddon, whereupon Christ would return to Jerusalem to commence his thousand-year reign. Dispensationalists flatly rejected the old evangelical hopes for building a Christian civilization and thus preparing the way for the Second Coming. In their view, the world was doomed. A grim assessment, perhaps, but with this ingenious consolation: the decline in literalist faith was now evidence of its veracity!

Such a dour and reactionary creed proved no match for the up-and-coming advocates of liberal modernism. Intent on reconciling Christianity with scientific advances and the new mood for social reform, the modernists marched with the spirit of the times and steadily gained control of the mainline Protestant denominations. Over the course of the 1920s, last-ditch efforts by fundamentalists to maintain denominational orthodoxy ended in abject failure, at least outside the South. Frustrated conservatives splintered off to form their own churches, sealing their own marginalization. Adding insult to injury was the 1925 Scopes trial, with its marquee showdown between William Jennings Bryan and Clarence Darrow. Bryan won the battle but lost the war: the young teacher, John Scopes, was duly convicted of teaching evolution in violation of Tennessee law, but the media circus surrounding the event exposed fundamentalists to widespread and merciless ridicule. With the repeal of Prohibition in 1933, the rout was officially complete. Theologically and socially conservative Protestantism, long the country's dominant faith, had lost its hold on American culture.

Yet the old-time religion did not die. In the South, in small towns and rural areas, among the less educated, the flame still burned. And shaking off their well-earned pessimism, a new generation of conservative religious leaders worked to rebuild dogmatic Protestantism as an active, if no longer preeminent, force in American life. Dissociating themselves from the now pejorative term "fundamentalist," they called themselves evangelicals. On matters of doctrine, the evangelicals dutifully toed the fundamentalist line. In their posture toward the outside world, however, they differed dramatically from those who continued to use the old label. Fundamentalists hunkered down in a defensive crouch, refusing any association with mainline denominations and focusing more on weeding out error in their ranks than adding to those ranks. The new evangelicals, by contrast, were intent on expansion and outreach. Thus, when the National Association of Evangelicals was founded in 1942, it adopted as its motto "Cooperation without compromise." "We would attempt to lead and love rather than vilify, criticize, and beat," explained Billy Graham, the celebrity superstar of the new movement, in 1955. "Fundamentalism has failed miserably with the *big stick* approach; now it is time to take the *big love* approach."[34]

Determined to spread the Gospel and increase their flock, evangelicals built up an entire, parallel cultural infrastructure—

a counterculture, by any other name. Religious radio programs in the postwar years included *Back to the Bible Hour, The Children's Gospel Hour, The Hour of Decision,* and *Old Fashioned Revival Hour.* New periodicals proliferated, among them *Christianity Today, Eternity, His,* and *Christian Life.* Organizations such as Youth for Christ and the Inter-Varsity Christian Fellowship catered to young people. Evangelical ministries—Billy Graham's foremost among them—grew in size and sophistication. A particular landmark was Graham's 1957 crusade in New York City's Madison Square Garden. Kicking off on May 15 and running through September 2, the campaign attracted over two million attendees—with 55,000 recorded "decisions for Christ." In June, ABC began televising live broadcasts of Graham's Saturday night services, and audiences in the millions tuned in. A Gallup poll taken after the initial telecast showed that 85 percent of Americans could identify Billy Graham—and 75 percent of them viewed him favorably.

The revival of the forties and fifties succeeded in putting dogmatic Protestantism back on the cultural map. Evangelicals had sloughed off the defeatism of fundamentalist despair; they had retooled their message to appeal to the unconverted; and they had constructed a robust network of churches and parachurch institutions within which believers could coalesce into a vital, thriving community. Yes, they remained outsiders, looked down upon when not ignored by the nation's metropolitan elites; only the exceptional Billy Graham, with his immense charisma and political skills, was a fully mainstream figure. Nevertheless, evangelicals were now a mass movement on the move. As the fifties drew to a close, the liberal "faith in faith" of the triple melting pot continued to dominate the nation's religious life—but not for long.

Though scorned by the cultural elite, evangelicals had consolidated their position in the nation's most economically dynamic region, and therefore the fulcrum of political change—the Sunbelt. The boom that began in the forties and fifties continued apace through the sixties and seventies. Between 1960 and 1980, the population of the South and the West climbed by 43 percent, compared to a 12 percent increase for the rest of the country. The region's political strength gained accordingly: Arizona, California, Florida, and Texas accounted for 94 electoral votes in 1972, up from 70 in 1960. The South, long the nation's economic laggard, played a game of rapid catch-up: per capita income rose from 79 percent of the national average in 1960 to 90 percent two decades later. As a result, by 1980, the South and the West combined to account for just over half of the nation's total personal income.

The fortunes of conservative Protestantism rose with those of its Sunbelt base. Evangelical congregations waxed with the inflow of migrants; rising incomes made more resources available for building churches and saving souls. The hum of expansion and upward mobility raised spirits as well. Increasingly self-confident and assertive, evangelicals counted their worldly blessings as signs of God's favor—and cast their bread upon the waters with redoubled zeal.

Conservative proselytizing found a receptive audience as countercultural chaos erupted around the country. Among what became known as the "great silent majority," including many Americans who considered themselves good liberals during the fifties, Aquarius and its tumults seemed like an outbreak of mass insanity. How could this happen? How could the most privileged children in history grow up to reject everything their parents held dear? Shaken by the radical assault on virtually every aspect of their way of life, many Americans hungered for something, anything, that could hold the line and restore some semblance of order and stability.

The mainline Protestant denominations had thrived as bulwarks of the postwar liberal ascendancy, but they faltered in the face of the Aquarian challenge. When civil rights activism flared up in the sixties, its prophetic energy awakened in many liberal clergy and church officials the craving for full-blown religious enthusiasm—a passion that had been singularly lacking during the prior decade. They satisfied that craving with a revival of the social gospel and immersion in the gathering spirit of protest. Thus, more than 5,000 churchpeople were arrested in demonstrations leading up to the passage of the Civil Rights Act. And as early as February 1965, the Methodist General Board of Christian Social Concerns was calling for the United States to refer resolution of the Vietnam conflict to the United Nations. A poll by *Lutheran* magazine in 1968 showed that 85 percent of Lutheran clergy felt that the church should support antiwar protests, while 58 percent of parishioners disagreed. The shepherds had wandered considerably to the left of their flocks.[35]

Meanwhile, they were also wandering ever farther from traditional Christian doctrine. Theologians such as Thomas Altizer, William Hamilton, and Paul van Buren caused a sensation with their advocacy of what became known as "death of God" theology. According to Altizer, "We must recognize that the death of God is a historical event: God has died in our time, in our history, in our existence." An extreme position for a theologian, to be sure, but symptomatic of the times. The 1964 slogan for the evangelicals' bête noire, the World Council of Churches, summed up the situation: "The world must set the agenda for the church." People who believed the world was going to hell thought such a slogan had things precisely backward.

The evangelical revival gave those people what they were looking for. For Americans anxious to defend their way of life against cultural upheaval, evangelicalism provided the resources with which to make a stand. It imbued believers with a fighting faith, granting them access to the same kinds of spiritual energies that animated the romantic rebellion—energies found only in the realms beyond reason. Such access was gained by dogmatic belief in the old biblical truths, but not by that means alone. Instead, as the evangelical faith surged during the sixties and seventies, fundamentalist focus on purity of doctrine receded ever more into the background. What took its place was an increasing emphasis on religious *experience*—specifically, on creating and maintaining and strengthening a personal, emotional bond with the divine. Exuberant worship, regular prayer, belief in present-day miracles and prophecy's glimpses of the future—these were the spiritual fortifications that could stymie the radical onslaught.

Here the influence of Pentecostalism was crucial. From its beginnings in the Azusa Street revival of 1906, the Pentecostal movement had been separate and distinct from more traditional fundamentalism. And the appeal of charismatic worship—with its howling and jumping and speaking in tongues and faith healing—was originally confined to the most marginal members of American society. But as Pentecostalism began to boom after World War II, and as the new, more ecumenical, evangelical movement came to define conservative Protestantism, lines began to blur and Pentecostals found a home within the evangelical tent. Billy Graham's 1967 dedication address at Oral Roberts University represented a major step forward in this new fusion. And so, over the course of the sixties and seventies, elements of the Pentecostal style diffused throughout the larger movement.

The result was a dramatic surge in the evangelical ranks. Between 1965 and 1975, at the same time the mainline denominations were shriveling, membership in the Church of the Nazarene increased by 8 percent, while Southern Baptists grew by 18 percent; membership in Seventh-Day Adventists and Assemblies of God leapt by 36 and 37 percent, respectively.[36] *Newsweek* declared 1976 "the year of the evangelical" as Jimmy Carter, who identified himself as one, took the presidency and Watergate felon Chuck Colson rode the best-seller charts with his confessional, *Born Again*. A Gallup poll that same year asked Americans, "Would you describe yourself as a 'born-again' or evangelical Christian?" Just over one-third of those polled said yes.

There is no point in mincing words: the stunning advance of evangelicalism marked a dismal intellectual regress in American religion. A lapse into crude superstition and magical thinking, credulous vulnerability to charlatans, a dangerous weakness for apocalyptic prophecy, and blatant denial of scientific reality—

the newfangled and resurgent brand of conservative Protestant-ism entailed a widespread and utterly gratuitous surrender of believers' critical faculties.

One case in point: the emergence of "creation science," a curi-ous tribute paid by superstition to reason. William Jennings Bryan had declared famously that "it is better to trust in the Rock of Ages than to know the ages of rock," but some believers in the Bible's literal truth were unwilling to cede the vast author-ity to modern science to godless evolutionists. Henry M. Morris was one such believer. A professor of hydraulic engineering, Morris teamed up with Bible scholar John C. Whitcomb to pro-duce the 1961 book, *The Genesis Flood,* the urtext of the "young earth" creation-science movement. Two years later, Morris and nine other evangelical scientists and engineers founded the Cre-ation Research Society. And in 1970, Morris and evangelist Tim LaHaye (now famous for his best-selling Left Behind series) es-tablished the Institute for Creation Research in San Diego. Such efforts, of course, were dismissed as laughable by mainstream scientists—and induced cringes in a fair number of evangelicals. No matter, though: they allowed literalist true believers to con-vince themselves that they weren't being irrational or antiscien-tific in clinging to the historical accuracy of Genesis. In so doing, they added further vigor and self-assurance to the evangelical cause.

And consider the top-selling religious book of the 1970s, which was indeed the number one selling "nonfiction" book of the de-cade: Hal Lindsey's *The Late Great Planet Earth,* which claimed that, according to the Book of Revelation, the world would end sometime during the eighties. Along the way, predicted the for-mer New Orleans tugboat captain, America would suffer an eco-nomic and military collapse, the Antichrist would lead a new United States of Europe to foil world communism and take con-trol of the Soviet Union and China, and Israel would become immensely rich and influential. "If I had been writing 15 years earlier," said Lindsey in 1977, "I wouldn't have had an audience. But a tremendous number of people were beginning to worry about the future, and they were looking everywhere for answers. The turn to the occult, astrology, Eastern religion, and other movements reflected the fear of what was going to happen in the future. And I'm just part of that phenomenon."[37] True enough: the celebration of unreason on the left had met its match on the right.

But having beat their intellectual retreat, evangelicals summoned up the fortitude to defend a cultural position that was, to a considerable extent, worth defending. In particular, they upheld values that after the Sturm und Drang of the sixties and seventies subsided would eventually garner renewed appreciation across the ideological divide—values of committed family life, personal probity and self-restraint, the work ethic, and unembarrassed American patriotism. By no means were they purely reactionary. On the contrary, in many important respects, religious conservatives were willing to change with the times.

Take race relations, for example. Despite the fact that many of them hailed from the South, the leading lights of the evangelical revival dissented from the reigning regional orthodoxies of white supremacy and segregation. For years, Billy Graham had waffled back and forth on the issue, but after the Supreme Court's 1954 *Brown* decision, he steadfastly refused to tolerate segregated seating at any of his crusades. "The ground at the foot of the cross is level," Graham said, and "it touches my heart when I see whites stand shoulder to shoulder with blacks at the cross."[38] In his breakthrough 1957 crusade at Madison Square Garden, Graham even invited Martin Luther King to join him on the podium, introducing him as one of the leaders of "a great social revolution" afoot in the country.[39] And Graham was not alone. The Southern Baptist Convention, bulwark of the Bible Belt, strongly endorsed the *Brown* decision and called for peaceful compliance. Pentecostalism, meanwhile, had begun as an integrated movement, led by the son of slaves. It was only natural, then, that charismatic churches were relatively quick to embrace more tolerant racial attitudes.

Though evangelicals hotly opposed the rampant hedonism

unleashed in the sixties, they nonetheless made measured concessions to mainstream popular culture. In this as in so much else, Oral Roberts was a pioneer. In 1969 he began a series of prime-time broadcasts that featured Hollywood talent as guest stars—starting with safe choices like Pat Boone, Dale Evans, and Anita Bryant, but then branching out to include such names as Jerry Lewis, Lou Rawls, Johnny Mathis, Della Reese, Burl Ives, and Johnny Cash. Wholesome, yes, but still a blurring of the lines between religion and secular entertainment. A leading attraction of the shows was a group of Oral Roberts University students known as the World Action Singers (in which, by the way, Kathie Lee Gifford got her start). Not afraid to show a little skin or sway to the beat of up-tempo rhythms, the group raised eyebrows among the stodgier of the faithful—and ratings among the rest. *Christianity Today* clucked at the World Action Singers' "animating singing and slithering," but Roberts was unperturbed as tens of millions tuned in. "These are clean young people," he insisted. "I like to see them move their bodies. Young people are in movement in this country and if you want to reach one of them you'd better move a little bit."[40]

Most important, evangelicalism moved decisively to align Christian faith with the central preoccupation of the affluent society: the new Holy Grail, self-realization. Unlike the classic bourgeois Protestantism of the nineteenth century, whose moral teachings emphasized self-restraint and avoidance of worldly temptation, the revitalized version of the old-time religion promised empowerment, joy, and personal fulfillment. A godly life was once understood as grim defiance of sinful urges; now, it was the key to untold blessings. "Something good is going to happen to you!" Oral Roberts proclaimed. His exuberant optimism anticipated and helped to shape the new evangelical mood. Thus, the 1960s saw the beginning of a huge boom in evangelical pop-psychology literature that exactly mirrored the corresponding phenomenon in the secular book trade. A few representative titles: Robert Schuller's *Self-Love* (1969) and *You Can Become the Person You Want To Be* (1973), Bruce Larson's

Dare to Live Now (1972), Lloyd Ahlem's *Do I Have to Be Me?* (1973), Tim LaHaye's *How to Win over Depression* (1974), Elmer Josephson's *God's Key to Health and Happiness* (1976), David Hubbard's *Happiness: You Can Find the Secret* (1976), and Henry Brandt's *I Want Happiness, Now!* (1978).[41]

The evangelicals' therapeutic turn, like that of the counterculture, moved with the powerful currents of psychic need sprung loose by mass affluence. Indeed, there was significant overlap between the two opposing religious revivals. The Jesus Freaks, or Jesus People, emerged out of the hippie scene in the late sixties, mixing countercultural style and communalism with evangelical orthodoxy. As the hippie phenomenon faded in the seventies, many veterans of the Jesus Movement made their way into the larger, socially conservative evangelical revival—and exerted a powerful influence on its development. For example, both the Calvary Chapel and Vineyard Christian Fellowship churches, two prominent examples of the "new paradigm" megachurch, trace their roots back to the Jesus Movement. So does the Contemporary Christian Music industry, which joins the instrumentation and rhythms of rock with evangelical lyrics.

The peculiar career of Arthur Blessitt provides an especially vivid illustration of evangelicalism's debt to the left. A Hollywood street preacher in the late sixties, Blessitt hosted a psychedelic nightclub called His Place on Hollywood's Sunset Strip, an establishment whose logo combined a cross and a peace sign. "Like, if you want to get high, you don't have to drop Acid. Just pray and you go all the way to Heaven," Blessitt advised in his delightfully dated tract called *Life's Greatest Trip*. "You don't have to pop pills to get loaded. Just drop a little Matthew, Mark, Luke, or John." In 1969, Blessitt began his distinctive ministry of carrying a 12-foot-tall cross around the country—and, later, around the world. On one of his countless stops along the way, at an April 1984 meeting in Midland, Texas, he received word that a local oilman, the son of a prominent politician, wanted to see him privately. The businessman told Blessitt that he was not comfortable attending a public meeting, but that he wanted to know Jesus better and learn how to follow him, whereupon the evangelist gave his witness and prayed with him. George W. Bush's subsequent conversion to evangelical Christianity, and its consequences for his life and the life of the nation, are now, of course, widely known.

Such crosscurrents of mutual influence were possible because, notwithstanding their obvious differences, evangelicals and Aquarians shared many things in common. Both sought firsthand spiritual experience; both believed that such experience could set them free and change their lives; both favored emotional intensity over intellectual rigor; both saw their spiritual lives as a refuge from a corrupt and corrupting world. That last point, of course, was subject to radically different interpretations. Aquarians rejected the world of the "establishment" because of its supposedly suffocating restrictions, while the evangelicals condemned its licentious, decadent anarchy. Even here, however, there was similarity. Both the antinomians of the left and the dogmatists of the right were united in their disaffection from the postwar liberal consensus—and, by extension, from the older form of therapeutic religiosity, the wan "faith in faith" that supported that consensus.

That shared discontent carried the day. Out of it emerged two great bursts of spiritual energy, the counterculture on the left and the evangelical revival on the right—one fervently committed to accelerating and radicalizing the cultural dynamism of mass affluence, the other committed just as fervently to arresting it. One, heedless of all limits, hurtled toward nihilism; the other, clinging to any limit that might hold, retreated into superstition. Between them, they left the social peace of the fifties in ruins.

No doubt that peace deserved to be disturbed. To its credit, it had calmed the passions of class conflict that shook the nation for decades during the transition from scarcity to abundance. But thus oriented to the problems of the past, the cautious, complacent liberalism of the fifties was ill suited to coping with the emerging conflicts of mass prosperity. It frustrated the aspirations of blacks, of women, and of the affluent young. It suppressed and distorted economic energies by throttling competition. Its spiritual life tended to the bland and shallow. Tough questions were dodged all around.

The problem, however, was that no new and improved social consensus emerged to take the place of the one that collapsed. Instead, over the course of the sixties and seventies, Americans split into hostile cultural factions, either joining or allying with one of the two rival religious awakenings. The realm of freedom was now divided against itself.

Learning to Fly

———— •◆• ————

Timothy Leary had just reached what he called the "the indisputable undeniable Dantean bottom"[1]—the maximum security "hole" of Folsom State Prison. His legal troubles began over seven years earlier, when in December 1965 he and his daughter Susan were busted for possession of marijuana while reentering the United States from Mexico. A few months later, on April 16, 1966, FBI agents, led by future Watergate felon and conservative talk-radio host G. Gordon Liddy, raided Leary's psychedelic retreat in Millbrook, New York. "The time will come," Leary told Liddy as he was led away in handcuffs, "when there will be a statue of me erected in Millbrook." Liddy smiled and shot back, "I'm afraid the closest you'll come is a burning effigy in the village square."[2]

After years of legal maneuverings and further busts, in May 1970, Leary wound up in a minimum-security prison in San Luis Obispo. But on September 12 of that year, Leary defied the authorities and the odds once again. In a wild stunt right out of Hollywood, he climbed a telephone wire from the roof of the prison to a pole outside the fence. Waiting for him below were members of the Weather Underground, the terrorist offshoot of Students for a Democratic Society, who provided his getaway.

Leary stayed at first with Black Panther Eldridge Cleaver in Algerian exile, but skipped out when Cleaver tried to put him under "arrest" as a "counterrevolutionary." He fled to Switzerland, then Afghanistan, but that last move proved costly. On January 17, 1973, Leary was apprehended in the Kabul airport. Extradited back to the United States, he was consigned a few months later to Folsom.

When Timothy Leary arrived in the prison's dreaded Section 4-A, he saw in the cell next to his a small man, long-haired and bearded, sitting on the floor in a lotus position. "So you finally made it," said Charles Manson, Leary's new neighbor. "I been watching you fall for years, man. . . . I've been wanting to talk to you for a long time. I wanted to ask you how come you blew it." When Leary asked him what he meant, the mass murderer replied, "You had everyone looking up to you. You could have led the people anywhere you wanted."[3]

Charles Manson had haunted the counterculture from the moment he was released from prison in March 1967. Having spent over half of his 32 years to date inside of institutions, he took full advantage of his newfound freedom and headed straight to Haight-Ashbury. There, as his fevered mind twitched back and forth between visions of a global race-war apocalypse and plans for a musical career that would outshine the Beatles', Manson began to assemble his "Family" of cultists and hangers-on. Held together by drugs, sex, and Charlie's curious charisma, subsisting on scrounging, scavenging, and petty crime, the group eventually included as many as a hundred people, including 30 hard-core disciples. At the end of 1967, Manson loaded up his followers in a black bus and left San Francisco for LA. For a while, he hung out with Hugh Romney (aka "Wavy Gravy") and the Hog Farmers, who would gain fame as the "Please Force" at Woodstock the same month Manson and his Family would gain infamy. Later Manson crashed with Dennis Wilson of the Beach Boys, and even convinced the group to record one of his songs. But by the summer of 1969, inspired by a Beatles song, Charles Manson was ready to unleash the atrocities of "Helter Skelter."

When members of the Manson Family slaughtered seven people over two nights in August 1969, the crimes grabbed national headlines. For one thing, one of the victims was a celebrity: the actress Sharon Tate, wife of director Roman Polanski and eight months pregnant. And the murders were diabolical. Victims were stabbed dozens of times, "Death to Pigs" and "Helter Skelter" were scrawled on the walls in their blood, and a fork was left stuck in one victim's stomach. When Manson and his followers were arrested that fall, the news of their bizarre death cult provoked horror in the psychedelic community: how could something so monstrous have arisen from among us?

The far reaches of the radical left, however, reacted differently. In June 1969, Students for a Democratic Society held their final annual convention. In the official crack-up of the student New Left, the militant Weatherman faction denounced its rivals as "objectively anticommunist" and "counterrevolutionary" and broke off from SDS proper. At Christmastime that year, the Weathermen held a "National War Council" in Flint, Michigan, before going underground for good. At the council, Manson's crimes were embraced as revolutionary acts. "Dig it!" exulted Bernardine Dohrn. "First they killed those pigs, then they ate dinner in the same room with them, then they even shoved a fork into the victim's stomach. Wild!" A four-fingered "fork" salute served as the greeting of choice at the Flint conclave.[4]

With that dismal scene of Timothy Leary and Charles Manson side by side in a cage, the curtain fell on the once-bright dream of romantic revolution. The dream had lasted only a few years, but for the people who shared in it, those were years lived at a fever pitch. "We had all the momentum; we were riding the crest of a high and beautiful wave . . . ," eulogized Hunter Thompson in 1971, sitting in his Las Vegas hotel room after 48 hours of chemically induced chaos. "So now, less than five years later, you can go up on a steep hill in Las Vegas and look West, and with the right kind of eyes you can almost *see* the high-water mark— that place where the wave finally broke and rolled back."[5]

What Thompson saw, as the tide receded, was that America's

basic social institutions had persevered. The radical assault on organized, commercialized, competitive society did not spread to the general populace. On the contrary, the assault provoked ferocious resistance. Even worse than the external hostility were the enemies that struck from within—the monsters hatched in the antinomian moral vacuum. And so, under attack from all sides, the utopian dream sputtered and died.

The revolutionary ambitions of the countercultural left had pursued two distinctive but interwoven paths. The political radicals of the New Left envisioned a novel form of communal intimacy known as "participatory democracy"—an idea best summarized by the informal slogan of the Student Nonviolent Coordinating Committee, "Freedom is an endless meeting."[6] Shared, all-consuming commitment to social change would first produce utopia in microcosm: the ecstatic union of the "movement." As the movement grew and advanced, utopia would spread. Meanwhile, cultural radicals sought psychological transformation. Rather than trying to change society, they would change themselves. Rather than resist, they would "drop out" and start anew in countless little communal utopias. Both paths, it turned out, were dead ends.

The New Left, after all the abstruse jargon was parsed, boiled down to an attempt to generalize the civil rights movement. The prophetic passion that had toppled Jim Crow would be redirected to all the rest of society's ills. At the same time, the leaderless unity of the movement, born of immersion in common ideals, would characterize social relations across the board. But where to start? By what succession of new targets could the energy and moral authority of the movement be maintained and augmented?

Such questions became increasingly urgent as the overwhelmingly white and well-educated leadership of the New Left found itself excluded from what continued to be called the civil rights movement. As segregation collapsed in the South, black activists shifted their attention to the ghettoes of the northern inner cities, and in the process moved steadily away from the ideal of integration and toward the new, ill-defined goal of self-determination expressed in the slogan "black power." Now consigned to the sidelines of the struggle that originally inspired them, white radicals soon discovered their own second act by opposing the escalating war in Vietnam. And growing out of antiwar agitation on college campuses was a broader campaign against the in loco parentis authority of university faculty and administrators. These two, entangled causes were inspired choices, perfectly suited to the youthful, privileged constituencies of the New Left. As people of draft age (if not actually subject to the draft themselves), young antiwar protesters could now assume the role of an oppressed minority. Further, as students, they could recast themselves as the "proletarians" of America's teeming "knowledge factories." And all could pour the full measure of their brimming, adolescent enthusiasm into one, unshakeable moral absolute: Stop the war!

With only one, ultimate demand—get the U.S. military out of Vietnam—protesters left themselves no possibilities for partial victories or incremental gains. The only alternatives were complete success and utter failure, and as the former failed to materialize, the protesters' pent-up frustration grew ever more combustible; their disaffection, ever more extreme. Members of the radical vanguard drifted away from simply opposing U.S. policy and began actively rooting for the other side. The flag of the Vietcong became the unofficial banner of the hard-core crowd, and chants of "Ho Ho Ho Chi Minh, dare to struggle, dare to win" wafted through the air along with tear gas. "We needed to feel that someone, somewhere in the world, was fighting the good fight and winning . . . ," recalled Todd Gitlin. "And so, increasingly, we found our exemplars and heroes in Cuba, in China, in the Third World guerilla movements, in Mao and Frantz Fanon and Che and Debray, most of all—decisively—in Vietnam."[7]

Such extremism was morally deranged—and utterly self-defeating. Although public opinion gradually soured on the war, it was much harsher in its condemnation of the antiwar movement. A 1968 poll conducted by the University of Michigan asked respondents to rate a variety of groups and individuals on a 100-point scale. One-third of those polled gave protesters a 0, the lowest possible rating, while only 16 percent ranked them in the upper half of the scale. "The whole world is watching," the young demonstrators chanted during the notorious "police riot" at the 1968 Democratic National Convention. Apparently, the world liked what it saw, as polls showed that a majority of Americans approved of the thuggish beatings administered by Chicago's finest.[8]

A year later, the New Left's self-destructive spiral had passed the point of no return. In that final 1969 convention of Students for a Democratic Society, when the Weathermen led the walkout that shattered the organization for good, their main rivals were the Maoists of the Progressive Labor faction. Just seven years after the lofty pieties of the Port Huron Statement, the organization that had sought to create a vital, post-Marxist left was reduced to choosing between totalitarians and terrorists.

Black radicalism followed a similar course. Heroic resistance to bigotry had defeated officially sanctioned segregation, but it could not create economic opportunities out of thin air for uneducated, unskilled blacks, nor could it stem the ghetto culture's catastrophic slide into ever deeper dysfunction. Mere defiance, however bold and provocative, would never remedy the complex problems that faced the black community, but maintaining the defiant stance of the angry prophet was a temptation that black leaders were unable to resist. Consequently, a movement once graced by sublime moral clarity fell under the malign influence of militant haters, shakedown artists, and thugs. Separatist, antiwhite militance came to the fore; "We shall overcome" gave way to "Burn, baby, burn."

The year 1966 marked a turning point. At the Student Nonviolent Coordinating Committee, the rabble-rousing Stokely Carmichael replaced John Lewis as president and soon voiced the movement's new rallying cry. "When you talk of black power," Carmichael thundered, "you talk of building a movement that will smash everything Western civilization has created."[9] Meanwhile, in Oakland, Huey Newton and Bobby Seale launched the Black Panther Party for Self-Defense. "We have two evils to fight, capitalism and racism," Newton proclaimed. "We must destroy both racism and capitalism."[10]

Unsurprisingly, such belligerence failed to impress the overwhelming majority of Americans. White backing of black demands made healthy gains over the course of the early sixties, but now began to dissolve. By the time of a 1968 Harris poll, only 28 percent of whites agreed that "progress in civil rights should be speeded up."[11] And while the Maoist mumbo jumbo spouted by the Black Panthers made for great television and played well with white radicals, their revolutionary program never caught on among ordinary African Americans. At their peak, the Panthers could claim only around 5,000 members in a dozen or so big cities.[12]

For the cultural revolutionaries of the Flower Power scene, manifestoes and marches and 10-point programs weren't the answer. And neither, certainly, was violence of any kind. Lovers rather than fighters, they sought a different route to utopia. Following Timothy Leary's mantra of "turn on, tune in, and drop out," they launched a large-scale social experiment in the possibilities of communal living. During the late sixties and early seventies, hundreds of thousands of young people—maybe as many as a million—lived for a time in thousands of separate communes or "intentional communities." Some were set up in cities, others went "back to the land"; some were religious or spiritual in orientation, others purely hedonistic. All, however, were dedicated to finding some radical alternative to American mass society.

The experiment failed. By the late seventies, the movement was in obvious decline, and most of the communes vanished as quickly as they first appeared. Yes, some communards soldiered on, and continue to do so still, but they do so in the sleepy, neglected margins of American life. Large-scale capitalist society was not replaced or even seriously challenged. Once romantic delusions are set aside, it should be obvious why combining "do your own thing" individualism with a total absence of institutional authority did not make for stable communities. One little utopia after another was brought to grief by the absence of clear rules and procedures for making decisions and settling disputes. In that vacuum, the committed unselfishness of the majority was usually no match for the outsized egos, free riders, and outright predators against whom anarchy was powerless to defend.

In Haight-Ashbury, the serpents entered the garden even before the mass influx of the Summer of Love. A broadside published by the Diggers in April 1967 and entitled *Uncle Tim'$ Children* (a reference to Timothy Leary) offered this withering assessment: "Pretty little 16-year-old middle class chick comes to the Haight to see what it's all about & gets picked up by a 17-year-old street dealer who spends all day shooting her full of speed again & again, then feeds her 3000 mikes and raffles off her temporarily unemployed body for the biggest Haight Street gang bang since the night before last. The politics & ethics of ecstasy. Rape is as common as bullshit on Haight Street."

Just as the phenomenon was peaking in the late sixties, Robert Houriet toured and studied dozens of communes. "Everywhere, cars that wouldn't run and pumps that wouldn't pump because everybody knew all about the occult history of tarot and nobody knew anything about mechanics," Houriet wrote in his book, *Getting Back Together.* "Everywhere, people who strove for self-sufficiency and freedom from the capitalist system but accepted food stamps and handouts from Daddy, a corporate sales VP. Sinks filled with dishes, cows wandering through gates left open, and no one to blame. Everywhere, instability, transiency. Somebody was always splitting, rolling up his bag, packing his guitar and kissing good-bye—off again in search of the truly free, unhungup community."[13] Eventually, most people wearied and called off the search.

The revolution may not have materialized, but the Aquarian awakening of the countercultural left was nonetheless an event of critical importance. Though it failed to overthrow American society, it did exert a powerful influence, reshaping political agendas and loyalties, redirecting social energies, and remaking popular culture. Was that influence for good or ill? Most decidedly, for both. On the one hand, the Aquarian impulse imparted new momentum to the ongoing drive to expand the range of choice in American life: to include outsiders, tolerate difference, and embrace the novel and the unconventional. Alas, however, this liberating impulse was marred by the besetting Aquarian vice of romanticism. Consequently, it exhibited an often reckless disregard for the restraint and discipline that are needed to make high ideals workable in practice.

AQUARIAN RADICALS SAW corporate America as the Enemy—materialistic, competitive, repressed, and repressive. Their hostility, however, was not reciprocated. At the same time that the countercultural left was emerging, savvy marketers and entrepreneurs were coming to the realization that romantic rebellion could be very good for business. And so, in a turn of events bemoaned ever since on the left and right flanks alike, Madison Avenue commercialized the Aquarian awakening and sold it to Middle America.

As early as 1963, a year before turmoil at Berkeley officially inaugurated the youth movement, soft drinks were being pitched to the free-spirited "Pepsi Generation." A couple of years later, Booth's House of Lords Gin—the primary ingredient in the archetypally square martini—was touted as a way of "taking a stand against conformity." According to a 1970 vodka ad, "Only Smirnoff is subtle enough to go where your soul moves you." "Join the Dodge Rebellion," proclaimed a car ad from 1965. "Express yourself" and "Freedom" were headlines for 1969 Suzuki motorcycle ads; others from the next year included "Suzuki takes on the country," "Suzuki expands life," and "Suzuki conquers boredom." "It lets me be me" was the 1971 slogan for Clairol Nice 'n Easy hair coloring. And in 1972, ads for Camel cigarettes bragged, "They're not for everybody. (But then, they don't try to be.)" Countercultural marketing, pitched to consumers who saw themselves (or wanted to see themselves) as rebellious individualists, quickly became ubiquitous.[14]

In the music and fashion industries, the products themselves, not just the advertising pitches, reflected the new spirit of rebellion. On August 28, 1964, the Beatles and Bob Dylan met for the first time during a reception at Manhattan's Hotel Delmonico. They ended up retreating to a private room and smoking pot together (the first time any of the Beatles had ever done so), and popular music was never the same. Following Dylan's lead, the Beatles were soon experimenting with increasingly bold and unconventional lyrics; following the Beatles' lead, Dylan soon went electric. Together, they obliterated rock 'n' roll's old, rigid formulas and inspired generations of musicians to explore the exhilarating possibilities for musical expression that they had discovered.

That exploration proved immensely profitable. During the early seventies, the music industry grew by 25 percent a year, and by the middle of the decade it had eclipsed sports and movies to become the leading form of entertainment in the country.[15] The cultural impact, meanwhile, was incalculable. In all its many phases and styles, modern pop music's enduring message, conveyed by the aphrodisiac of a pulsing bass beat, was as simple as it was subversive: surrender to the pleasures of the body. The Rolling Stones' bluesy satanic posturings, the Supremes' velvet Motown harmonies, Hendrix's pyrotechnics, Lynyrd Skynyrd's good-ole-boy bravado, the Sex Pistols' anarchic tantrums, the BeeGees' weightless disco confections—how many ecstasies, how many regrets, did they inspire and accompany?

The fashion industry, likewise, catered to the rising demand for mass nonconformity. What started on Carnaby Street in London soon swept the United States: the "Peacock Revolution" in men's clothing. In December 1967, Stan Gellers of *Men's Wear* magazine selected "The Rebel" as the "Man of the Year." "The rebel . . . isn't this the word that really describes the mood . . . the attitude . . . and the looks developing in all parts of the men's wear market?" he wrote. The man in the gray flannel suit was "out"; "in" came striped shirts, wide lapels, ties as loud as they were fat, medallions and flashy jewelry, big belts, and flared trousers. In February 1968, Johnny Carson wore a Nehru jacket designed by Oleg Cassini and started a blessedly short-lived sensation. The leisure suit, originally dubbed the "sport suit," made its debut in 1970 and stuck around considerably longer. Women's fashion, meanwhile, had long embraced constant change in styles, but the direction of change during the sixties and seventies was heavily influenced by countercultural symbolism. On the one hand, there was a dramatic turn toward greater sexual suggestiveness, with miniskirts, go-go boots, the braless look, hip-hugger jeans, hot pants, and, later, halter and tube tops. At the same time, the hippie "Earth Mother" look inspired mass markets for peasant blouses, maxi skirts, and granny dresses.

For those loyal to the glorious lost cause of romantic revolution, the commercialized diffusion of the rebellious spirit was "co-optation"—subverting the revolution by appropriating its style and symbols and draining them of their originally intended meaning. "Repressive tolerance," Herbert Marcuse called it in a remarkable turn of phrase. Taking a swipe at his old Brandeis colleague Maslow, Marcuse deplored the "publicity of self-actualization" within the existing structures of democratic capitalism. "[I]t encourages non-conformity and letting-go in ways which leave the real engines of repression in the society entirely intact," he wrote, "which even strengthen these engines by substituting the satisfactions of private and personal rebellion for a more than private and personal, and therefore more authentic, opposition."[16] Along the same lines, Theodore Roszak complained that "[t]he business of inventing and flourishing treacherous parodies of freedom, joy, and fullfillment becomes an indispensable form of social control under the technocracy."[17]

Such charges persist to the present day, as wrongheaded now as when they were first leveled. To begin with, the revolution did not fail because capitalist subterfuge dissipated its energies. The revolution never had a chance; its dream of some radical alternative to existing social institutions was just that—a fantasy. "Participatory democracy" never proceeded beyond the slogan stage. Communes did get off the drawing board, at least, but their organizational deficiencies prevented them from becoming anything more than a passing fad. If Aquarian values were to be propagated at all, capitalism would have to be the medium. There was no other.

Furthermore, the fact that commercialization frequently trivialized Aquarian values does not mean that it had no other impact. The assimilation of the counterculture into the American mainstream went far beyond advertising copy and skirt lengths and musical beats. What has been dismissed as co-optation was merely the beginning of a much broader process of cultural change. And, indeed, those apparently superficial shifts in consumption patterns were inextricably connected to deeper, more profound phenomena. By reconceiving their identities as consumers, by joining what Daniel Boorstin so evocatively called new "consumption communities," and by changing their appearance and their music, Americans were gradually accommodating themselves to a dramatically altered value system.

For a clue as to what was happening, consider the runaway success of Richard Bach's *Jonathan Livingston Seagull*. The eponymous hero of this slender tale was, of course, unlike all the other birds in his flock. While his fellow gulls flew for the sole purpose of getting from shore to food and back, Jonathan loved flying for the sheer joy of it. When, after a couple of pages of experimenting, he taught himself to do aerobatics, he was convinced he had discovered a new way of life. "How much more there is now to living! Instead of our drab slogging back and forth to the fishing boats, there's a reason to life! We can drag ourselves out of ignorance, we can find ourselves as creatures of excellence and intelligence and skill. We can be free! *We can learn to fly!*"[18] Alas, Jonathan's enthusiasm was less than infectious, and he was expelled from the flock for his unconventional behavior. The story, though, had a happy ending. After living out his life in solitude, Jonathan was reincarnated in a higher dimension and became a teacher of other high-flying seekers like himself. "He spoke of very simple things—that it is right for a gull to fly, that freedom is the very nature of his being, that whatever stands against that freedom must be set aside, be it ritual or superstition or limitation in any form." [19]

Jonathan Livingston Seagull was released in 1970, with virtually no marketing support and a print run of only 7,500. The book defied categorization: the original hardcover ran only 93 pages, over half of which were filled with photographs of gulls in flight. One of the few reviews, by *Publisher's Weekly*, sniffed that "the prose gets a might too icky poo for comfort." Yet word of mouth slowly spread, starting on the West Coast and especially college campuses, and gradually extending throughout the country. During 1971, the book went through eight additional printings, for a total of 140,000 copies. In July 1972, it reached the top of the *New York Times* best-seller list, where it remained for the next 10 months. By 1975, the book had sold an eye-popping nine million copies.

As went *Jonathan Livingston Seagull*, so went the country. Starting on the West Coast and especially college campuses, the sensibility that Richard Bach captured so pithily broke out of the countercultural underground and into Middle America over the course of the 1970s. Since the days when ground was first broken at Levittown, the mass pursuit of self-realization had been running at full gallop. Now that pursuit escaped the confines set by conventional definitions of the American Dream and set off in search of wider horizons. "[W]hatever stands against that freedom must be set aside, be it ritual or superstition or limitation in any form"—the gospel according to Jonathan summed up the decade in all its daring and excess.

AT THE CENTER of the tumultuous change in American values was the women's movement. In the space of a very few years, women provoked and won a far-reaching reappraisal of the relationship between the sexes. And the primary engine of their movement was women's desire to participate more fully in the commercialized division of labor. Although more radical feminists had other ideas, most women didn't want to beat capitalism; they just wanted to join it. Accordingly, the main thrust of the women's movement pushed toward a dramatic expansion of capitalism's domain—that is, precisely the opposite of what Aquarian radicalism intended. The cultural consequences of capitalism's expansion were enormous. Through pursuing expanded economic opportunity, women came to challenge a host of deep-seated cultural assumptions. Those assumptions had become barriers, and all barriers had to go. The result was a contentious rethinking of some of the most basic aspects of personal identity.

The sixties and seventies saw a marked acceleration in the long-standing trend toward more women in the workforce. In 1960, 34.5 percent of American women had a job or were looking for one; 20 years later, the figure had climbed to 51.2 percent. That 48 percent increase in the labor-force participation rate compared to an increase of 33 percent over the prior two decades. Much more impressive than the growing number of females on the job, though, was the growing number of jobs now available to females. As women who worked for paychecks became the norm, the traditional designation of most occupations as "man's work" came under furious attack and quickly gave way. The 1970s were the watershed decade. In 1972, only 3.8 percent of lawyers and judges were women; by 1981, the figure had jumped to 14.1 percent. In 1972, women chemists were only 10.0 percent of the total; by 1981, they accounted for 21.9 percent. The proportion of female mail carriers jumped from 6.7 percent to 15.7 percent between 1972 and 1981, that of female pharmacists rose from 12.7 percent to 25.7 percent, and that of female forklift operators increased from 1.0 percent to 5.7 percent.

The struggle for workplace equality propelled a broader campaign for full-fledged sexual equity. Working alongside men as peers caused women to question their traditionally subservient role in the domestic sphere. Meanwhile, the newfound ability to earn income gave women a financial independence that inevitably led to greater assertiveness. Consequently, a host of long-submerged questions suddenly emerged for red-hot public debate. Why should women do all the housework? How should kids be raised when both parents work? How can women's health issues be handled properly when female perspectives and experience are ignored? Why are some men so lousy in bed? Why don't some men understand that no means no? Why do so many men treat women as playthings or children rather than equals?

A critical reexamination so profound, and so deeply personal, couldn't help but unleash a considerable amount of confusion, bluster, and folly. The culprit, once again, was romantic excess, Aquarius's tragic flaw. A pair of assumptions, as baseless as they were mutually contradictory, encouraged the quixotic radicals who dreamed of "women's liberation" from "patriarchy": on the one hand, the belief that all sexual identity is socially constructed; on the other, the belief that women are naturally superior to men because they are more intuitive and empathetic. Ti-Grace Atkinson's radical distemper was a typical product of such thinking. The first New York chapter president of the National Organization for Women, Atkinson denounced marriage as "slavery," "legalized rape," and "unpaid labor."[20] And when, in 1968, the crazed Valerie Solanas wrote the crackpot *SCUM Manifesto* (SCUM stood for "Society for Cutting Up Men") and then shot Andy Warhol, Atkinson lionized her as "the first outstanding champion of women's rights."

Ultimately, of course, all the overheated fantasies of androgyny, or matriarchy, or some impossible combination of the two, were destined to go unfulfilled. Nevertheless, important changes, both practical and symbolic, did occur in rapid fashion. In 1973, the Supreme Court secured abortion rights in *Roe v. Wade*. In 1974, Michigan passed the first rape shield law. Two years later, Nebraska became the first state to declare it illegal for a husband to rape his wife. The 1973 publication of *Our Bodies, Ourselves* helped to launch the women's health movement, challenging the previously unquestioned authority of medical paternalism. Little League baseball admitted its first girls in 1974, and in 1979 the National Weather Service began naming hurricanes after men as well as women. The title "Ms." entered general circulation, while "male chauvinist" and "sexist" became epithets that men sought with increasing diligence to avoid. There was no turning back: integration into the capitalist organization of society had given women the material resources and self-confidence they needed to insist upon more equitable treatment.

Directly related to women's greater assertiveness was the breathtaking change in sexual mores that unfolded over the sixties and seventies. As women challenged one double standard after another, it was inevitable that the sexual double standard would come under attack as a relic from the patriarchal past. "During your best years you don't need a husband," advised Helen Gurley Brown in her 1962 best seller, *Sex and the Single Girl.* "You do need a man of course every step of the way, and they are often cheaper emotionally and a lot more fun by the dozen."[21] Other factors besides nascent feminism (which, indeed, would later become much more conflicted about "sexual liberation") pushed in the same direction. For one thing, the advent of the birth control pill—approved by the Food and Drug Administration on May 9, 1960—substantially reduced the potential costs of casual sex by making contraception reliable and convenient. More broadly, the fundamental cultural turn toward self-realization as the *summum bonum* was progressively reducing the old repressive restraints that had formerly held bodily desires in check. As the Aquarian awakening upped the stakes and declared war on self-restraint in all its forms, the "sexual revolution" become one more front in the general insurrection.

"Sexual intercourse began / in nineteen sixty-three / (which was rather late for me)," wrote Philip Larkin in "Annus Mirabilis," "Between the end of the *Chatterley* ban / and the Beatles' first LP." Larkin, actually, was a bit ahead of the curve: for most Americans, the breakthrough came in the seventies. In 1969, a Gallup poll showed that 69 percent of those surveyed believed that premarital sex was immoral; a mere four years later, according to the National Opinion Research Center's General Social Survey, only 47 percent still agreed.[22] Attitudes grew steadily more permissive as the decade wore on. By 1982, the NORC survey found that 36 percent of women now believed that premarital sex was "not wrong at all," up from just 20 percent ten years earlier.[23] The shift in attitudes reflected an underlying change in behavior. More than two-thirds of women who turned 18 during the fifties claimed to have slept with only one man by their thirtieth birthday. By contrast, only 2 percent of women who reached adulthood during the seventies would admit similar restraint.[24]

Sexuality didn't just become more unbuttoned; it grew dramatically more public as well. Long-standing taboos on sexually explicit verbiage and imagery vanished as the will to enforce them through censorship weakened and then collapsed. Philip Larkin noted the weakening that occurred in 1959, when the U.S. Post Office's ban on D. H. Lawrence's *Lady Chatterley's Lover* was overturned in federal court. The collapse came seven years later with the Supreme Court's decision in *Memoirs v. Massachusetts*, which held that material could be considered legally obscene only when it was "utterly without redeeming social value." Justice Tom Clark sputtered helplessly in dissent. "I have 'stomached' past cases for almost ten years without much outcry," he wrote. "Though I am not known to be a purist—or a shrinking violet—this book is too much even for me."[25] And what exactly was the smut that had exhausted Clark's considerable tolerance? The answer astounds with its quaintness: *Memoirs of a Woman of Pleasure,* better known as *Fanny Hill,* written by John Cleland back in 1749.

The door, however, had been opened for considerably raunchier fare. Six years after Clark's last stand, *Deep Throat,* shot for under $23,000, played widely in mainstream movie theaters and grossed over $100 million. Linda Lovelace, the esophageally agile star of the movie, appeared on *The Tonight Show* with Johnny Carson and made the cover of *Esquire.* Celebrities flocked to see what all the buzz was about, among them Frank

Sinatra, Warren Beatty, Truman Capote, and Watergate reporter Bob Woodward. Sammy Davis Jr. was such a fan that he and his wife ended up having group sex with Lovelace and her husband.

Despite the *Deep Throat* boomlet, hard-core pornography remained outside the cultural mainstream. But as the boundaries of the legally permissible ballooned, so did those of the socially acceptable. Nudity in movies became commonplace after Michelangelo Antonioni's *Blow-Up* broke the pubic-hair barrier in 1966. *Penthouse, Hustler,* and *Screw* joined the now-tame-by-comparison *Playboy* on the newsstands. Two sex manuals, 1969's *Everything You Always Wanted to Know about Sex (but Were Afraid to Ask),* by David Reuben, and 1972's decidedly bolder *The Joy of Sex,* by the delightfully named Alex Comfort, sold in the millions. Kathleen Woodiwiss's 1972 bodice-ripper *The Flame and the Flower* remade the romance-novel genre with its heavy sexual content. Donna Summer moaned orgasmically in the 1975 disco hit "Love to Love You Baby" while, that same year, Patti LaBelle belted out "Voulez-vous coucher avec moi ce soir?" in the chart-topping "Lady Marmalade." America had sex on the brain.

The country's new sexual openness even reached into the homosexual "closet." In the early hours of June 28, 1969, a police raid on the Stonewall Inn, a gay bar in Greenwich Village, quickly turned ugly as patrons resisted arrest. In prior years, harassment of gay bars had been common. New York bars could lose their liquor license for serving three or more homosexuals, and gays could be arrested on indecency charges for kissing, holding hands, or cross-dressing. In the late sixties, however, such crackdowns had become much less common, and with liberalization the old rules became harder to enforce. So when eight police officers walked into the Stonewall Inn and began to make arrests, they met with defiance. Before the night was done, a crowd of some 2,000 people was battling against over 400 cops. Two more nights of rioting followed over the next five days.

Stonewall inaugurated the modern gay rights movement, and with it the incorporation of homosexuality into American cultural pluralism. A major step in that direction occurred in 1973, when the American Psychiatric Association decided to remove homosexuality from its *Diagnostic and Statistical Manual of Mental Disorders*. What had been beyond the pale, condemned as diseased and criminal, was now a minority "lifestyle" or "orientation." While most Americans continued to disapprove of homosexuality as immoral, they came increasingly, if grudgingly, to the acknowledgment that gays were part of American society and ought to be, if not welcomed, at least tolerated. Gay influences were increasingly apparent in popular culture, as evidenced by the huge late-seventies hits scored by the Village People and the more enduring success of the rock group Queen. And in 1977, a young Billy Crystal became television's first recurring gay character in the ABC sitcom *Soap*. Meanwhile, an exuberant and often wildly decadent gay subculture flourished in New York, San Francisco, and other big cities.

The liberation of sexual appetites was only one part of a growing obsession with physical well-being. "Health foods," once a hippie enthusiasm, went mass-market. Wonder Bread gave way to whole-grain varieties, Quaker Oats introduced Granola in 1972, and General Mills acquired Yoplait Yogurt in 1974. In 1971, Alice Walker, a veteran of the Free Speech Movement, opened Chez Panisse in Berkeley, thereby launching the new "California cuisine" that focused on fresh, local ingredients. Per capita beef consumption began falling after 1976, and a big spike in wine drinking during the seventies was followed by a decline in the consumption of hard liquor. The proportion of Americans who smoked cigarettes fell from 42.4 percent in 1965 to 33.5 percent in 1979. Cigarette commercials were banned from television in 1971, and separate nonsmoking sections on airplanes were introduced in 1973. The Occupational Safety and Health Administration was created in 1970; the Consumer Product Safety Commission, two years later. The year after that, motorcycle helmets were required on interstate highways.

In the new health-conscious America, exercise and fitness were pursued with a kind of religious intensity. Physical exer-

tion, until recently an inescapable necessity, now became a path
to self-realization. The number of tennis players, according to
the U.S. Tennis Association, skyrocketed from 10.7 million in
1970 to 33.9 million five years later. Over that same period, bicycle sales more than doubled, from 6.9 million to 14.1 million.
And by 1978, according to a Gallup poll, 15 million Americans
were jogging regularly.[26] Jim Fixx, the leading guru of the running craze (until he had a fatal heart attack while running at the
age of 52), portrayed the sport he loved as a spiritual quest. "Having lost faith in much of our society—government, business,
marriage, the church and so on—" he wrote in the 1977 best
seller, *The Complete Book of Running*, "we seem to have turned
to ourselves, putting what faith we can muster in our own minds
and bodies." In this vein, Fixx popularized the idea of the
"runner's high," a "trance-like state, a mental plateau where they
feel miraculously purified and at peace with themselves and the
world."[27]

As Americans were rediscovering the suppressed urgings and
pleasures and possibilities of their physical natures, they were
recalling at the same time their forgotten sense of interdependence, and kinship, with the natural world around them. In retrospect, it was inevitable that the coming of mass affluence
would stir a heightened concern for preserving wilderness and
maintaining clean air and water. Interest in the aesthetics of
scenery, or even long-term health risks, was necessarily modest
when the vast bulk of the population was preoccupied with eking
out survival. Environmental quality is a luxury good, and once
America could afford it, Rachel Carson's *Silent Spring* and the
mass movement it launched came along like clockwork to rouse
demand.

To put the matter less flippantly, the new environmental consciousness was made possible by a fundamental change in the
terms of humanity's coexistence with the natural world. Throughout the 10 millennia of agricultural civilization, most people
lived their lives in direct confrontation with natural constraints.
Wresting their sustenance from the soil, subject to the vagaries

of weather, pests, and disease, they pitted their efforts against a pitiless foe and prayed for the best. Famines and plagues on the one hand, deforestation and soil erosion and extinctions on the other—such was the butcher's bill for the incessant and inconclusive struggle. Industrialization's alliance between science and technology, however, broke the long stalemate and won for humanity an epochal victory: the creation of a world of technological and organizational artifice, insulated from nature's cruelties and reflecting human purposes and aspirations. The cost of that triumph was immense, to humanity and the natural world alike. But when, in the middle of the twentieth century, Americans became the first people in history to achieve a durable conquest of nature, they were typically magnanimous in victory. Nature, the old adversary, became an ally to be cherished and protected; the environmental movement, a kind of Marshall Plan.

Yet, from its outset, that movement was afflicted with a heavy dose of victor's guilt. Writing in 1962, Rachel Carson set the tone with her overwrought denunciation of pesticides, which she condemned as irredeemably toxic and symptomatic of deeper ills. "The 'control of nature' is a phrase conceived in arrogance," she proclaimed in *Silent Spring*'s concluding lines, "born of the Neanderthal age of biology and philosophy, when it was supposed that nature exists for the convenience of man."[28] In an influential 1967 essay that broadened and deepened Carson's line of attack, the historian Lynn White located the roots of the "ecological crisis" in the most fundamental assumptions of Western civilization—that is, in the basic tenets of Christianity. "By destroying pagan animism, Christianity made it possible to exploit nature in a mood of indifference to the feelings of natural objects . . . ," White wrote. "Hence we shall continue to have a worsening ecologic crisis until we reject the Christian axiom that nature has no reason for existence save to serve man."[29]

The Aquarian awakening transformed the fledgling ecology movement into a major force for social change, infusing it with equal doses of soaring passion and deep-seated confusion. Romanticism, with its celebration of the wild and instinctual, was always attracted to nature worship, so it was hardly surprising that the spreading spirit of Aquarius would find in environmentalism an ideal outlet for its energies—or that a movement infused by that spirit's influence would be characterized by both its anticapitalist, Luddite tendencies and its apocalyptic fantasies of revolution. "The battle to feed all of humanity is over. In the 1970s the world will undergo famines—hundreds of millions of people are going to starve to death in spite of any crash programs embarked upon now."[30] Thus began Paul Ehrlich's 1968 best seller, *The Population Bomb*. Four years later, the Club of Rome issued its own prophecy of doom, *The Limits to Growth*. It was less lurid than Ehrlich's book, but no less Malthusian. "If the present growth trends in world population, industrialization, pollution, food production, and resource depletion continue unchanged, the limits to growth on this planet will be reached sometime within the next one hundred years," the Club of Rome concluded. "The most probable result will be a rather sudden and uncontrollable decline in both population and industrial capacity."[31]

Goaded by such hysteria, the environmentalist cause was quickly transformed from the concern of a tiny elite into a mass movement with, for a time at least, irresistible political momentum. On April 22, 1970, the nation's first Earth Day celebration made clear that a new issue now had a prominent place on the national agenda. The event was the brainchild of Senator Gaylord Nelson of Wisconsin, but the grassroots response to his call for a nationwide "teach-in" soon swamped his office's organizational resources. "That was the remarkable thing about Earth Day," Nelson recalled later. "It organized itself." All told, some 20 million people took part. Before the year was out, Congress had passed the Clean Air Act and the new Environmental Protection Agency had opened for business. And by 1973, the Clean Water Act and the Endangered Species Act were added to the nation's statute books.

Notwithstanding the antimarket animus of many of its activists, the environmental movement was yet another testament to capitalism's power to promote Aquarian values. The prosperity produced by economic dynamism had encouraged a shift in priorities. Values changed, and the economic and political systems responded to the new, greener sensibility. The response, of course, didn't satisfy everybody. Zealots, unreconciled to energy- and technology-intensive civilization, could never be placated. Meanwhile, the command-and-control regulatory structures erected to safeguard environmental quality were often crude and plagued by perverse incentives. Yet a rough balance was struck. Even subject to the new regulatory constraints, the capitalist process of wealth creation continued to trundle along. And at the same time, America's skies and lakes and rivers and streams grew cleaner.

THE CHURNING FLUX of urgent, new priorities and fading, old certainties left many Americans disoriented and groping for spiritual guidance. Increasing numbers of them came to the con- clusion that the established religious traditions didn't have the answers they were looking for. In particular, the mainline Prot- estant denominations, which once defined the country's reli- gious identity, went into a downward spiral. Between 1965 and 1975, the United Methodists lost 10 percent of their members; southern and northern Presbyterians lost 7 and 12 percent, re- spectively; membership in the United Church of Christ dropped by 12 percent; Episcopalians suffered the worst drop, losing nearly 17 percent of their membership in the space of a decade.[32] While the evangelical churches experienced rapid growth, and Roman Catholic membership edged up slightly, those gains did not offset the mainline losses. The proportion of Americans who identified themselves as neither Protestant, Catholic, nor Jew- ish, which stood at only 4 percent in 1957, rose to 10 percent by 1975.[33]

The decline in church membership was accompanied by a host of other indicators of creeping secularization. Weekly church attendance fell steadily from a peak of 49 percent of

Americans in 1955 to 40 percent in the early 1970s, with little or no recovery thereafter. Declines were particularly sharp among Roman Catholics after the liberalization of Vatican II.[34] The number of Americans who said that religion played a "very important" role in their lives slipped from 70 percent in 1965 to 55 percent 10 years later, stabilizing but not rising over the next decade.[35] In 1964, 77 percent of Americans said they had no doubts about the existence of God; by 1981, the figure had fallen to 62 percent.[36] In Muncie, Indiana, the heartland city that was the subject of the famous "Middletown" studies, only 41 percent of those polled in 1977 agreed that "Christianity is the one true religion" and "everyone should be converted to it." In 1924, when the question was asked originally, 94 percent of Middletowners had agreed.[37]

As traditional faith waned, Americans experimented with a multitude of other paths. According to a 1976 Gallup poll, six million Americans practiced transcendental meditation, another five million were performing yoga, and two million were involved with Eastern religions. Many paths, unfortunately, led in directions better left unexplored. Superstition and belief in the fantastic abounded. A wave of UFO sightings, including numerous claims of close encounters with aliens, swept the country during the fall of 1973. ESP, the Bermuda Triangle, Bigfoot, the Loch Ness monster, ancient astronauts, Uri Geller's bending spoons, Kirlian auras, pyramid power—the seventies were a golden age of pseudoscientific bunkum. Cults proliferated, as Scientology, the Hare Krishna movement, the Unification Church, and many, many others attracted and preyed upon the marginalized and psychologically vulnerable. Nothing, though, rivaled the horror that occurred in Jonestown, Guyana, when on November 18, 1978, Jim Jones convinced or coerced over 900 of his Peoples Temple followers, including 276 children, to kill themselves with cyanide-laced grape punch.

The main thrust of spiritual seeking, however, was nothing so sinister or bizarre. Rather, it was an updated version of that quintessentially American creed, the cult of self-improvement.

Whether they were being inspired by Ben Franklin, Horatio Alger, Dale Carnegie, or Norman Vincent Peale, Americans had always thrilled to the message that things could be better than they are, and that you have the power to make them so. What changed over time was the definition of "better"—from success and happiness through inner-directed discharge of bourgeois Protestant duty, to success and happiness through other-directed adjustment to social convention, to the latest twist on the perennial theme. And that new twist, that Aquarian twist, was to change the primary locus of duty. Duty to God and others receded to the background, while duty to self now took center stage.

The mass pursuit of personal fulfillment had begun decades before, as the triumph over scarcity allowed ordinary Americans to lift their sights from survival and security and aim for something higher. But with the deepening of affluence through continuing technological and organizational advances, and the rising of a new generation that had never known privation, the main path of pursuit headed off in a new direction. Summed up succinctly in a single phrase, it was the title of one of the top-selling books of 1977: *Looking Out for # 1.* "Looking out for Number One," explained the author, Robert Ringer, in the opening lines of the book's first chapter, "is the conscious, rational effort to spend as much time as possible doing those things which bring you the greatest amount of pleasure and less time on those which cause pain."[38] Alas, a task that is easier said than done!

Americans of the World War II generation had sought personal fulfillment in the achievement and enjoyment of prosperous stability: a house in the suburbs, filled with kids, efficiently run by Mom, and paid for by Dad's good, steady job. Their baby-boom offspring, however, hungered for more. Not that the old, conventional desiderata were necessarily rejected, but they were no longer seen as ends in themselves. "Instead of asking, 'Will I be able to make a good living?' 'Will I be successful?' 'Will I raise happy, healthy, successful children?'—the typical questions asked by average Americans in the 1950s and 1960s—Americans in the 1970s came to ponder more introspective matters," wrote the pollster Daniel Yankelovich in 1981. "We asked, 'How can I find self-fulfillment?' 'What does personal success really mean?' 'What kind of commitments should I be making?' 'What is worth sacrificing for?' 'How can I grow?' 'How can I best realize the commitment I have to develop myself?' "[39]

Abraham Maslow's concept of the hierarchy of needs captured the social dynamic unleased by mass affluence: the reorientation of human effort and concern away from basic needs and toward the higher needs of self-actualization. But in the early decades of the affluent society, the dynamic played out relatively unself-consciously. Few Americans in the fifties thought much about personal fulfillment in the abstract; instead, they thought about upward mobility and aquiring possessions and building families. By the 1970s, however, as the Aquarian awakening rippled out into the country, ordinary Americans by the tens of millions began to think about the choices they faced in explicitly Maslovian terms. Where once they pursued various proxies for personal fulfillment (money, success, family), now they wanted the real thing. And when they saw conflicts between chasing the proxies and chasing the real thing, they were increasingly inclined to opt for the latter.

The traditional American quest for self-improvement now became a spiritual quest—a quest to discover the "real me" and dutifully serve its needs. Urged on by group therapy sessions, 12-step recovery programs, support groups, and an endless parade of self-appointed self-help experts, a nation of Jonathan Livingston Seagulls took wing.

THE AQUARIUS-INSPIRED SHIFT in values brought many changes for the good. America became a more open, inclusive, and tolerant country. Blacks and women had more opportunities than ever in history. The demystification of sexual desire abated a great deal of pointless guilt and frustration. In music, fashion, films, and food, a proliferation of new styles and themes added variety and complexity to cultural experience. On the whole, if with obvious exceptions, religious attitudes grew less dogmatic and censorious. The realm of freedom was now, in many respects, considerably more open than before.

Those gains, however, came at a heavy price. As the spirit of romantic rebellion moved across Middle America, benighted prejudice and hidebound puritanism were hardly the only casualties. The rebellious aim was indiscriminate, and legitimate authority and necessary restraints were trashed in the general uproar. To blame was the naïve equation of the virtuous and the uninhibited, a proposition that collapsed the distinction between individualism and infantilism. As that proposition was put to the test during the sixties and seventies, the results were often less than edifying. Personal lives were thrown into turmoil, and the bonds of trust on which affluence and its possibilities depend loosened under the strain.

Much of the mayhem occurred behind closed doors, in the ranches and split-levels of suburbia. For if an antiseptic idealization of family life prevailed during the fifties, two decades later it was divorce that was being idealized. "It has been our experience with patients and friends that both spouses, after an initial period of confusion or depression, almost without exception look and feel better than ever before," enthused psychologists Susan Gettleman and Janet Markowitz in their 1974 book, *The Courage to Divorce*. "They act warmer and more related to others emotionally, tap sources of strength they never knew they had, enjoy their careers and children more, and begin to explore new vocations and hobbies."[40] And what about the kids? "No reason is sound enough to keep a crummy relationship together. The worst excuse of all is children," Robert Ringer declared flatly. "If kids are involved, give them a break. Get out of your mate's life so your children can enjoy both of you at your best—in happier states than they see you now."[41]

As such wishful thinking became the conventional wisdom, marriages by the millions unraveled and fell apart. The year

1965 saw 480,000 divorces nationwide; a decade later, the annual toll had zoomed to over a million. Law moved accommodatingly to scratch the increasingly irresistible itch. California became the first no-fault divorce state in 1969; within eight years, all but three states had followed suit. Religion, too, made its peace with the breaking of vows. In 1973, the Episcopal Church recognized civil divorce; between 1968 and 1981, the number of annulments doled out by the Roman Catholic Church soared an astonishing 77-fold.[42]

The accelerating demise of existing marriages was matched by a slowdown in the creation of new ones. Over the course of the seventies, the average age of the first-time bridegroom rose from 23 years old to nearly 25; that of his blushing bride, from under 21 to 22.[43] With marriage increasingly abandoned or avoided, the number of single adults rose to 22.5 percent of American households by 1980, up from 10.8 percent in 1950. And in the expanding middle ground between single life and marriage, over a million unmarried couples were living together by the late 1970s.

The flight from marriage meant a flight from raising children. By 1975, the birthrate for women between the ages of 15 and 44 had fallen below 67 per 1,000 women—lower even than during the Great Depression, and a nearly 50 percent drop from the peak of the baby boom. The number of legal abortions doubled from 745,000 in 1973 to over 1.5 million in 1980. And every year of the 1970s, roughly a million Americans had themselves sterilized.[44] For the dwindling number of children born, being raised by both parents could no longer be taken for granted. In 1970, 11.8 percent of children under 18 years old lived with only one of their parents (usually Mom); by 1981, that figure had risen to 20.0 percent. The decline of the two-parent family reflected not only the divorce boom, but also the precipitous increase in what it was no longer fashionable to call illegitimacy. Between 1960 and 1979, births to unwed white mothers shot from 2.3 percent of white total births to 9.4 percent.

No doubt the dark clouds gathering over the American family

had their silver linings. Many god-awful unions were mercifully dissolved, while many ill-considered ones were dodged. Smaller families made possible a greater degree of parental attentiveness to children's lives, a development that had its wholesome aspects. But make no mistake about it: personal fulfillment through freedom from family attachments was a seductive vision that, when chased after, often proved a mirage. Many divorcées, eager to sample the decadent pleasures of the seventies singles scene, found only frustration and loneliness. Many others purchased escape from their own problems at the expense of their children. Meanwhile, expected births per woman of childbearing age sank from 2.5 to 1.8 during the 1970s, slipping below the replacement rate of 2.1 and never recovering thereafter. Undoubtedly, there are many avenues for individual flourishing that do not involve having and raising children. But whatever its other virtues, a culture that cannot reproduce itself biologically is a culture that fails at least the most obvious test of vitality. When people do not believe enough in their way of life to provide for its future, they may be exhibiting symptoms of a deeper malaise.

The weakening of family bonds could be found throughout American society, but the black family in particular experienced a catastrophic collapse. Births to single black mothers already constituted a disturbing 21.6 percent of total black births back in 1960, but by 1979 the illegitimacy rate had soared to 54.7 percent. Daniel Patrick Moynihan identified and publicized the problem in 1965, when it was still in its relatively early stages. "At the heart of the deterioration of the fabric of Negro society is the deterioration of the Negro family . . . ," he warned. "[T]he family structure of lower class Negroes is highly unstable, and in many urban centers is approaching complete breakdown."

Despite its prescience, the Moynihan Report was quickly hooted down for "blaming the victim." "The family is a creature of the society," responded Andrew Billingsley, a Howard University professor, in typical fashion. "And the greatest problems facing black families are problems which emanate from the white racist, militarist, materialistic society which places higher priority on putting white men on the moon than putting black men on their feet on this earth." Anyway, Billingsley wrote elsewhere, "All the major institutions of society should abandon the single standard of excellence based on white European cultural norms."[45]

In that spirited defense of disastrous dysfunction can be seen one of the major causes of the crisis. Chaotic family life had long been a feature of southern sharecropper culture, and when that culture was transplanted in the anonymous northern ghetto, things only got worse. But the tipping point came when the fraying restraints of shame and shaming suddenly disappeared altogether. And what caused that? The spreading spirit of romantic rebellion, with its scorn for onerous duty and self-denial, was penetrating the inner city. And outside, the new permissiveness and indulgent relativism of enlightened liberal opinion were giving their blessing to the resulting wreckage.

Meanwhile, Aquarius-inspired rebelliousness was causing disruptions on the job as well as in the home. Not among the socioeconomic elite: there, changes in values and the changing nature of the workplace moved in happy unison. For the well educated and highly skilled, the desire for personal growth and creativity found a ready outlet in an increasingly postindustrial economy's rapid creation of intellectually challenging managerial and professional positions. And as the American economy's reliance on "knowledge workers" continued to deepen, corporate culture shifted to accommodate their growing need to express their individuality. William Whyte's *The Organization Man* was out; Robert Townsend's *Up the Organization* was in. Townsend, the CEO of the upstart car rental agency Avis, summed up the emerging "corporate maverick" ethos in his 1970 best seller's subtitle: *How to Stop the Corporation from Stifling People and Strangling Profits*. According to the new management thinking, hierarchy and conformism were uncool *and* bad for business.

If the spirit of Aquarius energized work life in the college-educated, white-collar ranks, its effects on other segments of the labor force were less salutary. In particular, for Americans with fewer employable skills and therefore more limited employment opportunities, the growing disdain for drudgery and routine undercut the willingness to put up with the daily grind. A deterioration in the work ethic became plainly visible in those lines of work in which strict discipline had previously held sway—in particular, on the assembly line and in the military. In the automobile industry, absences from the job at Ford and General Motors doubled between 1961 and 1970. On a typical day in 1970, 5 percent of GM's workers were missing; on Fridays and Mondays, absenteeism was more like 10 percent. The workers that did show up developed a predilection for vandalism and sabotage. "[S]crews have been left in brake drums," *Fortune* magazine observed, "tool handles welded into fender compartments (to cause mysterious, unfindable and eternal rattles), paint scratched, and upholstery cut." The troubles in Detroit were particularly severe, but by no means unique. A 1970 nationwide survey of business managers asked whether "hourly paid workers in your company are more conscientious about their work than a generation ago, or less." Some 63 percent of managers answered less, while only 2 percent said more.[46]

"Question authority" expressed a noble sentiment, to be sure, but one poorly suited to a properly functioning military. And so, as the Vietnam War's hapless draftees brought the counterculture with them into the armed forces, the results were predictably grim. Drug use became rampant; discipline grew ragged. A 1971 Defense Department survey estimated that between 25,000 and 37,000 soldiers serving in Vietnam were regularly using heroin. And between 1969 and 1973, at least 600 officers were murdered, or "fragged," by their own troops, while another 1,400 died mysteriously. After the war, efforts to build an all-volunteer fighting force did not begin promisingly. Recruiting goals went unmet, and consequently standards steadily slipped. By 1979, 46 percent of new Army recruits had IQ scores in the lowest acceptable category. To put that figure in perspective, consider that during the full-scale mobilization of World War II, when draft boards were hardly being choosy, only 21 percent of the country's soldiers had scores that low.[47] Given the Vietnam experience and the larger cultural hostility to the martial virtues, military service had become the employment option of last resort.

As with the unraveling of family ties, in the rebellion against the work ethic, it was the poor and especially inner-city blacks who suffered most. Promised liberation, they plunged instead into self-destruction and ruinous dependency. The courageous defiance that challenged white racism was now perverted into simple defiance of reality—specifically, a refusal to accept the rigorous self-discipline needed by the unskilled and uneducated to elevate their economic station.

That transition can be traced, with reasonable precision, to August 11, 1965. Just five days earlier, the signing of the epochal Voting Rights Act had marked the official end of Jim Crow and the crowning achievement of the mass movement that began a mere decade before on the streets of Montgomery. Yet now, in the predominantly black section of Los Angeles known as Watts, triumph turned to ashes. A minor altercation between white police officers and a black drunk driver exploded into five days of rioting. Thirty-four people were killed, another thousand were injured, and almost 4,000 people were arrested. A thousand businesses were destroyed by fire and vandalism and looting.

The overwhelming reaction, by black and white leaders alike, was to rationalize Watts as a continuation of the civil rights struggle. The riots showed, in Bayard Rustin's words, that blacks "would no longer quietly submit to the deprivation of slum life." Official Washington agreed. According to a presidential task force on crime, Watts "was a manifestation of a general sense of deep outrage, outrage at every aspect of the lives Negroes are forced to live, outrage at every element of the white community for forcing (or permitting) Negroes to live such lives."[48] Such indulgence of violence proved an incitement to more of the same, and 1965 was followed by a trio of "long hot summers" in which virtually every northern city of consequence was convulsed by unrest (interestingly, southern cities were largely spared). When the most devastating of these spasms hit Detroit in July 1967, it took a combination of state troopers, National Guardsmen, and elements of the 82nd and 101st Airborne Divisions to quell the disturbance. Before it was all over, 43 people died, 7,200 were arrested, and 2,500 businesses were damaged or destroyed. Detroit, which the *Washington Post* at the time called "the American model of intelligence and courage applied to the governance of a huge industrial city," never recovered.[49]

The riots of the late sixties were only the most spectacular examples of self-inflicted harm. The same blind rebelliousness that sparked the trashing of America's inner cities was simultaneously extinguishing the will to escape them. Specifically, dependence on the dole skyrocketed, as the number of Americans receiving welfare benefits increased from under 500,000 in 1966 to nearly a million four years later. Significantly, the big jump in reliance on government assistance occurred while unemployment was low and the economy was booming. The rise in dependency reflected not hard times, but a shift in preferences: more and more people were deciding that working just wasn't worth the bother. In reaching that conclusion, they were actively encouraged by the "welfare rights" movement of the late sixties, which encouraged the poor to abandon low-level, "dead-end" jobs and instead concentrate their energies on extracting income from the corrupt "system."

"Going downtown to mau-mau the bureaucrats got to be the routine practice in San Francisco," wrote Tom Wolfe in a lacerating 1971 piece for *Cosmopolitan*. "The poverty program *encouraged* you to go in for mau-mauing." According to Wolfe, clueless welfare bureaucrats "sat back and waited for you to come rolling in with your certified angry militants, your guaranteed frustrated ghetto youth, looking like a bunch of wild men. Then you had your test confrontation. If you were outrageous enough, if you could shake up the bureaucrats so bad that their eyes froze into iceballs and their mouths twisted up into smiles of sheer physical panic, into shit-eating grins, so to speak—then they knew you were the real goods. They knew you were the right studs to give the poverty grants and community organizing jobs to."[50]

The upshot was a large-scale, voluntary withdrawal of young black men from the nation's workforce. In 1965, 89.8 percent of black men aged 20 to 24 had jobs or were looking for work, compared to 85.3 percent of white men in the same age group. By 1980, the labor-force participation rate for young white men had nudged up to 87.1 percent, but for blacks it had fallen all the way to 78.9 percent. In 15 years, in other words, the differential between whites and blacks shifted by a whopping 12.7 percentage points.[51] As explained by Richard Cloward and Frances Fox Piven, two left-wing social scientists who championed the swelling of the welfare rolls, "When large numbers of people come to subsist on the dole, many of them spurning what little low-wage work may exist, those of the poor and the near-poor who continue to work are inevitably affected. From their perspective, the ready availability of relief payments . . . undermines their chief claim to social status: namely, that although poor they nevertheless earn their livelihood. If most of them react with anger, others react by asking, 'Why work?' "[52]

The inner city's moral wasteland of fatherlessness and joblessness would hatch a virulent outbreak of criminality. Between 1965 and 1980, the murder rate nationwide precisely doubled; aggravated assaults per 100,000 people rose by 165 percent; robberies, by 244 percent; burglaries, by 155 percent; car thefts, by 94 percent. Aiding and abetting the surge in lawbreaking was the well-intentioned excuse making that dominated educated opinion at the time. Ramsey Clark, Lyndon Johnson's attorney general (and Justice Tom Clark's son), typified the prevailing liberal outlook when he wrote in 1970, "[C]rime among poor blacks . . . flows clearly from the brutalization and dehumanization of racism, poverty, and injustice. . . . [T]he slow destruction of human dignity caused by white racism is responsible."[53]

Such thinking had clear and fateful implications for administration of the criminal justice system. The idea that rising crime should be fought with more aggressive policing and tougher sentencing was dismissed as hopelessly retrograde. The real solution lay in ending the victimization of the ghetto, not lashing out at those victims that struck back against the system. Indeed, a "tough-on-crime" policy would only worsen the problem by giving wider scope for abuses of power by police and correctional authorities, thus aggravating the poor's sense of oppression and encouraging even more crime. Guided by such analysis, liberal reformers in the nation's courts, mayor's offices, and police departments responded to soaring crime rates by tightening the reins on law enforcement.

In defense of the reformers, the treatment of suspects and prisoners was all too often deplorable. Cleaning up such abuses was a commendable goal, and ultimately the integrity and effectiveness of the criminal justice system were well served by higher standards and closer scrutiny. Alas, however, appropriate concern with civil liberties tended to go together with a casual disregard of the fundamental importance of catching and punishing criminals. Consequently, the old adage that crime doesn't pay began to look out of date. The proportion of robberies ultimately cleared by arrests sank from 37.6 percent in 1965 to 23.3 percent in 1980; for burglaries, the relevant figures dropped from 24.7 percent to 13.8 percent over the same period.[54] As the odds of getting caught declined, so did the severity of punishment for those who were caught. Between 1960 and 1980, the number of prisoners per 1,000 arrests fell from 232 to 124.[55]

The diffusion of Aquarian values was thus doubly culpable for the crime explosion. First, the reduced commitment to family and work obligations bred pathologies that encouraged criminality. On top of which, the naïve faith that repression is the root of all evil fostered a profound misunderstanding of the roots of crime. It was the lack of proper socialization, not an excess of social restrictions, that caused crime rates to shoot upward. Misdiagnosing the problem so utterly, liberal reformers were doomed to offer faulty prescriptions. In particular, by shifting blame away from criminals and their dysfunctional culture onto the larger structures of society, they reduced the stigma associated with illegal conduct. Moreover, fearful of contributing to the oppression they believed caused crime, they were unforgivably lax about the administration of justice. The sufferings of the poor, the primary victims of crime, were compounded as a result.

THE AQUARIAN AWAKENING was, like most historical movements, beset by internal contradiction. At the center of its wide-ranging and varied enthusiasms was the urge to widen the horizons of American life: to expand the moral imagination by embracing those previously excluded from full participation in the social enterprise; to expand consciousness by exploring realms of experience previously repressed or ignored. At the same time, however, it rejected the values and institutions that created and sustained the very possibility of Aquarius's exuberant expansionism. Without the immensely intricate division of labor developed and constantly elaborated by capitalism, there would have been no mass affluence; without mass affluence, there could have been no counterculture. Yet the radicals of the sixties denounced as banal and corrupt the corporate commercialism that surrounded them, and they held in equal scorn the conventional commitments to family and work that undergirded the capitalist division of labor. The Aquarian project was thus at war with itself.

The radical assault on capitalism proved a failure. After just a brief run of years, utopian braggadocio faded away, and childish fantasies were quietly abandoned. Yet the spirit of Aquarius lived on, propagated by the corporate commercialism that its true believers so despised. And as that attenuated strain of romantic rebelliousness permeated American society, its indiscriminate hostility to restraints on personal desire brought an inevitable mix of blessings and evils.

The mix was not evenly distributed. The shift in values that took place during the sixties and seventies concentrated its benefits on the upper and middling segments of society. Its harshest consequences, meanwhile, fell disproportionately on the working and lower classes. Why the disparate impact? The answer lies in this paradox: although freedom is experienced as the absence of restraint, it is experienced most fully when particular restraints are vigorously maintained. In other words, contrary to those under the spell of the romantic delusion, not all limitations on choice are the enemies of freedom. Rather, some are ultimately, and crucially, freedom enhancing. For those with the appropriate discipline, the Aquarian quest for self-realization usually led to a fuller, richer exploration of life's possibilities. But among those without that discipline, the turn toward self-assertiveness too often proved a cruel trap.

There is absolutely nothing natural about the freedom that the counterculture celebrated and sought to extend. Rather, the dramatic expansion of life choices made possible by mass affluence was a cultural achievement of the highest order, the result of an unprecedented mobilization of human energies combined with an immensely complex and intricate organization of social cooperation. And as Karl Marx himself recognized, that achievement was accomplished under the leadership of a particular class of people—the group Marx referred to as the bourgeoisie, and whose descendants served as the counterculture's bête noire. The bourgeoisie was distinguished by an intense commitment to a particular shared culture, one which turned out to be extremely well suited to promoting economic dynamism. In the United States, the Protestant bourgeois culture was so dominant as to constitute a kind of national civil religion—a fact that goes a long way toward explaining why the transition to mass affluence occurred first in America.

What made bourgeois culture so congenial to economic progress? Two features stand out as critically important: a focus on the long term, and a capacity for abstract loyalties. The Protestant work ethic was, of course, famous for its steely commitment to deferred gratification. And while stern self-denial was often practiced to an extent that makes little sense in our luxurious age, the firmly ingrained habit of rationally connecting means to ends over time—that is, of planning ahead and then sticking to one's plans—was an absolutely essential precondition for America's industrial takeoff. Without an unnatural fondness for tomorrow over today, how else could capital be saved from the press of current needs and patiently accumulated? How else could it be deployed in projects that took many years to reach fruition?

The stupendous levels of wealth enjoyed today require the ability to pursue large-scale as well as long-term projects. We depend, in other words, on the cooperation if not the kindness of strangers—anonymous millions who somehow trust each other enough to do business together, and even to put their lives in each other's hands. The Protestant bourgeois ethos greatly facilitated the emergence of such large-scale trust by providing a new and abstract form of unity founded on a shared faith and lifestyle. In their worship, dress, and manners, the members of America's Protestant establishment ostentatiously advertised their "respectability," and thus their trustworthiness in business dealings. The historical norm was for people to maintain only a narrow circle of personal loyalties, inherited connections based on family and birthplace. Bourgeois morality transcended such small-scale, organic unity and made possible a loyalty to common ideals and values. The result was an integrated national economy of unmatched productive power.

The bourgeois cultural innovations of future orientation and abstract loyalty remain at the heart of contemporary middle-class culture. Today, however, those essential, freedom-enhancing disciplines have been stripped of much of their original, nineteenth-century baggage. Two great waves of cultural change effected the transformation. The first took place over the first half of the twentieth century, as modern consumerism was born and the corporate organization of economic life gradually extended its reach. By midcentury, the old Protestant bourgeois ethos had lost its cultural dominance, ceding the stage to what David Riesman famously called the "other-directed" mentality. Dogmatic intolerance of other faiths gave way to the bland inclusiveness of the "triple melting pot"; narrow-minded bigotry softened as descendants of southern and eastern European immigrants began entering the middle class; suspicion of material self-indulgence was overwhelmed by the temptations of machine-made plenty.

Despite the dramatic changes, the other-directed suburbanites of the fifties still clung to many old-style bourgeois conventions. In particular, the ideal of distinctive male and female spheres, after losing ground for decades, enjoyed a spirited reaffirmation. Meanwhile, although the new pluralistic spirit moved to accommodate whites of non-northern-European descent, pervasive prejudice against African Americans made excuses for the perpetuation of their degrading mistreatment. And while sexual morality had loosened considerably, a vigorous and guilt-inducing repression still carried the day.

Then came the second wave. During the sixties and seventies, the Aquarian awakening did much to sweep away those remaining holdovers from the Protestant bourgeois past. But in so doing, it was only accelerating and exaggerating changes that were already well under way. Black subjugation under Jim Crow had been seriously undermined by agricultural mechanization and its twin effects: the demise of the sharecropping system and the mass migration of African Americans out of the South. Female participation in the labor market had been growing steadily for decades as the toil and drudgery of housework declined and opportunities for less physically demanding white-collar work for pay expanded. The sexual chemistry caused by young men and women at close quarters in schools and the workplace, combined with the availability of increasingly effective and convenient contraception, had rendered Victorian standards of decency as unenforceable as they were unnecessary.

As it reshaped middle-class values, the spirit of Aquarius was thus working in fundamental harmony with the logic of capitalist development. When, however, the romantic rebellion directly challenged that logic, it fell flat on its face. The countercultural left called for affluent, educated youth to abandon the large-scale, commercialized division of labor—in favor of either the wispy utopia of participatory democracy or the more tangible satisfactions of the hippie commune. All but a small minority declined the invitation, and most who accepted sooner or later found their way back to life inside the "system."

In other words, the American middle classes remained faithful to the core values of future orientation and impersonal interaction—and to the highly complex, organized, and competitive social order that is the living expression of those values. Though they now gave wider play to the romantic celebration of natural, bodily pleasures, they continued to believe in hard work and planning for the future. And despite the mounting stresses of life outside the womb of small-scale, face-to-face community, they continued to seek the diversity of opportunities that only an anonymous, abstract social order can provide.

Here, then, was a delicious irony. The radicals of the countercultural left dreamed of a utopia from which all traces of middle-class morality had been expunged. What they actually succeeded in accomplishing, however, was to foment cultural changes that broadened the scope within which core middle-class values could operate. The capitalist division of labor now expanded to create new opportunities for blacks and women. Sexual openness, rock music, the fitness boom, increased appreciation of the natural environment, and the quest for spiritual growth and self-help all launched large new markets for commercial exploitation—and causes for organized, nonprofit activism. In the process, American middle-class culture grew more inclusive, open-minded, and adventurous.

But for the less affluent and less educated, it was often a very different story. In the humbler reaches of American society, the values of future orientation and abstract loyalty were much weaker or even nonexistent. America's immigrant working classes originated, by and large, in the peasant cultures of Europe, and they brought with them to the New World the characteristic peasant ethos of fatalism and mistrust of strangers. A similar worldview was shared by the waves of African American migrants who fled the Deep South for the industrial cities of the North. And while many descendants of European peasants and black share-croppers absorbed and adopted middle-class values, many others remained firmly enmeshed in a distinctive working-class culture. Which is to say, in the first instance, that their capacity to plan for the long term was limited. In particular, they placed little value on education, and they were unlikely to think of work as a lifelong career with steady advancement and personal growth. And, in the second instance, their capacity to trust and work with strangers was limited. They tended to regard the "outside world"—the world beyond the peer group they grew up with—as a mysterious and hostile presence.

What distinguished the working class from the lower class, however, was a stoic devotion to hard work and family. That devotion, rooted in the sturdy peasant virtue of self-reliance, made for a work ethic of more modest ambitions than that of the bourgeoisie. In the working-class version of "respectability," the standard of success was simply holding one's own, not climbing the social ladder. Dreams of advancement, if they were seriously entertained, were invested in the children: work hard, save for the kids, and maybe they can have a better life. The more pressing motivation, though, was avoiding the shame of downward mobility—of being a "bum" who could not or chose not to support himself and his family.

If the Aquarian awakening made little headway in attacking the middle-class work ethic, it found the working-class version considerably more vulnerable. Those stuck in dull and arduous jobs could not savor the heady pleasures of high social status; they did not experience the bracing intellectual rigors of abstract, analytical work. In short, their work ethic was built mainly on self-denial. Compared to the middle-class analog, it offered much less scope for self-expression or personal growth. Consequently, when duty and respectability became passé and "follow your bliss" took their place, the conventional restraints of working-class culture began to loosen their hold.

For many, the old rules remained hard and fast, as conservative suspicion of novel and exotic ideas insulated them from the seductions of the counterculture. Others maintained their bearings by joining the evangelical revival; for them, a fervent religiosity that promised self-realization through communion with God and fellow believers provided the spiritual resources to keep faith with work and family. But a substantial number of working-class Americans, especially blacks in the inner city, were led by the Aquarian impulse to renounce the claims of self-discipline.

If they thought they were breaking free, they were wrong. Unlike middle-class Americans, they lacked the talent and the skill to combine the quest for self-realization with the work ethic. Unlike others in the working class, they lacked the self-control to honor work and family obligations that, at least in the short term, conflicted with personal desire. As a result, they wound up falling into the traps of alcoholism, drug addiction, crime, and chronic unemployment. Lured by the promise of self-actualization, they found self-destruction instead; in the name of freedom, they sank into dismal dependency. And through the chaos of their personal lives, they passed their pathologies on to the next generation. The result was a nightmarish expansion of what came to be known as the underclass.

Though inspired by a vision of all-embracing community, the Aquarian awakening ended up accentuating class divisions that had been relatively muted during those first decades after World War II. Specifically, the extremes at either end of the socioeconomic scale grew increasingly influential in setting the tone of American life. At the top was a highly educated, highly skilled elite, the group in whom the freedom-enhancing disciplines of foresight and trustworthiness were most highly developed. Because of the diffusion of the self-realization ethos, this elite was free to navigate the extended social networks of modern society with unprecedented freedom of movement. As a result, over the course of the eighties and nineties, its fusion of Aquarian and core middle-class values would unleash prodigious economic and cultural energies. At the bottom, meanwhile, was the underclass, utterly alienated from the extended social order around it and mired in dysfunction, dependency, and predatory behavior. Created during the sixties and seventies, it was the tragic conseqence of an attempt to transcend bourgeois morality by people who had not yet reached that level of cultural development.

In the elite and the underclass, respectively, both the promise and peril of the Aquarian awakening achieved their fullest realization. In the former, the hopes for progress and wider horizons came to bountiful fruition; in the latter, the neglected dangers of atavism and self-destruction exacted a horrific toll. Thus the spectacle of post-1960s America: the elite raised Babel to dizzying new heights, while the underclass sapped its foundations.

SIX

Realignment

———— •◆• ————

"It's morning again in America," said the deep, comforting voice. "Today, more men and women will go to work than ever before in our country's history. With interest rates and inflation down, more people are buying new houses, and our new families have confidence in the future. America today is prouder and stronger and better. Why would we want to return to where we were less than four short years ago?" Accompanying the narration were soft-focused, golden-lighted images of Americana: a cowboy in a horse corral; a station wagon, cruising through suburbia; a wedding; firefighters, raising the flag at the station as two young boys—one black, one white—look on in wonder; and finally, Old Glory, waving proudly and filling the screen.

Ronald Reagan's "Morning in America" television spots in 1984 brilliantly captured the dramatic changes in national circumstances and mood that the new decade, and new political leadership, had brought. Thanks to Orwell, the year 1984 had long loomed ominously in the popular imagination, its approach associated with the extinction of freedom and the crushing of the human spirit. The dreaded year had finally arrived, yet America's free society now seemed resurgent and emboldened with renewed self-confidence. A public opinion poll found that

51 percent of Americans believed their country was once again heading in the right direction, while only 32 percent felt it was on the wrong track. Just four years earlier, fully 70 percent had been in the pessimists' camp.

Economic prospects had brightened considerably. Inflation, which peaked at 13.5 percent in 1980, had fallen all the way to 4.3 percent. Interest rates were also coming down: after soaring to 18.9 percent in 1981, the prime rate charged by banks now averaged 12.1 percent. The sharp recession of 1981–1982 gave way to rollicking growth, as the real gross national product shot up 6.8 percent in 1984. Total employment rose by over four million in a single year.

The resumption of good times occurred against a backdrop of important changes in economic policy. Marginal income tax rates were slashed in August 1981, with the top rate falling from 70 to 50 percent. That same month, President Reagan fired over 11,000 illegally striking air traffic controllers, signaling a new firmness in resisting the demands of organized labor. And demands from sundry constituencies for government largesse met with similar resolve, as between 1981 and 1984 real federal discretionary spending on domestic programs shrank by 13.5 percent.[1] Such shifts in policy were promoted with a kind of libertarian rhetoric not heard from the White House in over a half century. "In this present crisis," Reagan famously declared in his first inaugural address, "government is not the solution to our problem; government is the problem."

Meanwhile, the country was shaking off its post-Vietnam funk and reasserting itself on the world stage. The Reagan administration's reinvigorated Cold War effort included a major ramp-up in defense spending, the deployment of intermediate-range nuclear missiles in Europe, aid for anticommunist insurgencies in Afghanistan and Nicaragua, and plans for a "Star Wars" missile-defense program. Furthermore, U.S. troops once again saw combat and tasted victory. On August 19, 1981, two Navy F-14s shot down a pair of Libyan planes that had attacked them in the Gulf of Sidra. And in October 1983, American forces invaded the tiny Caribbean island of Grenada and toppled the communist government there. Compared with military operations of prior and subsequent decades, those two engagements were small beer, yet at the time their boldness astounded.

As in politics, so in the popular culture: capitalism and patriotism were in fashion once again. Hippies and Yippies faded into distant memory; preppies and yuppies took their place. Power ties and suspenders, shoulder pads and big hair, fern bars and knicknacks from The Sharper Image—such were the trappings of the unabashed return to career-mindedness and enthusiasm for material possessions. The business world, once derided for its soulless routine, now buzzed with a sense of adventure. *Iacocca,* the memoirs of Chrysler's charismatic CEO, was the top-selling nonfiction book of 1984, while the exploits of corporate raiders on Wall Street and millionaire nerds in Silicon Valley alternately outraged and inspired—but never bored. And on television, *Dallas* and *Dynasty* stoked the nation's passion for glamour and glitz.

The patriotic fervor rekindled during the eighties was on prominent display in the 1984 release of Lee Greenwood's cornball anthem "God Bless the USA." The song only reached number seven on the country charts, but went on to gain a kind of immortality as a ritual chest thumper and tearjerker. In June that year, the fortieth anniversary of D-Day occasioned an outpouring of national pride that prior anniversaries had failed to elicit, highlighted by President Reagan's moving tribute to the now-gray-haired "boys of Pointe du Hoc." And the corporate-sponsored Olympic Games later that summer in Los Angeles featured an orgy of flag-waving as American athletes dominated in the absence of Soviet competition.

The "Morning in America" ads got one thing right: the country certainly had changed. And, in important respects, the change was for the good. At any rate, majorities in 49 of 50 states thought so when they gave Ronald Reagan a landslide reelection victory that November. But developments in the realm of freedom were far too messy and complicated to follow anybody's campaign script. Safe and reassuring images of old-fashioned, small-town values—cowboys and firemen and morning flag raisings—had little to do with the wrenching restructuring that American capitalism was undergoing. Neither did they jibe with the realities of contemporary culture.

For one thing, the newly conservative temper did not extend to matters of public decorum. On the contrary, the ongoing sexualization of pop culture proceeded apace. In September 1984, a then-obscure pop singer known simply as Madonna demonstrated her genius for mediagenic controversy during the inaugural MTV Video Music Awards show. Decked out in a combination bustier/wedding dress to perform the not-yet-released "Like a Virgin," she crawled and rolled and writhed her way through the number in simulated orgasmic abandon. The song went on to become Madonna's first number one single. This was also a big year for another one-named, sex-obsessed pop star, as Prince's *Purple Rain* film and sound track achieved a smashing success. One song on the album, "Darling Nikki," was lascivious enough ("I knew a girl named Nikki / I guess u could say she was a sex fiend / I met her in a hotel lobby / Masturbating with a magazine") to inspire Tipper Gore's campaign against naughty song lyrics. The sober efforts of the Parents Music Resource Center notwithstanding, *Purple Rain* went on to earn $68 million at the box office and sell 13 million records.

Considerably more troubling, the social pathologies of the underclass continued to fester. The violent crime rate in 1984 was down 10 percent from 1980, but still over two-and-a-half times higher than back in 1965. And over the following seven years, the frequency of violent crime would climb another 40 percent. The proportion of black babies born to unmarried mothers edged steadily upward, from 55 percent in 1980 to 59 percent in 1984. A decade later, the figure would top 70 percent. Meanwhile, a new symptom of social dysfunction gained public attention during the eighties: homelessness. Here was another unhappy legacy of the sixties, as an admirable if naïve solicitude for civil liberties led to deinstitutionalization of the mentally ill as well as new constitutional restrictions on vagrancy, loitering, and panhandling laws. As a consequence, street people and beggars became a distressingly common sight in the nation's cities.

Although the economy was booming in 1984, parts of the country could be excused for not noticing. In particular, America's industrial heartland had acquired a new nickname: the Rust Belt. Unemployment for blue-collar workers now stood at 11.5 percent, or half again the overall jobless rate. The figure would have been higher still, but for an exodus out of the battered factory towns of the Midwest in search of opportunities elsewhere. Between 1980 and 1984, the population of Flint, Michigan, fell by 6.6 percent; Youngstown, Ohio, 6.5 percent; Gary, Indiana, 5.8 percent, Pittsburgh, 5.0 percent; and Detroit, a whopping 9.5 percent. Overall, net migration out of Ohio, Indiana, Illinois, Michigan, and Pennsylvania topped 1.3 million during those four years.

The Rust Belt's distress reflected not just the cyclical pain of the recent, harsh recession, but also deeper, structural changes. Many of America's great industries were flailing in the face of foreign, and especially Japanese, competition. The share of the U.S. automobile market claimed by Japanese imports rocketed from 12 percent in 1975 to 27 percent five years later. In 1980, the "Big Three" American carmakers suffered a combined loss of $4 billion; layoffs of autoworkers topped 210,000 by year's end. In April of the next year, Japan was forced into a "voluntary restraint agreement" to limit its car exports to the United States. By 1984, a similar agreement was shielding American steel producers from a host of foreign competitors after import market share exceeded 25 percent. The year before, Harley-Davidson, the last American motorcycle maker, was rescued from the brink of bankruptcy by the imposition of import quotas. Japan was now dominant in consumer electronics: virtually all U.S. companies had exited color television production, and no American company was serving the fast-growing demand for videocassette recorders despite the fact that the VCR was invented here. Intel, which invented the DRAM memory chip in 1971, gave up on the business at the end of 1984 because it couldn't match the prices of its Japanese rivals.

Many observers, particularly those unsympathetic to Ronald Reagan's conservatism, believed that the turmoil in manufacturing portended some general economic disaster. "Deindustrialization" and the "disappearance of the middle class" were common diagnoses at the time. Such gloom and doom mistook metamorphosis for decline. In truth, the American economy was in the midst of a deep-seated restructuring that would raise productivity and overall living standards to new highs—and would, at the same time, render the small-town stability and simplicity celebrated in the "Morning in America" ads an ever more distant and irrelevant memory.

Unlike the postwar boom's general prosperity, the economic takeoff that began in the eighties was rather more selective in bestowing its blessings. Consider this assessment by the economist Richard McKenzie: "No one disputes the fact that during the 1970s and 1980s the incomes of many Americans floundered, even declined, nor that the rise in people's incomes was significantly slowed by historic standards. . . . Single parents and people with very limited education were especially hard hit. Union workers . . . frequently lost their protected bargaining positions due to growing domestic and international competition. As a consequence, many workers' real incomes sank, forcing their spouses to enter the labor force to maintain or improve their families' economic status."[2] That such a sobering analysis could appear in a book entitled *What Went Right in the 1980s* is telling, indeed. In the new economy that was struggling to be born, the class divisions aggravated during the sixties and seventies would be deepened still further.

In Ronald Reagan's America, the Aquarian awakening met its nemesis—a popular and well-organized conservative movement, dedicated to the proposition that the countercultural impulse had been an unmitigated moral disaster. By the 1980s, that movement had achieved considerable success, decisively realigning the political balance of power and exerting a weighty influence on the broader culture. The conservative movement, or the New Right as it was called at the time, drew inspiration and energy from another, very different religious awakening— the evangelical revival. From the revival of literalist Protestantism, opposition to the postwar liberal ascendancy gained a critical bloc of fervent supporters. The proselytizing passion of the evangelicals eventually translated into bold and innovative political activism; their ecumenical spirit led them to reach out and make common cause with tradition-minded Catholics and Jews. Thus were the antinomian excesses of the countercultural left countered with the dogmatic excesses of the religious right.

As liberal dominance was shaken by successive blows of social and economic turmoil, the New Right seized the opening and established conservatism as the country's most popular political creed. The conservative triumph, however, was steeped in irony. Capitalism's vigor was restored, and the radical assault on middle-class values was repulsed. But contrary to the hopes of the New Right's traditionalist partisans, shoring up the institutions of mass affluence did not, and could not, bring back the old cultural certainties. Instead, a reinvigorated capitalism brought with it a blooming, buzzing economic and cultural ferment that bore scant resemblance to any nostalgic vision of the good old days. Here, then, was conservatism's curious accomplishment: by marching under the banner of old-time religion, it made the world safe for the secular, hedonistic values of Aquarius.

AT THE TIME, Barry Goldwater's 1964 run for the White House seemed more like an extended, excruciating pratfall. After grabbing his party's nomination in a brilliantly organized grassroots campaign, "Mr. Conservative" found himself vilified and demonized, not only by liberals, but by the Republican establishment as well. "When in all our history," asked the eminent historian Richard Hoftstadter, "has anyone with ideas so bizarre, so archaic, so self-confounding, so remote from the basic American consensus, ever gotten so far?"[3] Reacting to Goldwater's acceptance speech at the GOP convention, notorious for the line that "extremism in the defense of liberty is no vice," California governor Edmund "Pat" Brown declared that he smelled the "stench of fascism."[4] Meanwhile, Goldwater's chief rival for the Republican nomination, New York governor Nelson Rockefeller, charged that his party was "in real danger of subversion by a radical, well-financed and highly disciplined minority."[5] And the *Saturday Evening Post,* normally solidly in the Republican column, could not stomach this nominee. "Goldwater is a grotesque burlesque of the conservative he pretends to be," sniffed a magazine editorial. "He is a wild man, a stray, an unprincipled and ruthless jujitsu artist like Joe McCarthy."[6]

The prickly Arizona senator responded by thumbing his nose at his detractors—and occasionally his supporters as well. He began speeches by naming people he didn't want to vote for him, including all "the lazy, dole-happy people who want to feed on the fruits of somebody else's labor."[7] He denounced the War on Poverty as "plainly and simply a war on your pocketbooks" in depressed West Virginia. He spoke out against cotton subsidies in North Carolina and Tennessee. And he warned that America's cities were being overrun with crime in sleepy, white-haired St. Petersburg. When an audience in Charlotte seemed unresponsive to his talk on the virtues of limited government, he turned on them. "There have been wealthy *slaves!*" he growled. "You can find justice in a *prison.*"[8]

The final result, in any event, had been all but predetermined nearly a year before Election Day, when John F. Kennedy was assassinated in Dallas. Whether Goldwater could have unseated JFK is doubtful, but defeating the memory of the fallen young leader would have taken a miracle. All the same, the scale of Lyndon Johnson's reelection victory was staggering. Johnson took 61 percent of the popular vote, eclipsing Roosevelt's 1936 demolition of Alf Landon as the greatest landslide in American history. In the Electoral College, Goldwater managed to win only six states—his native Arizona, and five Deep South states roiled by passage that year of the Civil Rights Act (which Goldwater had opposed). The debacle extended to congressional races, as Senate Democrats moved to a two-to-one advantage over Republicans while their colleagues in the House won the biggest Democratic majority since 1936. Eighteen of the 54 congressmen who officially endorsed Goldwater prior to his nomination went down to defeat.[9]

As a bid for power, the Goldwater candidacy was an abject failure. It was, however, a sign of things to come. For all the ham-handedness of his general election campaign, Barry Goldwater had succeeded in transforming scattered discontents with the liberal consensus into a coherent, unified, well-organized, national movement. In the 1960 election, Richard Nixon had received campaign contributions from 40,000 to 50,000 individual donors, while John F. Kennedy had relied on a donor base half that size. By comparison, Barry Goldwater received some 650,000 individual contributions. As New Right direct-mail guru Richard Viguerie noted, "[T]he Goldwater campaign was the first mass campaign in modern American history in terms of the number of people involved. An estimated four million men and women took an *active* part in the campaign, contacting many millions more."[10]

"The right-wing enthusiasts were justified, I believe, in the elation they expressed, even in defeat, over the Goldwater campaign," wrote Richard Hofstadter after the election, notwithstanding his own incredulous contempt for those enthusiasts and their leader. "They had less than nothing to show in practical results, but it is not practical results that they look for. They have demonstrated that the right wing is a formidable force in our politics and have given us reason to think that it is a permanent force."[11] As Hofstadter recognized, the conservative movement had now gained the national stage as the dominant faction within one of the country's great political parties. In subseqent years, it would build on that achievement with eminently practical results.

But before conservatism could win and exercise real power, the times would have to change and conservatism would have to change with them. Fulfilling those preconditions would not take long. Even as Goldwater was staggering toward humiliating defeat, the necessary changes were already under way. As the Aquarian awakening stirred and shook the country, only to be followed by a series of economic convulsions, the appeal of conservatism's incongruous mix of traditionalist and libertarian elements soon broadened rapidly. And the specific ingredients of that mix were reformulated to maximize its growing popularity.

Goldwater's brand of conservatism was the political expression of the rise of the Sunbelt. Over the course of the forties and fifties, the South and the West had experienced dramatic gains in population and income as those regions played catch-up with the nation's more advanced and densely settled industrial core. That economic takeoff, in turn, powered a revival of the old-time Protestant bourgeois ethos—no longer socially or culturally dominant, but now reasserting itself as a right-wing protest against the reigning, East Coast liberal establishment. The postwar Sunbelt right dreamed of nothing less than a restoration of the ancien régime—a wholesale repeal of the New Deal welfare and regulatory state, and a rejection of other-directed permissiveness and pluralism. Against that dream, it juxtaposed a nightmare alternative: communist infiltration and domination. By the lights of the passionate and sometimes paranoid anticommunism that served as the nascent movement's chief organizing principle, the New Deal was the first, large step down the slippery slope toward totalitarianism, while moral laxity was a communist plot to sap the country's capacity for self-defense.

Starting with an effort to draft him for the 1960 nomination, Barry Goldwater served as the standard-bearer for the Sunbelt bourgeois insurgency. Four years later, he and his army of "little old ladies in tennis shoes" succeeded in taking control of the Republican Party. At his moment of triumph, accepting his party's nomination at San Francisco's Cow Palace, Goldwater presented the ideology of the movement he led in blunt, unyielding terms. "The good Lord raised this mighty Republic to be a home for the brave and to flourish as the land of the free—not to stagnate in the swampland of collectivism, not to cringe before the bully of communism," he declared. "Now, my fellow Americans, the tide has been running against freedom. Our people have followed false prophets. We must, and we shall, return to proven ways—not because they are old, but because they are true."

According to Goldwater, the steady expansion of government power and unsettling signs of social decay were inextricably interrelated. "Rather than useful jobs in our country, people have been offered bureaucratic 'make work,' rather than moral leadership, they have been given bread and circuses, spectacles, and, yes, they have even been given scandals," he said. "Tonight there is violence in our streets, corruption in our highest offices, aimlessness among our youth, anxiety among our elders, and there is a virtual despair among the many who look beyond material success for the inner meaning of their lives." Turning to the international scene, Goldwater blasted the weakness of the Johnson administration, "which seems eager to deal with communism in every coin known—from gold to wheat, from consulates to confidence, and even human freedom itself." Rejecting anything that hinted of appeasement, he declared forthrightly that "we brand communism as the principal disturber of the peace today. . . . We here in America can keep the peace only if we remain vigilant and only if we remain strong."

With unrivalled prosperity at home and Cold War tensions diminishing abroad, Goldwater's jeremiad thrilled true believers but failed to connect with the great American center. The nucleus of today's conservative ascendancy had been created, but critical elements of the current coalition were missing. All told, in light of the domestic and international situation at the time, the numerous blunders of the Goldwater campaign, and the unmitigated savagery of the establishment's attacks on it, it is remarkable that two-fifths of the electorate voted for such an ideologically polarizing candidate. But for conservatism to rise higher, liberalism would have to stumble. And, of course, it soon did precisely that—badly and repeatedly.

THE NEW DEAL liberal order was, at bottom, a peace settlement. Its signal achievement was to broker an end to the bitter class conflicts that had raged during the rocky transition from scarcity to mass affluence. According to the settlement's basic terms, the capitalist system of private enterprise would be maintained, but in modified form. Government spending for public works and services increased dramatically; safety nets were erected to limit the hardships of the needy and jobless; regulatory protection against physical harm and fraud was shifted from courts to administrative agencies. And at the same time, the creative but unruly forces of competition in product, labor, and capital markets were stifled by a host of new restrictions.

Supporting this peace deal was a large and diverse coalition of interests, anchored by the working classes and led by an intellectual elite that was ideologically committed to government activism. But by the middle of the 1960s, a rift had opened up between the liberal elite and the working-class rank and file. A mere four years after LBJ's landslide win, that rift would leave the New Deal coalition in ruins. It would never be reassembled.

What happened? In short, the end of ideology got boring. After the bland, centrist politics of the fifties, the rising generation of the liberal elite grew restive, as quietly managing the New Deal order's sprawling technocratic apparatus failed to provide a sufficient challenge. Armed with vast government powers, blessed with unprecedented prosperity, and heady with ambition as the boom in college education swelled their ranks, liberals yearned for new causes and new victories. Which is to say, they sought to bring liberalism into the post-scarcity era. Lyndon Johnson, never really accepted by new-style liberals as one of their own, nonetheless gave voice to their Maslovian aspirations. "We're only at the beginning of the road to the Great Society . . . ," he said in his 1965 State of the Union address. "Ahead now is a summit where freedom from the wants of the body can help fulfill the needs of the spirit." [12]

In the new era, the interests of the white working classes no longer seemed a pressing concern. Factory workers, far from oppressed, were now enjoying middle-class incomes and moving to the suburbs. Labor unions, once romantic underdogs, had become large and powerful. And so, as the sixties dawned, twentieth-century liberalism's fundamental passion—to use the agencies of the state in support of social equality—redirected its ardor to needier and more appealing objects.

The civil rights movement, of course, was enthusiastically embraced by idealistic young liberals. And with the 1962 publication of Michael Harrington's *The Other America,* eliminating the nation's remaining "pockets of poverty" captured the liberal imagination. Disaffected from its elders' Cold War commitments, growing numbers of the new generation took to campaigning for nuclear disarmament and adopting a posture of "anti-anti-communism." As the decade progressed, support for civil rights and alleviating poverty fused into a preoccupation with solving the crisis of urban unrest, while the stalemate in Vietnam and the agonies of domestic antiwar protest sealed the demise of Cold War liberalism. At the same time, with the country convulsed by radical political and cultural dissent, safeguarding civil liberties took on a new urgency.

Moving into the seventies, feminism and environmentalism assumed their places as pillars of the reconstituted liberal program. Interestingly, in prior decades, both of those causes had been associated with the upper middle class, and thus with Republican Party conservatism. The Equal Rights Amendment was first proposed in Congress back in 1923 by Senator Charles Curtis and Representative Daniel R. Anthony Jr., two Republicans from Kansas. And in 1940, the GOP was the first major party to include support for the ERA in its party platform. Theodore Roosevelt's role in promoting the conservation movement is well known, but as recently as 1964, the Wilderness Act passed that year was cosponsored by Representative John Saylor, a staunchly anticommunist Republican from Pennsylvania.

The changing agenda of the liberal elite was taking on an increasingly Aquarian cast. Or, to put it another way, the triumph over scarcity shifted the primary focus of liberal egalitarianism from lack of material resources to lack of cultural acceptance. When most people were poor, and many desperately so, the great invidious distinction was between the haves and the have-nots, and liberals cast their lot with the latter. But with the arrival of widespread prosperity, liberal sympathies were redirected to the grievances of "belong-nots"—various groups of dissidents and outsiders that challenged or were excluded from America's cultural mainstream. Thus the increased attention to discrimination against blacks and women, harsh treatment of suspects and criminals, the problems of American Indians and migrant workers, and restraints on free speech and cultural expression. Even the long-standing liberal concern for the poor now gave greater emphasis to the stigma and sense of exclusion associated with poverty.

Post-scarcity liberalism was not content just to champion the needs of marginalized Americans. Fear that domestic inequalities were being replicated on the world stage fed the growing discomfort with American "imperialism" and its real and imagined depredations against the yellow, brown, and black peoples of the Third World. And, without stretching overly much, the embrace of environmentalism could be seen as a call for better treatment of an excluded "other"—in this case, the natural world.

The upshot of all this was that liberal policies and priorities lost touch with, and indeed grew increasingly antagonistic toward, the culture and values of the vast bulk of the American population—the constituency that as a result of this conflict came to be known as the Silent Majority or Middle America. When its egalitarianism challenged the *economic* status quo, liberalism had been a majoritarian creed, standing with the masses against the privileged few. Now, however, when it challenged instead the *cultural* status quo, liberalism put itself at odds with majoritarian sentiment. And when the tumult of the sixties led many to feel that their culture and values were under attack, the conditions were ripe for a swing toward conservatism.

California was a bellwether. In 1964, the state went heavily against Goldwater, 59 to 41 percent. In Orange County, a bastion of the Sunbelt restorationist insurgency, Goldwater carried 65 percent of the vote, but his fierce, unbending conservatism was just too much for nonideological middle- and working-class voters elsewhere in the state. They were too comfortable, and too optimistic, to think that any drastic change in leadership was needed. But that placid complacency would not last much longer. Beginning with the flare-up of the Free Speech Movement scarcely a month before the '64 election, Berkeley quickly became synonymous with student radicalism and antiwar protest. Watts went up in flames the following August. In September 1965, César Chávez and his National Farm Workers Association launched a contentious and widely publicized strike against grape growers in the Central Valley. And by 1966, the Bay Area hippie phenomenon was becoming increasingly conspicuous.

Consequently, in the governor's race of 1966, the electorate's mood was dramatically different than it had been just two years before. Taking full advantage of the mounting anxiety was political neophyte Ronald Reagan, catapulted into a new career by his impassioned, nationally televised speech in the waning days of the Goldwater campaign. "Not one in ten thousand takes the Reagan movement seriously," boasted California Democratic assemblyman Bill Bagley. "The Reagan movement is a remnant of the Goldwater movement. How in the Devil can a remnant expect to win an election?"[13] The oblivious Mr. Bagley failed to grasp that with every disturbance, with every new symptom of social disarray, the right-wing core that had supported Goldwater picked up additional converts and allies. On November 8, 1966, the newly created conservative majority gave Reagan a million-vote victory over incumbent Pat Brown.

Though detractors denigrated the former actor as a mere puppet of the Goldwaterite "radical right," Reagan skillfully softened the conservative message to broaden its appeal. Eager to avoid the intraparty rancor that had cost the GOP so dearly in '64, Reagan declared himself a believer in the 11th Commandment ("Thou shall not speak ill of any fellow Republican"). And he gamely reached out to Democrats and independents as well. Instead of launching another frontal assault on the New Deal, Reagan cheerfully admitted to having strongly supported both Roosevelt and Truman. Disavowing Goldwater's antiunion rhetoric, he cited his experience in the labor movement as president of the Screen Actors Guild and actively courted the blue-collar vote.

When Reagan chose to make his stand, he did so on the rock-solid ground of Middle American values. "Morality is the main issue of the campaign," he said on the campaign trail, "and the main focus of this issue is student conduct at Berkeley."[14] Once in office, he reveled in bashing student radicals and hippies (he once defined the latter as someone who "dresses like Tarzan, has hair like Jane, and smells like Cheetah").[15] "If it takes a blood-bath to silence the demonstrators," he vowed, "let's get it over with." On law-and-order issues generally, Reagan was unwavering in his support of the police. "For all our science and sophistication, for all our justified pride in intellectual accomplishment, the jungle is waiting to take over," stated an administration report. "The man with the badge helps to hold it back."[16] Here was a root-and-branch rejection of Aquarian romanticism, and Main Street loved it.

Reagan's victory in 1966 was only the most dramatic advance in a wider Sunbelt uprising. Claude Kirk became Florida's first GOP governor since Reconstruction, John Tower was the first Republican ever to win a full Senate term from Texas, Strom Thurmond won reelection to the Senate for the first time as a Republican, and Oklahoma and New Mexico elected their second and third GOP governors in history, respectively. Goldwater had engineered a conservative takeover of the Republican Party, but now conservative Republicans were actually winning.

Two years later, political realignment broke out of the Sunbelt and occurred nationwide. The year 1968 was an annus horribilis, for the country and liberalism alike. The Tet offensive and the end of hopes for victory in Vietnam, LBJ's decision not to seek reelection, the assassinations of King and Robert Kennedy, rioting in over a hundred cities in the wake of King's death, chaos and carnage in Chicago at the Democratic convention—the Great Society was falling apart. Indeed, society itself seemed to be falling apart. Post-scarcity liberalism had dreamed of promoting ever greater inclusiveness and open-mindedness, but it proved incapable of defending the social institutions that make those dreams of inclusiveness and open-mindedness achievable.

In the presidential election campaign that fall, the Democratic nominee, Vice President Hubert Humphrey, personified liberalism's agonies. Unfailingly decent, unquestionably well-meaning, Humphrey was trapped in a mind-set that made restoration of order, and the nation's confidence, impossible. In a telling comment about his Republican rival, Humphrey said, "For every jail Mr. Nixon wants to build, I'd like to build a house for a family. And for every policeman he wants to hire I'd like to hire another good teacher. It isn't either-or, it's both." [17] It would be hard to imagine a more fundamental failure to grasp the public mood. And so, four years after LBJ won a record-breaking 61 percent of the vote, Humphrey went down to defeat with under 43 percent.

The nearly 20-point swing in election results reflected deeper changes within the body politic. In 1963, according to a Gallup poll, 49 percent of Americans considered themselves liberal, edging out the 46 percent who claimed the conservative label. By 1969, self-identified conservatives had climbed to 51 percent, while the number of liberals plummeted to 33 percent. Rallying to the defense of embattled traditional values, Americans underwent an ideological realignment. That shift, in turn, was amplified by political realignment, as southern conservatives began leaving the Democratic Party for the more ideologically congenial GOP.

The rejection of the liberal ascendancy brought together not just Sunbelt Protestants, but northern and midwestern Catholics as well. Not just middle-class suburbanites and office workers, but also small-town and rural residents in addition to blue-collar workers and ethnic urban villagers. And what did the combination of all these disparate groups produce? Not just a genuine conservatism that sought to preserve a usable heritage in the face of inevitable change, but a marriage of convenience between that conservatism and the forces of blind reaction.

In particular, the growth of the New Right owed much to the rise in conservative and reactionary sentiment among the white working classes. Like the more tradition-minded members of the middle classes, rural southerners and blue-collar ethnics were aghast at new-style liberalism's disaffection from the work ethic, patriotism, and traditional religion. For working-class Americans, however, horror was mixed with a fair dose of resentment. What, after all, was the chief source of all the cultural tumult? The universities, which also conferred the degrees that were fast becoming the most important status marker in American society—a marker, of course, that members of the working classes conspicuously lacked. Meanwhile, liberalism's shift of sympathies to the most disadvantaged, and blacks in particular, was a bitter pill for working-class whites to swallow. First, there was the sense of betrayal: once their interests had been at the center of liberal concern, but now they felt thrown over and discarded. Next, there was status anxiety: as blacks advanced, the relative social position of working-class whites deteriorated. And for big-city urban villagers, the pain of wounded pride was compounded by much more tangible grievances. Open-housing laws broke up their tight-knit ethnic enclaves—and exposed them to rising crime and disorder. Forced busing further disrupted community life. And affirmative-action preferences expanded opportunities for blacks, but did so at the expense of blue-collar whites.

In the 1968 presidential campaign, the backlash of working-class whites against the liberal elite achieved heated, hysterical expression in the third-party candidacy of George Wallace. Alabama's former governor had made his name as a segregationist demagogue, but after the fall of Jim Crow, he found new life as the voice of a more general populist revolt. Running as the nominee of the newly created American Independent Party, Wallace jabbed incessantly at two hot buttons: resentment and fear.

"We are going to show them in November," he snarled, "that the average American is sick and tired of all those over-educated Ivory-tower folks with pointed heads looking down their noses at us." [18] Among his favorite targets: bureaucrats that "don't have enough sense to know how to get out of the bed in the morning," professors "who can't even park a bicycle straight," and student protesters who "take their tactics from Gandhi and money from Daddy." [19]

Wallace played the law-and-order card for all it was worth. As riots rocked Washington, Wallace called the nation's capital "a jungle . . . where you can't walk safely with your wife and children in the shadow of the White House." [20] When protesters lay down in front of LBJ's motorcade, he vowed that if something similar happened to him "that's going to be the last automobile they lie down in front of." [21] "I don't see how the police restrain themselves as much as they do," he offered at a rally in Cleveland. "If they could run this country for about two years," he said on other occasions, "they'd straighten it out." [22] Hecklers were a regular feature at Wallace events, and scuffles broke out frequently. Wallace, a former Golden Gloves boxer, reveled in the riotous atmosphere. "That's all right," he said to students who tried to shout him down in Grand Rapids, "because you've gotten me a half million votes here today." [23] "A good crease in the skull would stop this," he cracked during another disturbance. Violence and violent emotions were mother's milk for the Wallace campaign.

In late September, Wallace was running above 20 percent in public opinion polls. Humphrey, at 28 percent, was struggling to stay in second place. In the final weeks of the campaign, however, about a third of Wallace's support melted away, as many traditional Democrats returned to Humphrey in the end. Richard Nixon, running on what was effectively a modulated version of the Wallace message, came away with a narrow victory. "In a time when the national focus is concentrated upon the unemployed, the impoverished and the dispossessed," Nixon proclaimed at the Republican convention in Miami, "the working

Americans have become the forgotten Americans. In a time when the national rostrums and forums are given over to shouters and protestors and demonstrators, they have become the silent Americans. Yet they have a legitimate grievance that should be rectified and a just cause that should prevail."[24] Positioning himself between Humphrey's feckless liberalism and Wallace's rabid reaction, Nixon managed to augment support from traditional Republican business elites with enough of the Middle American vote to come out on top.

Once in office, Nixon was intent on consolidating the new conservative majority within the GOP. Central to his hopes was what he referred to as the "constituency of uneducated people." "In this period of our history, the leaders and the educated class are decadent . . . ," Nixon explained to his aide H. R. "Bob" Haldeman (who then recorded his boss's analysis in his diary). "When you have to call on the nation to be strong—on such things as drugs, crime, defense . . . the educated people and the leader class no longer have any character and you can't count on them. We can only turn for support to the noneducated people."[25]

Rallying Middle America against the liberal elite came naturally to Nixon. For him it wasn't just politics; it was personal. A graduate of tiny Whittier College and brand-new Duke Law School, Nixon dreamed of landing a position with a silk-stocking Wall Street law firm—only to suffer one humiliating rejection after another when he interviewed for jobs. Blocked from joining the eastern establishment, he returned to California and worked at a small-town Orange County law office before serving in World War II and then launching his political career. No matter how high he rose, Nixon continued to nurse a grudge against the East Coast's Ivy League aristocracy. Marrying his own brooding resentment to a canny reading of the political scene, Richard Nixon plotted the ultimate revenge. He would replace FDR's crumbling coalition with one of his own devising; thus securing his position at home, he would then remake world politics by playing the Soviets and the Chinese against each other. And maybe best of all, on his way to historical greatness he would humble the elites that excluded him by turning the masses against them.

In the end, these grandiose schemes fell victim to their architect's vindictiveness and paranoia. Plans for a "New Majority" and a new architecture of world peace collapsed in the moral squalor of Watergate, and Nixon himself was hounded from office in disgrace. Both the Republican Party and the conservative movement generally were badly, if temporarily, wounded as a result. In the 1974 congressional elections, Democrats picked up 48 seats in the House to gain a two-thirds majority, while a gain of four seats in the Senate gave the Democrats a three-fifths majority in the upper chamber. By 1975, the number of Americans who identified themselves as Republican had fallen to 21 percent, down nine percentage points from when Nixon was first inaugurated. Over the same period, those identifying themselves as conservatives dropped from 51 percent to 36 percent.[26]

Notwithstanding Nixon's crack-up, liberals proved incapable of rebuilding a governing consensus under their leadership. After the debacle of 1968, left-leaning supporters of a "New Politics" recognized that the New Deal coalition had broken up—and their response was a hearty good riddance. Liberated from their embarrassing dependence on the racist South, disenchanted with blue-collar ethnic whites, new-style liberals sought to construct their own coalition of blacks, feminists, the young, and college-educated suburbanites. Pursuing "the Catholic vote," according to Democratic strategist Fred Dutton, who served as Robert Kennedy's campaign manager, was no longer in the "party's political self-interest." "The net effect of these groups in relation to the dynamic of social change has become vastly different from thirty or sixty years ago," he wrote. "Then they were a wellspring of cultural diversity and political change; now they constitute an important bastion of opposition. They have tended, in fact, to become a major redoubt of traditional Americanism and of the antinegro, antiyouth vote."[27]

The McGovern Commission on reforming the Democratic Party's nominating process gave "New Politics" partisans their chance. Created to avoid any repetition of the bitter infighting of 1968, the commission ended up as a vehicle for Aquarian liberals to wrest control of the party from the old bulls and remake it in their own image. First, they boosted the role of primaries in delegate selection, thus cutting the percentage of delegates chosen by party bosses from 58 percent in 1968 to 40 percent four years later—and increasing the clout of the activists and the well educated, who tend to vote in primaries. Furthermore, under a new guideline backed by commission member Fred Dutton, state parties now had to give delegate slots to young people and women in "reasonable relationship" to their proportions in the state's general population. As a result, women made up 40 percent of the delegates at the 1972 Democratic convention, while young people constituted 21 percent—up from 13 and 4 percent, respectively, in 1968.

The commission chaired by George McGovern in 1969 led directly to a party headed by George McGovern in 1972. The Democratic convention in Miami, bragged commission staffer Ken Bode, "will be the most representative group ever gathered in one spot in our party's history." But representative of what? Surveying the other members of the California delegation, the actress Shirley MacLaine exulted that they looked "like a couple of high schools, a grape boycott, a Black Panther rally, and four or five politicians who walked in the wrong door."[28] Alas, the New Politics flopped ingloriously that November. Even without the complication of a significant third-party candidacy, Senator McGovern won less than 38 percent of the vote—five points below Humphrey's total.

Despite the embarrassing setback, Aquarian liberals hung on, and even flourished, as the Democratic Party's dominant faction. The new-style liberal coalition was large enough in parts of the country—the Northeast, the Pacific Coast, big cities of the Midwest, and heavily black areas of the South—to support a sizeable political class of mayors, state legislators, governors, and members of Congress. But at the national level, the reformulated liberal ideology was a minority taste. Even in 1975, when the opposing side was at a low ebb, only 27 percent of Americans described themselves as liberal—dropping another six points from 1969, and barely more than half the figure when JFK was president. Consequently, no national majority organized under self-consciously liberal leadership ever emerged again.

In 1976, a Democrat did succeed in retaking the White House, but Jimmy Carter was no Aquarian liberal. A Georgia peanut farmer and self-described born-again Christian, Carter assiduously courted the middle- and working-class voters of the Silent Majority. He pledged to ensure "that any decision our government makes is designed to honor and support and strengthen the American family"; he promised assistance to families that sent their children to parochial and other private schools; he even defended the "ethnic purity" of big-city, blue-collar neighborhoods.[29] Such appeals allowed him to win a narrow victory— once. But a rising conservative tide, swelled this time by economic distress, would sweep the conflicted and ineffective centrist from office after a single, disappointing term.

Between Goldwater's defeat and Carter's victory, a powerful backlash brought the conservative movement to political preeminence. From its Sunbelt base of bourgeois restorationists, the movement grew by attracting new constituencies among the middle and working classes—groups that had been content with the old postwar liberal consensus but now were alarmed by cultural upheaval and social disorder. Liberalism, under savage attack from the countercultural left, was unable or unwilling to defend itself. Instead, it remade itself in the Aquarian image— and, in the process, faltered in defending American society's most fundamental institutions and values. Where liberals abdicated, conservatives stepped in to fill the breach.

Conservatism's waxing strength effected a basic political realignment. In toppling the Great Society, the conservative backlash ruptured the New Deal coalition. Partisan realignment eventuated as well, with the steady diffusion of GOP power throughout the Sunbelt. Liberalism, reoriented to pursuing a post-scarcity agenda, found itself all too frequently at odds with majoritarian values. While liberals retained enormous cultural influence, their political muscle was now greatly reduced. Even after Watergate, when the uncommitted center of the American electorate bulked larger than either ideological flank, it was easier for conservatives to capture that center than it was for liberals. Consequently, even when avowed conservatives did not exercise power, those who did found the size and energy of the political right a powerful constraint on pursuing their own designs.

The rise of conservatism in the late sixties and early seventies was a response to liberation run amok. The response, predictably enough, combined a genuine conservative defense against nihilism with blind, reactionary opposition to liberating change. As the movement confronted the worsening economic climate of the seventies, however, conservatism took its own turn as an agent of liberation. While the New Right's early triumphs were the work of its traditionalist wing, now the libertarian wing began to gain adherents and win victories. With that development, contemporary conservatism came fully into its own: a paradoxical combination of promoting economic innovation while checking the cultural changes brought on by that innovation.

"WE HAVE LEARNED at last to manage a modern economy to assure its continued growth," Richard Nixon stated blandly in his 1969 inaugural address.[30] That single, complacent sentence was the most extensive mention of economic affairs in the whole speech. Despite the fact that he had reached the White House on a wave of resurgent conservatism, Nixon plainly saw no reason to challenge the prevailing liberal assumption of governmental omnicompetence in guiding economic affairs.

Over the course of his presidency, he continued to operate under that assumption even in the face of mounting contradictory evidence. Nixon created the bureaucracies of EPA and OSHA with little attention to the balance of burdens and benefits they caused; used revenue sharing with states and localities to throw money at social problems; okayed a fiscally irresponsible expansion of Social Security benefits; proposed a guaranteed income program without any work requirement; undermined the American-led international trading system by slapping an across-the-board, punitive tariff on imports; and, worst of all, in an egregious and senseless disruption of the competitive-market process, imposed comprehensive wage and price controls that started with a 90-day freeze and then persisted for over two years. For such actions, Richard Nixon has often been called, mischievously but not without justice, America's last liberal president.

In other words, while Nixon built upon the legacy of Goldwater conservatism when it came to defending traditional, mainstream values, he studiously ignored that legacy on the question of economic freedom. In so picking and choosing, Nixon was merely positioning himself in line with prevailing public opinion. Just as most Americans did not feel their values were threatened until there was chaos in the streets, they likewise were unperturbed by the sprawling extent of the regulatory and welfare state until the nation's economic performance began to suffer. And although the latter half of the sixties was bedeviled by a plague of social ills, it was blessed with a sizzling boom. Unemployment averaged only 4.5 percent in 1965, and then fell steadily to 3.5 percent during 1969; between 1964 and 1969, the country's gross national product grew at an average annual rate of 4.5 percent. Under such circumstances, political momentum for a sweeping overhaul of economic policy making was virtually nonexistent.

Yet almost as soon as Nixon entered office, the economic situation began to deteriorate. The dawn of a new decade marked the end of the go-go years, as the nation slipped into recession in 1970. And confounding Keynesian assumptions of an iron trade-off between inflation and unemployment, the rise in consumer prices accelerated to 5.9 percent from 5.4 percent the year before. A combination of deficit spending and profligate monetary expansion by the Federal Reserve revved up markets temporarily and ensured Nixon's reelection, but with the Arab oil embargo in 1973 the economy again faltered, this time badly. The inflation rate soared to 11.0 percent in 1974, while unemployment rose to 5.6 percent. What had begun as a mild, if irritating, cyclical dowturn now emerged as a full-blown, systemic crisis. After a quarter century of postwar prosperity, the economy had contracted the malady that would prove to be managerial liberalism's undoing: stagflation.

"If we are determined not to allow unemployment at any price, and are not willing to use coercion, we shall be driven to . . . a general and considerable inflation."[31] So wrote the economist F. A. Hayek in 1944. The greatest of a small band of dissident, promarket intellectuals, Hayek understood from the start that collectivist suppression of competition, far from the modern and enlightened advance in governance that its many supporters around the world imagined it to be, was in fact a crude and clumsy throwback. Sooner or later, warned Hayek and his colleagues, the limitations of technocratic, top-down control would reveal themselves. In the first decades after World War II, however, as America enjoyed unprecedented economic vitality, such warnings were taken seriously only in certain sections of the business community and among the ranks of free-market ideologues.

For all its real and ultimately terminal weaknesses, the New Deal economic order did boast one great virtue: its mishmash of collectivist and redistributionist improvisations sufficed to pacify the opponents of capitalism. An essential precondition for maintaining and expanding prosperity was thus satisfied. With the ideological struggles of the thirties behind them and a fair degree of industrial peace assured, businesses and investors were emboldened to face the peacetime future with confidence and optimism. Meanwhile, the unique conditions of the postwar years ensured that for a time at least the flaws of the New Deal system would not prevent robust economic growth. The continued spread of mass-production techniques and modern forms of business organization, the emergence for the first time of a truly integrated national market for goods and services, the untapped potential for commercial application of new technologies developed during World War II, and pent-up demand after decades of Depression and wartime rationing—all these factors combined to fuel capitalist wealth creation even in the face of misguided public policies. Furthermore, the American economy looked even stronger than it actually was, since the war's devastation of the rest of the industrialized world temporarily muted the feedback of foreign competition.

By the 1960s, the peculiar circumstances of the early postwar years had run their course. Whereupon Hayek's prophecy—the progressive worsening of inflationary pressures—began to work its inevitable curse. At the root of the problem were the coercive powers conferred upon organized labor. When wage concessions extracted by unions were in line with productivity gains, all was well. But when productivity growth slowed down, wage increases started to run ahead of market-clearing levels. At the same time, increasing imports from Europe and Japan began limiting the ability of businesses to pass along wage hikes in the form of higher prices. All of which threatened an increase in unemployment—the *summum malum* to be avoided however possible. What followed was an increasing resort to artificial stimulus, through expansionary monetary policy as well as increased federal spending (which, in turn, was accommodated by further monetary easing).

The election of John F. Kennedy on a pledge to "get the country moving again" after the 1958 recession inaugurated the inflationary era. Under the baleful influence of new-generation Keynesian economists like Walter Heller and James Tobin, the focus of macroeconomic policy making shifted from staving off depression to "fine tuning" (in Heller's cringe-inducing phrase) the economy in pursuit of maximum growth. Discounting the risks associated with pumping extra money into the economy, Tobin once cracked that the main cost of inflation was the extra shoe leather needed to walk to the bank more frequently. For a few years, the "New Economics" seemed to work masterfully. But then, under the pressure of Lyndon Johnson's spending binge at home and in Vietnam, the rate of inflation began to creep upward. Inflationary expectations set in, so that progressively larger doses of monetary stimulus were needed to keep the economy afloat.

Under Nixon, everything fell apart. Beginning with a policy of "gradualism," the new administration attempted to engineer a gentle disinflation while maintaining something close to full employment (defined arbitrarily as an unemployment rate of 4 percent). By 1971, with both inflation and unemployment still higher than when he took office, Nixon grew increasingly panicky about his reelection prospects. He had always blamed his 1960 loss to Kennedy on the Fed's tight-money policies, and he was determined that history would not repeat itself. And so, in a dramatic about-face, Nixon and Arthur Burns's Fed turned on all the spigots, with tax cuts on the fiscal side combined with a rollicking expansion of the money supply. In August 1971, Nixon stunned the world with his "New Economic Policy" (his advisers somehow missed that Lenin once had his own "NEP"), the centerpiece of which was a wage-and-price freeze, followed by controls, designed to tame inflation. While the NEP accomplished its political objectives—Nixon carried 49 states in 1972—the long-run economic fallout was disastrous. And the long run arrived less than a year after Election Day.

In the dismal crisis of 1974, the Achilles's heel of the New Deal system was at last revealed. Inflation was running out of control. And in a turn of events that the New Economics had deemed impossible, inflation was continuing to climb even as the economy swooned. Just as the liberal political consensus had been shattered by the social unrest of the sixties, now the liberal economic consensus was unraveling in the face of stagflation. It was therefore fitting, and not entirely coincidental, that F. A. Hayek, long a pariah in his profession, was named a winner of the 1974 Nobel Prize for economics.

Some fundamental change in the American economic system

was now unavoidable. "Capitalism is in crisis," Alan Greenspan, at the time chairman of Gerald Ford's Council of Economic Advisers, told Congress. The country, he said, had reached "the point of discontinuity" where business as usual was no longer sustainable.[32] It was imperative that order be restored—but by what means? On the one hand, government could reassert its authority with additional layers of controls, restrictions, and regimentation. Alternatively, government could assume a more modest role and allow market forces to bear greater responsibility for coordinating economic processes.

In the end, it wasn't a close call. As stagflation persisted throughout the seventies, and then dramatically worsened at the end of the decade, defenders of Big Government were badly discredited—much as defenders of small government had been discredited by the Great Depression. Disoriented and in disarray, many on the left simply panicked. In particular, they tended to blame the deteriorating economic situation not on bad policies, but on some unavoidable exhaustion of brighter possibilities. Misinterpreting the oil shocks of 1973 and 1979 as an "energy crisis," and the increased attention to environmental quality as an "ecological crisis," these counselors of despair pronounced that the mass affluence enjoyed for the quarter century after World War II would never return. As the economist Robert Lekachman told the *New York Times* in 1979, "The era of growth is over and the era of limits is upon us."[33] That kind of defeatism was hardly likely to rally the populace to collectivism's banner.

Meanwhile, economic mismanagement delivered only the latest in a series of blows to overall public confidence in government. Vietnam, Watergate, the crime explosion, the failure of the War on Poverty—together with joblessness, gas lines, and the rising cost of living, the cumulative effect was a profound skepticism about government's capacity to deliver on its promises. By 1980, only 25 percent of Americans trusted the federal government to do what is right most or all the time—down from 75 percent in 1964, and 53 percent as recently as 1972.[34] In this environment, there was virtually no chance that the country's economic troubles would create political momentum for further expansion of government powers over the economy. Proposals along those lines were doomed to fall flat.

With the left demoralized and the center disaffected, the libertarian right was poised to make its move. Having warned for decades about the perils of government interventionism, libertarians now tasted one of the sweetest of life's pleasures—the ability to say, "I told you so." And unlike their ideological opponents, they had clear and confidently held ideas about how to restore prosperity. As to subduing inflation, the task was straightforward, if unpleasant. "Inflation is always and everywhere a monetary phenomenon," declared Milton Friedman, leader of the "Chicago School" of free-market economists. Accordingly, to regain price stability it was necessary only to restrain the growth of the money supply. For an economy hooked on inflation, however, such a move was bound to cause a serious slump, and perhaps a prolonged one. How then to combine disinflation with healthy growth? By decollectivizing the economy—removing restrictions on competition and burdens on entrepreneurship, and thereby rendering economic relations more open to innovation and flexible in the face of change.

Deregulation and tax cuts were the tonics needed to restore the economy's lost vigor. In the transportation, energy, financial, and telecommunications sectors, controls on market entry and prices had been in place for decades, ostensibly to remedy "market failures" through enlightened regulatory oversight in the public interest. Over the course of the sixties and seventies, however, economic research spearheaded by the University of Chicago's George Stigler and Richard Posner was making abundantly clear that such controls' connection to the public interest was tenuous at best. All too often, regulatory agencies ended up "captured" by the regulated industries themselves, with the end result that prices and profits were higher than otherwise would have been the case. Swayed by these findings, even some on the left—notably, consumer advocate Ralph Nader and Senator Edward Kennedy—boarded the deregulatory bandwagon.

Tax rates, meanwhile, were a major contributor to stagflation—that is, they provided a critical link between inflation, on the one hand, and anemic growth, on the other. That link took the form of "bracket creep": by raising nominal dollar incomes, inflation was relentlessly pushing people into higher and higher income tax brackets. In 1980, for example, a family of four earning the median annual income of $30,000 faced a marginal tax rate of 28 percent—compared to the 19 percent rate that a median-income family had faced back in 1965. For a family earning double the median income, the marginal rate climbed from 22 percent to 49 percent over the same 15 years.[35] As pointed out by the champions of what became known as "supply-side economics," this punishing, unlegislated tax increase discouraged business creation and labor supply (especially among married women) while encouraging unproductive tax-avoidance schemes. In addition, and of crucial political significance, bracket creep greatly expanded the constituency for the free-market, small-government program.

The implentation of that program, identified most closely with the administration of Ronald Reagan, actually began under Jimmy Carter. (Carter's predecessor, Gerald Ford, also leaned against Nixonian interventionism, but his term in office was too brief and too overwhelmed by Watergate's aftermath to leave much in the way of tangible accomplishments.) On the regulatory front, Carter signed legislation deregulating the airline, trucking, and railroad industries and began the decontrol of oil and natural gas prices as well as bank interest rates. On taxes, he signed (albeit reluctantly) the 1978 Steiger amendment, an early supply-side measure that nearly halved the tax rate on capital gains. And, most fatefully, in July 1979, Carter nominated Paul Volcker as chairman of the Federal Reserve Board. Volcker, a well-known inflation hawk, lived up to his reputation as he proceeded immediately to slam the brakes on growth of the money supply. After just a few years of this unpleasant medicine, the inflationary fever was broken for good.

Despite his contributions to its success, Jimmy Carter had little enthusiasm for the free-market movement. On the contrary, convinced that the world was running out of fossil fuels, he believed that only massive government interventions—"the moral equivalent of war"—could save the American economy from the free market's heedless binging on nonrenewable energy. And when his sweeping energy-policy proposals were whittled away by Congress, Carter came to believe that the energy crisis was in fact a symptom of graver ills in the American body politic.

On July 15, 1979, he addressed the nation to offer his grim diagnosis. "Why have we not been able to get together as a nation to resolve our serious energy problem? It's clear that the true problems of our Nation are much deeper—deeper than gasoline lines or energy shortages, deeper even than inflation and recession." In what came to be known as the "malaise" speech (despite the fact that the word in question was never once used), Carter proclaimed that the country was suffering a "crisis of confidence." "The symptoms of this crisis of the American spirit are all around us. For the first time in the history of our country a majority of our people believe that the next five years will be worse than the past five years. Two-thirds of our people do not even vote. The productivity of American workers is actually dropping, and the willingness of Americans to save for the future has fallen below that of all other people in the Western world. As you know, there is a growing disrespect for government and for churches and for schools, the news media, and other institutions."

Jimmy Carter, like many Americans, thought the country was falling apart. In fact, it was only the New Deal economic order that was collapsing, but Carter was too much a creature of that order to see the distinction. Ronald Reagan, to his credit, saw it plainly. When announcing his presidential candidacy in November 1979, he took direct aim at Carter's limp pessimism. "Our leaders attempt to blame their failures on circumstances beyond their control, on false estimates by unknown, unidentifiable experts who . . . attempt to convince us our high standard of living,

the result of thrift and hard work, is somehow selfish extravagance which we must renounce in sharing scarcity. . . . The crisis
we face is not the result of any failure of the American spirit; it is
a failure of our leaders to establish rational goals and give our
people something to order their lives by."

With Reagan's convincing victory a year later, Americans once
again chose to rest their hopes on the continued elaboration of
the market-based division of labor. In the 1930s, when capitalism appeared to have broken down irreparably, voices on the left
were urging comprehensive central planning for the fulfillment
of basic needs and the steady reduction of paid work. Instead,
the New Deal order preserved the basic capitalist order (with
modifications and distortions, to be sure) and enshrined full employment, not ever shorter hours, as the goal of progressive policy. In the sixties, amidst unparalleled and seemingly automatic
prosperity, the New Left emerged to proclaim, once again, that
enough was enough—that now was the time to turn away from
the mobilization of social energies required by the mass-
consumption economy and move instead toward small-scale
participatory democracy and communal living. Except as a passing media spectacle, however, the revolution never got off the
ground. And now, in the seventies, when stagflation and the
specter of energy and environmental crises put the future of
mass affluence in doubt, the knee-jerk reaction of the left was
again to urge an abandonment of the consumerist ethos and its
reliance on coordination by impersonal market forces—this
time, through the imposition of technocratically managed limits
to growth and mandated acceptance of "small is beautiful" simplicity. And, once more, the American people would have none
of it. "The business of our nation goes forward," Ronald Reagan
announced in his January 1981 inaugural address, reflecting the
renewed popular mandate in favor of mass affluence. "I did not
take the oath I have just taken with the intention of presiding
over the dissolution of the world's strongest economy."

O F   C O U R S E ,   T H E   election of Ronald Reagan was a victory not just for libertarians, but for traditionalists as well. Back in 1966, Reagan had launched his political career by championing embattled Middle American values, and the late seventies provided no shortage of fresh outrages on which he could capitalize. Rising crime, welfare dependency, family breakdown, drugs, pornography—all served as ammunition for Reagan's assault on the Carter record.

Looking beyond domestic troubles, Reagan appealed to another traditional value, patriotism, when he vowed to rebuild America's military might and reassert American power overseas. Here Carter was especially vulnerable. "[W]e are now free of that inordinate fear of Communism which once led us to embrace any dictator who joined us in our fear," Carter had boasted in 1977, as he sought to reorient U.S. foreign policy away from rivalry with the Soviets and toward the general defense of human rights.[36] Noble in conception but at odds with the grim realities of the times, Carter's foreign policy imploded in the waning days of 1979—first, on November 4, when Iranian radicals stormed the U.S. Embassy in Tehran and took 66 Americans as hostages; next, on December 27, when Soviet troops poured into Afghanistan. The hostage crisis dragged on for 444 days and a rescue attempt failed ingloriously; the major U.S. responses to the Soviet invasion, a cutoff of grain sales and a boycott of the Moscow Olympics, were lamely ineffective. What had been touted as idealism now looked like weakness, and Reagan took full advantage. With his optimistic vision of "a city upon a hill," he gave Americans hope that their country's post-Vietnam slide into impotence could somehow be reversed.

Ronald Reagan made special efforts to cultivate a newly assertive traditionalist constituency—the so-called religious right. Since the "Year of the Evangelical" was declared in 1976, the "born-again" phenomenon was now national news. Its most visible manifestation was the growing number of "televangelists," who used their electronic pulpits to create huge nationwide followings. Billy Graham and Oral Roberts had led the way, but now Rex Humbard, Robert Schuller, Jimmy Swaggart, Jerry Falwell, Pat Robertson, and Jim Bakker all enjoyed audiences in the millions. A Gallup poll in the late seventies showed that a quarter of the nation's Protestants were regularly viewing or listening to religious broadcasts. And although many of the TV preachers stuck to purely spiritual themes, others began speaking out on social and political issues. "We have enough votes to run the country," Pat Robertson claimed with characteristic modesty.[37]

In 1976, a majority of white evangelicals had voted for Jimmy Carter as one of their own, but many were keenly disappointed with his failure to advance their agenda. "God, we have got to get this man out of the White House," Tim LaHaye prayed after a disappointing breakfast meeting with Carter that also included Jerry Falwell, Oral Roberts, Rex Humbard, and Jim Bakker. "And little did I know that several others prayed essentially the same prayer . . . ," LaHaye later recalled. "We all had made a commitment to God that day that, for the first time in our lives, we were going to get involved in the political process and do everything we could to wake up the Christians to be participating citizens instead of sitting back and letting other people decide who will be our government leaders."[38]

Republicans welcomed the disaffected with a 1980 GOP platform that supported voluntary prayer in schools and a constitutional amendment outlawing abortion. Reagan himself went even further, opposing the Equal Rights Amendment (about which the party platform was studiously silent) and endorsing the teaching of creationism as well as evolution. He closed his acceptance speech at the GOP convention in Detroit with a call to begin "our crusade" in a moment of silent prayer. And the next month, as the headlining speaker at a major gathering of evangelicals in Dallas, this divorced and remarried former movie actor who rarely attended church won over the crowd instantly with the opening line "I know you can't endorse me, but I want you to know that I endorse you."[39]

Come November, evangelicals did endorse Reagan at the ballot box. An exit poll conducted by CBS and the *New York Times* showed that self-identified "born-again" Christians voted for him over Carter by a margin of 61 percent to 34 percent. Newly formed groups like Christian Voice, the Religious Roundtable, and the Moral Majority campaigned hard on behalf of Reagan and other conservative candidates, using direct mail and a network of evangelical churches to register an estimated two million new voters and get them out to the polls.[40] With Reagan swept into office, and the Senate turned over to Republican control for the first time since 1954, Moral Majority leader Jerry Falwell crowed that the 1980 election was "my finest hour."[41]

The attraction of religiously conservative Protestants to right-wing politics was nothing new, since, from the beginning, they formed the backbone of the bourgeois insurgency out of which the New Right developed. What was novel, though, was political activism as an explicit expression of evangelical identity. Back in 1965, when mixing religion and politics meant civil rights marches, Jerry Falwell thought preachers should stay in their pulpits. "Believing in the Bible as I do, I would find it impossible to stop preaching the pure saving Gospel of Jesus Christ and begin doing anything else," he said to his Lynchburg, Virginia, congregation. "Preachers are not called to be politicians, but to be soul winners."[42] Later, he admitted frankly that such quietism was a "false prophecy." "I never thought the government would go so far afield. . . ," he explained. "Our lack of involvement is probably one of the reasons why the country's in the mess it is in. We have defaulted by failing to show up for the fight."[43]

In the immediate aftermath of the 1980 election, the hyperventilating mass media combined with self-promoting religious leaders to overstate the size, cohesion, and influence of politically organized evangelicalism. A postelection Harris poll supposedly found that followers of television evangelists swung the election—an assessment that Falwell and company were only too happy to second. But the demographic group in question was defined so broadly that the conclusion was essentially meaningless. By contrast, a more sober analysis of the CBS/*New York*

Times exit poll data showed that even if "born again" voters had flipped their allegiances and voted 61 to 34 for Carter instead, Reagan would have won regardless. And for a bit more perspective, consider that in 1972, seven years before the Moral Majority was founded, Richard Nixon carried over 80 percent of the evangelical vote in his rout of George McGovern.[44]

But if the influence of particular leaders and organizations on the religious right has sometimes been exaggerated, it is impossible to overstate the importance of the larger evangelical revival to the rise of the modern conservatism. Simply put, if dogmatic Protestantism had not staged its dramatic and unexpected comeback, the ideological and political realignment that has occurred since the mid-sixties would have been impossible.

The spread of evangelical and especially charismatic Christianity was a genuine religious awakening, a major sociological event. As with most historical phenomena of similar proportion, this one defied easy, black-or-white judgments. The retooled, kinder, gentler form of literalist bourgeois Protestantism answered real needs, and laid the foundation for durable and tight-knit families and communities. It offered impassioned and self-assured defense of socially wholesome values like hope for the future, belief in oneself, and commitment to marriage and family. However, it lent equal passion to upholding a stale, fusty mix of prudishness and intolerance, and pursuing a misguided absolutism on vexing, murky moral issues. And its complex mix of genuine conservatism, individualist libertarianism, and knee-jerk, zealous reaction was rooted in a shamelessly anti-intellectual faith, a lurch away from scientific rationality in favor of dogmatic belief. For good and for ill, this religious awakening asserted itself as an increasingly powerful cultural force, offering a strong and often effective counter to the twin, opposing forces of Aquarian secularism and its fellow traveler, liberal Protestantism.

The evangelical revival ensured that the center of American public opinion remained well to the right of where it otherwise would have drifted. Though conservative Protestants, along with other Americans, changed their views on such matters as race and the role of women outside the home, elsewhere they served as bulwarks of old-fashioned bourgeois morality. On abortion, sex outside of marriage, drugs, and pornography, evangelicals stoutly resisted the Aquarian encouragement of "if it feels good, do it." While defending traditional bourgeois asceticism, they likewise remained true to the bourgeois heritage of rugged individualism. Commitment to the work ethic and the competitive free-enterprise system, suspicion of welfare entitlements and centralized political power, and a strong preference for vigorous law enforcement over social policies designed to address the "root causes" of crime—all reflected the bourgeois ethos of personal responsibility, and all remained noticeably more pronounced within the evangelical camp than outside. Patriotic fervor and a belief in American exceptionalism, other legacies of the country's bygone bourgeois Protestant ascendancy, were also embraced by the born-again movement. For evangelicals, fidelity to these surviving elements of the old bourgeois creed was not simply incidental to religious conviction. Rather, adherence to traditional values was an integral aspect of evangelical identity. Resisting the proliferating temptations of the ambient secular culture was a proof of faith, a sign of the believer's commitment to Christ. Evangelicalism, in effect, consecrated what remained of the bourgeois ethos.

While enshrining social conservatism as unshakeable dogma, evangelicals proved quite flexible on doctrine generally. Cultivation of religious experience, and commitment to building and expanding religious communities, counted for far more than nuances of theology. Here evangelicals distinguished themselves from old-fashioned fundamentalists, and in so doing they transformed conservative Protestantism from an isolated backwater faith into a vital and self-confident movement. Furthermore, the reduced emphasis on doctrine made it possible for evangelicals to see themselves in a common cause with conservative Catholics and Jews against the encroachments of Aquarian "secular humanism." The traditionalist coalition that ruptured the New

Deal political order and spearheaded the nation's ideological re-alignment would not have emerged otherwise.

To grasp the distance traveled by the evangelical movement away from sectarian exclusiveness, consider the reaction of conservative Protestants to John F. Kennedy's 1960 presidential candidacy. Harold John Ockenga, a prominent evangelical minister, warned of the possible "Roman Catholic domination of America" and instructed fellow Protestants not "to aid and abet [that domination] by electing a President who has more power to advance such a goal than any other person." L. Nelson Bell, Billy Graham's father-in-law and executive editor of the flagship evangelical publication, *Christianity Today*, called the Catholic Church "a political system that like an octopus covers the entire world and threatens those basic freedoms and those constitutional rights for which our forefathers died in generations past." Such rhetoric was actually relatively temperate. "I remember being told that this was the last free election that the United States would ever see," recalled a former staffer for Campus Crusade. And according to a former student at Dallas Theological Seminary, a fundamentalist stronghold, "a guy stood up in the chapel and said that John F. Kennedy was 'the Beast' of Revelation, that he was the Antichrist, and under no circumstances could anybody vote for him." Years later, watching Kennedy's funeral, another fellow seminarian "was fairly sure [JFK] would rise out of the coffin and be the Antichrist."[45]

As the evangelical revival expanded, however, it outgrew the separatism of its fundamentalist roots and adopted a more inclusive vision of the Christian community. Billy Graham played a pioneering role. His overriding focus on spreading the Gospel and winning converts led him to stress the common ground among various Christian traditions and de-emphasize minor doctrinal differences. "I am far more tolerant of other kinds of Christians than I once was," Graham noted in a 1978 magazine interview. "My contact with Catholic, Lutheran and other leaders—people far removed from my own Southern Baptist tradition—has helped me, hopefully, to move in the right direction."[46] In particular, Graham came to the conclusion that theologically conservative Christians of whatever stripe had more in common with each other than with theological liberals in their own denominations. As early as 1964, in a televised conversation with Boston's Richard Cardinal Cushing, he stated that he was "much closer to Roman Catholic traditions than to some of the more liberal Protestants."[47]

In addition to blurring religious differences, evangelicals were also learning to work across them. Especially influential was Francis Schaeffer, the staunchly conservative theologian who popularized the concept of "cobelligerency." A strong advocate of greater political activism by evangelicals, particularly on the question of abortion, Schaeffer argued that conservative Protestants and social conservatives from other traditions, while not true allies, were at least "cobelligerents" in the struggle against "secular humanism." Theological differences, he insisted, should not preclude concerted action in defense of shared moral principles. "If I live in a suburb," he wrote, "and suddenly the sewer system begins to back up into the water system and all my neighbors are atheists, it does not mean we cannot sign a petition together or go to the city council or the mayor, to say we want our water system fixed. I do not have to wait for them to become Christians to do that. It is the same in the issues we are discussing. We should be glad for every co-belligerent who will stand beside us."[48]

More than anything else, the issue of abortion brought evangelicals and Catholics together. Not at first, however. The 1973 *Roe v. Wade* decision summoned the "right to life" movement into being, but initially evangelicals played little role in what was seen as largely a Roman Catholic affair. In 1971, before *Roe*, the Southern Baptist Convention had passed a resolution supporting legalized abortion; the year after *Roe*, in 1974, the resolution was reaffirmed. Jerry Falwell didn't deliver his first sermon on abortion until 1978. "[A] lot of Protestants reacted almost automatically—'If the Catholics are for it, we should be against it,'" commented Harold O. J. Brown, an evangelical theologian and ethicist. "That proved to be a very unwise position, but it took a while to realize that."[49] Francis Schaeffer was instrumental in changing evangelical attitudes. Together with a pro-life pediatric surgeon named C. Everett Koop (later Reagan's surgeon general), he produced a film series and companion book entitled *Whatever Happened to the Human Race?* that caused a sensation in the conservative Protestant community. "I wouldn't say it's the only thing that influenced the 'pro-life' movement," said Harold Brown, "but nothing has had an impact across the board that compares to the Schaeffer-Koop series. Today you won't find many who call themselves evangelicals who don't hold a very strong 'pro-life' position."[50]

The embrace of cobelligerency was showcased by the formation of the Moral Majority in June 1979. The organization was the brainchild of New Right activists Paul Weyrich, Richard Viguerie, and Howard Phillips—two Catholics and a Jew-turned-evangelical-convert, respectively. The front man, though, was Jerry Falwell, a Baptist who had dropped his earlier opposition to political involvement at the urging of Francis Schaeffer. "Listen, God used pagans to do his work in the Old Testament," Schaeffer had told Falwell, "so why don't you use pagans to do your work now?"[51] "When we announced that Moral Majority . . . welcomed Jews and Catholics and Protestants and Mormons and even non-religious people who shared our views on the family and abortion, strong national defense, and Israel," Falwell recalled, "a great deal of opposition erupted inside our own ranks." Such grumbling, though, quickly faded. "After one year of Moral Majority's explosion, our people realized that this is what the opposition had been doing all along."[52]

If the Moral Majority never really amounted to the political colossus that its promoters hoped for and its opponents feared, the idea behind it was one whose time had come. Out of the arid and acidic soil of fundamentalism, the evangelical revival had grown and blossomed into a major force in American life. And now it was combining with the conservative elements in other faiths to forge a larger, traditionalist ecumenism. On that religious foundation, increasingly organized and united, rested the new conservative ascendancy.

OVER THE COURSE of the sixties and seventies, American society was convulsed by two opposing religious movements: the
Aquarian awakening and the evangelical revival. At the core of
each was a vital half-truth, though the partisans on either side
were unsurprisingly oblivious to their own partiality. The devotees of the Aquarian awakening grasped that mass affluence
made possible wider horizons of experience and inclusiveness,
but they lacked proper appreciation of the institutions that in
turn made mass affluence possible. The leaders of the evangelical revival, on the other hand, were staunch in their defense of
affluence-creating institutions—and excessively rigid in their
suspicion of the new social and cultural possibilities created by
affluence.

By the 1980s, enough dust had settled for the broad outlines
of a resolution to become visible. The conservative movement,
bolstered and energized by the evangelical resurgence, now had
the upper hand in the struggle for political power. The Aquarian
left, however, had consolidated control over the country's major
cultural institutions. Each side enjoyed enough power to imagine that it could ultimately prevail, and so the so-called culture
wars dragged on. But, broadly speaking, the center held. The institutions of economic dynamism were preserved, as was the
cultural dynamism that those institutions unleashed.

In the clash of the one-eyed, each side achieved considerable
success where it saw clearly, and each failed miserably where it
was blind. The Aquarian awakening did create a more tolerant,
inclusive, and uninhibited America, but the revolution to overthrow capitalism and middle-class morality never materialized.
The evangelical revival, meanwhile, helped to preserve capitalism and middle-class morality, but the lost paradise of an endless 1950s—a never-never land where the cultural consequences
of mass prosperity remain forever latent—proved unrecover-
able.

What was emerging after two decades of upheaval was a decidedly more libertarian America. Which is to say, the essential
logic of mass affluence—the pursuit of self-realization through

participation in the extended division of labor—was now allowed to operate with unprecedented freedom of action. Government controls over free markets and free expression were scaled back; the constraints of morality and custom diminished and loosened. This state of affairs was neither sought nor anticipated by the great religious and political movements of the left and right. Rather, it was the accidental by-product of those movements' conflicting thrusts and counterthrusts. Each side was frequently checked by the other; neither could make much headway except when it moved with the currents of capitalism-driven social development. And thus the culture wars, even as they raged, gradually revealed their surprising result: to begin to set the realm of freedom free.

SEVEN

In Borges's Library

Jorge Luis Borges's short story, "The Library of Babel," describes a vast collection of books, its full extent unknown, whose volumes contain all possible combinations of alphabetic characters. "Everything is there," the narrator tells us: "the minute history of the future, the autobiographies of the archangels, the faithful catalogue of the Library, thousands and thousands of false catalogues, a demonstration of the fallacy of these catalogues, a demonstration of the fallacy of the true catalogue, the Gnostic gospel of Basilides, the commentary of this gospel, the commentary on the commentary of this gospel, the veridical account of your death, a version of each book in all languages, the interpolations of every book in all books."[1]

Most of the books, inevitably, contain only unreadable gibberish. "The impious assert that absurdities are the norm in the Library and that anything reasonable (even humble and pure coherence) is an almost miraculous exception." The narrator, however, has no sympathy for such heterodoxy. He admits freely that the best volume in the sections of the library under his administration is *The Combed Clap of Thunder,* and that other notable titles include *The Plaster Cramp* and *Axaxaxas Mlö.* But, he assures us, "[s]uch propositions as are contained in these titles, at first sight incoherent, doubtless yield a cryptographic or allegorical justification. . . . I can not combine certain letters, as *dhcmrlchtdj*, which the divine Library has not already foreseen in combination, and which in one of its secret languages does not encompass some terrible meaning. No one can articulate a syllable which is not full of tenderness and fear, and which is not, in one of those languages, the powerful name of some god."[2] What strikes one reader as arrant nonsense might well impress another as a work of sublime genius.

Borges's library provides an apt metaphor for contemporary America's pandemonium of social and cultural diversity. Out of the turmoil of the sixties and seventies came a new dispensation, one in which the space for economic and cultural development was now greatly expanded. Social peace and macroeconomic stability had been restored, but what followed was no return to normalcy. The old postwar liberal consensus, shattered by the rousing of passions on the left and the right, was gone for good. What took its place was an exuberant hyperpluralism, as old power structures—in economic life, in the organization of government and politics, and in popular culture—crumbled away and were replaced by a seething ferment of innovation and differentiation.

America's open society was flung wide open. Business empires were toppled, corporate hierarchies flattened. Big Labor was decimated. Party bosses and political machines ceded power. The mass media steadily lost market share and mind share. With computerization and globalization, consumer choice exploded. Broadened access to capital allowed dreamers tinkering in garages to create whole new industries. Grassroots activists and organized lobbying interests rewrote the rules of politics. Liberalized immigration brought unprecedented ethnic diversity. Alternative sources of information and entertainment proliferated. Subcultures and lifestyles bubbled up in mad profusion. Along every dimension of social endeavor, the discovery process of open-ended experimentation and adaptation was burgeoning.

"Plenitude" is the name that anthropologist Grant McCracken

has given to this new dispensation. "For us, plenitude is a matter of lifestyle, belief, behavior, and an ever-increasing variety of observable ways of living and being that are continually coming into existence . . . ," McCracken wrote in 1998. "Where once there was simplicity and limitation, everywhere there is now social *difference,* and that difference proliferates into ever more diversity, variety, heterogeneity."[3] The explosion of novelties produced much that was good—and much that was bad and ugly as well. Irrationality flourished, vulgarity and coarseness had a field day, and hunger for an increasingly indiscriminate public spotlight overwhelmed the old, wholesome restraints of humility and shame. In the cultural free-for-all, sublime genius and arrant nonsense jostled side by side—and telling the difference between the two was often hotly contested. Americans, it seemed, were remaking their country into something like Borges's library.

O N A P R I L F O O L S' Day in 1976, Steve Jobs and Steve Wozniak formed Apple Computer. A few months later they released the company's first product, the Apple I, featuring 8K bytes of memory and a built-in video terminal (the customer would need to supply his own monitor). A couple of college dropouts who were friends from high school, the pair's first commercial venture had been making and selling "blue boxes," illegal devices that allowed users to manipulate the telephone switching system to make free calls. Wozniak, a skilled hacker and habitual prankster, also ran a dial-a-joke service (he met his first wife when she called in) and once used a blue box to phone the pope while posing as Henry Kissinger (he hung up when he was told that His Holiness would be awakened to receive the call). Jobs, less talented as an engineer, was the dreamer and schemer of the two. Before teaming up with Wozniak to start Apple, he had become a vegetarian, lived on a commune, bummed around India in search of enlightenment, and pursued that same search pharmacologically. Even decades later, Jobs maintained that taking LSD was one of the most important things he had ever done.[4]

The connections between the sixties counterculture and the emerging computer culture extended far beyond Apple. Both were products of the Bay Area; both, in good romantic fashion, defied established authority. "Do not fold, spindle, or mutilate," a reference to computer punch cards, was a popular slogan during the sixties, as IBM's massive mainframes came to symbolize the antiseptic soullessness of centralized bureaucracy and technocratic control. A few years later, the hackers and hobbyists who launched the personal computer "revolution" took aim at the IBM monolith, not as a symbol, but as a technological reality. According to Jim Warren, the founder of the West Coast Computer Faire, the personal computer "had its genetic coding in the 1960s' . . . antiestablishment, antiwar, profreedom, antidiscipline attitudes."[5]

It should be unsurprising, then, that some of the most important shapers of the Silicon Valley sensibility came out of the psychedelic and antiwar scenes. Stewart Brand organized the legendary Trips Festival in January 1966, an outgrowth of Ken Kesey's acid tests, and later went on to greater fame as publisher of the hippie bible, *The Whole Earth Catalog*. Meanwhile, in 1968—the same year the first issue of the catalog was released— he helped engineer Douglas Englebart to stage "the mother of all demos," an early preview of such radical new computer technologies as the mouse, graphical user interface, videoconferencing, and hypertext. And in 1985, Brand founded The WELL, or Whole Earth 'Lectronic Link, an early online chat room and "virtual community." John Perry Barlow, a childhood friend of Grateful Dead member Bob Weir, sometimes wrote lyrics for the band's songs (his credits include "Mexicali Blues," "Looks Like Rain," and "Estimated Prophet"). Now a leading cyberspace guru, in 1990 he helped to create the Electronic Frontier Foundation, a group dedicated to "defending freedom in the digital world." Novelist William Gibson, who coined the term "cyberspace" in his 1984 sci-fi classic, *Neuromancer*, fled to Canada back in 1967 to avoid the draft and has lived there ever since. As a boy growing up in rural Virginia, he devoured the works of Beat authors William Burroughs, Jack Kerouac, and Allen Ginsberg. "The effect . . . ," he later recalled, "was to make me, at least in terms of my Virginia home, Patient Zero of what would later be called the counterculture."[6]

Running through the counterculture's dominant Luddism was a rich vein of quirky technophilia. Sound systems for rock bands, light shows, the mass media, and, of course, drugs—all these products of industrial civilization were embraced enthusiastically. So, too, were futurist prophets such as Marshall McLuhan and Buckminster Fuller, who preached that technological advance and technocratic control need not be a package deal. Accordingly, some on the romantic left imagined a post-scarcity utopia in which high-tech and back-to-nature simplicity were somehow reconciled.[7] "I like to think / (it has to be!) / of a cybernetic ecology / where we are free of our labors / and joined back to nature, / returned to our mammal / brothers and sisters, / and all watched over / by machines of loving grace," wrote the Beat poet Richard Brautigan in 1967. What emerged was a particular brand of utopianism that combined a love of gadgetry with commitment to do-it-yourself independence and a longing for technology on a more human scale. Out of it arose the personal computing movement and all that followed.

The Silicon Valley phenomenon was only the most pronounced and dramatic example of the sweeping changes that were transforming American capitalism. The postwar triumvirate of Big Business, Big Labor, and Big Government was giving way to a new, more open, more flexible, more dynamic economic order. Formerly, the foundations of mass prosperity had consisted of a huge stock of physical assets. Now, increasingly, the nation's wealth was the product of intangible ideas and "human capital" located in the heads of individual human beings. In the past, competitive success went to established corporate giants that controlled strategic physical assets. Now the laurels went to companies—old or new, big or small—that found and employed people with the right ideas and allowed them to put those ideas into action. Hence the popular appellation: the Information Age.

Manufacturing, the manipulation of matter, absorbed less and less of the nation's economic energies. Back in 1960, manufacturing accounted for 27 percent of gross domestic product; by 2000, the figure had fallen to 15 percent. The percentage of American workers employed in manufacturing fell concurrently—from 28 percent to 13 percent over the same period. None of which meant that the country was suffering from "deindustrialization": between 1980 and 2000, when said calamity was supposedly occurring, manufacturing output actually doubled. However, employment in particular industries (especially heavily unionized ones) did drop precipitously. The number of steelworkers, for example, declined from 752,000 in 1977 to 144,000 in 2000, while the number of clothing industry workers fell from 1.3 million to 526,000. As a result, private sector union membership, which peaked at 36 percent of the total workforce back in 1953, had slid all the way down to 9 percent by 2000.

As manipulating matter faded in relative importance, manipulating abstractions moved to the fore. Back in 1960, people employed primarily in handling and making use of information—managers, professionals, technicians, and clerical workers—constituted 37 percent of the workforce. By 2000, people in equivalent occupations made up 54 percent of the total. In other words, over half of working Americans could now be fairly classified as knowledge workers. Excluding clerical workers and administrative support staff does not affect the trend. In 1960, managerials, professional, and technical occupations—the elite of the information economy—accounted for 22 percent of all American jobs. By 2000, the figure had jumped to 34 percent.

In biology, "encephalization" refers to the growth in relative brain size during the evolution of a species. As the division of labor grew ever more elaborately complex, the evolving American economy was undergoing its own process of encephalization. From its inception, the competitive market order has been driven forward by experimentation and discovery, the goal of which is to find and apply socially useful knowledge. In earlier stages of economic development, this essential brain work was confined to a small circle of entrepreneurs, while everyone else was relegated to manual toil or tedious drudgery. Over time, with technological and organizational progress, physical capital became relatively plentiful and cheap, while human capital grew relatively scarce and precious. That is, people became more valuable for their heads than for their hands and backs. Capitalism thus has its own Maslow's pyramid: as people are released from the need for physical and routine work, they develop higher capacities in their work lives as well as their personal pursuits. They become knowledge workers.

The shift to an information economy made the perches of economic power less stable and secure than in the past. In the industrial era, ownership of the right physical assets allowed corporate Goliaths to exploit scale and scope economies and thereby enjoy huge competitive advantages over any potential new rivals. But when human capital became the key determinant of economic success, size and well-established position no longer counted for as much. The ability of a talented entrepreneur to play David was correspondingly enhanced. As shown by (among many others) Bill Gates, Michael Dell, Ted Turner, Rupert Murdoch, Fred Smith, and Sam Walton, the right idea at the right time could now upend whole industries. Between 1917 and 1976, the club of the largest hundred public companies took an average of 30 years to replace half its members. Between 1977 and 1998, the time needed to achieve the same amount of turnover had dropped to a mere 12 years.[8]

Adding to the precariousness of economic preeminence were new sources of competition and capital. The past few decades have witnessed a huge jump in international trade. In 2000, exports and imports combined equaled 26 percent of national income—up from 11 percent in 1970. And those figures actually understate the new intensity of international competition, since the so-called tradeable sectors of the economy—agriculture, mining, and manufacturing—have been a shrinking piece of the overall economic pie. Thus, U.S. merchandise exports as a percentage of total U.S. merchandise production rose from 15 percent to 40 percent during the last three decades of the twentieth century.[9] Similar trends can be found on the import side: between 1960 and 1993, imports as a percentage of domestic consumption rose from 1 percent to 15 percent for grapes, from 9 percent to 18 percent for tomatoes, from 2 percent to 64 percent for radios, televisions, and stereos, and from 3 percent to 40 percent for both machine tools and cars.[10] Competitive pressures have been augmented by international flows of capital as well as goods and services. U.S. multinationals created globalized production chains, often relocating labor-intensive operations south of the border or overseas. Capital flowed in as well: by the mid-nineties, foreign-affiliated firms accounted for almost 6 percent of U.S. gross product originating in private industries, and nearly 5 percent of total private-sector employment. The foreign presence in manufacturing was even greater, making up some 13 percent of output and 11 percent of employment.[11]

Broader access to capital domestically has been a major boost for entrepreneurs seeking to challenge the status quo. Financial markets grew much deeper, thus making it easier for people with ideas and people with resources to combine their forces. In 1970, the value of all listed U.S. stocks equaled about two thirds of GDP; stock market capitalization had risen to 1.5 times GDP by 2000.[12] Meanwhile, private equity markets, which include the venture capital firms that fund new enterprises, exploded from a mere $5 billion in investments back in 1980 to over $175 billion in 1999.[13] And high-yield or "junk" bonds, pioneered by financier Michael Milken, provided another important financing vehicle for promising upstarts. CNN and MCI, for example, were among the better-known Milken success stories. Despite the fact that Milken himself wound up doing a stretch in federal prison, his brainchild continued to grow: as of 2002, outstanding junk bonds topped $650 billion.[14]

The result of all these changes was to reduce the concentration of economic power. Between 1975 and 1996, the proportion of manufacturing workers employed by Fortune 500 companies sank from 79 to 58 percent, while the Fortune 500's share of manufacturing shipments fell from 83 percent to 75 percent. More broadly, the percentage of Americans working for establishments with over 1,000 employees fell nearly 30 percent between 1967 and 1985.[15] Small business owners, on the other hand, were on the rise. The ratio of business owners to total employment, after a century of decline, climbed from 8.2 percent in 1974 to 11.4 percent in 1996, a 38 percent increase.[16]

Of course, corporate giants still abounded, and in some industries concentration increased according to conventional measures. But make no mistake: a fundamental redistribution of power had occurred. Back in 1967, in *The New Industrial State,* economist John Kenneth Galbraith had celebrated the triumph of the corporate "technostructure" and its farsighted "planning system"—which he likened explicitly to communist central planning—over the old-fashioned confusion of blind market forces. "In the Soviet Union and the Soviet-type economies prices are extensively managed by the state. Production is not in response to market demand but given by the overall plan," Galbraith wrote. "In the Western economies markets are dominated by great firms. These establish prices and seek to secure a demand for what they have to sell. . . . The modern large Western corporation and the modern apparatus of socialist planning are variant accommodations to the same need."[17] Such visions of corporate omnipotence, plausible if exaggerated in Galbraith's day, bore no relation whatsoever to the new business realities. With competitors from around the globe in dogged pursuit, and with incessant pressure from Wall Street for higher returns, corporate chieftains now endured constant harrassment and second-guessing. Modern-day Gullivers, they wriggled and struggled under a thousand constraints.

Life inside the corporation changed to keep pace with altered external conditions. Where size was once touted as a sign and source of strength, now corporate leaders worried that large organizations were becoming "dinosaurs," too bulky and clumsy to adapt to a faster-paced world. "The most discouraging fact of big corporate life is the loss of what got them big in the first place: innovation," wrote management consultants Tom Peters and Robert Waterman in their influential 1982 best seller, *In*

Search of Excellence. "If big companies don't stop innovating entirely, the rate almost certainly goes way down."[18] In the new era, vertical integration and horizontal conglomeration were out; "lean and mean" were in. General Motors typified the trend toward "outsourcing." By selling off affiliated parts makers, GM went from producing eight million cars with 750,000 employees in 1989 to making 8.5 million cars with 362,000 employees 12 years later.[19] (Alas for poor GM, no matter what it did, it never seemed to get quite lean or mean enough.)

Spinning off nonessential units went hand in hand with thinning out corporate bureaucracy. The "Organization Man" of middle management, formerly the vital cog of the postwar economic machine, was now becoming redundant. Waves of corporate restructuring during the eighties and nineties worked to decentralize decision-making power and shorten chains of command, all in hopes of producing nimbler and more innovative companies. As described by Peters and Waterman, the best-run companies "were creating almost radical decentralization and autonomy, with its attendant overlap, messiness around the edges, lack of coordination, internal competition, and somewhat chaotic conditions, in order to breed the entrepreneurial spirit."[20] Middle managers, once tasked with pushing paper up and down the corporate hierarchy, were the prime casualties of this overhaul. Surveys by the American Management Association showed that between 1988 and 1993, over two-thirds of member companies engaged in downsizing—in other words, mass layoffs. And middle managers, who made up only 8 percent of corporate payrolls, received 19 percent of the pink slips.[21]

Aquarian values found fertile ground in the new business environment. In the sixties, the spirit of romantic rebellion made rapid inroads into the country's consumer culture, but corporate culture remained predominantly buttoned-down and bureaucratic. No longer, though: with the business world's growing emphasis on the need for constant change, countercultural rhetoric and style proved all but irresistible. "Thirty years after Woodstock and all the peace rallies," wrote David Brooks in *Bobos in*

Paradise, "the people who talk most relentlessly about smashing the status quo and crushing the establishment are management gurus and corporate executives."[22] The gray flannel suit gave way to casual Friday, and then casual everyday; flexible hours—and later, with cell phones and BlackBerrys, the blurring of any distinction between on and off the clock—replaced the nine-to-five routine. By the nineties, the hippie chic of Silicon Valley had gone nationwide.

DEREGULATED, GLOBALIZED, AND computerized, America's new economy gradually revealed itself as a formidable engine of innovation and growth. At every turn, however, knowledgeable naysayers were there to make grave pronouncements of decline and fall. Barry Bluestone and Bennett Harrison chronicled the woes of the Rust Belt and proclaimed, in the title of their 1984 book, *The Deindustrialization of America.* Clyde Prestowitz tapped into popular anxiety about foreign and especially Japanese competition with his 1988 best seller, *Trading Places: How We Allowed Japan to Take the Lead.* Pulitzer Prize–winning investigative journalists Donald Barlett and James Steele offered up a pair of jeremiads about the collapse of the American middle class: *America: What Went Wrong?* in 1992, and *America: Who Stole the Dream?* in 1996. And in March 1996, the *New York Times* ran a high-profile, multipart series bemoaning "The Downsizing of America."

Complementing the doom and gloom were healthy doses of hype and puffery. Overstating the effects of globalization was a popular nineties pastime, as exemplified by the title of management guru Kenichi Ohmae's 1996 book, *The End of the Nation State.* Nothing, though, could match the blue-sky boosterism inspired by the advent of the World Wide Web. "Governments of the Industrial World, you weary giants of flesh and steel, I come from Cyberspace, the new home of Mind," John Perry Barlow wrote in a 1996 essay entitled "A Declaration of the Independence of Cyberspace." "On behalf of the future, I ask you of the past to leave us alone. You are not welcome among us. You have no sovereignty where we gather." Such braggadocio was innocent enough, reflecting understandable exuberance about amazing new possibilities. But as the new millennium approached and the dot-com boom became the dot-com bubble, expectations slipped their tether to reality and a full-blown mania got under way. Stock market values soared into the ether; the flimsiest excuses for business plans obtained funding with ease; otherwise sober investors turned into trend-chasing fools; corner cutting and blatant corruption set in. And then—pop!—reality reasserted itself, with all its limitations, frustrations, and constraints.

Overshoots of optimism and pessimism are inevitable in the fog of economic development, especially when vision is distorted by ideology or interest. But looking back now with some measure of historical perspective, no fair assessment can deny that the new, more competitive, more entrepreneurial economic order has compiled an impressive record of accomplishment. Neither can it be denied, though, that the blessings of robust wealth creation have been unevenly distributed. Consequently, just as the cultural dynamism of the sixties and seventies opened deep rifts between those who embraced what was happening and those who deplored it, so did the economic dynamism of the eighties and nineties stir conflict between those on either side of the knowledge-economy divide.

At the macroeconomic level, the new economy's performance has been glittering. After the Great Inflation and the steep downturn that finally ended it, the past couple of decades have witnessed almost continuous economic expansion. Between the end of 1982 and the end of 2004, the real (i.e., inflation-adjusted) gross domestic product more than doubled, growing by over 5.6 trillion constant 2000 dollars. And in all of those 22 years, America experienced only 16 months of recession. By contrast, the prior 20 years (1963–1982) saw four recessions totaling 49 months in duration; between 1943 and 1962, there were five recessions that lasted a total of 47 months. Meanwhile, the two brief downturns of recent years were mild by historical standards. Unemployment peaked at 7.8 percent after the 1990–1991 recession, and at only 6.3 percent during the 2001 recession, as compared to the peak rate of 10.8 percent after the 1981–1982 slump. Considering the successive shocks that have rocked the country over the past few years—the dot-com bust, Enron and other corporate scandals, an extended bear market, the September 11 attacks and the continuing threat of terrorism, the war in Iraq, and the skyrocketing price of oil—the fact that the most recent slump was not more severe, and that the subsequent expansion was relatively vigorous, is testament to the new economy's resiliency. No, the business cycle has not been repealed, but its disruptive boom-and-bust fluctuations have been dampened.

Not only was the economy running more smoothly, but it was also running with increasing power. Beginning in the 1970s, for reasons not entirely clear, the productivity growth rate—the rate at which output per hour of work increases—suffered a sharp and sudden drop. And while the eighties boom brought a smart recovery in manufacturing productivity, the much larger service sector remained stubbornly sluggish. Thus, while the annual rate of productivity growth in the nonfarm business sector averaged 2.9 percent from 1947 to 1973, between 1973 and 1995 it averaged only 1.3 percent. And since productivity growth imposes the ultimate limit on how fast incomes and living standards can rise, the slowdown meant a corresponding slackening in the pace of prosperity's advance.

But in the mid-nineties, just as suddenly as the productivity slump had started, a new productivity boom began. Between the beginning of 1996 and the end of 2004, output per hour increased at an average annual rate of 2.9 percent, matching the rate attained during the "golden era" of the early postwar decades. However confused economists may be about the origins of the productivity slowdown, they are in overwhelming agreement regarding the cause of the new speedup: the accumulated effect of decades of spectacular advances in information and communications technologies, and the gradual diffusion of those technologies throughout the economy. Moore's law, according to which the number of transistors that can be squeezed onto a chip doubles every 18 months or so, has been in operation since the 1960s, but as late as 1987 the economist Robert Solow could state correctly, if somewhat snidely, that "you can see the computer age everywhere but in the productivity statistics."[23] In 1987, however, real investment in information technology amounted to only 1.7 percent of gross domestic product; by 2000, that figure had climbed to 6.8 percent.[24] As the scale of investment in computers and software reached critical mass, the payoff in the productivity statistics finally began to register.

The return to high productivity growth was a triumph, not just for the IT industry, but for the new economy as a whole. For the vast wealth-creating possibilities of the Information Age could be realized only through a thoroughgoing and often painful restructuring of economic life. And that restructuring, in turn, required a considerable measure of economic freedom as its essential precondition. Businesses had to rearrange their operations to take advantage of cheap computing power; whole new industries had to be created; old industries had to shrink or die. Without the conquest of inflation, the deregulation of key industries, the lowering of once-punitive tax rates, and continued openness to foreign competition and capital, the necessary restructuring would have been stunted if not aborted altogether. Silicon Valley could not have arisen without deep capital markets to nourish its growth; logistical breakthroughs like those pioneered by Federal Express and Wal-Mart could never have occurred if transportation and communications had not been thrown open to competition; the redeployment of manpower and resources throughout the economy was possible only because businesses were free to fire redundant workers and invest and source from abroad.

Sustained and now accelerated economic growth has rendered America's consumer cornucopia ever more lavish and various. Between 1970 and the mid-nineties, the average size of a new home increased 43 percent, from 1,500 square feet to 2,150. And since average household sizes have shrunk, the square footage per person actually climbed 70 percent. Some 81 percent of new homes built in 1997 had central heat and air-conditioning, while 87 percent had a built-in garage—up from 34 percent of new homes in 1970 with central heat and air, and 58 percent with a garage. Back in 1970, only 29 percent of households had two or more vehicles, 34 percent had a color television, 45 percent had a clothes dryer, and 27 percent had a dishwasher. By the mid-nineties, the number of households with two or more vehicles had risen to 62 percent, the number with a color television had jumped to 98 percent, 83 percent of households now had a dryer, and 55 percent had a dishwasher. In 1970, the number of annual air travel miles per person stood at 646; by the mid-nineties, that figure had more than tripled to 2,260. Roughly a half-million Americans took cruises in 1970; 4.7 million did so in 1997. In 1996, Americans placed 94.9 billion long-distance calls—up from 9.8 billion in 1970.[25]

Increased affluence involved much more than wider access to and greater use of existing products. Americans now enjoyed—or, more likely, took completely for granted—a host of products that didn't even exist a generation before. Just to name a few of them: microwave ovens, personal computers, the World Wide Web, e-mail, cellular phones, voice mail, laser printers, cable and satellite television, videocassettes and DVDs, compact discs and MP3, video games, airbags, antilock brakes, automatic teller machines, in-line skates, aspartame, LASIK surgery, CAT scans, ultrasounds, in vitro fertilization, soft contact lenses, home pregnancy tests, ibuprofen, and erectile dysfunction drugs.[26]

The dizzying variety of product offerings now bordered on the overwhelming. The typical supermarket in 2004 carried roughly over 30,000 different items, as compared to only 14,000 in 1980. At The Great Indoors, the Sears-affiliated home furnishing store that started up in the late nineties, customers could choose from 250 different faucets and over 1,500 styles of drawer pulls.[27] Ethnic dining options exploded, in smaller towns as well as urban centers. In the Washington, D.C., area, restaurant goers in 2005 could experience Afghan, Belgian, Brazilian, Caribbean, Ethiopian, Korean, Moroccan, Portuguese, Russian, Scandinavian, Turkish, and Vietnamese cuisine, as well as more traditional fare. Online retailing created virtual superstores that put vast inventories at customers' fingertips. Amazon.com offered two million book titles and then diversified into other products, while Netflix made 35,000 DVDs available for no-hassle rental. In response to the growing surfeit, Barry Schwartz's 2004 offering, *The Paradox of Choice: Why Less Is More*, was only one of a small library of books that sought to convince Americans that consumer plenty had become wretched excess. Books about too many options—yet another option to bedevil harried consumers!

Because of the productivity slowdown that began in the 1970s, there was a corresponding slowdown in the growth of wages and other income. This fact, together with the difficulties involved in comparing income across time periods, has given rise to commonly heard claims that living standards for all but the best-off Americans have stagnated or even declined over the past generation. To put the matter bluntly, such claims are purest nonsense. The quick glance provided in the paragraphs above makes clear that most Americans have enjoyed substantial improvements in material well-being. And consider, as further reinforcement, the following comparisons between households below the official poverty line in 1994 and all households in 1971. Among *poor* households in the mid-nineties, 72 percent had washing machines, compared to 71 percent of *all* households in 1971; 50 percent had clothes dryers, up from the 45 percent figure for all households in 1971; 98 percent had a refrigerator, while in 1971 only 83 percent of all households did; 93 percent had a color television, more than double the 43 percent figure for all households a generation earlier; 50 percent had an air conditioner, up from 32 percent of all households in 1971; and 60 percent had a microwave oven, a device fewer than 1 percent of all households possessed in 1971.[28] In many nontrivial respects, then, the poor

CARTE D'EMBARQUEMENT

BOARDING PASS

ETKT

BUSINESS

ELIT P DL2562269122

HERMAN/ERWIN

VOL FLIGHT	DATE DATE	DEPART TIME	DE FROM	A TO	EMBARQUEMENT/BOARDING PORTE/GATE HEURE/TIME	CLASSE CLASS	SIEGE SEAT	SEQ
DL 043	06OCT	11H45	CHARLES DE GAUL 2E CINCINNATI		E67 11H00	J	**06G**	162

in the mid-nineties had access to more material comforts and conveniences than the middle class did a generation earlier.

Nevertheless, it is true that the rising tide of prosperity did not lift all boats in equal measure. The emergence of the new knowledge economy was associated with a growing disparity in economic outcomes, in which the well-off reaped the largest gains in income while those in humbler stations fell farther and farther off the pace. Between 1947 and 1973, real income grew at an average annual rate of 3.0 percent for those in the bottom fifth of the income distribution, compared to 2.8 percent for the middle fifth and 2.5 percent for the top fifth. In other words, the bottom was catching up with the middle, and the middle was catching up with the top. Between 1973 and 2001, however, the situation was reversed. Average annual growth in real income was a measly 0.3 percent for those in the bottom fifth, improving to 0.8 percent for the middle fifth and 1.8 percent for the top fifth. Thus, in the past generation, the poor have been falling behind those in the middle, who have been falling behind the well-to-do.[29]

These widening disparities in economic achievement reflected the greater cultural freedom championed by the left as much as they did the greater economic freedom championed by the right. In particular, changes in family structure have been a major factor in the rise of income inequality. In 1979, married-couple households accounted for 74 percent of all adults and children; with continued high divorce rates and increasing rates of out-of-wedlock births, that figure had fallen to 65 percent by 1998. Since households headed by single women are much likelier to experience low income than are two-parent households, the marked increase in the former has worked to swell the ranks at the bottom of the income distribution. According to the economist Gary Burtless at the Brookings Institution, family breakdown alone accounts for between 21 and 25 percent of the overall increase in income inequality.[30]

The move of women into the workforce has also played a part. Since women's earnings have been growing faster than men's,

the switch from one- to two-earner households could have miti-
gated inequality by supplementing lagging male earnings with
more rapidly increasing female earnings. But because of the
prevalence of "assortative mating"—that is, marrying someone
of similar socioeconomic position—the rise in dual-income couples has ended up exacerbating income differences. Between
1979 and 1996, the proportion of working-age men with working wives rose by roughly 25 percent among those in the top fifth
of the male earnings distribution, while their wives' total earnings rose by over 100 percent.[31] Gary Burtless has calculated that
this unanticipated consequence of the women's movement accounts for another 13 percent of overall inequality.[32]

In addition to these changes in the composition of household
income, the increasing disparity in incomes also reflects a wider
dispersion of individual earnings. Here again, several factors
have been at play. One of particular significance has been the
surge in immigration during the past few decades. After the
enactment of restrictionist legislation in 1924, the great flood
of migrants from southern and eastern Europe slowed to a
trickle. The share of the American population born abroad,
which stood at 14.7 percent in 1910, sank all the way to 4.7 percent by 1970. With the passage of the Immigration and Nationality Services Act of 1965, however, a new period of mass
immigration began. By 2000, the foreign-born had climbed all
the way to 11.1 percent of the total population. Not only did the
numbers increase dramatically, but the ethnic composition
changed as well. Back in 1960, 84 percent of America's foreign-
born population were Canadian or European in origin; by 2001,
51 percent came from Latin America or the Caribbean, while
another 27 percent came from Asia. Between immigration and
high birthrates, America's Hispanic community exploded, growing from 6.4 percent of the population in 1980 to 13.7 percent in
2003, overtaking blacks in 2001 to become America's largest ethnic minority.

The rapid growth of America's Hispanic population spelled a
big increase in people at the lower levels of socioeconomic

achievement. As of 1999, 23 percent of Hispanics lived below the official poverty line, compared to 9 percent for whites. Some 44 percent of Hispanics lacked a high school diploma, compared to 16 percent for whites. As of 1995, 41 percent of all Hispanic births were to single mothers; for whites, the figure was 25 percent. In 2003, Hispanics made up 28 percent of all food-preparation workers, 37 percent of all dishwashers, 26 percent of all janitors, 39 percent of all maids and housekeepers, and 35 percent of all construction laborers—and only 5 percent of software engineers, 6 percent of accountants, 4 percent of lawyers, and 5 percent of physicians. By becoming more ethnically and culturally diverse, American society became more economically unequal.

Meanwhile, the gradual transformation from an industrial to a knowledge economy precipitated a major shift in the demand for labor—one that caught millions of Americans unprepared. The prior phase change, from agricultural to industrial, had been what economists call "skill neutral"; in other words, workers displaced from declining sectors were able with relative ease to find jobs in growth industries. Thus, the mechanization of agriculture and falling farm prices may have dried up opportunities in rural areas and small towns, but workers willing to move to the country's burgeoning industrial cities could find factory jobs that paid as well as or better than what they were accustomed to.

But as America's industrial heartland degenerated into the Rust Belt during the seventies and eighties, laid-off workers encountered significantly greater difficulty in finding new jobs with comparable pay. What did it matter to someone who had spent decades on the assembly line that Silicon Valley was booming? He lacked the education and skills to avail himself of the new economy's exciting opportunities. The turning point for blue-collar workers came during the recessions of 1980 and 1981–1982: between January 1979 and January 1984, 5.1 million workers who had held their positions for at least three years lost those jobs due to plant closings or job eliminations, and about half of them had been employed in manufacturing. For most, losing their jobs meant downward mobility. According to a survey taken in January 1984, 30 percent of displaced workers had found other jobs that paid as well or better, 30 percent had found other work but taken a pay cut, and a full 40 percent were still unemployed or had dropped out of the labor force altogether.[33]

Although good times soon returned for the economy overall, for blue-collar workers things were never the same. A large "skill bias" had opened up: whereas a recent college graduate in 1980 could expect to earn about 35 percent more than a high school graduate, by the early nineties the "college premium" had jumped to nearly 60 percent, and it has remained around there ever since. The premium for graduate degrees has risen even more steeply: from around 40 percent in 1980 to almost 115 percent in 1997.[34] While median, inflation-adjusted earnings generally rose for white-collar occupations, between 1979 and 1996 they fell 11 percent for craftsmen and precision workers, 8 percent for machine operators, 14 percent for transport equipment operators, and 16 percent for handlers and laborers.[35]

As prospects for upward mobility dimmed for the working classes, for the elite they soared into the stratosphere. At the very pinnacle, the number of billionaires in the country rose from 12 in 1982 to 268 in 1999.[36] More generally, Census Bureau data show that the percentage of households with inflation-adjusted incomes above $100,000 a year doubled from 1979 to 2004.[37] The phenomenon at work is familiar to sports fans. In professional sports, the introduction of free agency has led to a huge increase in players' salaries, as teams are now free to compete for the best talent and that competition bids up the price. A kind of free agency has come to the larger economy as well. Competition in most industries has intensified, which raises the stakes for who gets the best personnel. As a result of more-robust competition, organizational loyalty isn't what it used to be, which means that the top talent is free to chase the top dollar. And with the elimination of punitively high marginal tax rates, one former restraint on bidding wars (namely, that most of the bid price wouldn't go to the person being sought) has been lifted. Consequently, the most economically productive members of society are now better able to capture for themselves the market value they produce.

So what are we to make of the rise in income inequality? Critics of the more market-oriented policies that underlie the new economy have seized upon the widening spread in earnings as evidence of the failure of those policies. Their case, however, is a weak one. Regardless of valiant and ingenious efforts to torture the data into saying otherwise, there has been no mass immiserization of the poor and working classes. It is true that with the productivity slowdown between the early seventies and the mid-nineties, growth in wages and household income slowed and even reversed in the middling and lower levels of the income distribution. Income measures, however, do a poor job of capturing changes in what can be bought for a given amount of money—especially those due to the invention of new products and increases in quality and variety. In terms of actual consumption, it is beyond serious argument that most Americans have made significant gains in material welfare over their counterparts of a generation ago.

As to the rise of income inequality, much of it can be attributed to demographic and cultural changes rather than the operation of the economic system. For one thing, the statistics would look appreciably rosier if the great wave of Hispanic immigration had somehow been prevented. Yet most of the poor immigrants who came here from Mexico and Central America surely bettered their lot in doing so—is that fact to be deplored? Some top surgeons, jealous of maintaining their gaudy success rates, shy away from tough cases with long odds. America, by opening her borders to the poor and uneducated from poor, underdeveloped countries, chose a riskier, more rewarding course. America chose doing good over looking good.

Disparities in income have also been exacerbated by the sharp increase in single motherhood and the associated emergence of a permanent underclass. Those social pathologies, the lamentable consequences of the Aquarian awakening, are surely serious problems. At their root, however, is an absolute lack of spiritual and cultural resources, not a relative lack of material resources. The latter is largely a symptom of the former.

To the extent that widening income inequality has resulted from changes in the country's economic system, the primary reason has been that the knowledge economy is in greater need of highly educated, highly skilled workers than the old industrial economy was. This is good news! What if the opposite were true, and the economy was devaluing education and skills and insatiable in its demand for physical toil and clerical tedium? Would that be cause for celebration? The existence of the college premium lends vigorous encouragement to the development of human capital—in other words, the stretching of minds and expansion of intellectual capacities. That kind of incentive structure is surely a positive feature of the new economy, not a shortcoming.

And incentives do matter. Economists Kevin Murphy and Finis Welch have tracked the relation between trends in the college premium and college attendance. With the boom in college education during the sixties and early seventies, the portion of men and women between the ages of 21 and 25 with at least some college experience rose to nearly 45 percent by 1974. At that point, however, the supply of college-educated workers had raced ahead of demand, and consequently the college premium fell over the course of the seventies from nearly 50 percent in 1971 down to 35 percent in 1980. As the returns to college education fell, so did college attendance: by 1981, the portion of 21- to 25-year-olds with college experience had dropped below 40 percent. With the return to economic vitality in the eighties, however, the college premium began to rise again, and so did college attendance. In 1987, the fraction of 21- to 25-year-olds with college experience passed the former 1974 peak, and by the mid-nineties was approaching 50 percent. "The clear implication of these data," Murphy and Welch concluded, "is that investment in human capital responds to the rate of return."[38]

Nevertheless, the fact is that many Americans have been unable to take proper advantage of the new economy's immense possibilities. That fact must be considered a major disappointment—and one that is not easily remedied. For while economic incentives matter, sometimes culture matters more. And many Americans have been raised in a working-class culture that does not sufficiently encourage education or long-term planning. As a result, they lack the skills that are now so highly rewarded—and what is worse, they lack the capacity to develop those skills. Until relatively recently, working-class culture was consistent with upward mobility. But things have changed, and low-skill, high-paying jobs are increasingly a thing of the past. Consequently, the anti-intellectual mentality that remains deeply engrained in large segments of the American populace has become a socio-economic dead end.

IN THE EIGHTIES and nineties, the structure of economic life was transformed by new sources of competition and new methods of communication. At the same time, the structure of American political life would experience a similar metamorphosis. In politics as in economics, stable systems of top-down control, dominated by powerful insiders, were replaced by ones that were more open, more unruly, and sometimes more divisive.

Just as the seventies witnessed the toppling of the Big Business/Big Labor/Big Government triumvirate, so it saw the demise of America's reigning political establishment. The following milestones marked the changing of the guard. On May 2, 1972, J. Edgar Hoover died in his sleep after leading the FBI for 48 years. On October 7, 1974, Washington, D.C., police pulled over a drunken Wilbur Mills along with Argentine stripper Fanne Foxe, who promptly dived into the Tidal Basin. The scandal forced Mills to relinquish his chairmanship of the House Ways and Means Committee, a post he had held since 1957. And on December 20, 1976, Chicago mayor Richard Daley died of a heart attack during his 21st year in office. All three men had en-

joyed careers of unprecedented duration: Hoover was the lon-
gest-serving head of a federal agency in American history, Mills
was chairman of Ways and Means longer than anybody before
or since, and Daley's tenure as Chicago's mayor remains the longest ever (though his son is catching up with him). All three,
likewise, amassed enormous power. With his notorious secret
files, Hoover was untouchable and all but unaccountable; Mills's
immense influence over tax and spending bills earned him the
reputation as "the most powerful man in Washington"; Daley's
iron grip on Chicago made him a kingmaker in presidential politics. When these giants passed from the scene, their like was
never seen again. A whole world had died with them.

The system that produced those men and their remarkable careers no longer exists. To a significant degree, it was a holdover
from the age of scarcity, premised on social realities that were
rapidly becoming obsolete. Specifically, it was adapted to a society with an electorate dominated by unsophisticated rural and
urban-immigrant voters. Under those conditions, American democracy was a rather closely held affair. Yes, outsiders barged
in, but that was the exception. And yes, the general public got a
direct veto now and again. But the day-to-day business of politics was usually run by tight little oligarchies, whether at the
municipal, state, or federal level. The bosses controlled access to
many types of public office, and they used that control to direct
elaborate systems of patronage. The role of lesser officials in this
system—that is, the beneficiaries of said patronage—was not to
help mold policy, but to do what they were told. A typical if late
example of the dutiful functionary was John G. Fary, who, after
two decades in the Illinois legislature, won election to Congress
in 1975. "I will go to Washington to help represent Mayor Daley,"
he promised on election night. "For twenty-one years, I represented the mayor in the legislature, and he was always right." [39]
Out in the general public, meanwhile, relatively few constituencies were organized to participate meaningfully in the political
process. In the voting booth, instinctive, often inherited loyalties
and a further level of patronage were the dominant influences

on decision making. The vast majority of the electorate, the vast majority of the time, was politically inert.

As American society grew ever richer, more complex, and more intricately organized, so did its political sphere. In particular, active participation by the general public in the political process, whether through directly lobbying government officials or through joining or donating money to lobbying groups, skyrocketed over the past several decades. Gale Research's *Encyclopedia of Associations* listed fewer than 5,000 organizations back in 1956; by 1970, the figure had jumped to 10,000, and by 1990 it topped 20,000. Virtually every conceivable economic interest became organized, as this sampling by journalist Jonathan Rauch attests: "the National Paint Varnish and Lacquer Association; the Possum Growers and Breeders Association; the American Association of Sex Educators, Counselors, and Therapists; the Bow Tie Manufacturers Association; the Association of Metropolitan Sewerage Agencies; the Frozen Pizza Institute." As the number of groups grew, membership in particular organizations grew as well. The National Association of Home Builders was founded back in 1942, but its membership expanded more than threefold between 1967 and 1982.[40] Corporations grew more politically active: the number of corporate Washington offices increased by a factor of 10 between 1961 and 1982.

Business groups were the early leaders of the organizing craze, but beginning in the 1960s public-interest groups started forming in large numbers. Ralph Nader was a pivotal figure on the left: under the umbrella of Public Citizen, founded in 1971, an army of young "Nader's Raiders" crusaded against corporate power and its influence on government policy. The ecology movement launched a flurry of organizing, as the number of environmental groups reached some 7,000 by the early nineties. Between the early seventies and 1990, the membership of the National Resources Defense Council tripled, that of the Environmental Defense Fund quintupled, the Sierra Club's membership grew sevenfold, and the National Audubon Society's grew almost eightfold. On the conservative side, the New Right's rise to power was propelled in no small part by grassroots activist groups like Phyllis Schlafly's Eagle Forum, Paul Weyrich's Free Congress Foundation, Howard Phillips's Conservative Caucus, and Jerry Falwell's Moral Majority. By 1990, seven out of 10 Americans belonged to at least one association, while one-quarter of Americans belonged to four or more.[41]

Technological progress played an important role in promoting the mad rush to engage in political action. Jet aircraft, television commercials, and cheap long-distance service via WATS lines reduced the costs of mobilizing large and farflung constituencies; fax machines, e-mail, and Web sites pushed costs down yet further. Organizational innovations like direct mail allowed activists to find, raise money from, and communicate with like-minded fellow citizens. Cultural change was crucially important as well. As more and more Americans joined the middle classes and adopted middle-class values, they developed the capacity for abstract loyalties that allowed them to band together with strangers on matters of common interest.

The ballooning size of government was both a cause and consequence of interest-group proliferation. The epochal shift in the 1930s toward larger and more activist government doubtless created strong incentives for the creation of interest groups. A rapidly expanding federal budget was a trough that tempted droves of claimants to muscle their way up for a taste; Washington's sprawling regulatory apparatus encouraged both offense-minded interests seeking some change in the rules, and defensive interests content with the status quo, to organize themselves for competition in the legislative and bureaucratic arenas. Similar dynamics operated as well at the state and local levels. At the same time, the rapid proliferation of interest groups due to technological, organizational, and cultural changes created a swarm of new constitutencies dedicated, in one way or another, to the growth of government. Yet the ultimate impact on policy change was often unclear, since every new proposal now was forced to run a gauntlet of opposition groups clamoring to exercise a veto. Gridlock and drift were more typical outcomes than decisive movement in one direction or the other.

If the effect of interest-group proliferation on the substance of political decision making was ambiguous, the effect on the style of politics was unmistakable. Namely, the power of a few bosses and dominant insiders to control events was rapidly slipping away. The politics of smoke-filled rooms assumed that the number of relevant actors could fit in a single room. As the general public roused itself and organized, that assumption grew increasingly untenable.

Insider control was challenged, not simply by the public at large, but within the political class as well. The rebellion by young Turks against their elders was of a piece with larger trends. As the spirit of Aquarius swept the country, all authority came into question; all hierarchies were suspect. In the public sector, these broad currents of cultural change were accelerated by the changing nature of the political vocation. In the old system, political office was generally a part-time job; only those who occupied or aspired to the very apex of power treated politics as a full-time career. Not until the 1960s did Congress start to remain in session throughout the year; election campaigns used to be ridiculously quick and cheap by contemporary standards. But as America's overall division of labor grew ever more complex, specialization came to the political sphere as it did everywhere else. With the rise of professional politicians at all levels of government, the deference shown by lesser or junior officeholders to the bosses and old bulls began to erode.

"It is true that the modern professional politician does not have to sweat his way through long and expensive academic preparation," wrote the journalist Alan Ehrenhalt in his insightful *The United States of Ambition*. "But if by age thirty he has managed to maneuver his way onto a city council, or a state legislature, he has done so at the expense of years of unglamourous work that are, for him, the equivalent of professional training." Having made such an investment, the modern politician is as allergic to hierarchy and authority as his fellow professionals in law or medicine. "It is not logical to expect someone in that position to show up for the first day of elective office and ask where he can receive his orders," Ehrenhalt continued. "He wants to legislate, to make policy."[42]

In the U.S. Congress, the decisive break with the past came in the wake of the 1974 elections. Those contests, occurring in the immediate aftermath of Nixon's resignation, brought a huge influx of new blood into the House of Representatives: 93 incoming freshmen, 75 of whom were Democrats. The "Watergate babies," as the Democratic members of that Class of '74 came to be known, were young (half were under 40 years old), college educated, and more closely tied to the antiwar movement than to the Democratic Party machinery. A new generation, dedicated to a New Politics of Aquarian-tinged liberalism, the Watergate babies had no interest in following the old rules. In particular, they made clear that the long-established seniority system for committee chairmanships was no longer in effect. Existing chairmen would now need to court the rank-and-file members, and in particular the large new freshman class, if they expected to retain their posts. Such uppitiness did not sit well with F. Edward Hébert, the 73-year-old chairman of the House Armed Services Committee, who chose to address the incoming members as "boys and girls." He and two other old bulls—the 75-year-old William R. Poage (House Agriculture Committee) and the 81-year-old Wright Patman (House Banking Committee)—were subsequently ousted from their posts.

The same developments that were rendering the general populace more organized and politically active, and the political class more open and competitive, were simultaneously redefining the relationship between politicians and public. Specifically, technological and organizational innovations worked to enhance the ability of individual politicians to communicate directly with voters, and that of politically active citizens to choose and support their politicians. Television campaign spots, improved polling techniques, the shift to a primary system for nominating presidential candidates, the growth of political action committees, C-SPAN, 24-hour cable news, the Internet—all empowered political entrepreneurs, whether professional politicians, lobbyists, or activists, to advance their own individual careers and causes. The political parties, which previously were the leading institutions that mediated between politicians and the public, consequently lost much of their power. It was the age of the free agent.

In the new style of American politics, bottom-up replaced top-down. With the decline of bosses and parties, there was no longer anybody in overall charge. Which is to say, there were no longer well-established, generally recognized gatekeepers with the power to decide who ran for office and what issues got on the political agenda. Candidates were by and large self-selected: for anyone with the ambition and talent to raise money, get media attention, and build public support, the path to power was open. Likewise, new issues could bubble up from the most unexpected quarters. Activists with the right timing and the skills needed to persuade, motivate, and organize could push their causes to the center of public debate regardless of what the current political elite might think.

The altered structure of American politics had important consequences for the focus and tenor of political life. The new, more open and entrepreneurial system caused politics to be much more ideological than it had been in the past. The old networks of patronage and mutual back-scratching had broken down; what took their place were networks of shared values and enthusiasm. As a consequence, the rivalry between the two great, opposing religious movements of mass affluence—the Aquarian awakening and the evangelical revival—gradually emerged as the central organizing principle of political debate. With their unmatched capacity to rouse profound passions, those movements were ideal breeding grounds for political organization and participation. With their tendency toward Manichean overstatement, they were ideally suited to attracting the attention of mass media that thrived on sensationalism and controversy. The age of the free agent, it turned out, was also the age of the zealot.

The two major political parties grew more ideologically consistent. Liberal Republicans and conservative Democrats, once commonplace, became endangered species. Formerly, partisan differences had turned on sectional, ethnic, and economic divisions; now, increasingly, religious identity drove party affiliation. Back in the fifties, there was no discernible difference between Republicans and Democrats with respect to church attendance. In the seventies, by contrast, a small gap had opened up: the share of nonchurchgoers who identified themselves as Democrats was 7 percentage points higher than that of regular church attendees. By 1986, the gap had expanded to 35 percentage points, as regular churchgoers were more likely to identify themselves as Republican by 22 percentage points, while nonchurchgoers swung Democratic by a 13 point margin.[43]

A survey of delegates at the 1992 Republican and Democratic conventions revealed stark differences and deep animosities along religious lines. Over 60 percent of first-time white Democratic delegates were either avowedly secular or did not attend church regularly. Among Republicans, on the other hand, 56 percent of first-time delegates were either evangelicals or regularly attendees at mainline Protestant or Catholic churches.[44] The survey also measured attitudes on a 0-to-100 scale of favorability (0 the lowest, 100 the highest). Especially noteworthy was the depth of animus against religious traditionalists among Democratic delegates. More than half the delegates assigned the lowest possible score of 0 to Christian fundamentalists, while the average rating was a sternly disapproving 11.[45]

The same polarization could also be found in the electorate at large. George H. W. Bush won 81 percent of the white evangelical vote in 1988 and 61 percent in 1992 (most of his drop in support went to Ross Perot). In 2000, 76 percent of white evangelicals voted for George W. Bush.[46] Meanwhile, according to an analysis by political scientists Louis Bolce and Gerald De Maio, over three-quarters of so-called secularists—the roughly one-sixth of the electorate in which Aquarian cultural attitudes ran most strongly—voted for Bill Clinton in 1992, while some two-thirds supported Al Gore in 2000.[47]

The parallels between economic and political developments were striking. In both realms, relatively closed and insider-dominated systems were upended by the progress of mass afflu-ence. Concentrations of power dissipated; competition intensified; bold entrepreneurship took advantage of the absence of hem-ming restraints. And with expanded freedom of action came the accentuation of differences. In the new economy, a widen-ing spread in economic outcomes highlighted the distinction between a knowledge-worker elite and the less-educated, low-skilled working classes. The era of hyperpluralism and profes-sional politicians, meanwhile, brought ideological polarization. Although most voters resided in the broad, nonideological center, most of the energy and passion could be found on the two flanks. As a result, whether they wanted to or not, voters were forced to choose sides in an irreconcilable conflict between rival sets of true believers.

DOUGLAS COUPLAND, A young sculptor from Vancouver, launched himself on a writing career when he happened to read Paul Fussell's *Class*. A mordant take on American social stratifi-cation published in 1983, the book concluded with a description of "X people" who stood outside the traditional class structure. "X people constitute something like a classless class," Fussell wrote. "They occupy the one social place in the U.S.A. where the ethic of buying and selling is not all-powerful. Impelled by inso-lence, intelligence, irony, and spirit, X people have escaped out the back doors of those theaters of class which enclose others."[48] Anticipating the "bobos," or bourgeois bohemians, of David Brooks's invention, Fussell was trying, at the close of an extended exercise in categorization, to come to grips with the fact that de-fying categorization was becoming increasingly commonplace.

Fussell's musings clicked with Coupland's sense of his con-temporaries' resistance to pigeonholing. "[T]he frightening sci-ence fiction–like aspect of it is that all baby boomers seem to agree," Coupland later explained. "It's like one entity divided amongst a million separate little beings, whereas I think if you were to ask younger people who are, well, of this generation that . . . refuses to be named, you know, what do you, as a group, think about a certain issue, they'll say well, I think this person-ally, but I'm not going to speak for anyone else and I think that's presumptuous and I'd never presume to speak for anyone else."[49] And so, in a 1988 article for *Vancouver* magazine, Coupland in-troduced the term "Generation X" to describe what followed the baby boom. He then moved to Palm Springs and worked the idea into a first novel, the celebrated 1991 zeitgeist guide entitled *Generation X: Tales for an Accelerated Culture.*

A confection combining equal measures of incisive trendspot-ting and whining self-pity, *Generation X* told the stories of three young friends who fled their "McJobs" in the "veal-fattening pens" of office cubicles and tried to start over. Quite literally, it told their stories: what passed for a plot was little more than an excuse for the friends to entertain each other, and us, with a suc-cession of confessions, fables, and fantasies. In the book's wide margins, Coupland embellished the tale-telling with a dictionary of neologisms (including "McJob" and "veal-fattening pen"), a sprinkling of Liechtensteinian cartoon panels (sample dialog bubble: "Don't worry, Mother . . . If the marriage doesn't work out, we can always get divorced"),[50] and the occasional bumper-sticker koan ("You must choose between pain and drudgery," "You are not your ego," "Simulate yourself," "Control is not con-trol").

This strange mélange cohered, more or less, as an extended meditation on all-consuming, self-consuming disillusionment. The characters in the book, inheritors of Holden Caulfield's self-aborbed, angst-ridden legacy, navigated a cultural landscape overwhelmed by accumulated artifice: the abstract intangibility of work life in an incomprehensibly complex, service sector–dominated economy; the heaping profusion of gadgets, novel-ties, brands, jingles, catchphrases, hit singles, celebrities, and TV and movie plots and characters that comprise the pop-culture pantheon. Holden Caulfield had a keen eye for spotting what he regarded as "phony"; Douglas Coupland's creations, by contrast, now saw phoniness as ubiquitous. Consequently, and paradoxically, the run-amok excess of contemporary information overload stood revealed as "a land that is barren—the equivalent of blank space at the end of a chapter—and a land so empty that all objects placed on its breathing, hot skin become objects of irony." [51]

Generation X succeeded in capturing an emerging new sensibility—a way of thinking and living that resulted when the Aquarian defiance of authority turned back upon itself. During the sixties and seventies, there had been a clear distinction between countercultural rebels and the embattled establishment. By the eighties and nineties, however, the baby boomers were becoming the new establishment—and finding their own pretensions mocked by their successors in adolescent rebellion. For the new generation of rebels, excessive earnestness of any type, whether traditionalist or romantic, was to be skewered and lampooned. What began with the youth culture of the fifties had now come full circle. Now, even antiauthoritarianism had lost its authority. Protest was replaced by ironic detachment.

Such detachment did not have to take the alienated form exhibited by the precious protagonists of *Generation X*—or the real-life variations on that theme by those in the slacker, punk, and grunge scenes. (And to his credit, Coupland always insisted that the story of his crowd was not everybody's story.) Preppies and yuppies, for example, may have accepted conventional definitions of material and career success, but they did so with a knowing wink. Distancing themselves psychologically, if only just a bit, from the roles they assumed, they were willing to poke fun at themselves and the games they were playing. Recall, in this regard, Douglas Coupland's predecessor as subculture tour guide: Lisa Birnbach, author of the 1980 best seller, *The Official Preppy Handbook*. Written as pure parody (on the book's cover, just below the title: "Look, Muffy, a book for us"), Birnbach's *Handbook* nonetheless won an enthusiastic audience as a how-to guide for all those not born in Greenwich but who wanted to adopt preppy styles, mannerisms, and patois. Though frequently depicted as throwbacks to precounterculture values, the preppy and yuppie phenomena were in fact suffused with post-Aquarian irony.

And consider, in a similar vein, the change in TV comedy. In the sixties and seventies, the hip comedies, the ones that most successfully connected with young audiences, were those that used traditional bourgeois and working-class attitudes as their foils. *Rowan & Martin's Laugh-In* and *The Smothers Brothers Comedy Hour* pioneered the antiestablishment satire and parody later employed on *Saturday Night Live; All in the Family* exploited Archie Bunker's working-class bigotry for laughs; *M*A*S*H* pitted a pair of bighearted rebels, Hawkeye and Trapper John, against Frank Burns and Hot Lips Houlihan's puritanical officiousness and hypocrisy. But with the 1982 debut of *Late Night with David Letterman,* a very different kind of comedy began to catch on. Letterman's absurdist, pop-culture-obsessed, and studiously apolitical style made a clean break from the earnestly engaged stance that once constituted comic daring. Smirking, aloof, cynical, Letterman was totally disengaged—detachment was the very essence of his shtick. And following Letterman's lead were the two best sitcoms of the nineties: *Seinfeld* and *The Simpsons*. "No hugs, no learning" was the unofficial *Seinfeld* motto—can you get more disengaged than a "show about nothing"? *The Simpsons'* equal-opportunity authority bashing, meanwhile, fired brilliant satirical shots in every conceivable direction.

Across the wide and complex currents of American culture, disillusionment and irony gave rise to a distinctive new style. Among other places, it could be seen in the architecture of Philip Johnson and Michael Graves, with their playful juxtaposition of disparate elements from prior periods, and their use of ornament for ornament's sake. It could be seen in the pastiche of genres and nonlinear storytelling of Quentin Tarantino's movies. And it could be seen in the sampling techniques of rap artists and canny musical scavengers like Beck and Moby. The common style here, often referred to as postmodern, was actually an antistyle: a refusal to accept the old notion that each time and place had its own distinctive set of forms. It was fitting that the term "postmodern," like "Generation X," said nothing about its subject. For both the post-boomer cohort itself and the culture it produced and consumed were distinguished precisely by their slippery, protean undefinability.

The attraction to variety and permutation went hand in hand with a genial, nonjudgmental relativism. "There is one thing a professor can be absolutely certain of: almost every student entering the university believes, or says he believes, that truth is relative." With those words, expressed with deep regret, the conservative scholar Allan Bloom began his 1987 opus, *The Closing of the American Mind.*[52] A decade later, liberal sociologist Alan Wolfe saw much the same thing, although he was rather more cheery about it. "To exclude, to condemn, is to judge, and middle-class Americans are reluctant to pass judgment on how other people act and think," Wolfe observed in *One Nation, After All.*[53]

Though the new sensibility was denounced by ideologues of the traditionalist right, it was equally disappointing to their counterparts of the romantic left. Back in the sixties, after all, countercultural radicals had had no difficulty in passing judgment on the uptight squares of the establishment. And in the eighties and nineties, those who remained wedded to the failed utopian dream were quick to condemn the reticence of the rising generation as apathy and self-centeredness.

The charge of self-centeredness was not entirely out of line, though it hardly stung when coming from aging baby boomers. But apathy? On the contrary, a thousand flowers were set to bloom. The new tolerance, and its accompanying suspicion of all exclusivist claims to truth, gave impetus to an exuberant outpouring of cultural experimentation and subcultural proliferation.

Headbangers, Goths, punks, ravers, rappers, slam poets, krump dancers, swing dancers, ovo-lacto-vegetarians, vegans, fruitarians, Wiccans, JuBus, hashers, sluggers, NASCAR fans, rodeoers, Corvair enthusiasts, birders, comet hunters, role-playing gamers, reading-club members, soccer moms, metro-sexuals, buppies, yachters, skateboarders, BASE jumpers, marathoners, Burning Man attendees, ham radio operators, 12-step groupies, Esperanto speakers, Civil War reenactors, zine publishers, bloggers—these and countless other subcultures, lifestyles, and mix-and-match identities have sprung up, grown, and mutated in the new culture of plenitude.

Recent years have seen a good deal of intellectually fashion-able hand-wringing about Americans' increasing self-absorption and withdrawal from community life. Concerns about declining "social capital" have been raised most prominently by Robert Putnam, the Harvard political scientist and author of *Bowling Alone.* More people are bowling than ever before, he argued, using his famous example, but membership in organized bowl-ing leagues is declining—as is membership in a host of other or-ganizations, from Shriners and Jaycees to the League of Women Voters, PTAs, and labor unions. "Of course, membership is down even more dramatically in the Grand Army of the Republic (GAR), easily the largest social/civic group in post–Civil War America; and in the Anti-Saloon League, an association which energized millions of Protestant Americans in towns across the country . . . ," responded Everett Carll Ladd, head of the Roper Center for Public Opinion Research.[54] With that mocking retort, Ladd exposed the fundamental flaw in the "bowling alone" the-sis—namely, confusing the fortunes of particular organizations with the overall state of American sociability and civic-mindedness. Only such myopia could explain the failure to ap-preciate the phenomenal profusion of new affinity groups and communities.

"New species of social life," wrote the theorist of plenitude Grant McCracken, "form everywhere in the culture of commo-tion: around a football team (e.g., Raiders fans), a rock group (e.g., Deadheads), a TV series (e.g., Trekkers), a leisure activity (e.g., line dancing), an economic downturn (e.g., slackers), an economic upturn (e.g., preppies), a means of transport (e.g.,

Hell's Angels), a modernist aesthetic (e.g., space-age bachelor-pad music), a sports activity (e.g., Ultimate Frisbee), a movie (e.g., *Rocky Horror Picture Show*), and a communications technology (e.g., geeks)."[55] Like shipwrecks that come to serve as sea-life habitats, even the most banal and throwaway products of consumer society could be refashioned into the stuff of community and personal meaning. "Anything can be a sunken ship— a point around which a species of social life can muster," McCracken wrote. "But, strictly speaking, the metaphor has its limits. After all, real sunken ships draw only existing species while the metaphorical ones of the contemporary world actually help invent new ones."[56]

According to a popular argument among critics of consumerism, the ongoing pileup of material plenty has brought little in the way of increased happiness because so many of our possessions are valued primarily as "positional goods," or status symbols. Since the quantity of social status is fixed, the argument goes, consumerism has amounted to a kind of arms race in which we must strive unceasingly just to maintain our relative positions. So what if you keep moving into bigger and bigger houses, stocked with more and more stuff, if the Joneses remain one step ahead of you?

There is some force to the argument, to be sure, but it is easily overstated. Flat-screen TVs and vacations in the Galápagos are, after all, enjoyable on their own merits, not merely for the bragging rights they confer. And furthermore, the assumption that status seeking is a zero-sum game, in which one contestant's gain is necessarily and unavoidably another's loss, makes less and less sense in a culture of plenitude. Every new subculture, every new lifestyle grouping, has created its own little status hierarchy, with rich rewards in esteem and camaraderie for those who participate successfully in this or that little corner of social endeavor.[57]

Consider, in this regard, a social setting long known for its brutal status competition: high school. "In the 1950s, for instance, there were only two categories of teen," Grant McCracken observed. "As one respondent put it, 'When I was 16, you could be mainstream or James Dean. That was it. You had to choose.' "[58] With such limited options, fitting in proved next to impossible for depressingly large numbers of people. Today, thanks to subcultural proliferation, the chances of finding a niche have improved. A young member of the Goth scene explained to McCracken how she found hers: "We were Goth, namely because of our environments. Suburbia, a high school that came straight out of *Heathers*, and we just didn't fit. Our 'peers' and our parents let us know every single chance they got. I'd like to think of it as a protective mechanism. . . . We weren't perfect and [we were] tired of pretending."[59]

The same kind of dynamic could be found in the adult world as well. The increasing complexity of American society meant that the diversity of viewpoints, interests, passions, and aptitudes was increasing as well. And with the Internet and other connective technologies, the ability of people with similar interests to find each other improved by leaps and bounds. The march of consumerism, therefore, brought both wealth creation and status creation—and with both, richer opportunities for self-realization.

The explosion of new identities and communities has been fueled by ongoing advances in information and communications technologies. Once highly centralized and aimed at the lowest common denominator of public appeal and acceptability, the mass media were transformed by new entrants that took advantage of falling costs to offer increasingly specialized fare. The number of periodicals in circulation soared from 6,960 in 1970 to more than 11,000 by 1994. Cable and satellite systems now offered hundreds of channels; the broadcast networks, which commanded 85 to 90 percent of the prime-time viewing audience in the 1960s, saw their share of that audience drop below 50 percent by 2001. The Internet, meanwhile, brought the proliferation of information sources to levels beyond prior imagining. As of the end of 2005, the popular search engine Google had indexed more than eight billion Web pages, while another search engine, Technorati, was tracking over 26 million weblogs. World-wide e-mail traffic approached 50 billion messages a day in 2006, not counting the spam that dwarfs regular traffic.

Decades of liberal immigration policies have been a major contributor to the country's teeming cultural diversity. Over 28 million people spoke Spanish at home as of 2000; more than two million spoke Chinese; 1.2 million spoke Tagalog (the language of the Philippines); nearly 900,000 spoke Korean; 615,000 spoke Arabic. By 2001, the number of adults identifying themselves as Muslims, Buddhists, and Hindus exceeded those who identified themselves as Jews.

America as Babel, indeed. In recent decades, interrelated and mutually reinforcing processes of economic, political, and cultural differentiation and competition have triggered a mad expansion of social complexity and variety. The Aquarian dream of widened horizons came true, after a fashion, but only after the idol-smashing radicalism of the sixties was first checked by a conservative backlash, then swallowed up by a more comprehensive iconoclasm. Ironic origins for an ironic age.

Americans reacted to the enlarged social space of the eighties and nineties as they have always reacted to the opening of new frontiers: with a pell-mell rush into the unknown. They came in search of riches, power, new forms of self-expression and community, and the quiet pleasures of increased elbow room. But could they tame this moral wilderness? Perhaps they would lose themselves in all the vast choices, like the lonely, autistic savants of Borges's library. Perhaps they would dissipate their energies in ill-considered and self-destructive pursuits. Or perhaps they would be at each others' throats, locked in intractable ideological and religious conflict. By the early twenty-first century, Americans had reached the realm of freedom and begun its exploration. Could they hold on to it now? Could they prove worthy of its blessings?

EIGHT

E Pluribus Unum?

———•◆•———

The horrors of September 11, 2001, occasioned an immense outpouring of raw patriotic sentiment, unembarrassed by irony or self-consciousness. Amidst their shock and sorrow and anger and fear, Americans found themselves, often unexpectedly, overwhelmed with love—love for a bleeding, threatened country and its unique and suddenly fragile way of life.

Wal-Mart reported sales of 450,000 flags in just the first three days after the terrorist attacks. Polls later in the month showed that some 80 percent of Americans were displaying Old Glory at their homes or on their cars or clothes. Joining in were many for whom flag-waving was an unaccustomed pleasure. "A few days after the World Trade Center massacre, my wife and I hung out a flag on our balcony in Greenwich Village. Our desire was visceral—to express solidarity with the dead, membership in a wounded nation, and affection for the community of rescue that affirmed life in the midst of death, springing up to dig through the nearby ashes and ruins."[1] So wrote Todd Gitlin, onetime leader of Students for a Democratic Society. A generation earlier, members of that organization typically had visceral reactions to the Stars and Stripes of an entirely different sort.

New heroes were celebrated and mourned—ordinary, worka-day Americans who, in the extremity of their final hours, re-vealed the moral grandeur that underlies even the most routine aspects of life in the realm of freedom. Cops on the street, fire-fighters responding to a call, men and women jetting across a continent and back to make their livings—the prosaic was sud-denly transfigured. Among the brave were Todd Beamer and Mark Bingham, two of the passengers aboard United Airlines Flight 93 whose efforts to rush the cockpit prevented the doomed plane from reaching Washington. Beamer, a New Jersey–based account manager at the software firm Oracle, was an evangelical Christian who recited the Lord's Prayer with a phone operator shortly before dying. Bingham, the head of his own public rela-tions firm in the Bay Area, was a gay Berkeley graduate who also happened to be a former rugby star and a proud Republican. The courage of these men and their fellow passengers saved the Capitol, or perhaps the White House, from fiery destruction. Such complex lives, so characteristically American in their mix-ing of identities and scrambling of stereotypes, thus were sacri-ficed for the country that made them possible.

Patriotic acts, big and small, were accompanied by decidedly more patriotic attitudes. One January 2002 poll found that 60 percent of those surveyed felt more patriotic after September 11, while another poll showed that 87 percent appreciated their country more. In November 2001, 74 percent of Americans ex-pressed the view that the country was united about the most im-portant values, while a quarter reported that the country was divided. In 1998, by contrast, 66 percent had said the country was divided.[2] Literally and figuratively, Americans were rallying around the flag.

Four years after the attacks on New York and Washington, di-saster struck another American city. This time the cause was, not terrorism, but blind nature. This time there was no feel-good silver lining. On the morning of August 29, 2005, Hurricane Ka-trina made landfall in eastern Louisiana, bringing devastation to much of the Gulf Coast. Although New Orleans avoided the brunt of the storm, multiple breaches in the city's levee system soon left three-quarters of the entire metropolitan area under water. Most residents had evacuated in time, but many tens of thousands stayed behind—a situation attributable at least partly to the fact that the poverty rate in mostly black New Orleans stood at a dismal 38 percent. What followed was a descent into chaos. The confirmed death toll in Louisiana topped 1,100 (more than 200 Mississippians also perished). Among the dead were 34 nursing home patients, left to drown in their beds. Survivors, meanwhile, faced horrific conditions. Desperate throngs huddled in the Superdome and Convention Center without power or adequate supplies. Outside, understandable looting for necessities degenerated quickly into wild crime sprees by predators out for fun and profit. Snipers fired on relief workers. Sensational early reports of worse atrocities were eventually dismissed, but reality was bad enough.

Government responses to the storm and its aftermath were a study in clownish incompetence. The levee system was badly defective. The city's evacuation plans failed to address the fact that more than a quarter of the population lacked access to private transportation. A couple of hundred New Orleans police officers simply abandoned the city after the storm, while others joined in the looting. Food, water, and other basic supplies took many days to reach the stranded; there were numerous reports that bumbling federal and state officials blocked the relief efforts of private and other outside agencies. The unqualified and buffoonish head of the Federal Emergency Management Agency, Michael Brown, was recalled from New Orleans during the debacle and resigned soon thereafter. Just a week or so earlier, during his first on-site visit to the disaster area, President Bush had praised his FEMA chief with the line, much mocked afterward, "Brownie, you're doing a heckuva job."

While the trauma of September 11 brought Americans closer together, Katrina's devastation had the opposite effect. Specifically, the country's oldest and deepest wound, the division between whites and blacks, was reopened and liberally salted.

According to a September 2005 Gallup poll, 60 percent of African Americans believed that one reason for the federal government's slow response was that most of the victims were black; only 12 percent of whites agreed. During a live fund-raiser for hurricane relief broadcast on NBC, rapper Kanye West declared flatly, "George Bush doesn't care about black people." Provocative, to be sure, but hardly atypical: only 21 percent of African Americans disagreed according to that same Gallup poll. More depressing yet, it was widely rumored in New Orleans that the levees were detonated intentionally to flood the city's black neighborhoods.

The historian Arnold Toynbee, once renowned but now nearly forgotten, argued that the rise and fall of civilizations could be explained by a pattern of "challenge and response." All societies face changing conditions, whether physical or technological or intellectual in nature, that threaten established arrangements. For some, a given ordeal provides an impetus for growth; for others, it initiates a pattern of retreat and decline.

So what did the challenges of 9/11 and Katrina reveal about the health and future prospects of the American civilization? America's unity after the terrorist attacks expressed the hidden strengths that underlie the country's swarming and cacophonous diversity. Faced with a clear external threat, the great bulk of the citizenry responded as true citizens—members with a stake in, and a proud attachment to, the country where they lived and the rambunctious, raucous lifestyle they were learning to make work. And what powers such shared commitment put in their joint possession! Consider, without necessarily approving how they were expended, the enormous resources at the country's disposal. Here was a nation that, when provoked, responded by changing the governments of two countries a half a world away, with combined populations fully one-sixth as large as its own, all with just a few percent of its national income. By the most basic existential criteria, that was an impressive achievement, however well or haplessly executed—and it was inextricably linked to the populace's firm fundamental preference for jostling self-assertion.

As the threat grew less well defined, however, the self-consciousness of solidarity in freedom inevitably faded. Domestic conflicts reasserted themselves; the consensus over Afghanistan ruptured in Iraq. George W. Bush, after enjoying sustained approval ratings in excess of 80 percent, hung on to win a second term but then found himself badly weakened and short of options. Katrina merely put the exclamation mark on the proposition that unity in extremis does not mean an absence of serious social ills. When Islamist fanatics made war on America, Americans naturally contrasted their own way of life with that of their adversaries—and realized how much they cherished what they had. But in more normal times, America compares itself not to the evil of its enemies, but to the possibilities of its potential. And that comparison always invites discontent. The random tackings of Katrina, and its collision with a once-great city, put some of America's most troubling discontents on painful display. The cultural dysfunction of the underclass, the political dysfunction of urban corruption and federal bureaucratic bungling and ideological feuding—all were showcased, and all continue to fester.

After a half century of mass affluence, American society has undergone transformative changes. Many were for the good; others took a tragic toll. But while most of the attention, celebratory and condemnatory alike, has focused on the breakdown of traditional worldviews, norms, and institutions, an ultimately more consequential story has been unfolding at the same time. A new kind of social order has been emerging—one better adapted than the ancien régime to the wider possibilities created by increasing technological and organizational complexity. Notwithstanding the Aquarian rebellion against order of any kind, recent years have seen at least a partial regeneration of those healthy bonds that hold society together. And notwithstanding the blind-versus-blind ideological conflict that the Aquarian rebellion commenced, a new and workable modus vivendi has been taking shape in the broad center of American public opinion. The unity and strength revealed after 9/11 were not just vestiges of a long-standing but badly depleted stock of social and moral capital. Rather, they were a sign that this stock has been renewing itself in recent years.

The fact that things are better than many people think is certainly no cause for smugness. For, most assuredly, American society today is rife with squandered potential. But if genuine improvements are to be made, they will come from building on existing strengths. And, although the prevailing ideologies of left and right do their best to obscure this fact, America's new, post-Aquarian, middle-class culture has been the indispensable foundation for recent renewal—and in expanding its reach lies the only real hope for mitigating the country's real and lamentable shortcomings.

DURING THE NINETIES, cultural pessimism was rampant on both sides of the ideological divide. On the right, increasingly lurid sexual and violent content on television and in movies and music confirmed dark forebodings of accelerating moral decline (the fact that Bill Clinton won two elections and survived impeachment didn't help, either). On the left, the ebullience of the economic boom provoked acute dyspepsia regarding the spiritual hollowness and ecological unsustainability of it all.

Two of the more intemperate formulations of this ambidextrous gloom came, strikingly enough, from two of the more prominent figures in American politics. In the best-selling *Slouching towards Gomorrah*, Robert Bork, the Supreme Court justice manqué, denounced his country as an "enfeebled, hedonistic," and "degenerate society" that threatened to "slide into a modern, high-tech version of the Dark Ages." The breeding ground of America's afflictions, Bork argued, was nothing other than mass prosperity itself. "Affluence brings with it boredom," he wrote. "Of itself, it offers little but the ability to consume, and a life centered on consumption will appear, and be, devoid of meaning. Persons so afflicted will seek sensation as a palliative, and that today's culture offers in abundance."[3] The devil's workshop churns on!

Vice President Al Gore managed to outdo even Bork's full-throated hysteria. Toward the end of his environmentalist jeremiad, *Earth in the Balance,* Al Gore condemned the spiritual sickness of consumer society with this utterly unhinged analogy. "In Nazi Germany, dysfunctional thinking was institutionalized in the totalitarian state, its dogma, and its war machine," he wrote. "Today, a different dysfunction takes the form of a ravenous, insatiable consumptionism, its dogma, and the mechanisms by which ever more resources are obtained. Totalitarianism and consumptionism have led to crises peculiar to advanced industrial civilization: both are examples of alienation and technology run amok."[4] Analysis like that inspired a popular Internet quiz in which passages from *Earth in the Balance* were placed alongside others from the Unabomber's manifesto and readers were challenged to tell them apart.

Undeterred by such dire assessments, Americans during the nineties embarked upon a remarkable process of moral and cultural renewal. During the sixties and seventies, the spreading spirit of romantic rebellion, in addition to its many positive accomplishments, also served to undermine those healthy forms of self-restraint that make the enjoyment of freedom possible. The damage inflicted was widespread, but the worst effects were reserved for those at the lower levels of socioeconomic status. In the nineties, the damage began to heal. Basic indicators of the strength of social bonds, after decades of disturbing trends, reversed course and started to improve.

Crime rates, after peaking in the early nineties, began a sudden and precipitous drop. The number of violent crimes in a year per 100,000 people fell from its 1992 high of 758 all the way down to 475 by 2003—a 37 percent decline. In particular, the frequency of murders dropped 39 percent; robbery, 46 percent; and aggravated assault, 33 percent. Over the same period, the frequency of property crimes (burglary, larceny, car theft) fell by 27 percent. Numerous theories have been adduced to explain these wholesome developments: demographic change (specifically, fewer crime-prone 18- to 24-year-old men as a percentage of the total population); the subsidence of crack cocaine's popularity; better policing techniques. Surely, though, the most obvious piece of the puzzle was the huge jump in incarceration: the total number of inmates in jails and state and federal correctional facilities leaped by 72 percent between 1990 and 2000, from 1.1 million to 1.9 million. The lenient and lackadaisical approach to law enforcement that arose during the sixties was unceremoniously abandoned.

Welfare dependency also declined sharply. The number of families on public aid stood at over 5 million in 1994; a decade later, the figure had fallen below 2 million. Considerable credit must be given to landmark welfare reform legislation enacted in 1996. Fulfilling Bill Clinton's promise to "end welfare as we know it," the act rescinded welfare's entitlement status, instituted a work requirement, and placed a five-year cap on receipt of benefits. Not unrelated was the fall in births to unwed black mothers and the percentage of black births to teen mothers. Although the illegitimacy rate for African American babies has continued to hover just under 70 percent, the total number of births to single black mothers fell 15 percent between 1990 and 2002. Meanwhile, the share of total black births to teen mothers fell from 23 percent in 1995 to 18 percent in 2002.

The slide toward family breakdown was arrested across American society. The divorce rate in 2003 stood at 3.8 per 100,000 people—down 17 percent from a decade earlier and the lowest since 1971. Along with stronger marital bonds came something of a baby boomlet—the Echo Boom—as the first generation born in mass affluence began creating the next. In the mid-seventies, total live births bottomed out at under 3.1 million a year. By the early twenty-first century, the figure had climbed above 4.0 million. Fertility rates recovered from the 1976 nadir of 1.7 expected births per woman to 2.0 in 2002. The most recent figure still fell below the population-maintaining replacement rate of 2.1 births per woman, but Census Bureau projections estimate that this threshold will be exceeded again by 2010. The increase in fertility may have owed something to the declining resort to abortion.

In 1981, abortions peaked at 29.3 per 1,000 women, with the ratio to live births equaling 43 percent. By 2002, abortions had fallen over 30 percent to 20.8 per thousand women, and now totaled only 32 percent of live births—the least depressing statistics since 1974, the year after *Roe v. Wade*.

Social theorist Francis Fukuyama has referred to the unraveling of freedom-enhancing self-restraint during the sixties and seventies as the "Great Disruption"—a serious but temporary deterioration in the moral climate that accompanied the transition from industrial to information economy. Norms suited to an earlier and simpler way of life became obsolete and fell into disrepute; the Aquarian awakening, throwing the baby out with the bathwater, called all hierarchy and all authority into question. Consequently, even as Jim Crow and retrograde attitudes about the role of women in society were being overthrown, basic commitments to abiding by the law, working for a living, and raising a family were also being weakened. "During the Great Disruption, the culture produced many cognitive constructs that obscured from people the consequences of their personal conduct on people close to them," Fukuyama observed. "They were told by social scientists that growing up in a single-parent family was no worse than growing up in an intact family. They were reassured by family therapists that children were better off if the parents divorced than if they remained in a conflict-strained household."[5] They were also told that crime was an understandable, even heroic response to deprivation, and that working in a menial job was beneath their dignity.

The damage done was real, but not irreversible. "[S]ocial order, once disrupted, tends to get remade once again, and there are many indications that this is happening today," argued Fukuyama. "We can expect this to happen for a simple reason: human beings are *by nature* social creatures, whose most basic drives and instincts lead them to create moral rules that bind themselves together into communities. They are also by nature rational, and their rationality allows them to create ways of cooperating with one another spontaneously. Religion, often helpful to this process, is not the sine qua non of social order, as many conservatives believe. Neither is a strong and expansive state, as many on the Left argue."[6]

Using their inborn capacities for reason and sociability, Americans have been repairing and reweaving their frayed and snapped social bonds. When it became clear that the promise of liberation was being marred by disorder and anomie, people came to realize that all restraints on self-assertion are not created equal—and they began the process of reconciling greater freedom and choice with necessary self-restraint. According to Fukuyama, we are in the midst of a "Great Reconstruction," not unlike that which occurred with the Second Great Awakening during the country's transition from agricultural to industrial economy. In the present case, the move from Industrial Age to Information Age norms was accompanied not by one religious revival, but by a pair of diametrically opposed ones. Out of the antitheses of the Aquarian awakening and the evangelical revival came the synthesis that is emerging today.

At the heart of that synthesis is a new version of middle-class morality—more sober, to be sure, than the wild and crazy days of "if it feels good, do it," but far removed from old-style bourgeois starchiness or even the genial conformism of the early postwar years. Core commitments to family, work, and country remain strong, but they are tempered by broad-minded tolerance of the country's diversity and a deep humility about telling others how they should live. "Above all moderate in their outlook on the world," summarized sociologist Alan Wolfe in *One Nation, After All*, "they believe in the importance of living a virtuous life but are reluctant to impose values they understand as virtuous for themselves on others; strong believers in morality, they do not want to be considered moralists."[7]

Liberal attitudes on race and the role of women in society have now become subjects of overwhelming consensus. Consider interracial dating, once among the most ferociously enforced of taboos. According to a 2003 survey, 77 percent of Americans agreed with the proposition "I think it's all right for blacks and whites to date each other," up from 48 percent in 1987. Even 59 percent of southerners agreed—a remarkable transformation.[8] Meanwhile, as of 1998, 82 percent of Americans approved of married women working outside the home—with less than a percentage point of difference between male and female responses.[9]

And while most Americans still reject the notion that homosexuality is normal, they nonetheless are willing to live and let live. Over 50 percent of respondents in a 2001 survey continued to hold that homosexual sex is always wrong, though the figure has declined from more than 70 percent in the early seventies. Nevertheless, some nine in 10 Americans endorsed equal job opportunities for gays and lesbians as of 2003; over 60 percent extended that endorsement to include teaching positions in elementary schools.[10] Meanwhile, a 2005 poll found that supporters of gay marriage or civil unions outnumbered opponents, 48 percent to 44 percent.[11]

Progressive attitudes on race and sex have been bolstered by new and strict rules of etiquette. Ethnic jokes, once a staple of American humor, are now considered bad manners or worse. Goatish behavior in the workplace is proscribed by strict rules against sexual harassment. "Homophobia" is zealously guarded against. Although the aversion to giving offense is a creditable one, it has veered all too frequently into killjoy puritanism, as exemplified by the widely noted absurdities of "political correctness." Overzealous moralism and humorless busybodyism are abiding American temptations; today they are simply being indulged in on behalf of new causes. Notwithstanding the excesses, the fact that certain forms of casual bigotry are no longer quite so casual must be regarded as a genuine improvement.

These deep bows toward the influence of Aquarius, while highly significant, are nonetheless highly selective. On issues of crime and punishment, for instance, Americans continue to support a hard line. A 2003 survey found that 65 percent of respondents thought the criminal justice system wasn't tough enough, while 26 percent thought it was about right. Only 6 percent said it was too tough. Capital punishment still enjoys strong support, as 74 percent of those answering a 2005 poll favored the death penalty in cases of murder.[12] Enthusiasm for vigorous law enforcement is matched by a strong belief in the right to self-defense. Asked whether they favored a ban on private ownership of handguns, 63 percent of Americans responding to a 2004 survey said no. Moderate restrictions on gun ownership, however, do command majority support.[13]

Although the principle is often honored in the breach, Americans in overwhelming numbers recognize the importance of two-parent families. A 1996 survey showed that 86 percent of Americans regarded out-of-wedlock births as a very serious or critical problem; in that same survey, 81 percent said that divorces involving parents with small children are a problem of equal severity.[14] Meanwhile, belief in the work ethic remains strong. According to a 1994 survey, 74 percent of Americans still believe that "if you work hard you can get ahead—reach the goals you set and more."[15] Along related lines, 66 percent of the participants in Alan Wolfe's detailed study of middle-class suburbanites endorsed the statement that "the problems of America's inner cities are largely due to people's lack of personal responsibility for their own problems." And though they are more alert to its past and present failings than earlier generations, Americans remain unfailingly patriotic. Some 92 percent of Wolfe's sample group said that despite its problems, the United States is still the best place in the world to live.[16]

What has emerged, then, in the broad center of American public opinion is a kind of implicit libertarian synthesis, one which reaffirms the core disciplines that underlie and sustain the modern lifestyle while making much greater allowances for variations within that lifestyle. Though reasonably coherent and sturdy, it remains implicit because it cuts across the ideological lines of left and right that still dominate the definition of cultural and political allegiances and discourse. Lacking affirmative articulation as a mainstream public philosophy in its own right, the libertarian synthesis operates as a largely unspoken modus vivendi, a compromise between the overreaching of the left and right's conflicting half-truths.

Explicitly libertarian thought has exerted considerable influence in recent decades, but mostly indirectly. F. A. Hayek's seminal critique of collectivism, Milton Friedman and the Chicago school's rigorous economic analysis, James Buchanan and the "public-choice" school's insights into the political process, the lonely iconoclasm of development economist Peter Bauer, Robert Nozick's intellectual virtuosity in response to John Rawls, the law-and-economics movement, the novels and polemical writings of Ayn Rand—all have figured prominently in America's postwar intellectual history. Yet the primary channel of libertarian influence has been through the conservative movement's amalgam of free-market economics and traditionalist elements. An avowedly libertarian political movement, conceived as an alternative to both the collectivist left and the traditionalist right, has existed since the sixties, but it has never succeeded in advancing beyond the fringes of American political life. A Libertarian Party was established in 1971, and its presidential candidate in 1980 did win nearly a million votes, but that was the highwater mark. Far too rationalistic and utopian to ever appeal to mass tastes, it quickly sank into crankish obscurity and irrelevance.

The implicit libertarian synthesis that today informs the country's cultural and political center developed, not as the successful program of a self-conscious movement, but as the accidental result of the left-right ideological conflict. Unsurprisingly, that synthesis is therefore hardly a model of consistency. Widespread economic illiteracy, combined with vested interests in the status quo, weaken public support for rough-and-tumble market competition, especially when the competitors are "too big" (e.g., Microsoft, Wal-Mart, oil companies) or, worse yet, foreigners. The bloated middle-class entitlement programs, Social Security and Medicare, remain highly popular despite (or, perhaps, precisely because of) their fiscal unsustainability. And the quixotic "war on drugs" continues to enjoy broad public backing.

Nevertheless, in its broad outlines at least, centrist public opinion comports reasonably well with the reflexive libertarianism often described as "fiscally conservative, socially liberal." And contrary to all the recent talk about a highly polarized electorate divided into right-wing "red" states and left-wing "blue" states, the fact is that a purplish centrism is culturally and politically dominant in America today. According to 2004 survey data, 66 percent of Americans consider themselves either moderate, slightly conservative, or slightly liberal. By contrast, only 21 percent label themselves conservative or extremely conservative, while a mere 13 percent call themselves liberal or extremely liberal.[17] Meanwhile, the divide between red and blue states, while real, is hardly dramatic. Survey data from 2000 showed that self-identified conservatives comprised 31 percent of voters in red states (i.e., states won by Bush in the 2000 election) and 24 percent of voters in blue states (i.e., states won by Gore); liberals constituted 11 percent of red-state voters and 20 percent of blue-state voters.[18]

Consider what is generally regarded as the most polarizing of all the so-called culture war issues: the bitter and agonizing debate over abortion. Notwithstanding the dominance of that debate by impassioned advocates of the more extreme positions, most Americans take the more nuanced (muddled? ambivalent?) view of "yes, but . . ." when it comes to a woman's legal right to end a pregnancy. Pro-choice sentiment generally predominates: a 2005 survey showed that 55 percent of those surveyed believed that decisions about abortion should be left up to a woman and her doctor; 29 percent felt that abortion should be legal only in cases of rape, incest, or risk to the mother's life; and 14 percent maintained that abortion should be illegal under all circumstances. Nevertheless, there is broad support for a variety of moderate restrictions on abortion. Thus, a 2005 poll show that 73 percent favored laws requiring women under 18 to obtain parental consent; 70 percent believed that "partial-birth" abortions should be made illegal unless the mother's life is in danger; and 78 percent supported laws that require a 24-hour waiting period.[19]

Nonideological moderation between the left and right's op-posing claims thus dwarfs the committed partisanship of either flank. Here is the nub of the matter: America is an exuberantly commercial and intensely competitive society, a fact of which true believers on the left sternly disapprove; it is, simultaneously and not unrelatedly, an exuberantly secular and intensely hedo-nistic society, to the deep chagrin of true believers on the right. America is the way it is because the vast majority of Americans choose to make it that way, so it should come as no great shock that excessively vigorous condemnation of the contemporary American way of life meets with broad public disfavor. Ideo-logues, who define themselves by their dissent from America's prevailing cultural synthesis, must temper that dissent in their public pronouncements or else face marginalization.

None of which is meant to imply that ideological conflict is not real. It is all too real, and all too rancorous. But, in the end, it has proved inconclusive. Despite their best efforts, both sides have failed to capture the prize of the great unconverted middle. Moreover, in attempting to do so, both sides have made key con-cessions along the way, so that the very definitions of left and right have shifted toward the cultural center. Today's typical red-state conservative is considerably bluer on race relations, the role of women, and sexual morality than his predecessor of a generation ago. Likewise, the typical blue-state liberal is consid-erably redder than his predecessor when it comes to the impor-tance of markets to economic growth, the virtues of the two-parent family, and the morality of American geopolitical power.

The bell curve of ideological allegiance—with the committed tails dominated by a centrist bulge—is mirrored by a similar bell curve of religious and spiritual identity. As of 1996, 25 percent of Americans belonged to evangelical denominations, while those reporting no religious affliation (the group in which Aquarian attitudes are most prevalent) comprised 15 percent of the popu-lation. The religious center was still occupied by mainline Prot-estants and Catholics, together representing 44 percent of the population. Meanwhile, just as "red" and "blue" sentiments have faded and blurred over the past generation, so too has the intensity of religious commitment. A study by the Pew Research Center divided evangelicals, mainline Protestants, and Catholics into "committed" and "other" on the basis of religious practices (church attendance, prayer, declared importance of religion in one's life) and adherence to traditional beliefs (certainty about the existence of God and belief in life after death, heaven, and hell). Between 1965 and 1996, evangelicals grew from 23.9 to 25.4 percent of the population, but committed evangelicals shrank from 16.9 to 15.8 percent; as the portion of Americans in mainline Protestant denominations fell from 27.2 to 22.1 percent, committed mainline Protestants dropped from 10.1 percent to 6.9 percent; and as Catholics dipped from 23.9 percent of the population to 21.8 percent, committed Catholics plummeted from 16.1 percent to 8.7 percent.[20]

And in the same way that nonideological moderation dominates American political opinion, nonjudgmental tolerance now holds sway in religious opinion. Among Alan Wolfe's sample group of middle-class suburbanites, 84 percent agreed with the statement that "there are many different religious truths and we ought to be tolerant of all of them"; only 10 percent disagreed.[21] A corollary of such relativism: active proselytizing, with its implied or explicit criticism of other faiths, is widely frowned upon. When asked whether it is most important for churches to teach people to live better lives, convert them to a set of beliefs, or do both, 73 percent of respondents in a 1996 survey gave the first answer. The number of evangelicals giving either the second or third answer fell from 74 to 48 percent between 1965 and 1996; for mainline Protestants, the decline was from 35 to 17 percent; for Catholics, from 44 to 15 percent.[22]

The American Babel has thus proved more stable, and more peaceable, than is commonly realized. Yes, the social and cultural dynamism unleashed during the sixties and seventies inflicted significant damage on the bonds that maintain trust and order. In the latest version of an old, old story, liberty once again demonstrated its tendency to degenerate into license. But the story doesn't end there, for liberty contains within it the seeds not only of its own corruption, but of its self-renewal as well. Confronted with the grim consequences of runaway romantic rebellion, Americans began putting greater emphasis on the personal responsibility that is freedom's essential complement. Recent years have, as a consequence, seen a strengthening of social bonds and a return to greater stability.

It is true that increased social dynamism has released powerful centrifugal forces. In economics, politics, and culture, a frenzy of innovation and differentiation has scattered Americans over a vastly expanded social space. From the underclass to the superrich, from survivalist militias to black-clad anarchists, from Christian reconstructionists to neopagans, the extremes of American life are farflung indeed, and the shared values and experiences that produce social cohesion have grown increasingly thin and abstract.

It turns out, however, that this thin and abstract libertarian synthesis is surprisingly robust and resilient. Aside from extreme circumstances like the September 11 attacks, the gossamer bonds of unity in freedom are hardly sensed at all. But they are there all the same, and they exert a moderating influence that marginalizes the extremes and thereby tempers conflict. Indeed, the very diversity of America's boiling, bubbling pluralism serves to strengthen that moderating influence. Because the political and cultural marketplaces are so competitive, no group can take its current size and status for granted. The natural desire to see one's own values and priorities prevail in the larger world—to gain new enthusiasts or converts, to wield more power, to win elections—thus forces groups to engage that larger world and take differing perspectives into account. To be sure, groups that set themselves apart from the larger world can thereby gain recruits. But not too far apart: alienation and paranoia can build and sustain a tiny splinter cell, but any group that is at all serious about wider influence must restrain its centrifugal tendencies.

Furthermore, the fact of pluralism—in other words, the inability of any ideology or sect or lifestyle to dominate the social landscape—gives all groups a shared stake in encouraging mutual tolerance. There can be no doubt, then, that the same relativism which has promoted subcultural proliferation has also been promoted by it. Here is one of the most outstanding, and most underappreciated, virtues of contemporary American society. Criticized on the right as nihilism with a smiley face, and on the left as stuporous apathy in the face of oppression, the prevailing ethos of tolerance in reality marks a truly great achievement. To be sure, relativism has its dangers. The recognition that all human truth is partial and contingent is a profound insight poised on a knife's edge: fall off by forgetting that some truths are more complete than others, and you risk descending into a self-swallowing tolerance of intolerance. But maintained within proper bounds, relativism makes possible the immense diversity that Americans now enjoy. It is the wholesome anesthetic that soothes the pain of difference and allows variety to flourish.

WHILE RECENT DEVELOPMENTS afford solid ground for cultural optimism, it is optimism of a subdued and guarded sort. Contrary to the fevered premonitions of left and right, the apocalypse is not right around the corner. But neither, most assuredly, is the millennium. Adapting to the novel conditions of the realm of freedom, Americans have bested the skeptics and built a social order that, to a remarkable degree, combines incredible complexity with unity and stability. Yet it is painfully obvious that this new social order suffers from a host of nagging and even debilitating ills. America in the early years of the twenty-first century can fairly make this stupendous claim: never before in human history, including any previous era of American history, has a way of life given so many people so many rich opportunities to live healthy, challenging, and fulfilling lives. Yet the claim invites this sharp rebuke: those opportunities are far too often wasted.

The fact that the point is often overstated does not make it any less true: unprecedented cultural freedom has loosed a flood tide of prurience and vulgarity. Howard Stern, Jerry Springer, *Beavis and Butt-Head, South Park,* the Pam and Tommy sex video and a string of lesser imitations, Monicagate, *Girls Gone Wild, Who Wants to Marry a Multimillionaire? Fear Factor,* Janet Jackson's "wardrobe malfunction," porn star Jenna Jameson's giant billboard in Times Square, the 13,600 new hard-core pornographic videos produced in 2005 (up from 1,250 in 1991), and on and on and on—too much is never enough! Contrary to the shrill warnings of hyperventilating prudes, such coarseness is not precipitating a general breakdown of public morals. But neither is it anything to be proud of.

In his delightfully contrarian *Everything Bad Is Good for You,* science writer Steven Johnson makes a convincing case that contemporary popular entertainment, including such widely derided forms as reality TV shows and video games, is actually much more sophisticated and cognitively demanding than the standard fare of more wholesome yesteryears. "For decades, we've worked under the assumption that mass culture follows a steadily declining path toward lowest common-denominator standards, presumably because the 'masses' want dumb, simple pleasures and big media companies want to give the masses what they want," Johnson wrote. "But in fact, the exact opposite is happening: the culture is getting more intellectually demanding, not less."[23] If you harbor doubts, tune into *24* or *Lost* for the very first time and try to figure out what is going on, and then compare the experience to that of viewing a random episode of *Kojak* or *Love Boat.* Or if you have teenage boys around the house, get them to try to teach you how to play Halo 2, and then recall how much easier learning to play Monopoly was.

Still, the fact remains that commercial popular culture is geared to serving the tastes of adolescents and young adults, for the simple reason that their large discretionary income and lack of well-developed brand loyalty make them advertisers' most coveted audience. "Very little entertainment, let alone information, flows your way because no one is willing to pay the freight to send it . . . ," wrote James Twitchell, the perceptive analyst of consumer culture, in a passage directed to older readers. "Ironically, the only way to return to a culture that served the mature would be if everyone over forty made it a habit to change brands of everything every week or so just like the kids."[24]

The logic of consumer capitalism therefore dictates that mass popular culture will, for the time being at least, be dominated by the puerile and sensational. And the continued hold of Aquarian sentiments (most particularly, *épater le bourgeois*) on the entertainment industry, combined with highly diverse and competitive media outlets scrambling for audiences, have ensured that sex and violence, those guaranteed pushers of adolescent buttons, are portrayed with ever-increasing frequency and provocative "edginess."

It is undeniable that, in the vast selections available in this media-saturated culture, there are great treasures available. Contemporary artists are producing a wealth of intelligent, imaginative, and challenging offerings; at the same time, the whole library of past masterworks is more accessible than ever before. But in terms of what is actually consumed, works of quality are swamped by immense, seemingly limitless quantities of dross and dreck. Even in material marked by excellent craftsmanship and some level of higher ambition, there is chronic overreliance on "shock and awe" in preference to depth and believability. None of which amounts to a mortal threat to the republic: the vices of America's "carnival culture," to use James Twitchell's apt phrase, are minor and relatively benign. Consumed in moderate amounts, and mixed with more substantive experiences, a little bawdiness and raucous thrill riding make for simple, undemanding pleasure—and a break from the stresses and pressures of workaday life. Like junk food, much of pop culture is enjoyable on occasion if unhealthy as a regular diet. Yet one suspects that overindulgence in the latter is as widespread as that in the former—and that those morbid bulges of belly fat, so depressingly common these days, have their counterparts tucked away inside people's skulls.

The coarseness of pop culture goes beyond sex, violence, banality, and empty spectacle. There is also the incessant, ubiquitous bombardment of advertising, promotion, and spin. Yes, of course, such bombardment is an indispensable aspect of freedom: a world with a surfeit of choices is necessarily a world saturated with attempts at persuasion. And to be sure, we are far from defenseless, having developed thick, protective shells of skepticism and irony in response to the endless assault. Still, there is no sense pretending that the relentless barrage of insincerity and special pleading is on balance an edifying experience.

In his charming essay, *On Bullshit*, philosopher Harry Frankfurt distinguished between the subject of his study and simple lying. "Someone who lies and someone who tells the truth are playing on opposite sides, so to speak, of the same game," Frankfurter observed. "Each responds to the facts as he understands them, although the response of the one is guided by the authority of the truth, while the response of the other defies that authority and refuses to meet its demands. The bullshitter ignores these demands altogether. He does not reject the authority of the truth, as the liar does, and oppose himself to it. He pays no attention to it at all. By virtue of this, bullshit is a greater enemy of the truth than lies are." And where has this contempt for truth been developed to corrosive perfection? Frankfurt gives the obvious answer: "The realms of advertising and of public relations, and the nowadays closely related realm of politics, are replete with instances of bullshit so unmitigated that they can serve among the most indisputable and classic paradigms of the concept."[25]

Constant exposure to the hard and soft sell is, at its best, wearisome and cynicism inducing. For those less resistant to the nonstop seduction, there are heavier burdens to bear. The awful spectacle of devoted, tearful fans gathered outside Michael Jackson's courtroom, or the more common sight of ordinary folk degrading themselves on TV talk shows in pursuit of their Warholian quarter hours, reveals the woeful psychological consequences of partaking too uncritically in the pop-culture worship of wealth and fame. Consider also the nearly 1.6 million personal bankruptcy petitions filed in 2004, up from under 300,000 two decades earlier. Here is clear evidence of the dysfunction that ensues when the spur of acquisitiveness digs too deeply.

Ideologues of both the left and the right are united in their high dudgeon against the vulgarity of commercialism and pop culture. But from their moralists' perches, they inundate the culture with their own species of vulgarity: the intellectual sloth of superstition and unreason. A few depressing statistics will serve to illustrate the point. According to a 2005 Gallup poll, 53 percent of Americans believe that God created man in his present form, just as the Bible says. A 2002 Time/CNN poll, meanwhile, showed that 59 percent believe that the events in Revelation will someday come true. That latter fact helps to explain the stunning commercial success of the *Left Behind* series of books by Tim LaHaye and Jerry Jenkins. These 12 books, which dramatize events from the biblical end-times, have enjoyed combined sales in excess of 60 million copies.

Americans' credulity, meanwhile, extends well beyond the confines of fundamentalist Christianity. According to 2005 Gallup polling data, 41 percent of Americans believe in extrasensory perception, 25 percent believe in astrology, 24 percent think that the earth has been visited by extraterrestrial beings, 20 percent believe in reincarnation, 21 percent think it is possible to communicate with the spirits of the dead, and 21 percent also believe in witches.

For those ideologically hostile to old-time religion, the fantasies of New Age spirituality offer plentiful avenues of escape from the jurisdiction of fact and reason. Channeling, crystals, crop circles, angels, Atlantis, feng shui, auras, herbal medicine, homeopathy, iridology—a whole rummage sale of hokum is available for Aquarians looking to cobble together a do-it-yourself spiritual life. The popularity of such foolishness is yet another unfortunate consequence of the indiscriminate Aquarian rebellion against authority—including the authority of scientific rationality. In a darkly amusing example of turnabout as fair play, the religious right is now making use of the romantic left's science-bashing techniques for its own purposes. Thus the so-called intelligent design movement, creationism's latest disguise, uses arguments against evolution—"it's just a theory"—that were cribbed from left-wing rants against the "tyranny" of "white Western phallocentric" science.

These characteristic vices of contemporary American society—crassness, materialism, superstition—impose their heaviest burdens on the working and lower classes. Not that the better off are immune—certainly not. But, generally speaking, the same skills that enable America's middle classes and elites to succeed in the economic sphere also advantage them in the cultural realm. In the contemporary knowledge economy, the critical determinant of economic success is a well-developed capacity for abstract thinking, which makes possible long-term planning, large-scale organization, and use of extremely arcane and specialized knowledge. At the low end of the skills continuum, members of the underclass operate within such narrow time horizons and circles of trust that their lives are plagued by chronic chaos and dysfunction. At the high end, members of the managerial and professional elite amass high levels of human capital in the form of expertise and relationships, which allows them to produce significant economic value and claim commensurate rewards.

That human capital also pays off in leisure hours. People with college educations are more likely to read books, follow current events, travel abroad, and attend the theater and symphony as well as more aesthetically ambitious movies—not avoiding trash culture, by any means, but extending their intellectual horizons well beyond it. Likewise, they are less likely to succumb to the escapist credulity of lowbrow spirituality. As to materialism, its appeal cuts across all class lines. It is, however, a romantic delusion to suppose that those of humbler station are on the whole any less susceptible to its charms than people at higher earning levels. Furthermore, people with greater earning power tend to possess the self-discipline that allows them to manage their acquisitiveness with less disruption to the rest of their lives.

It therefore follows that the single greatest failing of America's new social order is this: far too many people lack the middle-class skills and habits needed to thrive in contemporary life. Those who suffer that critical deficit are, with too few exceptions, condemned to relative unproductiveness, and thus to lower standards of living and socioeconomic status. They must do without the comforts and conveniences that the better off enjoy; they must suffer the anxiety that comes with little or no cushion to absorb the shock of adverse events; they do not possess the broader perspective that makes fuller, richer, more challenging lives possible; they are prone to dysfunctional and dangerous behaviors, including dropping out of school, having children out of wedlock, divorce, substance abuse, and crime; and they lack the imagination and discipline to better their situation. In short, they are without the resources, material and cultural, required for taking full advantage of mass affluence's opportunities while at the same time skirting the worst consequences of its temptations.

This failing should be understood as a relative one—relative only to America's own high potential. As an actually existing social order, contemporary American society compares favorably to anywhere else on earth or any prior era of the country's past. Yes, the persistence of the underclass is a serious blot: the existence of such deep social pathologies in such dismal concentrations, and the terrible suffering that they inflict on the innocent, are—or ought to be—sources of national shame. By contrast, the division between the working and middle classes is problematic only insofar as membership in the latter remains too small: better cultural discipline could expand the ranks of those well equipped to make the most of mass affluence. But even in the best of all currently possible worlds, a large fraction of America's population would lack either the ability or the drive to pursue postsecondary education or otherwise develop employable analytical skills. Which means they would continue to occupy a decent and honorable position in American life, one in which comfortable lives full of challenges and successes and good times remain widely available. And there are still paths to upward mobility for the non–college educated if they have technical training, good people skills, a talent at small business management, or just pure doggedness. Warnings that the continued advance of meritocracy could leave America with a kind of IQ-based caste system may serve to promote a useful alertness to risks along those lines, but they do not seem plausible at present. There is still a real possibility of advancement for those willing to work hard.

Even so, we can do better. Many more Americans than have yet done so should be able to develop the skills and habits that give the best chance for success and fulfillment. To refer to current levels of social inequality as a failing, rather than a necessary and irremediable condition, is therefore to assert grounds for optimism. And those grounds do exist, though their emergence is one of the more breathtaking novelties of the age.

For all of human history until the past generation or so, no society that ever existed had more than a modest need for people with abstract reasoning skills. Until industrialization, all the highest and most prized achievements of civilization amounted to a tiny oasis in a vast desert of cruel deprivation. The overwhelming bulk of humanity was fated to suffer, not just relative unproductiveness, but absolute poverty—trapped in lives of tradition-bound manual labor and barely capable of eking out survival. With the coming of technology-intensive production, and the resulting transition to mass affluence, the encephalization of social cooperation began in earnest. Still, however, the industrial economy required for its functioning large quantities of cognitively undemanding manual and clerical labor. Only with the recent shift to the new knowledge-based economy has the demand for cool heads outstripped that for warm bodies.

The implications of this most recent development are widely misunderstood. What has attracted considerable attention, and strenuous disapproval, is the fact that low-skill jobs no longer offer a dependable path to upward socioeconomic mobility—a situation that has contributed to the recent rise in economic inequality. And without a doubt, the declining demand for low-skilled workers has been a source of real misfortune and bitter disappointment for many. But the flip side of the reduced need for low-skilled workers is the growing demand for high-skilled workers. And, consequently, the flip side of today's misfortune and disappointment is greater opportunity for better lives tomorrow. In the past, most people didn't develop abstract reasoning skills because there was no practical benefit in doing so. Now there is. As a result, the prospects for expanding the golden circle of mass affluence's full promise are less constrained than ever before.

Today many people do not live as fully as they might. It has always been thus. Formerly, though, the fact was an unavoidable corollary of scarcity: the division of labor was too crude to allow any but a small minority to develop their intellectual capacities. Today the main problem is the comparatively much more tractable one of cultural lag. The division of labor has now attained such a level of complexity that there are more openings for people with high skills than there are people to fill them. At present, then, the primary obstacle that prevents more people from living better is the persistence of cultures maladapted to current circumstances. Working-class culture has become, to a significant extent, obsolete: it does not raise people to develop the planning, networking, and analytical skills that are the admission ticket to the golden circle. Underclass culture, meanwhile, has been dysfunctional since its inception.

To state such facts should not be confused with blaming the victim. People do not choose their parents or the other circumstances of their birth and childhood. Some people are somehow able to rise above those circumstances; most are not. This is not a statement of moral judgment; it is a statement of fact. From that fact it follows that if people are born into unpromising circumstances, most of them will carry that burden throughout their lives. And in the Information Age, any culture that fails to inculcate long-term planning, working cooperatively with others, and analytical thinking qualifies as unpromising circumstances. Accordingly, if we are sincerely interested in improving American society, we cannot flinch from recognizing that culture matters a great deal. And that, on balance, some cultures have more to offer than others.

So how can beneficent cultural change be encouraged? A frightfully difficult question, the only completely honest answer to which is that nobody really knows. As mentioned above, one part of the answer is the present course of economic development, which is now offering a potent array of both carrots and sticks that encourage greater investment in human capital. Accordingly, public policies that maintain a positive climate for innovation and growth, and that preserve the strong incentives to build human capital, are of critical importance. Improving the educational system would seem to provide another important piece of the puzzle. A parasitical public-education establishment, including immensely powerful teachers' unions, fiercely resists the only workable system of greater accountability for school performance: competition. If public funding of education allowed free choice among traditional government-run schools on the one hand, and charter, home, and privately run schools on the other, the same competitive forces that promote innovation and productivity throughout the economy would at last be allowed into the classroom. A chicken-and-egg problem arises here, though, since one of the most potent forces for improving the schools (including by reforming education policy) would be more parents who cared more about the quality of their kids' education.

The task of encouraging the wider adoption of middle-class skills and habits is complicated significantly by the current high levels of immigration from poor, underdeveloped countries. Coming from backgrounds not unlike those of the southern and eastern European peasants that arrived here a century ago, these new immigrants must make their way in a society vastly more complex than that which awaited the entrants at Ellis Island. In other words, the problem of cultural lag is truly daunting. Worse, many immigrants today come illegally and thus are all but incapable of integrating themselves into normal society. A return to more restrictionist immigration policies, while an understandable temptation, is not so much a solution as it is a form of surrender—an admission that the noble goal of incorporating new people into the American Dream is no longer worth the bother. Taking that goal seriously, though, would require taking assimilation seriously: providing a legal channel for low-skilled immigrants from Mexico and elsewhere and then requiring use of that channel with proper enforcement; ending the failed experiment in bilingual education; and revisiting social policies that encourage ghettoization and sterile identity-group politics.

More generally, our ability to mitigate the ills of present-day social inequality would be greatly aided by a clearer understanding of the nature and sources of the problem. Much of the focus has been on income differences, but these are symptoms, not causes. Unfortunately, when it comes to grappling with the fundamental issues, a lack of cultural self-confidence inhibits efforts to encourage wider assimilation into upwardly mobile middle-class culture. The dominance of political discourse by ideologies of the left and right undermines that self-confidence, as each side has a stake in trashing the prevailing libertarian synthesis. Because of the persistence of ideological polarization, the modus vivendi that has emerged in recent years—and which provides the most promising way of life yet devised for people in mass society—is an unspoken and unloved compromise rather than a well-articulated and widely embraced consensus. As a result, the path of progress through the realm of freedom's vast, alluring, and treacherous landscape remains obscure to our blinkered vision.

The continued ability of ideological minorities to set the terms of public debate is attributable to the decentralized politics made possible by mass affluence. Not the politics alone, though, but its operation in the context of sensational and shallow mass media and a relatively unsophisticated and inattentive electorate. Agenda setting now occurs through a bottom-up process of organization and advocacy, a state of affairs that gives disproportionate influence to impassioned true believers. Activists, meanwhile, need to *activate*—they must generate the money, staff, volunteers, media attention, or voter turnout that they need to further their causes. And they have found that subtlety and nuance are not the keys to the kingdom.

At this state of the nation's political development, what sells are bold, provocative positions that can be conveniently labeled so they appeal to well-defined core constituencies. And to reach beyond the already committed, political entrepreneurs must attract the attention and assistance of large numbers of people who may take only the most casual interest in political matters. Once again, calm tones and judicious, balanced judgments are not the best way to divert public attention away from the multitude of possible distractions. The mass media bear significant responsibility here. Operating in a more decentralized and competitive market than ever before, the large television outlets in particular offer dumbed-down reporting, well marbled with tabloid fat, and with debate between opposing views usually presented at high decibels and wedged into a simplistic, red-versus-blue framework. But the media act the way they do for a reason: they provide the content that gets the biggest audience. Activists often behave the same way in their efforts to reach mass audiences on their own. Direct-mail letters, with their underlining, red ink, capitalized passages, and exclamation marks, are paragons of the browbeating hard sell.

Here, then, is the hard truth: we get the politics we deserve. The low overall quality of political discourse and the persistence of the sterile, left-right impasse both reflect the fundamental fact that the public doesn't demand better. The upside is that major improvements are possible. The decentralized political system is relatively new, and there is reason to think that further development and more sophistication are achievable goals. The Internet's effect thus far on politics has been ambivalent, but one thing is clear: opportunities for being well informed about the larger world have never been better. If the costs of being knowledgeable have plummeted, it is reasonable to expect increasing consumption of knoweldge. At the same time, the employment market's continued strong preference for college degrees is also pushing toward a better-informed electorate. There is thus a reasonable prospect that conditions may eventually allow a breakout from the current ideological alignment.

Lurches in that direction have already been visible. Witness the recurrent appeal of charismatic outsiders like Ross Perot, Jesse Ventura, Arnold Schwarzenegger, and John McCain—men who promise to transcend partisan bickering and the old, tired ideological categories. But thus far no coherent alternative has emerged, because there is no underlying movement—no distinctive, well-understood body of ideas, no mass of self-identified supporters, to combine with the appropriate political personality.

For such a movement to offer a viable alternative to the prevailing ideologies, it would need to start with forthright affirmation of the libertarian cultural synthesis—and equally forthright rejection of the left and right's illiberal baggage. A movement so grounded would probably not yield an explicitly libertarian politics, since it would need to include constituencies that incline toward more activist government. More likely, it would articulate an intellectual common ground shared by small-government conservatives, libertarians, and promarket liberals. It is at least possible that such common ground could be discovered if policy issues were at last delinked from the long-running cultural conflict. What might the resulting consensus look like? Perhaps something along these lines: it would be neither anticorporate nor overly chummy with the K Street business lobby; it would maintain a commitment to noninflationary growth; it would support an ample safety net, but one focused on helping (rather than rendering permanently dependent) poor people and people in temporary need, not sloshing money from one part of the middle class to the other (in particular, the elderly); it would oppose corporate welfare; it would endorse vigorous environmental protection while rejecting green Luddism and refusing to accept that the command-and-control regulatory status quo is the final word on the subject; it would shed the left's hostility to law enforcement and middle-class values while insisting that civil liberties and social tolerance are respected; and it would part company with all grand ideological pipe dreams in the realm of foreign affairs (including pacifism as well as neoconservative adventurism), insisting instead that American power is a positive force in the world but one that ought to be used cautiously.

At present, no viable hybrid of this or any other description exists or even appears to be germinating. For the time being, then, we are stuck with the continuing battle of half-truths. But comparing our situation with that in most other countries of the world, it is difficult to summon up too much self-pity regarding our predicament.

IN OCTOBER 1990, V. S. Naipaul, the Nobel Prize–winning novelist and travel writer, gave a lecture in New York entitled "Our Universal Civilization." Born to Indian parents in colonial Trinidad, an emigrant to Great Britain who was eventually knighted, and an inveterate traveler and gifted and sympathetic observer, Naipaul spoke on a theme that has been central to both his own life and his life's work: the global spread of liberal values and institutions, and the confused clash between them and the traditional societies they confront and transform. In his particular emphasis on the troubled relationship between Islam and liberal modernity, he presciently identified one of the twenty-first century's greatest and most dangerous challenges.

Naipaul nonetheless chose to end on a hopeful note—namely, "the beauty of the idea of the pursuit of happiness." "This idea of the pursuit of happiness is at the heart of the attractiveness of the civilization to so many outside it or on its periphery," he stated at the conclusion of the lecture. "I find it marvelous to contemplate to what an extent, after two centuries, and after the terrible history of the earlier part of this century, the idea has come to a kind of fruition. It is an elastic idea; it fits all men. It implies a certain kind of society, a certain kind of awakened spirit. I don't imagine my father's parents would have been able to understand the idea. So much is contained in it: the idea of the individual, responsibility, choice, the life of the intellect, the idea of vocation and perfectibility and achievement. It is an immense human idea. It cannot be reduced to a fixed system. It cannot generate fanaticism. But it is known to exist; and because of that, other more rigid systems in the end blow away." [26]

Although, as Naipaul correctly notes, the idea of the pursuit of happiness is too powerful to be confined to any one country, it has been central to the American experience from the beginning. The phrase itself comes from the country's founding document, its birth announcement to the world. From that moment of deliberate self-creation, this nation was the purest and most enthusiastic expression of a new kind of society, one in which the idea of a right to the pursuit of happiness was now possible.

The roots of this new civilization trace back to the ancient Greeks, but what we commonly call Western modernity first emerged in Europe a few centuries ago. Volumes may be devoted to outlining its distinguishing characteristics and course of development, but here it suffices to say that the new civilization's defining feature was its ever-deepening reliance on open-ended experimentation and discovery. In "natural philosophy," or science, a never-completed process of advancing and testing provisional and refutable hypotheses came to supplant the static truths of revelation and established authority. In economic life, free-floating market transactions and ongoing technological and organizational innovation took the place of the "just price" and time-honored practice. In politics, democratic government, in which power arises from the people and changes hands in contests of persuasion, overthrew the divine right of kings and hereditary aristocracies. And in social life, a new ethos of individual and group advancement began to challenge the ancient demarcations of status; "making your own way" started to substitute for "knowing your place." The cake of custom fissured and crumbled, and through the widening cracks the open-ended pursuit of happiness began.

America brought all these elements together and proclaimed the birth of what the Great Seal of the United States refers to as *novus ordo seclorum,* or a new order of the ages. To a greater extent than anywhere else, America embodied the intertwining and mutually reinforcing traditions of the new "open society"— which, when seen as a coherent whole, came to be known as the liberal tradition. And as the young nation grew, it became the chief proving ground for the liberal tradition's further development. In particular, beginning in the second half of the nineteenth century, America pioneered the most advanced form of a radically new economic order, born of the union of science and technology: the prodigiously productive system of mass production, mass distribution, and large-scale corporate enterprise. The result was the greatest discontinuity in human history: the triumph over scarcity and the achievement of mass affluence. Social freedom begat material freedom.

Which, in turn, begat further social freedom. Since the 1950s, as a result of mounting prosperity and continued economic development, the open society's process of experimentation and discovery has accelerated even as it has grown dramatically more inclusive. With respect to the pursuit of knowledge, in 1940 fewer than 25 percent of adult Americans had graduated high school, while college education was reserved for the privileged few. Today, a college degree is virtually a precondition for high socioeconomic status, while failure to graduate high school now indicates acute underlying pathologies. In economics, the static oligopolies of the New Industrial State, and the clock-punching conformism of factory hands and Organization Men, have been blown away by a renaissance of entrepreneurship and dizzying technological change. In politics, the reign of party bosses and insiders has been supplanted by a feverish free-for-all of interest groups and grassroots activists. And the pursuit of happiness has exploded through the restraints of tradition and now roams freely over an enormously expanded space of social possibilities. The fall of Jim Crow and the feminine mystique, the rise of Aquarian and evangelical enthusiasm, the mad proliferation of subcultures and identities—these are the consequences of the pursuit's spirited exploration of the realm of freedom.

America in the era of mass affluence has thus given the liberal tradition of the open society an exhilarating elaboration. During the sixties and seventies, the phenomenal social energies released by prosperity often seemed to threaten chaos, or to provoke reactions that would lead to a general retreat from liberal openness. The experience of recent years, however, has made it increasingly clear that the center did hold. It takes the form of today's modus vivendi, a libertarian synthesis of core middle-class values and inclusive tolerance. Though rife with discontents and grounds for discontent, contemporary American society offers a ringing affirmation of the liberal tradition's continued vitality and creative power.

Alas, however, under the influence of rival religious awakenings, the representation of that tradition in social and political discourse has been split between two hostile camps. The prevailing ideologies of left and right are mirror images of one another, each containing a mixture of liberal and illiberal elements. The Aquarian left celebrates mass affluence's diversity and inclusiveness, while lacking due appreciation for the institutional and moral framework that sustains and advances progressive values. The right, on the other hand, defends that framework, but does so on the basis of dogmatic beliefs that remain unreconciled to mass affluence's cultural openness. As a result, Americans of predominantly liberal disposition—which, these days, means the majority who are comfortable with the prevailing libertarian synthesis—are left to choose which illiberal bedfellows they dislike least. Those who are most repelled by the left's collectivism and antipathy to middle-class values drift rightward; those who cannot stomach the religious right drift to the left. People with equal hostility to both ideological flanks are stranded in the political wilderness.

Poised on freedom's far frontier, American society has suffered great convulsions over the past half century. Despite everything, though, the realm of freedom has endured. In wild, unruly
fashion, it has even flourished. Muddling through in resilient,
adaptable, pragmatic confusion has long been the American
way. If we are able to carry on in that fashion, there are surely
worse fates. But can we?

Nothing casts a darker shadow on the country's future prospects than the specter of additional, and worse, terrorist attacks.
A suitcase nuke or smallpox outbreak would not only claim a
terrible toll in human lives; such a cataclysm, in addition, could
provoke a panicked abandonment of civil liberties and a wider
withdrawal toward more authoritarian values. In an age when
small bands of extremists can wield the power of mass destruction, the openness we have come to enjoy takes on the quality of
a high-wire act.

Even if such tragedies can be avoided, other shocks and
stresses are doubtless in store. The forward press of America's
economic dynamism will continue to put strains on the social
fabric. Globalization, combined with ongoing developments in
information technology, will render millions of jobs—including
high-skill, white-collar jobs—obsolete. The upshot will be an
economy that generates new and wider opportunities for creative and challenging work, as well as grievances and resentment
from those whose skills are no longer marketable.

Nothing on the horizon holds more exhilarating promise, and
stokes deeper fears, than the accelerating pace of breakthroughs
in biotechnology. Miraculous new cures, the extension of the
normal life span, genetic engineering to root out defects and ac-
centuate desirable traits—all are possible in the decades ahead.
When manipulation of the genome becomes feasible, human nature itself will leave the realm of necessity and enter that of free
choice.

Peering ahead, one can spy the glittering prizes of new treasures and chances—and the looming menace of great powers
misused. Whatever our technological prowess and the vastness

of our riches, there is no escape from conflict and turmoil; there is no "happily ever after." Freedom, like Pandora's box, always besets us with a host of vexing ills. We should recall, though, that Pandora's box also gave humanity its most cherished blessing. It gave us hope.

Notes

———◆———

INTRODUCTION

1. F. Scott Fitzgerald, "The Rich Boy," in *The Short Stories of F. Scott Fitzgerald: A New Collection,* ed. Matthew J. Bruccoli (1926; repr., New York: Scribner, 1995), p. 317.

2. David Riesman, *The Lonely Crowd,* with Nathan Glazer and Reuel Denney (1961; repr., New Haven, Conn.: Yale University Press, 1989), p. 247.

3. John Kenneth Galbraith, *The Affluent Society* (1958; repr., New York: Houghton Mifflin, 1998), pp. 210–211.

4. Tom Wolfe, *Mauve Gloves and Madmen, Clutter and Vine* (1976; repr., New York: Bantam Books, 1977), pp. 152, 154.

5. Ronald Inglehart, *Modernization and Postmodernization: Cultural, Economic, and Political Change in 43 Societies* (Princeton, N.J.: Princeton University Press, 1997), p. 28.

6. Ibid., pp. 27, 31, 40.

7. Ibid., pp. 38, 281.

8. Quoted in Morris P. Fiorina, Samuel J. Abrams, and Jeremy C. Pope, *Culture War? The Myth of a Polarized America* (New York: Pearson Longman, 2005), p. 4.

9. Quoted in James Q. Wilson, "How Divided Are We?" *Commentary,* February 2006.

10. Jonathan Chait, "Mad about You," *New Republic,* September 29, 2003.

11. See Wilson.

12. Figures derived from National Election Survey data. See also Edward L. Glaeser and Bryce A. Ward, "Myths and Realities of American Political Geography," Harvard Institute of Economic Research Discussion Paper 2100, January 2006.

13. Alan Wolfe, *One Nation, After All: What Americans Really Think about God, Country, Family, Racism, Welfare, Immigration, Homosexuality, Work, the Right, the Left and Each Other* (New York: Penguin Books, 1999); Fiorina, Abrams, and Pope.

14. David Brooks, *Bobos in Paradise: The New Upper Class and How They Got There* (New York: Touchstone, 2000), p. 10.

ONE: THE REALM OF FREEDOM

1. Sources for this account include "The Two Worlds: a Day-Long Debate," *New York Times*, July 25, 1959; "Better to See Once," *Time*, August 3, 1959; Richard M. Nixon, *Six Crises* (Garden City, N.Y.: Doubleday, 1962), pp. 252–263; Richard M. Nixon, *RN: The Memoirs of Richard Nixon* (New York: Grosset & Dunlap, 1978), pp. 203–209.

2. Nixon, *Six Crises*, pp. 259–260.

3. Robert C. Tucker, ed., *The Marx-Engels Reader*, 2nd ed. (1972; repr., New York: W. W. Norton, 1978), p. 441.

4. Genesis 2:8–9, 3:19 (New Revised Standard Version).

5. Hesiod, *Theogony and Works and Days*, trans. M. L. West (New York: Oxford University Press, 1988), p. 40.

6. Herman Pleij, *Dreaming of Cockaigne: Medieval Fantasies of the Perfect Life*, trans. Diane Webb (1997; repr., New York: Columbia University Press, 2001).

7. See Angus Maddison, *The World Economy: A Millennial Perspective* (Paris: Organisation for Economic Co-operation and Development, 2001); Robert E. Lucas Jr., "The Industrial Revolution: Past and Future," *Region*, Federal Reserve Bank of Minneapolis, 2003 Annual Report Issue.

8. Quoted in Pleij, p. 261.

9. Richard Hakluyt, *Voyages and Discoveries: Principal Navigations, Voyages, Traffiques, and Discoveries of the English Nation*, ed. Jack Beeching (1598–1600; repr., New York: Penguin Classics, 1985), p. 274.

10. Quoted in Jack Larkin, *The Reshaping of Everyday Life, 1790–1840* (New York: Harper & Row, 1988), pp. 127–128; for description of homes, see ibid., pp. 121–148.

11. The discussion below relies heavily on ibid., pp. 72–85.

12. Quoted in ibid., p. 79.

13. W. J. Rorabaugh, *The Alcoholic Republic: An American Tradition* (New York: Oxford University Press, 1979), app. 1, table A1.2.; pp. 10–11.

14. Quoted in David Boaz, ed., *The Libertarian Reader: Classic and Contemporary Writings from Lao-tzu to Milton Friedman* (New York: Free Press, 1997), p. 83.

15. An invaluable source of many of the figures cited in the remainder of this chapter is U.S. Bureau of the Census, *The Statistical History of the United States from Colonial Times to the Present* (New York: Basic Books, 1976).

16. Quoted in William Leach, *Land of Desire: Merchants, Power, and the Rise of a New American Culture* (New York: Vintage Books, 1993), p. 16.

17. Ibid., p. 40.

18. Jacob A. Riis, *How the Other Half Lives: Studies among the Tenements of New York* (1890; repr., Cambridge, Mass.: Belknap Press of Harvard University Press, 1970), p. 34.

19. Ibid., p. 155.

20. Ibid., p. 132.

21. Daniel Horowitz, *The Morality of Spending: Attitudes toward the Consumer Society in America, 1875–1940* (Chicago: Ivan R. Dee, 1985), pp. 14, 16.

22. Benjamin Harrison, First Annual Message to Congress, December 3, 1889.

23. Robert William Fogel, *The Fourth Great Awakening and the Future of Egalitarianism* (Chicago: University of Chicago Press, 2000), p. 141.

24. Ibid., p. 140.

25. Stanley Lebergott, *Wealth and Want* (Princeton, N.J.: Princeton University Press, 1975), p. 46.

26. Stanley Lebergott, *Pursuing Happiness: American Consumers in the Twentieth Century* (Princeton, N.J.: Princeton University Press, 1993), p. 97.

27. Ibid., p. 123.

28. Fogel, *Fourth Great Awakening*, p. 141.

29. W. Michael Cox and Richard Alm, *Myths of Rich and Poor: Why We're Better off Than We Think* (New York: Basic Books, 1999), p. 57.

30. All the figures cited in this paragraph are from Lebergott, *Pursuing Happiness*.

31. Robert S. Lynd and Helen M. Lynd, *Middletown: A Study in Modern American Culture* (1929; repr., New York: Harvest Books, 1959), p. 251.

32. John Kenneth Galbraith, *The Affluent Society* (1958; repr., New York: Houghton Mifflin, 1998), p. 2.

33. Tucker, p. 477.

34. Ibid., pp. 475–476.

35. Quoted in Daniel T. Rodgers, *The Work Ethic in Industrial America,*

1850–1920 (1974; repr., Chicago: University of Chicago Press, 1978), pp. 5–6.

36. Alexis de Tocqueville, *Democracy in America,* trans. George Lawrence (New York: Perennial Library, 1988), p. 54.

37. Quoted in Max Weber, *The Protestant Ethic and the "Spirit" of Capitalism,* trans. and ed. Peter Baehr and Gordon C. Wells (New York: Penguin Books, 2002), p. 10.

38. Ibid., p. 11.

39. Letter from Thomas Jefferson to Dr. Benjamin Waterhouse, June 26, 1822.

40. Jon Butler, *Awash in a Sea of Faith: Christianizing the American People* (Cambridge, Mass.: Harvard University Press, 1990), p. 270.

41. Quoted in William G. McLoughlin, *Revivals, Awakenings, and Reform: An Essay on Religion and Social Change in America, 1607–1977* (Chicago: University of Chicago Press, 1978), p. 119.

42. Quoted in ibid., p. 129.

43. Quoted in Daniel Feller, *The Jacksonian Promise: America, 1815–1840* (Baltimore, Md.: Johns Hopkins University Press, 1995), p. 107.

44. Rorabaugh, app. 1, table A1.2, p. 233.

45. Larkin, p. 199.

46. Charles Sellers, *The Market Revolution: Jacksonian America, 1815–1846* (New York: Oxford University Press, 1991), p. 248.

47. Larkin, p. 300.

48. Sellers, p. 366.

49. Quoted in Liah Greenfeld, *The Spirit of Capitalism: Nationalism and Economic Growth* (Cambridge, Mass.: Harvard University Press, 2001), p. 410.

50. *The Annals of America* (1839; repr., Chicago: Encyclopedia Britannica, 1976), vol. 6, p. 511.

51. Alfred D. Chandler Jr., *The Visible Hand: The Managerial Revolution in American Business* (Cambridge, Mass.: Belknap Press of Harvard University Press, 1977), p. 43.

52. John Micklethwait and Adrian Wooldridge, *The Company: A Short History of a Revolutionary Idea* (New York: Modern Library, 2003), pp. 58–59.

53. Peter Drucker, *Concept of the Corporation* (1946; repr., New Brunswick, N.J.: Transaction Books, 2001), pp. 6–7.

54. Chandler, p. 482.

55. Tocqueville, p. 513.

56. Robert H. Wiebe, *The Search for Order, 1877–1920* (New York: Hill & Wang, 1967), p. xiii.

57. Quoted in Sellers, p. 268.

58. Rodgers, *Work Ethic,* pp. 162–163.

59. Quoted in ibid., pp. 155–156.

60. Quoted in Robert Kanigel, *The One Best Way: Frederick Winslow Taylor and the Enigma of Efficiency* (New York: Viking, 1997), p. 446.

61. Quoted in E. Digby Baltzell, *The Protestant Establishment: Aristocracy and Caste in America* (1964; repr., New Haven, Conn.: Yale University Press, 1987), p. 101.

62. Quoted in McLoughlin, p. 144.

63. Quoted in Richard Hofstadter, *Social Darwinism in American Thought* (1944; repr., Boston: Beacon Press, 1992), p. 57.

64. Quoted in McLoughlin, p. 173.

65. Quoted in Hofstadter, p. 73.

66. Quoted in Baltzell, p. 176.

67. Quoted in Hofstadter, p. 83.

68. For a pathbreaking analysis of changes in American legal doctrine during the nineteenth century, see Morton J. Horwitz, *The Transformation of American Law, 1780–1860* (Cambridge, Mass.: Harvard University Press, 1977).

69. Edward Bellamy, *Looking Backward: 2000–1887* (1888; repr., New York: Signet Classic, 1960), p. 166.

70. Thorstein Veblen, *The Theory of Business Enterprise* (New York: Charles Scribner's Sons, 1910), pp. 27, 39.

TWO: CLIMBING MASLOW'S PYRAMID

1. Abraham Maslow, *Motivation and Personality* (New York: Harper & Brothers, 1954), p. 83.

2. The following discussion relies heavily on Edward Hoffman, *The Right to Be Human: A Biography of Abraham Maslow* (Los Angeles: Jeremy P. Tarcher, 1988).

3. Maslow, p. 83.

4. Ibid., p. 91.

5. Thorstein Veblen, *The Theory of the Leisure Class* (1899; repr., New York: Dover, 1994), pp. 17–20.

6. Simon N. Patten, *The New Basis of Civilization* (1907; repr., Honolulu: University Press of the Pacific, 2004), pp. 9, 129, 213, 215.

7. Quoted in Daniel T. Rodgers, *The Work Ethic in Industrial America, 1850–1920* (1974; repr., Chicago: University of Chicago Press, 1978), p. 11.

8. Quoted in ibid., pp. 96–97.

9. Bruce Barton, *The Man Nobody Knows: A Discovery of the Real Jesus* (1925; repr., Chicago: Ivan R. Dee, 2000), pp. 4, 34, 64, 66, 67.

10. Quoted in William Leach, *Land of Desire: Merchants, Power, and*

the Rise of a New American Culture (New York: Vintage Books, 1993), p. 3.

11. Quoted in Robert S. Lynd and Helen M. Lynd, *Middletown: A Study in Modern American Culture* (1929; repr., New York: Harvest Books, 1959), p. 340.

12. Quoted in Daniel J. Boorstin, *The Americans: The Democratic Experience* (1973; repr., New York: Vintage Books, 1974), p. 159.

13. Quoted in Lynd and Lynd, p. 160.

14. Quoted in Stuart Ewen, *Captains of Consciousness: Advertising and the Social Roots of the Consumer Culture* (1976; repr., New York: Basic Books, 2001), p. 131.

15. Ernest Rutherford Groves and William Fielding Ogburn, *American Marriage and Family Relationships* (New York: Henry Holt, 1928), p. 346.

16. Twelve Southerners, *I'll Take My Stand: The South and the Agrarian Tradition* (1930; repr., Baton Rouge: Louisiana State University Press, 1977), p. xlvii.

17. Quoted in Ewen, p. 53.

18. Edward Filene, "Mass Production Makes a Better World," *Atlantic Monthly*, May 1929.

19. Quoted in Michael J. Sandel, *Democracy's Discontent: American in Search of a Public Philosophy* (Cambridge, Mass.: Belknap Press of Harvard University Press, 1996), p. 186.

20. Quoted in ibid., p. 198.

21. "The Treaty of Detroit," *Fortune*, July 1950; "The U.S. Labor Movement," *Fortune*, February 1951.

22. William D. Haywood and Frank Bohn, *Industrial Socialism* (Chicago: Charles H. Kerr, 1911), p. 62.

23. Quoted in Alan Brinkley, *Liberalism and Its Discontents* (Cambridge, Mass.: Harvard University Press, 1998), p. 50.

24. Quoted in William H. Whyte Jr., *The Organization Man* (Garden City, N.Y.: Doubleday Anchor Books, 1956), p. 19.

25. Ibid., p. 19.

26. Quoted in Lizabeth Cohen, *A Consumers' Republic: The Politics of Mass Consumption in Postwar America* (New York: Alfred A. Knopf, 2003), p. 119.

27. David M. Potter, *People of Plenty: Economic Abundance and the American Character* (Chicago: University of Chicago Press, 1954), p. 70.

28. Cohen, p. 124.

29. James Truslow Adams, *The Epic of America* (Boston: Little, Brown, 1931), p. 404.

30. Quoted in Cohen, p. 302.

31. Quoted in David Halberstam, *The Fifties* (New York: Fawcett Books, 1993), p. 280.

32. Quoted in ibid., p. 573.

33. Quoted in Ardis Cameron, introduction to *Peyton Place*, by Grace Metalious (1956; repr., Boston: Northeastern University Press, 1999), p. xv.

34. Dwight Macdonald, *Against the American Grain: Essays on the Effects of Mass Culture* (1962; repr., New York: Da Capo Press, 1983), p. 59.

35. Ernest Havemann, "The Age of Psychology in the U.S.," *Life*, January 7, 1957.

36. Ibid.

37. "Pills for the Mind," *Time*, March 7, 1955.

38. Havemann, "Age of Psychology in the U.S."

39. Norman Vincent Peale, *The Power of Positive Thinking* (1952; repr., New York: Ballantine, 1996), p. 13.

40. See Philip Rieff, *The Triumph of the Therapeutic: Uses of Faith after Freud* (New York: Harper & Row, 1966).

41. Sloan Wilson, *The Man in the Gray Flannel Suit* (1955; repr., New York: Four Walls Eight Windows, 1983), pp. 251–252.

42. Michael Elliott, *The Day before Yesterday: Reconsidering America's Past, Rediscovering the Present* (New York: Simon & Schuster, 1996), p. 65; see Kenneth T. Jackson, *Crabgrass Frontier: The Suburbanization of the United States* (New York: Oxford University Press, 1985).

43. Jackson, pp. 233–238; Halberstam, pp. 131–143; "Up from the Potato Fields," *Time*, July 3, 1950.

44. "Up from the Potato Fields."

45. Quoted in Whyte, p. 316.

46. Herbert J. Gans, *The Levittowners: Ways of Life and Politics in a New Suburban Community* (New York: Columbia University Press, 1967), p. 254.

47. Quoted in Whyte, p. 328.

48. Gans, *Levittowners*, p. 166.

49. Elliott, p. 76.

50. Will Herberg, *Protestant-Catholic-Jew: An Essay in American Religious Sociology* (1955; repr., Chicago: University of Chicago Press, 1983), pp. 47, 50, 66.

51. Quoted in ibid., p. 278.

52. Quoted in ibid., p. 152.

53. Ibid., p. 191.

54. Quoted in ibid., p. 84.

55. Quoted in ibid., p. 89.

56. David Riesman, *The Lonely Crowd*, with Nathan Glazer and Reuel Denney (1961; repr., New Haven, Conn.: Yale University Press, 1989), p. 18.

57. Ibid., p. 25.

58. James H. Leuba, *The Belief in God and Immortality: A Psychological, Anthropological and Statistical Study* (Boston: Sherman, French, 1916), p. 250; James H. Leuba, "Religious Beliefs of American Scientists," *Harper's*, August 1934.

59. Sinclair Lewis, *Babbitt* (1922; repr., New York: Bantam Books, 1998), pp. 3, 105.

60. Richard J. Herrnstein and Charles Murray, *The Bell Curve: Intelligence and Class Structure in American Life* (New York: Free Press, 1994), p. 30.

61. Quoted in ibid., p. 30.

62. Quoted in Cohen, pp. 125, 292.

63. "The U.S. Labor Movement," *Fortune*, February 1951.

64. Herbert J. Gans, *The Urban Villagers: Group and Class in the Life of Italian-Americans* (1962; repr., New York: Free Press, 1982), p. 121.

THREE: HOWL

1. Daniel Bell, *The End of Ideology: On the Exhaustion of Political Ideas in the Fifties* (Glencoe, Ill.: Free Press of Glencoe, Illinois, 1960), p. 374.

2. Daniel Bell, "First Love and Early Sorrows," *Partisan Review* 48, no. 4 (1981).

3. Bell, *End of Ideology*, p. 374.

4. Lionel Trilling, *The Liberal Imagination: Essays on Literature and Society* (Garden City, N.Y.: Doubleday, 1950), p. 5.

5. Ibid., pp. 6, 8, 9.

6. Lorraine Hansberry, *A Raisin in the Sun* (1958; repr., New York: Vintage Books, 1994), p. 74.

7. Ibid., pp. 48, 65, 73–74.

8. C. Vann Woodward, *The Strange Career of Jim Crow*, 3rd rev. ed. (1955; repr., New York: Oxford University Press, 1974), p. 85.

9. W. E. B. DuBois, *Writings* (New York: Library of America, 1986), p. 364.

10. Nicholas Lemann, *The Promised Land: The Great Black Migration and How It Changed America*, (1991; repr., New York: Vintage Books, 1992), pp. 3–5.

11. Quoted in David Halberstam, *The Fifties* (New York: Fawcett Books, 1993), p. 444.

12. Alan Ehrenhalt, *The Lost City: The Forgotten Virtues of Community in America* (New York: Basic Books, 1995), p. 158.

13. Quoted in Alan Brinkley, *Liberalism and Its Discontents* (Cambridge, Mass.: Harvard University Press, 1998), p. 78.

14. Stephan Thernstrom and Abigail Thernstrom, *America in Black and White: One Nation, Indivisible* (1997; repr., New York: Touchstone, 1999), p. 83.

15. Quoted in Taylor Branch, *Parting the Waters: America in the King Years, 1954–1963* (1988; repr., New York: Touchstone, 1989), p. 140.

16. Quoted in ibid., p. 149.

17. Martin Luther King Jr., "Our Struggle," *Liberation*, April 1956.

18. Ferdinand Lundberg and Marynia F. Farnham, M.D., *Modern Woman: The Lost Sex* (New York: Harper & Brothers, 1947), p. 235.

19. Agnes E. Meyer, "Women Aren't Men," *Atlantic*, August 1950.

20. Betty Friedan, *The Feminine Mystique* (1963; repr., New York: W. W. Norton, 1997), p. 44.

21. Robert Coughlan, "Changing Roles in Modern Marriage," *Life*, December 24, 1956.

22. Quoted in Friedan, *Feminine Mystique*, p. 50.

23. Quoted in Ruth Rosen, *The World Split Open: How the Modern Women's Movement Changed America* (New York: Penguin Books, 2000), p. 43.

24. Friedan, *Feminine Mystique*, pp. 357–358.

25. Betty Friedan, *Life So Far* (New York: Simon & Schuster, 2000), p. 103.

26. Friedan, *Feminine Mystique*, p. 315.

27. Thorstein Veblen, *The Theory of Business Enterprise* (New York: Charles Scribner's Sons, 1910), pp. 48–49.

28. Quoted in Butler Shaffer, *In Restraint of Trade: The Business Campaign against Competition, 1918–1938* (Lewisburg, Pa.: Bucknell University Press, 1997), p. 123.

29. Quoted in ibid., p. 109.

30. Quoted in John M. Jordan, *Machine-Age Ideology: Social Engineering and American Liberalism, 1911–1939* (Chapel Hill: University of North Carolina Press, 1994), pp. 57–58.

31. Quoted in E. J. Dionne Jr., *Why Americans Hate Politics* (New York: Touchstone, 1992), p. 172.

32. William H. Whyte, *The Organization Man* (Garden City, N.Y.: Doubleday Anchor Books, 1956), p. 152.

33. Quoted in John Strohmeyer, *Crisis in Bethlehem: Big Steel's Struggle to Survive* (Pittsburgh: University of Pittsburgh Press, 1986), p. 29.

34. Quoted in ibid., p. 71.

35. See Raymond Arsenault, "The End of the Long Hot Summer: The Air Conditioner and Southern Culture," *Journal of Southern History* 50, no. 4 (1984): 597–628.

36. Quoted in Kevin P. Phillips, *The Emerging Republican Majority* (New Rochelle, N.Y.: Arlington House, 1969), p. 444.

37. Quoted in Lisa McGirr, *Suburban Warriors: The Origins of the New American Right* (Princeton, N.J.: Princeton University Press, 2001), p. 96.

38. Quoted in E. Digby Baltzell, *The Protestant Establishment: Aristocracy and Caste in America* (1964; repr., New Haven, Conn.: Yale University Press, 1987), p. 284.

39. Benjamin Spock, M.D., *The Pocket Book of Baby and Child Care* (New York: Pocket Books, 1946), p. 3.

40. Ibid., p. 4.

41. Ibid., p. 266.

42. Ibid., p. 265.

43. Halberstam, p. 475.

44. James B. Twitchell, *Lead Us into Temptation: The Triumph of American Materialism* (New York: Columbia University Press, 1999), p. 93.

45. J. D. Salinger, *The Catcher in the Rye* (1951; repr., New York: Bantam Books, 1964), pp. 2, 3, 9, 13, 137.

46. Jack Kerouac, *On the Road* (1957; repr., New York: Signet, 1982), p. 11.

47. Norman Mailer, *Advertisements for Myself* (New York: G. P. Putnam's Sons, 1959), pp. 337–358.

48. Herbert Marcuse, *Eros and Civilization: A Philosophical Inquiry into Freud* (1955; repr., Boston: Beacon Press, 1966), p. 3.

49. Ibid., pp. 16–17.

50. Ibid., pp. 151–153.

51. Abbie Hoffman, *The Autobiography of Abbie Hoffman* (1980; repr., New York: Four Walls Eight Windows, 2000), pp. 26–27.

FOUR: SIGNS AND WONDERS

1. Mike Mahoney, "Good Hippies' Summer Plans," *San Francisco Chronicle*, April 6, 1967.

2. Quoted in Martin Torgoff, *Can't Find My Way Home: America in the Great Stoned Age, 1945–2000* (New York: Simon & Schuster, 2004), pp. 91–92.

3. Quoted in Charles Perry, *The Haight-Ashbury: A History* (1984; repr., New York: Vintage Books, 1985), p. 122.

4. Quoted in Todd Gitlin, *The Sixties: Years of Hope, Days of Rage* (1987; repr., New York: Bantam Books, 1993), pp. 209–210.

5. Quoted in David E. Harrell Jr., *Oral Roberts: An American Life* (Bloomington: Indiana University Press, 1985), p. 207.

6. Quoted in ibid., p. 5.

7. Quoted in ibid., p. 66.
8. Quoted in Gitlin, p. 51.
9. Quoted in David L. Chappell, *A Stone of Hope: Prophetic Religion and the Death of Jim Crow* (Chapel Hill: University of North Carolina Press, 2004), p. 38.
10. Quoted in ibid., p. 80.
11. Quoted in ibid., p. 91.
12. See ibid., pp. 44–86.
13. Gitlin, p. 82.
14. Quoted in Chappell, p. 75.
15. Quoted in ibid., p. 88.
16. Gitlin, p. 83.
17. Quoted in Torgoff, p. 111.
18. Quoted in ibid., p. 30.
19. Quoted in ibid., pp. 108–109.
20. Quoted in ibid., p. 82.
21. Quoted in ibid., p. 104.
22. Theodore Roszak, *The Making of a Counter Culture: Reflections on the Technocratic Society and Its Youthful Opposition* (1969; repr., Berkeley: University of California Press, 1995), p. 51.
23. Edward Bellamy, *Looking Backward: 2000–1887* (1888; repr., New York: Signet Classic, 1960), pp. 190–191.
24. Tom Hayden, *The Port Huron Statement* (1962; repr., New York: Thunder's Mouth Press, 2005), p. 52.
25. Roszak, *Making of a Counter Culture*, p. 55.
26. Murray Bookchin, "Toward a Post-Scarcity Society: The American Perspective and the SDS," May 1969.
27. Roszak, *Making of a Counter Culture*, p. 41.
28. Gitlin, p. 417.
29. Alan W. Watts, *Beat Zen, Square Zen, and Zen* (San Francisco: City Lights Books, 1959), p. 17.
30. Edward Hoffman, *The Right to Be Human: A Biography of Abraham Maslow* (Los Angeles: Jeremy P. Tarcher, 1988), p. 272.
31. Quoted in Walter Truett Anderson, *The Upstart Spring: Esalen and the American Awakening* (Reading, Mass.: Addison-Wesley, 1983), p. 90.
32. Gitlin, p. 237.
33. Jerry Rubin, *Do It! Scenarios of the Revolution* (New York: Simon & Schuster, 1970), p. 256.
34. Quoted in William Martin: *A Prophet with Honor: The Billy Graham Story* (New York: William Morrow, 1991), p. 212.
35. A. James Reichley, *Faith in Politics* (Washington, D.C.: Brookings Institution Press, 2002), pp. 236, 238, 240.

36. David Frum, *How We Got Here: The 70s, the Decade that Brought You Modern Life (for Better or Worse)* (New York: Basic Books, 2000), p. 153.

37. Quoted in ibid., p. 157.

38. Quoted in Martin, *Prophet with Honor*, p. 170.

39. Quoted in ibid., p. 235.

40. Quoted in Harrell, p. 269.

41. James Davison Hunter, *American Evangelicalism: Conservative Religion and the Quandary of Modernity* (New Brunswick, N.J.: Rutgers University Press, 1983), pp. 93–98.

FIVE: LEARNING TO FLY

1. Timothy Leary, *Flashbacks: A Personal and Cultural History of an Era* (1983; repr., New York: Jeremy P. Tarcher/G. P. Putnam's Sons, 1990), p. 336.

2. Jay Stevens, *Storming Heaven: LSD and the American Dream* (New York: Grove Press, 1987), p. 271.

3. Leary, p. 337.

4. Quoted in Todd Gitlin, *The Sixties: Years of Hope, Days of Rage* (1987; repr., New York: Bantam Books, 1993), p. 399.

5. Hunter S. Thompson, *Fear and Loathing in Las Vegas: A Savage Journey to the Heart of the American Dream* (1971; repr., New York: Vintage Books, 1998), p. 68.

6. Gitlin, p. 307.

7. Ibid., pp. 262–263.

8. Richard M. Scammon and Ben J. Wattenberg, *The Real Majority: An Extraordinary Examination of the American Electorate* (New York: Coward-McCann, 1970), pp. 161–162.

9. Michael T. Kaufman, "Stokely Carmichael, Rights Leader Who Coined 'Black Power,' Dies at 57," *New York Times*, November 16, 1998.

10. "Interview with Huey P. Newton," *Movement*, August 1968.

11. Scammon and Wattenberg, pp. 97–98.

12. James T. Patterson, *Grand Expectations: The United States, 1945–1974* (New York: Oxford University Press, 1996), p. 661.

13. Robert Houriet, *Getting Back Together* (New York: Coward, McCann & Geoghegan, 1971), p. xxxiv.

14. Thomas Frank, *The Conquest of Cool: Business Culture, Counterculture, and the Rise of Hip Consumerism* (Chicago: University of Chicago Press, 1997), pp. 137–139, 150, 159, photographs.

15. George M. Plasketes, "Taking Care of Business: The Commercialization of Rock Music," in *America's Musical Pulse: Popular Music in Twentieth-Century Society*, ed. Kenneth J. Bindas (Westport, Conn.: Greenwood Press, 1992), p. 151.

16. Herbert Marcuse, "Repressive Tolerance," in *A Critique of Pure Tolerance*, by Robert Paul Wolff, Barrington Moore Jr., and Herbert Marcuse (1965; repr., Boston: Beacon Press, 1969), pp. 114–115.

17. Theodore Roszak, *The Making of a Counter Culture: Reflections on the Technocratic Society and Its Youthful Opposition* (1969; repr., Berkeley: University of California Press, 1995), p. 15.

18. Richard Bach, *Jonathan Livingston Seagull* (1970; repr., New York: Avon Books, 1973), pp. 30–31.

19. Ibid., p. 114.

20. William Manchester, *The Glory and the Dream: A Narrative History of America, 1932–1972* (Boston: Little, Brown, 1973), p. 1106.

21. Helen Gurley Brown, *Sex and the Single Girl* (1962; repr., New York: Barnes & Noble Books, 2003), p. 4.

22. Jon C. Pennington, "It's Not a Revolution but It Sure Looks Like One," *Radical Statistics*, 83 (2003): 104–116.

23. David Frum, *How We Got Here: The 70s, the Decade that Brought You Modern Life (for Better or Worse)* (New York: Basic Books, 2000), p. 191.

24. Ibid., p. 191.

25. *Memoirs v. Massachusetts*, 383 U.S. 413 (1966).

26. Frum, p. 173.

27. Quoted in ibid., p. 174.

28. Rachel Carson, *Silent Spring* (1962; repr., New York: Houghton Mifflin, 2002), p. 297.

29. Lynn White, "Historical Roots of Our Ecological Crisis," *Science* 155 (1967): 1203–1207.

30. Paul R. Ehrlich, *The Population Bomb* (New York: Ballantine Books, 1968), p. xi.

31. Donella H. Meadows, et al., *The Limits to Growth: A Report for the Club of Rome's Project on the Predicament of Mankind* (New York: Universe Books, 1972), p. 23.

32. Jackson W. Carroll, Douglas W. Johnson, and Martin E. Marty, *Religion in America: 1950 to the Present* (San Francisco: Harper & Row, 1979), p. 15.

33. Ibid., p. 9.

34. Ibid., p. 21.

35. Robert Wuthnow, *The Restructuring of American Religion: Society and Faith since World War II* (Princeton, N.J.: Princeton University Press, 1988), p. 164.

36. Ibid., p. 165.

37. Daniel Yankelovich, *New Rules: Searching for Fulfillment in a World Turned Upside Down* (New York: Random House, 1981), p. 88.

38. Robert J. Ringer, *Looking Out for # 1* (New York: Fawcett Crest, 1977), p. 10.

39. Yankelovich, pp. 4–5.
40. Quoted in Frum, pp. 74–75.
41. Ringer, p. 325.
42. Frum, p. 80.
43. Ibid., p. 96.
44. Yankelovich, p. xiv.
45. Quoted in Nicholas Lemann, *The Promised Land: The Great Black Migration and How It Changed America* (1991; repr., New York: Vintage Books, 1992), p. 177.
46. Frum, p. 21.
47. Ibid., p. 89.
48. Quoted in Edward C. Banfield, *The Unheavenly City Revisited* (1970; repr., Prospect Heights, Ill.: Waveland Press, 1990), p. 211.
49. Quoted in Stephan Thernstrom and Abigail Thernstrom, *America in Black and White: One Nation, Indivisible* (1997; repr., New York: Touchstone, 1999), p. 160.
50. Tom Wolfe, *Radical Chic and Mau-Mauing the Flak Catchers* (1970; repr., New York: Bantam Books, 1971), pp. 117–118.
51. Charles Murray, *Losing Ground: American Social Policy, 1950–1980* (New York: Basic Books, 1984), p. 248.
52. Frances Fox Piven and Richard A. Cloward, *Regulating the Poor: The Functions of Public Welfare* (New York: Pantheon Books, 1971), p. 343.
53. Quoted in Myron Magnet, *The Dream and the Nightmare: The Sixties' Legacy to the Underclass* (San Francisco: Encounter Books, 1993), p. 163.
54. Murray, p. 256.
55. Ibid., p. 261.

SIX: REALIGNMENT

1. Veronique de Rugy and Tad DeHaven, "On Spending, Bush Is No Reagan," Cato Institute Tax & Budget Bulletin no. 16, August 2003.
2. Richard B. McKenzie, *What Went Right in the 1980s* (San Francisco: Pacific Research Institute for Public Policy, 1994), p. 129.
3. Quoted in Lisa McGirr, *Suburban Warriors: The Origins of the New American Right* (Princeton, N.J.: Princeton University Press), p. 142.
4. Quoted in ibid., p. 141.
5. Quoted in John Micklethwait and Adrian Wooldridge, *The Right Nation: Conservative Power in America* (New York: Penguin Press, 2004), p. 55.
6. Quoted in ibid., p. 56.
7. Quoted in ibid., p. 56.
8. Quoted in Rick Perlstein, *Before the Storm: Barry Goldwater and the Unmaking of the American Consensus* (New York: Hill & Wang, 2001), p. 430.

9. Lee Edwards, *Goldwater: The Man Who Made a Revolution* (Washington, D.C.: Regnery, 1995), p. 338.

10. Richard Viguerie and David Franke, *America's Right Turn: How Conservatives Used New and Alternative Media to Take Power* (Chicago: Bonus Books, 2004), p. 83.

11. Quoted in E. J. Dionne Jr., *Why Americans Hate Politics* (New York: Touchstone, 1992), pp. 185–186.

12. Quoted in McGirr, pp. 188–189.

13. Quoted in ibid., p. 195.

14. Quoted in ibid., p. 203.

15. Quoted in Todd Gitlin, *The Sixties: Years of Hope, Days of Rage* (1987; repr., New York: Bantam Books, 1993), p. 217.

16. Quoted in McGirr, p. 204.

17. Quoted in Jules Witcover, *The Year the Dream Died: Revisiting 1968 in America* (New York: Warner Books, 1997), p. 362.

18. Quoted in Jonathan Rieder, "The Rise of the 'Silent Majority,' " in *The Rise and Fall of the New Deal Order, 1930–1980,* ed. Steve Fraser and Gary Gerstle (Princeton, N.J.: Princeton University Press, 1989), p. 250.

19. Quoted in "Wallace's Army: The Coalition of Frustration," *Time,* October 18, 1968; quoted in Witcover, p. 391.

20. Quoted in Witcover, p. 280.

21. Quoted in ibid., p. 382.

22. Quoted in "Wallace's Army."

23. Quoted in Witcover, p. 382.

24. Quoted in Rieder, pp. 260–261.

25. Quoted in Allen J. Matusow, *Nixon's Economy: Booms, Busts, Dollars, and Votes* (Lawrence: University of Kansas Press, 1998), pp. 2–3.

26. Gallup poll.

27. Quoted in Mark Stricherz, "Goodbye, Catholics: How One Man Reshaped the Democratic Party," *Commonweal,* November 4, 2005.

28. Penn Kemble and Josh Muravchik, "The New Politics and the Democrats," *Commentary,* December 1972.

29. Quoted in William Martin, *With God on Our Side: The Rise of the Religious Right in America* (New York: Broadway Books, 1996), p. 155.

30. Quoted in Matusow, p. 9.

31. F. A. Hayek, *The Road to Serfdom* (1944; repr., Chicago: University of Chicago Press, 1972), pp. 207–208.

32. Quoted in David Frum, *How We Got Here: The 70s, the Decade that Brought You Modern Life (for Better or Worse)* (New York: Basic Books, 2000), p. 302.

33. Quoted in ibid., p. 313.

34. American National Election Studies, University of Michigan.

35. Lawrence B. Lindsey, *The Growth Experiment: How the New Tax Policy Is Transforming the U.S. Economy* (New York: Basic Books, 1990), pp. 41–42.

36. Quoted in Frum, p. 309.

37. Quoted in A. James Reichley, *Faith in Politics* (Washington, D.C.: Brookings Institution Press, 2002), p. 297.

38. Quoted in Martin, *With God on Our Side*, p. 189.

39. Quoted in ibid., pp. 216–217.

40. Reichley, p. 298.

41. Quoted in Martin, *With God on Our Side*, p. 220.

42. Quoted in ibid., pp. 69–70.

43. Quoted in ibid., p. 202.

44. Dionne, p. 234.

45. Quoted in Martin, *With God on Our Side*, pp. 48–53.

46. James Michael Beam, "I Can't Play God Anymore," *McCall's*, January 1978.

47. Quoted in William Martin, *A Prophet with Honor: The Billy Graham Story* (New York: William Morrow, 1991), p. 310.

48. Francis A. Schaeffer, et al., *Plan for Action: An Action Alternative Handbook for Whatever Happened to the Human Race?* (Old Tappan, N.J.: Fleming H. Revell, 1980), p. 68.

49. Quoted in Martin, *With God on Our Side*, p. 193.

50. Quoted in ibid., p. 194.

51. Quoted in ibid., p. 197.

52. Quoted in ibid., p. 204.

SEVEN: IN BORGES'S LIBRARY

1. Jorge Luis Borges, *Ficciones* (New York: Grove Press, 1962), p. 83.

2. Ibid., p. 86.

3. Grant McCracken, "The Politics of Plenitude," *Reason*, August–September 1998.

4. John Markoff, *What the Dormouse Said: How the 60s Counterculture Shaped the Personal Computer Industry* (New York: Viking, 2005), p. xix.

5. Quoted in Leander Kahney, *The Cult of Mac* (San Francisco: No Starch Press, 2004), p. 32.

6. William Gibson, "Since 1948," William Gibson—Official Web site, http://www.williamgibsonbooks.com/source/source.asp.

7. See Theodore Roszak, *From Satori to Silicon Valley: San Francisco and the American Counterculture* (San Francisco: Don't Call It Frisco Press, 1986).

8. W. Michael Cox and Richard Alm, *Myths of Rich and Poor: Why We're Better Off Than We Think* (New York: Basic Books, 1999), p. 123.

9. Douglas A. Irwin, *Free Trade under Fire* (Princeton, N.J.: Princeton University Press, 2002), p. 8.

10. Ibid., p. 10.

11. Mahnaz Fahim-Nader and William J. Zeile, "Foreign Direct Investment in the United States," *Survey of Current Business*, June 1998.

12. Raghuram G. Rajan and Luigi Zingales, *Saving Capitalism from the Capitalists: Unleashing the Power of Financial Markets to Create Wealth and Spread Opportunity* (New York: Crown Business, 2003), p. 68.

13. Ibid., 70–71.

14. Ibid., p. 72.

15. Ibid., p. 81.

16. Ibid., p. 80.

17. John Kenneth Galbraith, *The New Industrial State* (1967; repr., New York: Mentor, 1986), pp. 30–31.

18. Thomas J. Peters and Robert H. Waterman Jr., *In Search of Excellence: Lessons from America's Best-Run Companies* (1982; repr., New York: HarperBusiness, 2004), p. 200.

19. Rajan and Zingales, p. 81.

20. Peters and Waterman, p. 201.

21. Charles Heckscher, *White-Collar Blues: Management Loyalties in an Age of Corporate Restructuring* (New York: Basic Books, 1995), p. 3.

22. David Brooks, *Bobos in Paradise: The New Upper Class and How They Got There* (New York: Touchstone, 2000), p. 110.

23. Robert Solow, "We'd Better Watch Out," *New York Times Book Review*, July 12, 1987.

24. J. Bradford DeLong, "Productivity Growth in the 2000s," unpublished manuscript, March 2002.

25. Cox and Alm, p. 7, table 1.1; p. 129, table 6.7.

26. Ibid., p. 26, table 2.1.

27. Virginia Postrel, *The Substance of Style: How the Rise of Aesthetic Value Is Remaking Commerce, Culture, and Consciousness* (New York: HarperCollins, 2003), pp. 40–41.

28. Cox and Alm, p. 15, table 1.2.

29. Gary Burtless and Christopher Jencks, "American Inequality and Its Consequences," in *Agenda for the Nation*, ed. Henry Aaron, James Lindsay, and Pietro Nivola (Washington, D.C.: Brookings Institution Press, 2003), p. 65, fig. 3-2.

30. Gary Burtless, "Effects of Growing Wage Disparities and Changing Family Composition on the U.S. Income Distribution," Brookings

Institution Center on Social and Economic Dynamics Working Paper no. 4, July 1999.

31. Burtless and Jencks, p. 72.

32. Burtless.

33. Paul O. Flaim and Ellen Sehgal, "Displaced Workers of 1979–83: How Well Have They Fared?" *Monthly Labor Review,* July 1985.

34. Kevin M. Murphy and Finis Welch, "Wage Differentials in the 1990s: Is the Glass Half-Full or Half-Empty?" in *The Causes and Consequences of Increasing Inequality,* ed. Finis Welch (Chicago: University of Chicago Press, 2001), p. 346, fig. 12.2.

35. Figures derived from Frank Levy, *The New Dollars and Dreams: American Incomes and Economic Change* (1988; repr., New York: Russell Sage Foundation, 1998), p. 84, table 5.2.

36. Roy C. Smith, *The Wealth Creators: The Rise of Today's Rich and Super-Rich* (New York: Truman Talley Books, 2001), p. 5.

37. Levy, pp. 119–120.

38. Murphy and Welch, p. 354.

39. Alan Ehrenhalt, *The Lost City: The Forgotten Virtues of Community in America* (New York: Basic Books, 1995), p. 8.

40. Jonathan Rauch, *Government's End: Why Washington Stopped Working* (1994; repr., New York: Public Affairs, 1999), pp. 42, 44, 46.

41. Ibid., pp. 47, 50.

42. Alan Ehrenhalt, *The United States of Ambition: Politicians, Power, and the Pursuit of Office* (1991; repr., New York: Times Books, 1992), p. 34.

43. Thomas Byrne Edsall, "The Changing Shape of Power: A Realignment in Public Policy," in *The Rise and Fall of the New Deal Order, 1930–1980,* ed. Steve Fraser and Gary Gerstle (Princeton, N.J.: Princeton University Press, 1989), pp. 284–285.

44. Figures derived from Geoffrey Layman, *The Great Divide: Religious and Cultural Conflict in American Party Politics* (New York: Columbia University Press, 2001), p. 106, table 3.1.

45. Louis Bolce and Gerald De Maio, "Our Secularist Democratic Party," *Public Interest,* Fall 2002.

46. A. James Reichley, *Faith in Politics* (Washington, D.C.: Brookings Institution Press, 2002), pp. 331, 334.

47. Bolce and De Maio.

48. Paul Fussell, *Class: A Guide through the American Status System* (1983; repr., New York: Touchstone, 1992), p. 186.

49. Interview on CNN's *Heads Up,* May 28, 1994.

50. Douglas Coupland, *Generation X: Tales for an Accelerated Culture* (New York: St. Martin's Press, 1991), p. 154.

51. Ibid., p. 16.

52. Allan Bloom, *The Closing of the American Mind: How Higher Education Has Failed Democracy and Impoverished the Souls of Today's Students* (New York: Simon & Schuster, 1987), p. 25.

53. Alan Wolfe, *One Nation, After All: What Americans Really Think about God, Country, Family, Racism, Welfare, Immigration, Homosexuality, Work, the Right, the Left and Each Other* (New York: Penguin Books, 1999), p. 54.

54. Everett C. Ladd, *The Ladd Report* (New York: Free Press, 1999), p. 25.

55. Grant McCracken, *Plenitude 2.0*, Beta version, 1998, http://cultureby.com/books/plenit/html/Plenitude2.htm, p. 48.

56. Ibid., p. 49.

57. I am indebted to Will Wilkinson for this point.

58. McCracken, *Plenitude 2.0*, p. 23.

59. Ibid., p. 27 (capitalization added).

EIGHT: *E PLURIBUS UNUM*?

1. Todd Gitlin, "America's Left Caught between a Flag and a Hard Place," *San Jose Mercury News,* November 2, 2001.

2. Karlyn Bowman, "Pride and Patriotism: Sept. 11 Affects American Feelings," *Roll Call,* June 27, 2002.

3. Robert H. Bork, *Slouching towards Gomorrah: Modern Liberalism and American Decline* (New York: ReganBooks, 1996), pp. 2, 4, 7, 8–9.

4. Albert Gore: *Earth in the Balance: Ecology and the Human Spirit* (Boston: Houghton Mifflin, 1992), p. 275.

5. Francis Fukuyama, *The Great Disruption: Human Nature and the Reconstitution of Social Order* (New York: Touchstone, 1999), p. 273.

6. Ibid., p. 6.

7. Alan Wolfe, *One Nation, After All: What Americans Really Think about God, Country, Family, Racism, Welfare, Immigration, Homosexuality, Work, the Right, the Left and Each Other* (New York: Penguin Books, 1999), p. 278.

8. "Evenly Divided and Increasingly Polarized: 2004 Political Landscape," Pew Research Center for the People and the Press, November 5, 2003, p. 45.

9. National Opinion Research Center, General Social Survey.

10. Morris P. Fiorina, Samuel J. Abrams, and Jeremy C. Pope, *Culture War? The Myth of a Polarized America* (New York: Pearson Longman, 2005), pp. 58, 60.

11. Gallup poll.

12. Gallup poll.

13. Gallup poll.
14. Gallup poll.
15. Everett C. Ladd, *The Ladd Report* (New York: Free Press, 1999), p. 109.
16. Alan Wolfe, pp. 177, 205, 270.
17. National Opinion Research Center, General Social Survey.
18. Fiorina, Abrams, and Pope, p. 15.
19. "Abortion, the Court and the Public," Pew Research Center for the People and the Press, October 3, 2005.
20. Andrew Kohut, et al., *The Diminishing Divide: Religion's Changing Role in America's Politics* (Washington, D.C.: Brookings Institution Press, 2000), pp. 18, 32.
21. Alan Wolfe, p. 62.
22. Kohut et al., pp. 27, 31.
23. Steven Johnson, *Everything Bad Is Good for You: How Today's Popular Culture Is Actually Making Us Smarter* (New York: Riverhead Books, 2005), p. 9.
24. James B. Twitchell, *Lead Us into Temptation: The Triumph of American Materialism* (New York: Columbia University Press, 1999), p. 29.
25. Harry G. Frankfurt, *On Bullshit* (Princeton, N.J.: Princeton University Press, 2005), pp. 22, 60–61.
26. V. S. Naipaul, "Our Universal Civilization," Wriston Lecture, Manhattan Institute, October 30, 1990, http://www.manhattan-institute.org/html/wl1990.htm.

Bibliography

———————— ·◆· ————————

Aaron, Henry, James Lindsay, and Pietro Nivola, eds. *Agenda for the Nation*. Washington, D.C.: Brookings Institution Press, 2003.

Abbott, Carl. *The New Urban America: Growth and Politics in Sunbelt Cities*. Chapel Hill: University of North Carolina Press, 1981.

Adams, Donald R. "The Standard of Living during American Industrialization: Evidence from the Brandywine Region, 1800–1860." *Journal of Economic History* 42, no. 4 (1982): 903–917.

Adams, James Truslow. *The Epic of America*. Boston: Little, Brown, 1931.

Anderson, Walter Truett. *Reality Isn't What It Used to Be: Theatrical Politics, Ready-to-Wear Religion, Global Myths, Primitive Chic, and Other Wonders of the Postmodern World*. San Francisco: HarperSanFrancisco, 1990.

———. *The Upstart Spring: Esalen and the American Awakening*. Reading, Mass.: Addison-Wesley, 1983.

Arsenault, Raymond. "The End of the Long Hot Summer: The Air Conditioner and Southern Culture." *Journal of Southern History* 50, no. 4 (1984): 597–628.

Atack, Jeremy, and Fred Bateman. "How Long Was the Workday in 1880?" *Journal of Economic History* 52, no. 1 (1992): 129–160.

Bach, Richard. *Jonathan Livingston Seagull*. 1970. Reprint, New York: Avon Books, 1973.

Baltzell, E. Digby. *The Protestant Establishment: Aristocracy and Caste in America*. 1964. Reprint, New Haven, Conn.: Yale University Press, 1987.

Banfield, Edward C. *The Moral Basis of a Backward Society.* New York: Free Press, 1958.

———. *The Unheavenly City Revisited.* 1970. Reprint, Prospect Heights, Ill.: Waveland Press, 1990.

Barone, Michael. *Our Country: The Shaping of America from Roosevelt to Reagan.* New York: Free Press, 1990.

Bartley, William W., III. *The Retreat to Commitment.* London: Chatto & Windus, 1964.

Barton, Bruce. *The Man Nobody Knows: A Discovery of the Real Jesus.* 1925. Reprint, Chicago: Ivan R. Dee, 2000.

Bell, Daniel. *The Coming of Post-Industrial Society.* 1973. Reprint, New York: Basic Books, 1976.

———. *The Cultural Contradictions of Capitalism.* New York: Basic Books, 1978.

———. *The End of Ideology: On the Exhaustion of Political Ideas in the Fifties.* Glencoe, Ill.: Free Press of Glencoe, Illinois, 1960.

———. "First Love and Early Sorrows." *Partisan Review* 48, no. 4 (1981): 532–551.

Bellamy, Edward. *Looking Backward: 2000–1887.* 1888. Reprint, New York: Signet Classic, 1960.

Beniger, James R. *The Control Revolution: Technological and Economic Origins of the Information Society.* Cambridge, Mass.: Harvard University Press, 1986.

Bettmann, Otto L. *The Good Old Days—They Were Terrible!* New York: Random House, 1974.

Bindas, Kenneth J., ed. *America's Musical Pulse: Popular Music in Twentieth-Century Society.* Westport, Conn.: Greenwood Press, 1992.

Bloom, Allan. *The Closing of the American Mind: How Higher Education Has Failed Democracy and Impoverished the Souls of Today's Students.* New York: Simon & Schuster, 1987.

Boaz, David, ed. *The Libertarian Reader: Classic and Contemporary Writings from Lao-tzu to Milton Friedman.* New York: Free Press, 1997.

Boorstin, Daniel J. *The Americans: The Democratic Experience.* 1973. Reprint, New York: Vintage Books, 1974.

Borges, Jorge Luis. *Ficciones.* New York: Grove Press, 1962.

Bork, Robert H. *Slouching towards Gomorrah: Modern Liberalism and American Decline.* New York: ReganBooks, 1996.

Borus, Daniel H. "The Strange Career of American Bohemia." *American Literary History* 14, no. 2 (2002): 376–388.

Branch, Taylor. *Parting the Waters: America in the King Years, 1954–1963.* 1988. Reprint, New York: Touchstone, 1989.

Brecher, Jeremy. *Strike!* Boston: South End Press, 1997.

Brinkley, Alan. *Liberalism and Its Discontents.* Cambridge, Mass.: Harvard University Press, 1998.

Brittan, Samuel. *Capitalism and the Permissive Society.* London: Macmillan, 1973.

Brody, David. *Workers in Industrial America: Essays on the Twentieth Century Struggle.* 1980. Reprint, New York: Oxford University Press, 1993.

Brooks, David. *Bobos in Paradise: The New Upper Class and How They Got There.* New York: Touchstone, 2000.

Brown, Helen Gurley. *Sex and the Single Girl.* 1962. Reprint, New York: Barnes & Noble Books, 2003.

Browne, Harry. *How I Found Freedom in an Unfree World: A Handbook for Personal Liberty.* 1973. Reprint, Great Falls, Mont.: Liam Books, 1997.

Burtless, Gary. "Effects of Growing Wage Disparities and Changing Family Composition on the U.S. Income Distribution." Brookings Institution Center on Social and Economic Dynamics Working Paper no. 4, July 1999.

Burtless, Gary, and Christopher Jencks. "American Inequality and Its Consequences." In *Agenda for the Nation,* edited by Henry Aaron, James Lindsay, and Pietro Nivola. Washington, D.C.: Brookings Institution Press, 2003.

Butler, Jon. *Awash in a Sea of Faith: Christianizing the American People.* Cambridge, Mass.: Harvard University Press, 1990.

Cameron, Ardis. Introduction to *Peyton Place,* by Grace Metalious. 1956. Reprint, Boston: Northeastern University Press, 1999.

Carroll, Jackson W., Douglas W. Johnson, and Martin E. Marty. *Religion in America: 1950 to the Present.* San Francisco: Harper & Row, 1979.

Carson, Rachel. *Silent Spring.* 1962. Reprint, New York: Houghton Mifflin, 2002.

Chandler, Alfred D., Jr. *The Visible Hand: The Managerial Revolution in American Business.* Cambridge, Mass.: Belknap Press of Harvard University Press, 1977.

Chappell, David L. *A Stone of Hope: Prophetic Religion and the Death of Jim Crow.* Chapel Hill: University of North Carolina Press, 2004.

Cobb, James C. *The Selling of the South: The Southern Crusade for Economic Development, 1936–1980.* Baton Rouge: Louisiana State University Press, 1982.

Cohen, Lizabeth. *A Consumers' Republic: The Politics of Mass Consumption in Postwar America.* New York: Alfred A. Knopf, 2003.

Coontz, Stephanie. *The Way We Never Were: American Families and the Nostalgia Trap.* 1992. Reprint, New York: Basic Books, 2000.

Coupland, Douglas. *Generation X: Tales for an Accelerated Culture.* New York: St. Martin's Press, 1991.

Cox, W. Michael, and Richard Alm. *Myths of Rich and Poor: Why We're Better off Than We Think.* New York: Basic Books, 1999.

Cross, Gary. *An All-Consuming Century: Why Commercialism Won in Modern America.* New York: Columbia University Press, 2000.

Dass, Ram. *Be Here Now.* 1971. Reprint, Kingsport, Tenn.: Kingsport Press, 1978.

Dionne, E. J., Jr. *Why Americans Hate Politics.* New York: Touchstone, 1992.

Doblin, Rick. "Pahnke's 'Good Friday Experiment': A Long-Term Follow-Up and Methodological Critique." *Journal of Transpersonal Psychology* 23, no. 1 (1991): 1–28.

Drucker, Peter. *Concept of the Corporation.* 1946. Reprint, New Brunswick, N.J.: Transaction Books, 2001.

DuBois, W. E. B. *Writings.* New York: Library of America, 1986.

Edwards, Lee. *Goldwater: The Man Who Made a Revolution.* Washington, D.C: Regnery, 1995.

Ehrenhalt, Alan. *The Lost City: The Forgotten Virtues of Community in America.* New York: Basic Books, 1995.

———. *The United States of Ambition: Politicians, Power, and the Pursuit of Office.* 1991. Reprint, New York: Times Books, 1992.

Ehrlich, Paul R. *The Population Bomb.* New York: Ballantine Books, 1968.

Elliott, Michael. *The Day before Yesterday: Reconsidering America's Past, Rediscovering the Present.* New York: Simon & Schuster, 1996.

Ewen, Stuart. *Captains of Consciousness: Advertising and the Social Roots of the Consumer Culture.* 1976. Reprint, New York: Basic Books, 2001.

Feller, Daniel. *The Jacksonian Promise: America, 1815–1840.* Baltimore, Md.: Johns Hopkins University Press, 1995.

Fiorina, Morris P., Samuel J. Abrams, and Jeremy C. Pope. *Culture War? The Myth of a Polarized America.* New York: Pearson Longman, 2005.

Fitzgerald, F. Scott. "The Rich Boy." In *The Short Stories of F. Scott Fitzgerald: A New Collection,* edited by Matthew J. Bruccoli. 1926. Reprint, New York: Scribner, 1995.

Flaim, Paul O., and Ellen Sehgal. "Displaced Workers of 1979–83: How Well Have They Fared?" *Monthly Labor Review,* July 1985.

Fogel, Robert William. *The Escape from Hunger and Premature Death, 1700–2100: Europe, America and the Third World*. New York: Cambridge University Press, 2004.

———. *The Fourth Great Awakening and the Future of Egalitarianism*. Chicago: University of Chicago Press, 2000.

Fox, Robert W., and, T. J. Jackson Lears. *The Culture of Consumption: Critical Essays in American History, 1880–1980*. New York: Pantheon Books, 1983.

Frank, Thomas. *The Conquest of Cool: Business Culture, Counterculture, and the Rise of Hip Consumerism*. Chicago: University of Chicago Press, 1997.

Frankfurt, Harry G. *On Bullshit*. Princeton, N.J.: Princeton University Press, 2005.

Fraser, Steve, and Gary Gerstle, eds. *The Rise and Fall of the New Deal Order, 1930–1980*. Princeton, N.J.: Princeton University Press, 1989.

Friedan, Betty. *The Feminine Mystique*. 1963. Reprint, New York: W. W. Norton, 1997.

———. *Life So Far*. New York: Simon & Schuster, 2000.

Frum, David. *How We Got Here: The 70s, the Decade that Brought You Modern Life (for Better or Worse)*. New York: Basic Books, 2000.

Fukuyama, Francis. *The Great Disruption: Human Nature and the Reconstitution of Social Order*. New York: Touchstone, 1999.

Fussell, Paul. *Class: A Guide through the American Status System*. 1983. Reprint, New York: Touchstone, 1992.

Galbraith, John Kenneth. *The Affluent Society*. 1958. Reprint, New York: Houghton Mifflin, 1998.

———. *The New Industrial State*. 1967. Reprint, New York: Mentor, 1986.

Gans, Herbert J. *The Levittowners: Ways of Life and Politics in a New Suburban Community*. New York: Columbia University Press, 1967.

———. *The Urban Villagers: Group and Class in the Life of Italian-Americans*. 1962. Reprint, New York: Free Press, 1982.

Gilder, George. *Microcosm: The Quantum Revolution in Economics and Technology*. New York: Touchstone, 1989.

Ginsberg, Allen. *Howl, and Other Poems*. 1956. Reprint, San Francisco: City Lights Books, 2002.

Gitlin, Todd. *The Sixties: Years of Hope, Days of Rage*. 1987. Reprint, New York: Bantam Books, 1993.

Glaeser, Edward L., and Bryce A. Ward. "Myths and Realities of American Political Geography." Harvard Institute of Economic Research Discussion Paper 2100, January 2006.

Goff, Brian, and Arthur A. Fleisher III. *Spoiled Rotten: Affluence, Anxiety, and Social Decay in America*. Boulder, Colo.: Westview Press, 1999.

Gordon, John Steele. *An Empire of Wealth: The Epic History of American Economic Power*. New York: HarperCollins, 2004.

Gore, Albert. *Earth in the Balance: Ecology and the Human Spirit*. Boston: Houghton Mifflin, 1992.

Greenfeld, Liah. *The Spirit of Capitalism: Nationalism and Economic Growth*. Cambridge, Mass.: Harvard University Press, 2001.

Groves, Ernest Rutherford, and William Fielding Ogburn. *American Marriage and Family Relationships*. New York: Henry Holt, 1928.

Hakluyt, Richard. *Voyages and Discoveries: Principal Navigations, Voyages, Traffiques and Discoveries of the English Nation*. Edited by Jack Beeching. 1598–1600. Reprint, New York: Penguin Classics, 1985.

Halberstam, David. *The Fifties*. New York: Fawcett Books, 1993.

Hansberry, Lorraine. *A Raisin in the Sun*. 1958. Reprint, New York: Vintage Books, 1994.

Harrell, David E., Jr. *Oral Roberts: An American Life*. Bloomington: Indiana University Press, 1985.

Havemann, Ernest. *The Age of Psychology*. New York: Simon & Schuster, 1957.

Hayden, Tom. *The Port Huron Statement*. 1962. Reprint, New York: Thunder's Mouth Press, 2005.

Hayek, F. A. *The Road to Serfdom*. 1944. Reprint, Chicago: University of Chicago Press, 1972.

Haywood, William D., and Frank Bohn. *Industrial Socialism*. Chicago: Charles H. Kerr, 1911.

Heath, Joseph, and Andrew Potter. *Nation of Rebels: Why Counterculture Became Consumer Culture*. New York: HarperBusiness, 2004.

Heckscher, Charles. *White-Collar Blues: Management Loyalties in an Age of Corporate Restructuring*. New York: Basic Books, 1995.

Herberg, Will. *Protestant-Catholic-Jew: An Essay in American Religious Sociology*. 1955. Reprint, Chicago: University of Chicago Press, 1983.

Herrnstein, Richard J., and Charles Murray. *The Bell Curve: Intelligence and Class Structure in American Life*. New York: Free Press, 1994.

Hesiod. *Theogony, and Works and Days*. Translated by M. L. West. Oxford: Oxford University Press, 1988.

Hoffman, Abbie. *The Autobiography of Abbie Hoffman*. 1980. Reprint, New York: Four Walls Eight Windows, 2000.

Hoffman, Edward. *The Right to Be Human: A Biography of Abraham Maslow.* Los Angeles: Jeremy P. Tarcher, 1988.

Hofstadter, Richard. *Social Darwinism in American Thought.* 1944. Reprint, Boston: Beacon Press, 1992.

Horowitz, Daniel. *Betty Friedan and the Making of the Feminine Mystique.* 1998. Reprint, Amherst: University of Massachusetts Press, 2000.

———. *The Morality of Spending: Attitudes toward the Consumer Society in America, 1875–1940.* Chicago: Ivan R. Dee, 1985.

Horwitz, Morton J. *The Transformation of American Law, 1780–1860.* Cambridge, Mass.: Harvard University Press, 1977.

Houriet, Robert. *Getting Back Together.* New York: Coward, McCann & Geoghegan, 1971.

Hunnicutt, Benjamin K. "The New Deal: The Salvation of Work and the End of the Shorter Hours Movement." In *Worktime and Industrialization: An International History,* edited by Gary Cross. Philadelphia: Temple University Press, 1989.

Hunter, James Davison. *American Evangelicalism: Conservative Religion and the Quandary of Modernity.* New Brunswick, N.J.: Rutgers University Press, 1983.

Inglehart, Ronald. *Culture Shift in Advanced Industrial Society.* Princeton, N.J.: Princeton University Press, 1990.

———. *Modernization and Postmodernization: Cultural, Economic, and Political Change in 43 Societies.* Princeton, N.J.: Princeton University Press, 1997.

———. *The Silent Revolution: Changing Values and Political Styles Among Western Publics.* Princeton, N.J.: Princeton University Press, 1977.

Irwin, Douglas A. *Free Trade under Fire.* Princeton, N.J.: Princeton University Press, 2002.

Jackson, Kenneth T. *Crabgrass Frontier: The Suburbanization of the United States.* New York: Oxford University Press, 1985.

Johnson, Steven. *Everything Bad Is Good for You: How Today's Popular Culture Is Actually Making Us Smarter.* New York: Riverhead Books, 2005.

Jordan, John M. *Machine-Age Ideology: Social Engineering and American Liberalism, 1911–1939.* Chapel Hill: University of North Carolina Press, 1994.

Kahney, Leander. *The Cult of Mac.* San Francisco: No Starch Press, 2004.

Kanigel, Robert. *The One Best Way: Frederick Winslow Taylor and the Enigma of Efficiency.* New York: Viking, 1997.

Kaus, Mickey. *The End of Equality.* 1992. Reprint, New York: Basic Books, 1996.

Kerouac, Jack. *On the Road.* 1957. Reprint, New York: Signet, 1982.

Keynes, John M. "Economic Possibilities for Our Grandchildren." *Essays in Persuasion.* 1930. Reprint, New York: W. W. Norton, 1963.

Kohut, Andrew, John C. Green, Scott Keeter, and Robert C. Toth. *The Diminishing Divide: Religion's Changing Role in America's Politics.* Washington, D.C.: Brookings Institution Press, 2000.

Ladd, Everett C. *The Ladd Report.* New York: Free Press, 1999.

Larkin, Jack. *The Reshaping of Everyday Life, 1790–1840.* New York: Harper & Row, 1988.

Layman, Geoffrey. *The Great Divide: Religious and Cultural Conflict in American Party Politics.* New York: Columbia University Press, 2001.

Leach, William. *Land of Desire: Merchants, Power, and the Rise of a New American Culture.* New York: Vintage Books, 1993.

Lears, T. J. Jackson. *No Place of Grace: Antimodernism and the Transformation of American Culture, 1880–1920.* 1983. Reprint, Chicago: University of Chicago Press, 1994.

Leary, Timothy. *Flashbacks: A Personal and Cultural History of an Era.* 1983. Reprint, New York: Jeremy P. Tarcher/G. P. Putnam's Sons, 1990.

Lebergott, Stanley. *Pursuing Happiness: American Consumers in the Twentieth Century.* Princeton, N.J.: Princeton University Press, 1993.

———. *Wealth and Want.* Princeton, N.J.: Princeton University Press, 1975.

Lemann, Nicholas. *The Promised Land: The Great Black Migration and How It Changed America.* 1991. Reprint, New York: Vintage Books, 1992.

Leuba, James H. *The Belief in God and Immortality: A Psychological, Anthropological and Statistical Study.* Boston: Sherman, French, 1916.

Levy, Frank. *The New Dollars and Dreams: American Incomes and Economic Change.* 1988. Reprint, New York: Russell Sage Foundation, 1998.

Lewis, Sinclair. *Babbitt.* 1922. Reprint, New York: Bantam Books, 1998.

Lichtenstein, Nelson. *The Most Dangerous Man in Detroit: Walter Reuther and the Fate of American Labor.* New York: Basic Books, 1995.

Linden, Eugene. *Affluence and Discontent: The Anatomy of Consumer Societies.* New York: Viking Press, 1979.

Lindsey, Lawrence B. *The Growth Experiment: How the New Tax Policy Is Transforming the U.S. Economy.* New York: Basic Books, 1990.

London, Paul A. *The Competition Solution: The Bipartisan Secret behind American Prosperity.* Washington, D.C.: AEI Press, 2005.

Lucas, Robert E., Jr. "The Industrial Revolution: Past and Future." *Region.* Federal Reserve Bank, 2003 Annual Report Issue.

Luckmann, Thomas. *The Invisible Religion: The Transformation of Symbols in Industrial Society.* New York: Macmillan, 1967.

Lundberg, Ferdinand, and Marynia F. Farnham, M.D. *Modern Woman: The Lost Sex.* New York: Harper & Brothers, 1947.

Lynd, Robert S., and Helen M. Lynd. *Middletown: A Study in Modern American Culture.* 1929. Reprint, New York: Harvest Books, 1959.

Macdonald, Dwight. *Against the American Grain: Essays on the Effects of Mass Culture.* 1962. Reprint, New York: Da Capo Press, 1983.

Maddison, Angus. *The World Economy: A Millennial Perspective.* Paris: Organisation for Economic Co-operation and Development, 2001.

Magnet, Myron. *The Dream and the Nightmare: The Sixties' Legacy to the Underclass.* San Francisco: Encounter Books, 1993.

Mailer, Norman. *Advertisements for Myself.* New York: G. P. Putnam's Sons, 1959.

Manchester, William. *The Glory and the Dream: A Narrative History of America, 1932–1972.* Boston: Little, Brown, 1973.

Marber, Peter. *Money Changes Everything: How Global Prosperity Is Changing Our Needs, Values, and Lifestyles.* Upper Saddle River, N.J.: Financial Times Prentice Hall, 2003.

Marchand, Roland. *Advertising the American Dream: Making Way for Modernity, 1920–1940.* Berkeley: University of California Press, 1985.

Marcuse, Herbert. *Eros and Civilization: A Philosophical Inquiry into Freud.* 1955. Reprint, Boston: Beacon Press, 1966.

———. *One-Dimensional Man.* 1964. Reprint, Boston: Beacon Press, 1991.

Markoff, John. *What the Dormouse Said: How the 60s Counterculture Shaped the Personal Computer Industry.* New York: Viking, 2005.

Marsden, George. *Understanding Fundamentalism and Evangelicalism.* Grand Rapids, Mich.: William B. Eerdmans, 1991.

Martin, William. *A Prophet with Honor: The Billy Graham Story.* New York: William Morrow, 1991.

———. *With God on Our Side: The Rise of the Religious Right in America.* New York: Broadway Books, 1996.

Maslow, Abraham. *Motivation and Personality.* New York: Harper & Brothers, 1954.

——. *Toward a Psychology of Being*. New York: Van Nostrand Rein-
hold, 1968.

Matusow, Allen J. *Nixon's Economy: Booms, Busts, Dollars, and Votes*.
Lawrence: University of Kansas Press, 1998.

May, Elaine T. *Homeward Bound: American Families in the Cold War
Era*. New York: Basic Books, 1988.

McCracken, Grant. *Plenitude 2.0*. Beta version. 1998, http://cultureby
.com/books/plenit/html/Plenitude2.htm.

McCrossen, Alexis. *Holy Day, Holiday: The American Sunday*. Ithaca,
N.Y.: Cornell University Press, 2000.

McGirr, Lisa. *Suburban Warriors: The Origins of the New American
Right*. Princeton, N.J.: Princeton University Press, 2001.

McKenzie, Richard B. *The American Job Machine*. New York: Universe
Books, 1988.

——. *What Went Right in the 1980s*. San Francisco: Pacific Research
Institute for Public Policy, 1994.

McLoughlin, William G. *Revivals, Awakenings, and Reform: An Essay
on Religion and Social Change in America, 1607–1977*. Chicago:
University of Chicago Press, 1978.

Meadows, Donella H., Dennis L. Meadows, Jørgen Randers, and Wil-
liam H. Behrens III. *The Limits to Growth: A Report for the Club of
Rome's Project on the Predicament of Mankind*. New York: Universe
Books, 1972.

Micklethwait, John, and Adrian Wooldridge. *The Company: A Short
History of a Revolutionary Idea*. New York: Modern Library, 2003.

——. *The Right Nation: Conservative Power in America*. New York:
Penguin Press, 2004.

Murphy, Kevin M., and Finis Welch. "Wage Differentials in the 1990s:
Is the Glass Half-Full or Half-Empty?" In *The Causes and Conse-
quences of Increasing Inequality*, edited by Finis Welch. Chicago:
University of Chicago Press, 2001.

Murray, Charles. *Losing Ground: American Social Policy, 1950–1980*.
New York: Basic Books, 1984.

Naipaul, V. S. "Our Universal Civilization." Wriston Lecture, Manhattan Institute, October 30, 1990, http://www.manhattan-institute
.org/html/wl1990.htm.

Nelson, Daniel. *Shifting Fortunes: The Rise and Decline of American
Labor, from the 1820s to the Present*. Chicago: Ivan R. Dee,
1997.

Nixon, Richard M. *RN: The Memoirs of Richard Nixon*. New York:
Grosset & Dunlap, 1978.

——. *Six Crises*. Garden City, N.Y.: Doubleday, 1962.

Patten, Simon N. *The New Basis of Civilization.* 1907. Reprint, Honolulu: University Press of the Pacific, 2004.

Patterson, James T. *Grand Expectations: The United States, 1945–1974.* New York: Oxford University Press, 1996.

Peale, Norman Vincent. *The Power of Positive Thinking.* 1952. Reprint, New York: Ballantine Books, 1996.

Pennington, Jon C. "It's Not a Revolution but It Sure Looks Like One," *Radical Statistics* 83 (2003): 104–116.

Perlstein, Rick. *Before the Storm: Barry Goldwater and the Unmaking of the American Consensus.* New York: Hill & Wang, 2001.

Perry, Charles. *The Haight-Ashbury: A History.* 1984. Reprint, New York: Vintage Books, 1985.

Peters, Thomas J., and Robert H. Waterman Jr. *In Search of Excellence: Lessons from America's Best-Run Companies.* 1982. Reprint, New York: HarperBusiness, 2004.

Phillips, Kevin P. *The Emerging Republican Majority.* New Rochelle, N.Y.: Arlington House, 1969.

Piven, Frances Fox, and Richard A. Cloward. *Regulating the Poor: The Functions of Public Welfare.* New York: Pantheon Books, 1971.

Pleij, Herman. *Dreaming of Cockaigne: Medieval Fantasies of the Perfect Life.* Translated by Diane Webb. 1997. Reprint, New York: Columbia University Press, 2001.

Postrel, Virginia. *The Substance of Style: How the Rise of Aesthetic Value Is Remaking Commerce, Culture, and Consciousness.* New York: HarperCollins, 2003.

Potter, David M. *People of Plenty: Economic Abundance and the American Character.* Chicago: University of Chicago Press, 1954.

Rajan, Raghuram G., and Luigi Zingales. *Saving Capitalism from the Capitalists: Unleashing the Power of Financial Markets to Create Wealth and Spread Opportunity.* New York: Crown Business, 2003.

Rauch, Jonathan. *Government's End: Why Washington Stopped Working.* 1994. Reprint, New York: Public Affairs, 1999.

Rayback, Joseph G. *A History of American Labor.* New York: Macmillan, 1964.

Reichley, A. James. *Faith in Politics.* Washington, D.C.: Brookings Institution Press, 2002.

Restad, Penne L. *Christmas in America: A History.* New York: Oxford University Press, 1995.

Revel, Jean-Francois. *Without Marx or Jesus: The New American Revolution Has Begun.* Translated by J. F. Bernard. Garden City, N.Y.: Doubleday, 1971.

Rieff, Philip. *The Triumph of the Therapeutic: Uses of Faith after Freud.* New York: Harper & Row, 1966.

Riesman, David. *The Lonely Crowd.* With Nathan Glazer and Reuel Denney. 1950. Reprint, New Haven, Conn.: Yale University Press, 1989.

Riis, Jacob A. *How the Other Half Lives: Studies among the Tenements of New York.* 1890. Reprint, Cambridge, Mass.: Belknap Press of Harvard University Press, 1970.

Ringer, Robert J. *Looking Out for # 1.* New York: Fawcett Crest, 1977.

Rodgers, Daniel T. *The Work Ethic in Industrial America, 1850–1920.* 1974. Reprint, Chicago: University of Chicago Press, 1978.

Rorabaugh, W. J. *The Alcoholic Republic: An American Tradition.* New York: Oxford University Press, 1979.

Rosen, Ruth. *The World Split Open: How the Modern Women's Movement Changed America.* New York: Penguin Books, 2000.

Roszak, Theodore. *From Satori to Silicon Valley: San Francisco and the American Counterculture.* San Francisco: Don't Call It Frisco Press, 1986.

———. *The Making of a Counter Culture: Reflections on the Technocratic Society and Its Youthful Opposition.* 1969. Reprint, Berkeley: University of California Press, 1995.

Rubin, Jerry. *Do It! Scenarios of the Revolution.* New York: Simon & Schuster, 1970.

Rustin, Bayard. "From Protest to Politics: The Future of the Civil Rights Movement." *Commentary,* February 1965, p. 25.

Salinger, J. D. *The Catcher in the Rye.* 1951. Reprint, New York: Bantam Books, 1964.

Sandel, Michael J. *Democracy's Discontent: American in Search of a Public Philosophy.* Cambridge, Mass.: Belknap Press of Harvard University Press, 1996.

Scammon, Richard M., and Ben J. Wattenberg. *The Real Majority: An Extraordinary Examination of the American Electorate.* New York: Coward-McCann, 1970.

Schaeffer, Francis A., C. Everett Koop, M.D., Jim Buchfuehrer, and Franky Schaeffer V. *Plan for Action: An Action Alternative Handbook for Whatever Happened to the Human Race?* Old Tappan, N.J.: Fleming H. Revell, 1980.

Sellers, Charles. *The Market Revolution: Jacksonian America, 1815–1846.* New York: Oxford University Press, 1991.

Selvin, Joel. *Summer of Love: The Inside Story of LSD, Rock and Roll, Free Love and High Times in the Wild West.* 1994. Reprint, New York: Cooper Square Press, 1999.

Shaffer, Butler. *In Restraint of Trade: The Business Campaign against Competition, 1918–1938.* Lewisburg, Pa.: Bucknell University Press, 1997.

Shils, Edward. "Dreams of Plenitude, Nightmares of Scarcity." In *Students in Revolt,* edited by Seymour Martin Lipset and Philip G. Altbach, pp. 1–35. Boston: Houghton Mifflin, 1969.

Singer, Max. *Passage to a Human World: The Dynamics of Creating Global Wealth.* New Brunswick, N.J.: Transaction Publishers, 1989.

Smith, Roy C. *The Wealth Creators: The Rise of Today's Rich and Super-Rich.* New York: Truman Talley Books, 2001.

Somers, Christina H., and Sally Satel, M.D. *One Nation under Therapy: How the Helping Culture Is Eroding Self-Reliance.* New York: St. Martin's Press, 2005.

Spock, Benjamin, M.D. *The Pocket Book of Baby and Child Care.* New York: Pocket Books, 1946.

Stevens, Jay. *Storming Heaven: LSD and the American Dream.* New York: Grove Press, 1987.

Stricker, Frank. "Affluence for Whom? Another Look at Prosperity and the Working Classes in the 1920s." *Labor History* 24 (Winter 1983): 5–33.

Strohmeyer, John. *Crisis in Bethlehem: Big Steel's Struggle to Survive.* Pittsburgh: University of Pittsburgh Press, 1986.

Susman, Warren I. *Culture as History: The Transformation of American Society in the Twentieth Century.* Washington, D.C.: Smithsonian Institution Press, 2003.

Talese, Gay. *Thy Neighbor's Wife.* Garden City, N.Y.: Doubleday, 1980.

Thernstrom, Stephan, and Abigail Thernstrom. *America in Black and White: One Nation, Indivisible.* 1997. Reprint, New York: Touchstone, 1999.

Thompson, Hunter S. *Fear and Loathing in Las Vegas: A Savage Journey to the Heart of the American Dream.* 1971. Reprint, New York: Vintage Books, 1998.

Tiffany, Paul A. *The Decline of American Steel: How Management, Labor, and Government Went Wrong.* New York: Oxford University Press, 1988.

Timberlake, Richard H. *Monetary Policy in the United States: An Intellectual and Institutional History.* 1978. Reprint, Chicago: University of Chicago Press, 1993.

Tocqueville, Alexis de. *Democracy in America.* Translated by George Lawrence. New York: Perennial Library, 1988.

Torgoff, Martin. *Can't Find My Way Home: America in the Great Stoned Age, 1945–2000.* New York: Simon & Schuster, 2004.

Townsend, Robert. *Up the Organization: How to Stop the Corporation from Stifling People and Strangling Profits.* 1970. Reprint, London: Coronet Books, 1971.

Trilling, Lionel. *The Liberal Imagination: Essays on Literature and Society.* Garden City, N.Y.: Doubleday, 1950.

Tucker, Robert C., eds. *The Marx-Engels Reader,* 2nd ed. 1972. Reprint, New York: W. W. Norton, 1978.

Twelve Southerners. *I'll Take My Stand: The South and the Agrarian Tradition.* 1930. Reprint, Baton Rouge: Louisiana State University Press, 1977.

Twitchell, James B. *Lead Us into Temptation: The Triumph of American Materialism.* New York: Columbia University Press, 1999.

U.S. Bureau of the Census. *The Statistical History of the United States from Colonial Times to the Present.* New York: Basic Books, 1976.

Veblen, Thorstein. *The Theory of Business Enterprise.* New York: Charles Scribner's Sons, 1910.

———. *The Theory of the Leisure Class.* 1899. Reprint, New York: Dover, 1994.

Viguerie, Richard, and David Franke. *America's Right Turn: How Conservatives Used New and Alternative Media to Take Power.* Chicago: Bonus Books, 2004.

Walicki, Andrzej. *Marxism and the Leap to the Kingdom of Freedom: The Rise and Fall of the Communist Utopia.* Stanford, Calif.: Stanford University Press, 1995.

Watts, Alan W. *Beat Zen, Square Zen, and Zen.* San Francisco: City Lights Books, 1959.

Weber, Max. *The Protestant Ethic and the "Spirit" of Capitalism.* Translated and edited by Peter Baehr and Gordon C. Wells. New York: Penguin Books, 2002.

White, Lynn. "Historical Roots of Our Ecological Crisis." *Science* 155 (1967): 1203–1207.

Whyte, William H., Jr. *The Organization Man.* Garden City, N.Y.: Doubleday Anchor Books, 1956.

Wiebe, Robert H. *The Search for Order, 1877–1920.* New York: Hill & Wang, 1967.

Wilson, Sloan. *The Man in the Gray Flannel Suit.* 1955. Reprint, New York: Four Walls Eight Windows, 1983.

Witcover, Jules. *The Year the Dream Died: Revisiting 1968 in America.* New York: Warner Books, 1997.

Wolfe, Alan. *One Nation, After All: What Americans Really Think about God, Country, Family, Racism, Welfare, Immigration, Homosexuality, Work, the Right, the Left and Each Other.* New York: Penguin Books, 1999.

Wolfe, Tom. *The Electric Kool-Aid Acid Test.* 1968. Reprint, New York: Bantam Books, 1969.

————. *Mauve Gloves and Madmen, Clutter and Vine.* 1976. Reprint, New York: Bantam Books, 1977.

————. *Radical Chic and Mau-Mauing the Flak Catchers.* 1970. Reprint, New York: Bantam Books, 1971.

Wolff, Robert P., Barrington Moore Jr., and Herbert Marcuse. *A Critique of Pure Tolerance.* 1965. Reprint, Boston: Beacon Press, 1969.

Woodward, C. Vann. *The Strange Career of Jim Crow.* 3rd rev. ed. 1955. Reprint, New York: Oxford University Press, 1974.

Wuthnow, Robert. *The Restructuring of American Religion: Society and Faith since World War II.* Princeton, N.J.: Princeton University Press, 1988.

Yankelovich, Daniel. *New Rules: Searching for Fulfillment in a World Turned Upside Down.* New York: Random House, 1981.

Index